2 KEYSTONE PARISH EDITION

SADLIER'S
Coming to Faith Program
Parish Annotated Guide

COMING TO JESUS

Dr. Gerard F. Baumbach
Dr. Eleanor Ann Brownell
Joan B. Collins
Moya Gullage
Helen Hemmer, I. H. M.
Gloria Hutchinson
Dr. Norman F. Josaitis
Rev. Michael J. Lanning, O. F. M.
Dr. Marie Murphy
Karen Ryan
Joseph F. Sweeney
Patricia Andrews

The Ad Hoc Committee to Oversee the Use of the Catechism, National Conference of Catholic Bishops, has found this catechetical series to be in conformity with the *Catechism of the Catholic Church.*

Official Theological Consultant
The Most Rev. Edward K. Braxton, Ph. D., S. T. D.

Scriptural Consultant
Rev. Donald Senior, C. P., Ph. D., S. T. D.

Catechetical and Liturgical Consultants
Dr. Gerard F. Baumbach
Dr. Eleanor Ann Brownell

Pastoral Consultants
Rev. Msgr. John F. Barry
Rev. Virgilio P. Elizondo, Ph.D., S. T. D.

Catechist's Guide Collaborators
Judene Leon
Mary Sharon Obrimski, I.H.M.

William H. Sadlier, Inc.
9 Pine Street
New York, New York 10005-1002
http://www.sadlier.com

CONTENTS

UNIT 2: THE SACRAMENT OF RECONCILIATION

Unit 3: The Sacrament of the Eucharist

UNIT 4: WE CELEBRATE THE EUCHARIST

William H. Sadlier, Inc. has long been committed to developing quality materials for Catholic Religious Education.

Our new **KEYSTONE EDITION K–8** continues this tradition.

Sadlier meets the needs of both school and parish by providing programs for each of them. Now every child will be able to develop the foundations of faith and gain a strong sense of Catholic identity.

Sadlier is proud to present the two components of the **KEYSTONE EDITION** for grades K–8; ***Coming to Faith*** and ***Faith and Witness***.

Religion K–8

SCHOOL

Coming to Faith provides a rich, authentic, complete presentation of our Catholic faith for Grades K–6. ***Faith and Witness*** challenges adolescents with topic-specific courses of study. Each presentation fosters commitment to the teachings and tradition of our Catholic Church.

Sadlier is proud that the **KEYSTONE EDITION** has been found by the Ad Hoc Committee to Oversee the Use of the Catechism, National Conference of Catholic Bishops, to be **in conformity with the *Catechism of the Catholic Church*.**

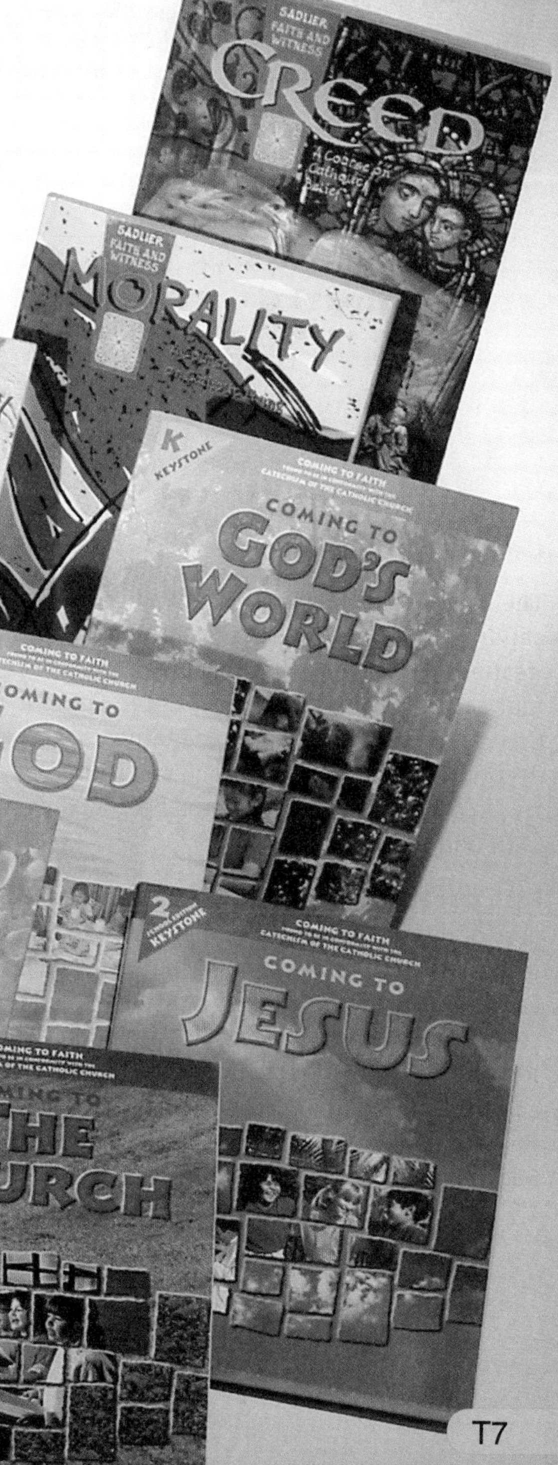

Keystone Parish

The Ad Hoc Committee to Oversee the Use of the Catechism, National Conference of Catholic Bishops, has found this catechetical series to be in conformity with the *Catechism of the Catholic Church.*

4360-1 4362-8 4364-4 4365-2

4361-X 4363-6 4366-0

Coming to Faith

The **KEYSTONE EDITION** of ***Coming to Faith*** initiates children into the heart and beauty of Catholic teaching. The treatment of the catechetical content is based on each of the four sections of the *Catechism of the Catholic Church*: the Creed, Sacraments, the Commandments, and Prayer, and is deeply rooted in Scripture. The curriculum of the ***Coming to Faith Program*** carefully blends child development with faith and moral development.

Each text contains numerous features that help turn the richness of our Catholic heritage into a lived faith. Beautiful **art** makes the text come alive and sparks the child's imagination. **Faith Words** in each chapter provide the child with an extensive vocabulary to develop **Catholic literacy. Our Catholic Identity** is a 16 page tear-out booklet that features Catholic customs, traditions, and heritage. Texts also contain **Catholic Belief Booklets: My Catholic Faith Book** (grades K–3) and **Sharing Our Faith as Catholics** (grades 4–6).

4361-X

Liturgy Lessons are an important component of each text and are designed to enhance the child's understanding of the ebb and flow of the liturgical seasons and celebrations.

Sadlier strives for **Family involvement.** Every chapter concludes with **Faith Alive at Home and in the Parish.** These practical tear-out pages summarize the lesson for the parent, engage the family in creative activities, and encourage review of the chapter's content. A **Family Scripture Moment** also encourages the family to read and discuss a weekly Scripture passage that appears in each lesson.

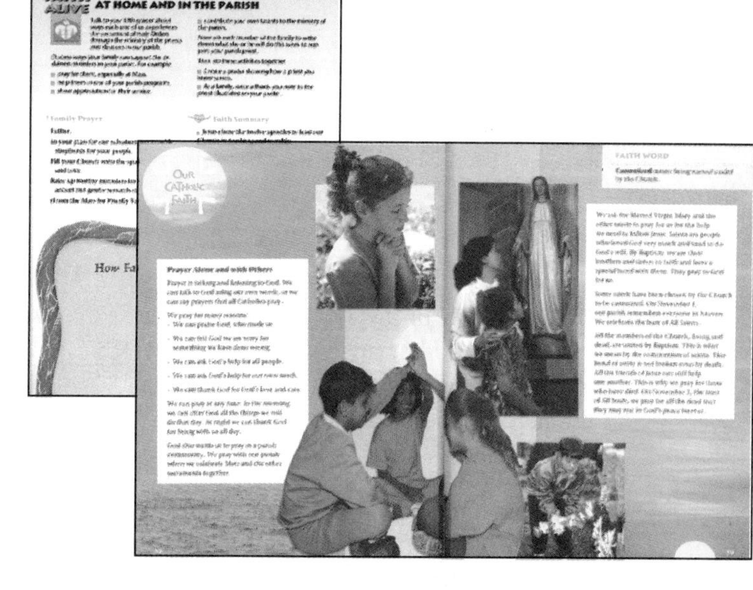

4373-3

Catechist's Guides are clear, concise, and easy to use! One of the most useful features of the Guide is the **Catechist's Workshop,** a wonderful catechist training tool. Every lesson plan begins with **Adult Background**. **Liturgical** and **Justice and Peace Resources** are provided as well. **Wraparound Lesson Plans** feature clearly stated objectives and activities for each reduced child's page and are easy to follow. **Enrichment** and **Optional Activities** are provided, as well as **Special Needs Activities** that focus on visual, auditory, and tactile-motor needs. *Catechism of the Catholic Church* references occur in each chapter making this a useful and practical reference.

Enrichment Materials include **Activity Books** for each grade level. These provide creative activities that reinforce the theme of each lesson. Age-appropriate **Music** is available for grades K–4 in **cassettes**. A **Blackline Testing Program** is available for each grade level from 1–6, including chapter, unit, and cumulative tests. An **Assessment Program** containing quarterly assessments in standardized test format with a reproducible report for families is also available in paks of 20.

3343-6

3420-3

3320-2

The Ad Hoc Committee to Oversee the Use of the Catechism, National Conference of Catholic Bishops, has found this catechetical series to be in conformity with the *Catechism of the Catholic Church.*

Faith and Witness

The **KEYSTONE EDITION** of the ***Faith and Witness Program*** is a series of **semester texts** that invites and challenges young people to become committed members of the faith community! It is a creative response to the needs of **adolescents** in the Catholic Church.

Each **semester text** provides a topic-specific course that involves adolescents as active and responsible partners in the learning process. Every lesson incorporates a **Forum Activity** that involves the young person immediately and interactively in the day's work. **Art** is the cornerstone of each session's opening **Prayer Activity**, as well as a powerful learning-teaching tool.

Abundant features focus on **Catholic identity** and **heritage**, **Catholic teachings**, **Scripture Updates**, and highlight **heroes of faith**.

A **Journal** is available for each semester title to furnish the adolescents with a directed reflection on their thoughts, dreams, and questions regarding the theme as it relates to their lives.

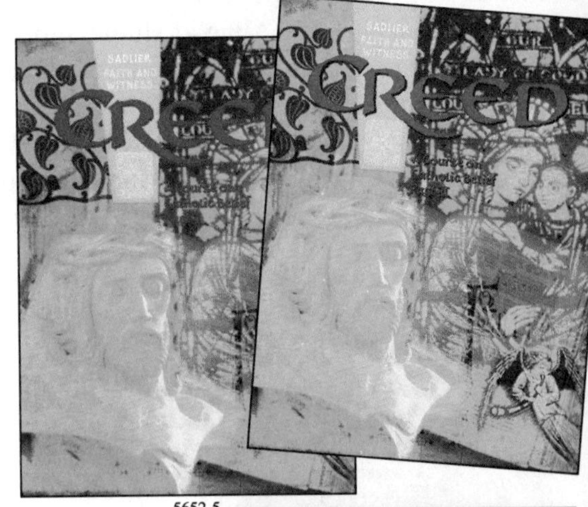

5652-5
5653-3

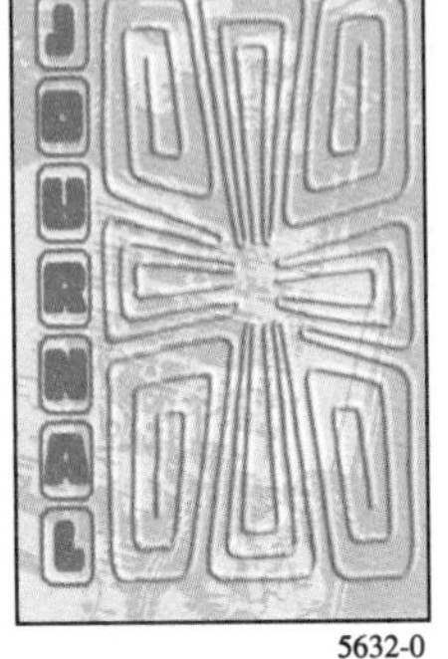

5632-0

5654-1

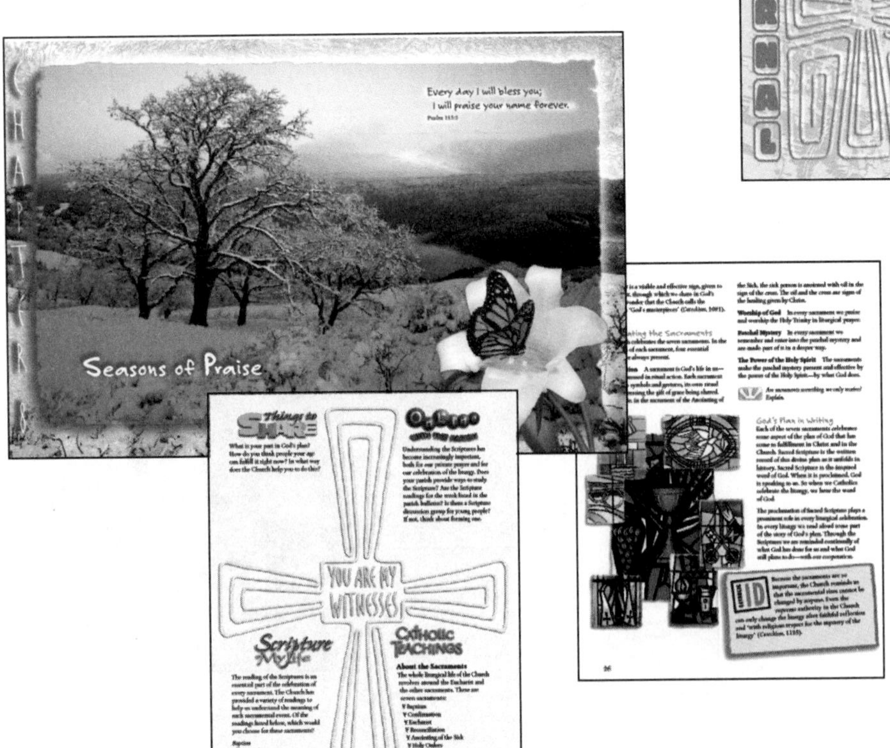

5651-7

New Testament

Because support for the catechist is essential, an easy to use **Catechist's Guide** has been developed. Guides are arranged in a **Wraparound Format**. The activities for the session surround the corresponding text page. Every session begins with an **Adult Focus** for background. The **Teaching Resources Page** outlines everything necessary for the session's work. Three **Reproducible Masters** are incorporated into each session of the Guide. These include an **Activity Handout**, **Assessment Page**, and **Highlights for Home**.

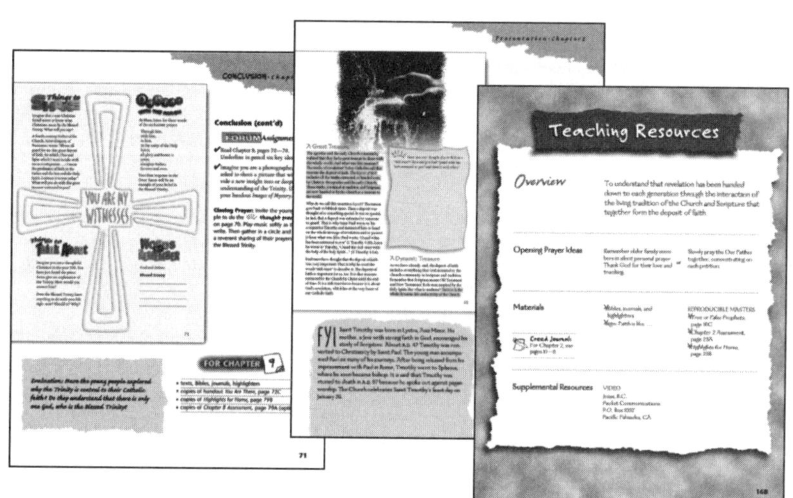

SADLIER FAITH AND WITNESS

MORALITY

A Course on Catholic Living

Annotated Edition

5664-9

Additional resources include **Posters** featuring the beautiful art of selected chapter openers and **Blackline Master Test Books** which provide additional assessment for each of the semester texts.

Church History: A Course on the People of God is a 15-chapter resource text providing an age-appropriate introduction to the people, events, and movements in the story of our Church. **Prayer Celebrations for the Liturgical Year** provides adolescents with the opportunity to work together to plan their own prayer celebrations for different seasons of the liturgical year. **Parish Guides** are available for fifteen-chapter editions of **Morality** and **Creed**, should you choose the option of one year-long course of study.

SADLIER FAITH AND WITNESS

NEW TESTAMENT

Edition

5661-4

SCOPE & SEQUENCE

• *Catechism of the Catholic Church* references for the Grade 2 text are on pages T14–T17.

GRADE	Doctrine	Prayer and Worship	Scripture
K			**Family Scripture Moment: Psalms and New Testament**
Unit 1	**Life:** God gives us life; God made and loves us; we have gifts of senses and feelings; God wants us to love others; *the Bible*	Prayers of friendship, thanksgiving for gifts of life, senses, feelings, people; Bible celebration; Scripture prayers	Genesis 1:26, 31; 2:18 1 John 4:10–11 Isaiah 43:4
Unit 2	**Creation:** God made all things—light and water, plants and flowers, animals, birds, and fish. God wants us to care for the world; *Advent; Christmas*	Prayers of thanksgiving and praise for creation—water, light, earth, plants, animals; celebrations of life; Scripture; Advent and Christmas celebrations	Genesis 1:1–27, 1:1–5, 9–10, 11–12, 16–18, 20–25, 28–30; 31 Psalm 66:3; 24:1; 104:24 Luke 2:4–16
Unit 3	**Mary, Jesus:** Mary is the Mother of God and our mother, too; we call Jesus, Mary, and Joseph the Holy Family; Jesus is our friend and our teacher; *Palm Sunday*; the Hail Mary	Scripture prayer; prayers to Mary, Jesus, the Holy Family; **Hail Mary**; Palm Sunday	Luke 1:26–38; 2:4–7, 8–15 Mark 12:29–31, 10:13–16 John 12:12–13 Matthew 28:1, 5, 6
Unit 4	**Church:** We belong to God's family, the Church, through our Baptism; God's family helps and cares for one another as Jesus cared for others; Jesus is with us always; the Sign of the Cross; *holy water*	Prayers of thanksgiving for family; introduction to the Mass; Mass responses; prayer songs to Jesus; the **Sign of the Cross**	Genesis 1:1–31 Psalm 138:1, 7, 8 John 15:17 Matthew 28:20
GRADE **1**			**Family Scripture Moment: Gospel of Luke**
Unit 1	**God made the world;** all creation is good; God made us to be like Him; God gives us grace; He knows and loves us; Blessed Trinity; God is with us always; the Bible; saints; *All Saints*	Prayers of thanksgiving for creation; celebrating life; prayers of thanksgiving for gifts of life and love; thanking people who show God's love; **Sign of the Cross**; prayer of thanksgiving to God for loving us always; Bible celebration; All Saints celebration	Genesis 1:3–4, 10–13, 24–25, 26, 27–31; 2:8—3:15 1 John 3:1 Isaiah 7:14; 41:1, 10 Matthew 5:6
Unit 2	**Story of Jesus;** Jesus: human and divine, one of us and God's own Son; Jesus shows us God's love; Jesus is our friend and teacher; prayer and Law of Love; Last Supper, death, and resurrection of Jesus; *Advent; Christmas*	Prayer for our family; song of praise to Jesus; praying to Jesus; **Our Father**; Holy Communion; Jesus is with us always; Advent calendar; Christmas celebration	Luke 1:26–28; 2:1–16; 4–7; 5:20; 6:27; 11:1–2; 22:14–20 Mark 4:35–41; 12:29–31 John 14:9 Revelation 22:20–21
Unit 3	**Sending of the Spirit** at Pentecost as Helper; birth of the Church; the Church is for everyone; Baptism; children of God; grace: God's own life and love; the Mass: what we say and hear; God's Word; our gifts; Holy Communion; *Lent; Easter*	Prayer to the Holy Spirit; following Jesus; celebrating our Baptisms; letter to Jesus; Mass; Lenten prayer; Easter celebration	John 14:16–17, 26; 15:12; 20:11–18 Acts 2:2–6
Unit 4	**Our Parish;** our Church celebrates sacraments, prays, helps people to be fair, brings peace and God's forgiveness, shares good news; Reconciliation; God's eternal love	Helping in our parish; **Hail Mary**; prayer to Jesus for help; **Our Father**; living as a child of God; prayer service for forgiveness	Luke 15:11–24; 21:36 Matthew 18:22–34 John 14:27 Mark 10:13–16 I Peter 2:9

GRADE 2	Doctrine	Prayer and Worship	Scripture
			Family Scripture Moment: Gospel of Matthew
Unit 1	**Believing in God:** Father, Son, and Holy Spirit; Jesus, God's only Son, human and divine, risen; Holy Spirit and the Church; Church membership, service, worship; parish family: mission and service; sacraments: Baptism, Reconciliation, Eucharist; prayer; *the Bible, God's Word*	Letter to God; **Sign of the Cross**; showing our love; asking help of the Spirit; Mass; Baptism; the parish Church: Jesus' community of friends; prayer service; Bible prayer service	Mark 1:16–18 Genesis 1:1–31; 2:7, 21–22 Luke 2:41–49; 4:18 Acts 2:1–12, 38–42 John 5:24; 13:34–35 Psalm 119:105
Unit 2	**Jesus reveals God's love:** shows how to love; help of the Holy Spirit; choices: love and sin; Law of Love, Ten Commandments; God's will; forgiveness; sacrament of Reconciliation; celebrating the sacrament; *Advent*; *Christmas*	Being a caregiver; choosing love; **Act of Contrition**; asking forgiveness; celebrating Reconciliation; preparing and blessing of Advent wreath and candles; Christmas prayer service	Mark 12:28–31 Luke 1:26–38; 2:4–14; 15:1–6; 19:1–10 Matthew 18:21–23 Exodus 20:1–17 Psalm 19:8
Unit 3	**Jesus gives us the Mass** as a special meal and sacrifice; preparing for Eucharist: Liturgy of the Word and of the Eucharist; the Mass: sent to love and serve; *Lent*; *Easter*	Making a Mass book; Mass; Prayer of the Faithful; celebrating Mass together: Introductory Rites, Liturgy of the Word, Liturgy of the Eucharist, Concluding Rite; Lenten Prayer Service; Easter Play	Mark 8:1–8; 12:30–31 Luke 22:14–20 Matthew 26:26–28 John 20:1–10
Unit 4	**First Communion:** preparing, receiving, thanking; the real presence of Christ in the Eucharist; Jesus with us always: at Mass, in others, in our Church, our parish, our family; Mary, Mother of Jesus and our mother; *Reconciliation celebration*	First Communion: preparation and receiving; Blessed Sacrament; helping others; **Hail Mary**; **Our Father**; **Glory to the Father**; song to Jesus; Reconciliation celebration	Luke 1:38, 42; 15:4–6; 24:13–35 Matthew 18:20; 25:40

GRADE 3			**Family Scripture Moment:** Gospel of Mark
Unit 1	**Jesus is our Friend**; Jesus' mission and teaching; the calling of the apostles; Jesus' death and resurrection; the Holy Spirit: Pentecost; the Church carries on Jesus' mission; the parish, a place of prayer and worship; *Reconciliation*; *Eucharist*	Being Jesus' disciple; prayer for help in following Jesus; prayer to the Holy Spirit; bringing about the kingdom of God; visit to the Blessed Sacrament; celebrating forgiveness; planning and celebrating the Mass	Isaiah 43:1 Mark 10:13-16 Matthew 4:18–20; 12:50; 25:40; 28:19, 20 John 13:34–35; 15:9–14 Luke 5:27–28 Acts 2:1–12, 33, 38, 42 I Corinthians 12:12–27
Unit 2	**Our parish prays:** kinds of prayer, praying to Mary and the saints, praying for the dead; the sacraments; God's life and love in us: grace; sacraments of initiation, healing, and service; sacrament of Reconciliation; celebrating the Mass and the Eucharist; the parts of Mass; *Advent*; *Christmas*	Evening prayer; living sacrament; Absolution; **Our Father**; invitation to Mass; Sunday Mass; Advent prayer; Christmas celebration	Luke 2:1–20; 12:38–42; 15:11–32 Matthew 26:26–28 Psalm 95
Unit 3	**The Bible:** Old and New Testament; the Church passes on the good news; missionaries; the parish church community: pope, bishops, pastors, lay people, the family; vocations; justice and peace for all; the kingdom of God; parables; *Lent*; *Easter*	Praying with the Bible; sharing good news; vocations: working for God's kingdom; peacemakers; **Our Father**; Stations of the Cross; a Lenten prayer; Jesus' resurrection: an Easter play	Matthew 6:10; 13:3–8; 33, 44; 28:16–20 Acts 9:1–5; 11:3 Luke 14:15–24; 24:1–10 John 18:29—19:17
Unit 4	**Marks of the Church:** one, holy, catholic, apostolic; ecumenical movement: Jews, Christians, Protestants; Roman and Eastern Rites; Mary, Mother of the Church; members of the Church; *Prayer*, *the Saints*	**Apostles' Creed**; prayer for Church leaders; prayer for Christian unity; immaculate conception; prayer to Mary; making a "Faith Book"; **Hail Mary**; **Grace Before Meals**; **Act of Contrition**; **Glory to the Father**; prayers to the saints; prayer for vocation	John 11:41–42; 17:21; 19:26, 27 Matthew 16:18 Luke 1:26–38

SCOPE & SEQUENCE
GRADE 2

UNIT 1 Our Catholic Faith

	Chapter	Our Life	Sharing Life	Our Catholic Faith	Coming to Faith	Practicing Faith
1	*We Believe in God*	I take an imaginary trip through God's world.	We share what we see, hear, and do on our trip.	**The Blessed Trinity** God the Father, Son, and Holy Spirit cares for us.	We show we are glad to be alive. We recall the Persons of the Blessed Trinity.	I write a thank You prayer to God.

• Doctrinal Correlation to the *Catechism of the Catholic Church*: paragraph 237 *Our Catholic Identity*: The Blessed Trinity

	Chapter	Our Life	Sharing Life	Our Catholic Faith	Coming to Faith	Practicing Faith
2	*Jesus Christ Is God's Son*	I tell the stories I know about Jesus.	Share experiences of Jesus' presence in our lives.	**Jesus Christ** Present an overview of Jesus' life and that Jesus Christ is both human and divine.	We recall who Jesus is and how He shows us to love.	I choose someone to whom I will be kind.

• Doctrinal Correlation to the *Catechism of the Catholic Church*: paragraph 444

	Chapter	Our Life	Sharing Life	Our Catholic Faith	Coming to Faith	Practicing Faith
3	*The Holy Spirit Is Our Helper*	I read a poem about times people are afraid.	We share experiences of being helped when we are afraid.	**Our Helper the Holy Spirit** Present the action of the Holy Spirit in the early Church and today.	We recall the coming of the Holy Spirit on Pentecost.	I decide how I will ask the Holy Spirit to help me.

• Doctrinal Correlation to the *Catechism of the Catholic Church*: paragraph 731 *Our Catholic Identity*: The Holy Spirit

	Chapter	Our Life	Sharing Life	Our Catholic Faith	Coming to Faith	Practicing Faith
4	*We Belong to the Catholic Church*	I talk about a club where everyone is welcome.	We share what it is like to belong to Jesus' special group.	**The Catholic Church** Present the essential structure and role of the Catholic Church as a community of Jesus' followers.	We recall what we like best about belonging to Jesus' community.	I decide what I will do to show I belong to the Catholic Church.

• Doctrinal Correlation to the *Catechism of the Catholic Church*: paragraph 737 *Our Catholic Identity*: The Holy Father

	Chapter	Our Life	Sharing Life	Our Catholic Faith	Coming to Faith	Practicing Faith
5	*We Belong to Our Parish*	I read a story about being part of a family.	We share what we like best about having a family. We share how God wants us to live in our parish family.	**Our Parish Family** In our parish we help others and work to bring about God's kingdom on earth.	We recall how we work in our parish for the kingdom of God.	I decide one way I will help my parish to be a community of Jesus' followers.

• Doctrinal Correlation to the *Catechism of the Catholic Church*: paragraph 752 *Our Catholic Identity*: Mary in Our Family and Parish

	Chapter	Our Life	Sharing Life	Our Catholic Faith	Coming to Faith	Practicing Faith
6	*Prayer*	I help to write a letter to someone far away.	We share ways we talk to God.	**Prayer** We learn to listen and talk to God.	We recall the ways that we can pray.	I choose a prayer to pray this week and join in a prayer celebration.

• Doctrinal Correlation to the *Catechism of the Catholic Church*: paragraph 2567

	Chapter	Our Life	Sharing Life	Our Catholic Faith	Coming to Faith	Practicing Faith
7	*The Bible*	We talk about how we learn about new things.	We share ways we learn about God.	**The Word of God** The Bible shows us how to love God today and always.	We recall what we learn from Bible stories.	I decide to tell or act out a Bible story.

• Doctrinal Correlation to the *Catechism of the Catholic Church*: paragraph 104

The **Coming to Faith** program makes inclusive use of the four signs of catechesis as called for in the *National Catechetical Directory* (NCD): biblical, liturgical, ecclesial, and natural. In this Scope and Sequence, the signs are noted by these symbols:

Biblical which show how God is revealed in the Scriptures.

Liturgical which flow from the sacramental life of the Church.

Ecclesial which include doctrinal and creedal formulations.

Natural which are expressed in the environment, arts, science, and culture.

UNIT 2 The Sacrament of Reconciliation

	Chapter	Our Life	Sharing Life	Our Catholic Faith	Coming to Faith	Practicing Faith
8	*God Loves Us Always*	I talk about how people show love.	We discuss why we need to love and ways to do it.	**The Law of Love** Present Jesus' Law of Love and how the Holy Spirit helps us live it.	Deepen understanding of love for God, others, and ourselves.	I decide how to help someone in need.

• Doctrinal Correlation to the *Catechism of the Catholic Church*: paragraph 2052 *Our Catholic Identity*: What is a Shepherd?

	Chapter	Our Life	Sharing Life	Our Catholic Faith	Coming to Faith	Practicing Faith
9	*We Make Choices*	Explore feelings about making choices.	We share how to know when something is wrong to do.	**Choosing Love** Present the Ten Commandments as positive rules that tell us what God wants us to do.	Deepen understanding of the idea that we can choose to love or not to love.	I choose a commandment and tell how I will live it.

• Doctrinal Correlation to the *Catechism of the Catholic Church*: paragraph 2054

	Chapter	Our Life	Sharing Life	Our Catholic Faith	Coming to Faith	Practicing Faith
10	*God Forgives Us*	I read the Zacchaeus story about asking for forgiveness.	We share ways of showing we are sorry.	**Reconciliation** We become God's friends again in the sacrament of Reconciliation. Act of Contrition.	We recall forgiveness in the story of Zacchaeus.	I join in a Reconciliation circle and prayer.

• Doctrinal Correlation to the *Catechism of the Catholic Church*: paragraph 1446 *Our Catholic Identity*: Vestments

	Chapter	Our Life	Sharing Life	Our Catholic Faith	Coming to Faith	Practicing Faith
11	*We Prepare for Reconciliation*	I choose how to respond to a situation of wrongdoing.	We share our feelings on being wronged and how we would respond.	Present the way to examine one's conscience and for celebrating Reconciliation by ourselves.	We recall how we can bring God's peace to others.	I decide how I will show I am sorry for hurting someone in my life.

• Doctrinal Correlation to the *Catechism of the Catholic Church*: paragraph 1456

	Chapter	Our Life	Sharing Life	Our Catholic Faith	Coming to Faith	Practicing Faith
12	*We Celebrate Reconciliation*	Discuss Jesus' words about forgiveness.	We share reasons for always forgiving others.	Present the communal rite of Reconciliation and how it helps us to grow in love.	Deepen understanding of how the parish celebrates Reconciliation together.	I choose a way to show I am sorry and join in a prayer celebration.

• Doctrinal Correlation to the *Catechism of the Catholic Church*: paragraph 1480 *Our Catholic Identity*: A Sign of Forgiveness

	Chapter	Our Life	Sharing Life	Our Catholic Faith	Coming to Faith	Practicing Faith
13	*Advent*	I read a story about Mary.	We share what we might do while we wait for Christmas.	**Preparing for Jesus** During Advent we prepare to celebrate Jesus' birth. Advent wreath.	We recall how we can prepare during Advent.	I decide to join in an Advent wreath prayer.

• Doctrinal Correlation to the *Catechism of the Catholic Church*: paragraph 1171

	Chapter	Our Life	Sharing Life	Our Catholic Faith	Coming to Faith	Practicing Faith
14	*Christmas*	I read a story about the first Christmas.	We share how the shepherds felt when they saw Jesus.	**Celebrating Christmas** The symbols of Christmas remind us of Jesus' birth.	We celebrate a Christmas prayer service.	We recall the joyful news of Christmas.

• Doctrinal Correlation to the *Catechism of the Catholic Church*: paragraph 1172

SCOPE & SEQUENCE
GRADE 2

UNIT 3 The Sacrament of the Eucharist

	Chapter	Our Life	Sharing Life	Our Catholic Faith	Coming to Faith	Practicing Faith
15	*Jesus Gives Us the Mass*	I talk about the story of Jesus feeding the people.	We talk about Jesus' sensitivity to the needs of the people.	**Bread of Life** The Mass is our celebration of Jesus' special meal and sacrifice.	We come to a deeper understanding of Jesus' gift of Himself at Mass.	I make a Mass book for our Sunday celebration.

• Doctrinal Correlation to the *Catechism of the Catholic Church*: paragraph 1323 *Our Catholic Identity*: Blessed Be God Forever

	Chapter	Our Life	Sharing Life	Our Catholic Faith	Coming to Faith	Practicing Faith
16	*We Prepare for Eucharist*	I talk about experiences of family prayer at mealtime.	We share ways to thank God by helping those who have no food.	**Our Greatest Prayer** The Mass is the great thanksgiving meal of the Church.	We recall how we can participate in the Mass.	I write a prayer to prepare for Mass.

• Doctrinal Correlation to the *Catechism of the Catholic Church*: paragraph 1348 *Our Catholic Identity*: Why Catholics Genuflect

	Chapter	Our Life	Sharing Life	Our Catholic Faith	Coming to Faith	Practicing Faith
17	*The Liturgy of the Word*	I play a listening game.	We share about how we listen.	**Liturgy of the Word** We listen carefully to God's word as it is read to us from the Bible.	We recall what happens in the Liturgy of the Word.	I decide how I will listen more carefully at Mass next Sunday.

• Doctrinal Correlation to the *Catechism of the Catholic Church*: paragraph 1349

	Chapter	Our Life	Sharing Life	Our Catholic Faith	Coming to Faith	Practicing Faith
18	*The Liturgy of the Eucharist*	I talk about gift giving.	We share about the gifts God has given us and what we can give to God.	**The Liturgy of the Eucharist** The bread and wine become Jesus Himself.	We recall what happens to our gifts of bread and wine at Mass.	I write a prayer to thank God for one gift.

• Doctrinal Correlation to the *Catechism of the Catholic Church*: paragraph 1352 *Our Catholic Identity*: Our Communion Prayer

	Chapter	Our Life	Sharing Life	Our Catholic Faith	Coming to Faith	Practicing Faith
19	*We Are Sent to Love and Serve*	I talk about how people show love for God.	We share ways Jesus wants us to serve others.	**To Love and Serve** Each day we find ways to love and serve others.	We recall that we are sent from Mass to love and serve one another.	I choose one way that I will live the Eucharist.

• Doctrinal Correlation to the *Catechism of the Catholic Church*: paragraph 1396 *Our Catholic Identity*: Lamb of God

	Chapter	Our Life	Sharing Life	Our Catholic Faith	Coming to Faith	Practicing Faith
20	*Lent*	I talk about how things change and grow.	We share feelings about a world where nothing changed or grew.	**A Time to Grow** During Lent, we prepare for Easter.	We recall how we can be better friends to Jesus during Lent.	I decide how I will love God and others during Lent.

• Doctrinal Correlation to the *Catechism of the Catholic Church*: paragraph 618

	Chapter	Our Life	Sharing Life	Our Catholic Faith	Coming to Faith	Practicing Faith
21	*Easter*	I make up a springtime poem.	We share how we feel about the season of new life.	**New Life** The symbols of Easter remind us of Christ's new life.	We recall why we celebrate Easter.	I decide what I will do to celebrate Jesus' new life at Easter.

• Doctrinal Correlation to the *Catechism of the Catholic Church*: paragraph 1169

UNIT 4 We Celebrate the Eucharist

	Chapter	Our Life	Sharing Life	Our Catholic Faith	Coming to Faith	Practicing Faith
22	*We Celebrate First Holy Communion*	We talk about who is helping us prepare for our First Holy Communion.	I name people who will help me.	**Receiving Communion** We have grown in our faith and can receive Communion.	We recall how to receive Communion.	I choose how I will get ready for Communion.

• Doctrinal Correlation to the *Catechism of the Catholic Church*: paragraph 1391

	Chapter	Our Life	Sharing Life	Our Catholic Faith	Coming to Faith	Practicing Faith
23	*We Celebrate Our Life with Jesus*	I talk about making a cassette for someone far away.	We share how we feel when someone we love is far away.	**Jesus' Presence** Jesus is with us in the Eucharist and in other people.	We recall that Jesus is always with us.	I recognize the times that Jesus will be with me this week.

• Doctrinal Correlation to the *Catechism of the Catholic Church*: paragraph 1404 *Our Catholic Identity*: The Tabernacle

	Chapter	Our Life	Sharing Life	Our Catholic Faith	Coming to Faith	Practicing Faith
24	*Jesus Christ Is with Our Community*	I talk about how I need the help of others.	We list ways Jesus wants us to help others.	**Community** Jesus is present when we work together to love and serve one another and those in need.	We recall how Jesus is with us in the sacraments and in one another.	I decide how I will be a more loving member of the Church, my parish, and my family.

• Doctrinal Correlation to the *Catechism of the Catholic Church*: paragraph 1369 *Our Catholic Identity*: Lord I Am Not Worthy

	Chapter	Our Life	Sharing Life	Our Catholic Faith	Coming to Faith	Practicing Faith
25	*Mary, Our Mother*	I talk about praying to Mary.	We share a favorite prayer to Mary and how Mary is our mother.	**Mary** Mary is part of God's plan.	We recall that Mary is our mother, too.	I decide how I will honor Mary.

• Doctrinal Correlation to the *Catechism of the Catholic Church*: paragraph 494 *Our Catholic Identity*: The Rosary

	Chapter	Our Life	Sharing Life	Our Catholic Faith	Coming to Faith	Practicing Faith
26	*Jesus Christ Is with Us Forever*	I talk about ways I have grown this year.	We share what we have learned and how we have grown in faith.	**Forever in Heaven** Jesus promised His friends that they would be with God forever in heaven.	We tell how we feel about being disciples of Jesus.	I decide how I will live as Jesus' disciple.

• Doctrinal Correlation to the *Catechism of the Catholic Church*: paragraph 1716 *Our Catholic Identity*: Aspirations

	Chapter	Our Life	Sharing Life	Our Catholic Faith	Coming to Faith	Practicing Faith
27	*A Reconciliation Celebration*	I remember the times I hurt someone.	We think about how much God loves us.	**The Good Shepherd** Jesus shows us God's love and forgiveness.	We recall our need to be sorry.	I will forgive others and be a peacemaker.

• Doctrinal Correlation to the *Catechism of the Catholic Church*: paragraph 1465

	Chapter	Our Life	Sharing Life	Our Catholic Faith	Coming to Faith	Practicing Faith
28	*My Mass Book*	I learn how to make My Mass Book.	We share our Mass Books.	**Praying the Mass** We use our Mass Books to celebrate.	We recall what happens at Mass.	I decide to use My Mass Book.

• Doctrinal Correlation to the *Catechism of the Catholic Church*: paragraph 1346

The Catechism of the Catholic Church

What Is the Catechism?

After many years of intense work and preparation, the *Catechism of the Catholic Church* was officially promulgated by His Holiness, Pope John Paul II, in 1992, some thirty years after the beginning of the Second Vatican Council.

What is this catechism and why is it such a gift to our Church? A catechism is a faithful presentation of the truths of the Catholic Church. These include the teachings of Sacred Scripture, the Tradition of the Church, and the teachings of the magisterium of the Church. A catechism does not teach new doctrine but faithfully hands on the received doctrine of the Church. However, the content of a catechism is often presented in a new way to help answer the questions and issues raised in each age.

That is why we have been given this gift of the new *Catechism of the Catholic Church*, to pass on to the faithful in our day the authentic teaching of the Catholic Church and to help us answer in adult language the challenges that are ours at the end of the twentieth century and those that will come in the new millennium. The *Catechism* is not in a question-and-answer format, and does not address the kinds of methodologies available for handing on the faith to our children, young people, and adults. Rather, it concerns itself with the clear presentation of Catholic teaching on the truths of faith.

For Whom Is It Written?

The *Catechism of the Catholic Church* is addressed, first of all, to bishops, who are the principal teachers of our Catholic faith. It is also addressed to those who prepare catechetical materials, priests, catechists, and all those who wish to know what the Catholic Church believes. It is not intended to replace local catechisms or deny cultural differences throughout the world, but to help preserve the unity of faith and fidelity to the deposit of faith.

Sadlier's Involvement

For over 165 years, William H. Sadlier, Inc., has worked in service to the Catholic Church. We welcome the publication of the *Catechism of the Catholic Church* as a reference for the development of our future catechetical materials. We have always ensured that our books accurately reflect the authentic teachings of the Church. This new catechism, the first such major catechism in more than 400 years, provides us with an essential standard for the presentation of Church teaching. As we revise existing works and develop new materials for the generations to come, we will certainly look to the *Catechism of the Catholic Church* for guidance and inspiration.

The *Coming to Faith* Program meets the high standards set by this gift of the *Catechism* and the four pillars that provide its basic framework. Indeed, the *Catechism's* fourfold emphasis on creed, sacraments, the moral life of the Christian, and prayer, rooted in and supported by the Scriptures, is an emphasis and structure with which we feel a particular compatibility. In addition, Sadlier's methodology and pedagogy have long supported and provided for the authentic presentation of Catholic doctrine, and will continue to do so in the future.

We are proud that we are co-publishers of the *Catechism of the Catholic Church* in the United States in both English and Spanish editions. May it be and remain a work of reference, resource, and renewal.

Easy Reference for the Catechist

To assist you in understanding the relation between the *Catechism of the Catholic Church* and the *Coming to Faith* Program, there are the following references in the program's annotated guides:

- In the **Scope and Sequence Chart**, a reference to the appropriate *Catechism* paragraph for each major chapter theme;

- For each lesson, a reference to the pertinent *Catechism* paragraph in the **For the Catechist—Spiritual and Catechetical Development** pages.

Catechist's Workshop

The *Catechist's Workshop* is a way to introduce you to teaching the *Coming to Faith* Program. You are encouraged to use it as a self-directed workshop or with other catechists or teachers in your parish.

If we can be of any service, please call our catechetical specialists at 1-800-582-5437.

Congratulations!

You Are a Catechist

The Church is responsible for continuing the mission of Jesus to proclaim and teach about the kingdom of God. Through its ministry of the word, the Catholic Church invites people such as yourself to share in this responsibility.

You have been called to a very special ministry in the Church. You have been chosen to be a catechist, a minister of the word in your parish or school. Each time you gather to share the faith of the Church, you are proclaiming the good news that Jesus Christ is risen and present in our lives. Think:

- Why were you invited to be a catechist?
- What gifts or talents do you believe you bring to this ministry?

What is Catechesis?

Through catechesis, we discover and learn the Christian message passed on by the community of faith. We are challenged as believers to justice, peace, and service as we are formed within the worshiping community. As Pope John Paul II reminds us in describing the early Church's catechetical efforts, catechesis is about "making disciples" (*Catechesi Tradendae*, 1).

Sharing the Light of Faith, the *National Catechetical Directory* (NCD), provides this comprehensive statement about catechesis: "Catechesis refers to efforts which help individuals and communities acquire and deepen Christian faith and identity through initiation rites, instruction, and formation in conscience. It includes both the message presented and the way in which it is presented" (NCD, 5).

What Role Do Parents Play in Catechesis?

It is within the family that faith is nurtured and grows. Parents have a vital role in their children's faith development. Indeed, families catechize by their attitudes, values, and beliefs. As a catechist you are called to assist families. As the NCD reminds us, "parents, catechists, and community all have roles in the catechesis of the young" (NCD, 181).

God promises you as God promised the prophet Jeremiah:
I chose you before I gave you life. Before you were born I selected you....
Do not be afraid....
I am giving you the words you must speak.
From Jeremiah 1:5, 8, 9

What Do Catechists Do?

As a catechist your role is to lead young people to an understanding of their Catholic faith and to encourage them and their families to participate actively in the parish community.

As a catechist you promote important catechetical goals:

- *information*—religious concepts and content presented according to the age and readiness of your group
- *formation*—prayer and worship experiences that invite and engage the young believers to adhere to and deepen their faith
- *instruction*—in Creed, the Scriptures, sacraments and ritual, Christian living and morality, and our common prayer heritage

Go and make disciples of all peoples!
From Matthew 28:19

Your *Catechist's Annotated Guide* will help you to prepare yourself by studying the teachings of our faith, by deepening your understanding of Catholic doctrine, and by becoming more familiar with the teachings of Scripture. It will also enable you to plan your lessons creatively so that you may present the good news of the Catholic faith with enthusiasm and confidence.

What Is Important When Teaching Second Graders?

You have been asked to help bring a group of young children to understand and live their Catholic faith according to their age and readiness. It is neither necessary nor expected that the children will come to an adult understanding of the teachings of our faith. It is important, however, that each child begin to develop a relationship with God, that he or she learn to praise God and to experience God through prayer. This is the beginning of a lifelong experience with God.

What Is Helpful to Know About Second Graders?

- Second graders are delightfully unpredictable. Changes take place not only from day to day but often from moment to moment. That is because they are moving from an egocentric stage to a more concrete operational stage. They will need help in this development.

- One way to help is to provide many opportunities for collaborative work and for sharing. The most effective way of influencing this development is through personal interaction—your own, and the child's peers.

- Second graders sometimes show a lack of reversibility. This means that they can often come up with correct answers but have difficulty supplying reasons. They can supply a conclusion but cannot retrace the steps that got them there.

How Can You Help Your Second Graders Grow in Faith?

- Appreciate and cultivate the sense of wonder that is integral to these children. It is the natural foundation for developing a lifelong attitude of awe before the wonderful mysteries of God.

- Keep catechist talk to a minimum, and do not prolong activities. The children's attention span is about seven minutes. Plan each "seven minutes" well, and then change the activity.

- Include times of silence and prayer. These should be brief but frequent. Such moments can be valuable times of renewal and rest as well as an introduction to a beautiful kind of personal prayer.

THE LEARNING/TEACHING PROCESS

- Shared Christian Praxis is the learning/teaching process you will be using in the *Coming to Faith* Program.
- This process helps you to see the relationship between our life and our faith.
- The process begins with a focusing prayer.
- Shared Christian Praxis is made up of five movements, described briefly below.

Movement One

Our Life

Invites the children to think about and name a personal or faith experience related to the theme of the lesson.

Movement Two

Sharing Life

Invites the children to critical reflection by using their memories, imaginations, and reasoning abilities. The children are encouraged to think, share, or talk with God, one another, and/or the catechist about the life or faith experiences named in *Our Life*.

Movement Three

Our Catholic Faith

Presents the Catholic Church's Story and Vision, which includes:

- Doctrine
- Scripture
- Tradition
- Liturgy
- Faith stories of our Catholic Church

Following the presentation of *Our Catholic Faith* comes an explanation of how we might apply it to our lives today.

Movement Four

Coming to Faith

Offers questions and activities to help the children learn, understand, and relate our Catholic faith to their own lives.

Movement Five

Practicing Faith

Challenges the children to decide how to live the Catholic faith today in their homes and parish.

FAITH ALIVE AT HOME AND IN THE PARISH

The *Faith Alive at Home and in the Parish* (FAAHP) pages are designed to help the family reinforce what the children have learned and to encourage them in the practice of their faith. These pages are filled with a variety of activities for the family, including the new *Family Scripture Moment*, which engage the family in partnership with the catechist and parish to bring the child to a knowledge of and lived response to faith.

Each lesson has a *Faith Summary* accompanied by a "Learn-by-Heart" symbol: Learn by heart The symbol reminds you and/or the parent to help the child learn the *Faith Summary* by heart.

The *Review* on the back of this page gives the family and the catechist a way to determine the child's growth in faith.

A WAY TO LEARN AND TEACH THAT MAKES FAITH COME ALIVE

Overview of the Lesson

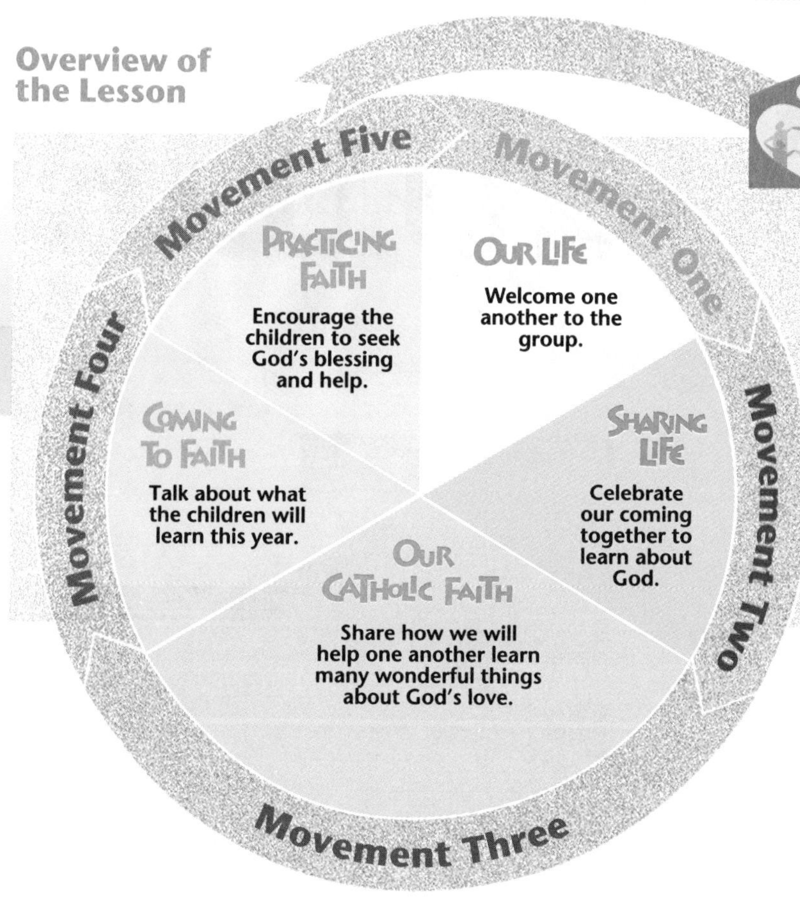

Faith Alive at Home and in the Parish

Family and child share ways that they can experience the wonders of God around us through the gift of our senses.

The FAAHP symbol represents the joining together of child, family, and catechist within the context of home and parish.

How to Plan Your Lesson Time

In planning your lesson it is important to know how to use your time wisely. Each lesson has a *Beginning*, a *Middle*, and *End*. To help you determine how many minutes should be devoted to each part, recommended percentages are given here.

Using *Our Catholic Identity*

This new feature supplements 15 chapters and is found after page 201 as perforated pupil pages. The middle section of each designated lesson plan contains suggestions for the best use of these pages.

You may also use the *Our Catholic Identity* pages at any other appropriate time during the year. It is suggested that the children remove the section at the end of the year to use as a reminder of their Catholic heritage.

Beginning

25%________ min.

FOCUSING PRAYER

Invites the child to prayer

Movement One

OUR LIFE

Focus on and name a life or faith experience.

Movement Two

SHARING LIFE

Reflect on and talk about that experience.

Middle

50%________ min.

Movement Three

OUR CATHOLIC FAITH

Learn the Story and Vision of our Catholic faith.

End

25%________ min.

Movement Four

COMING TO FAITH

Understand and make the faith their own.

Movement Five

PRACTICING FAITH

Decide through prayer or action to live the faith.

Enrichment and Optional Activities

The *Enrichment* activities and optional activities may be used to extend the time period of your lesson.

FAAHP Pages

Reinforce learning and encourage the practice of a living faith both in the family and in the parish.

TEXT&GUIDE

Teaching the *Coming to Faith* Program
The text and guide are your most important resources. Familiarize yourself with both. They are designed to help you proclaim the good news, filled with confidence and enthusiasm.

Look at the cover of the children's text. The mosaic you see pictured represents major themes of our Catholic faith, as outlined in the Scope and Sequence.

Open the child's text to the *Table of Contents* (see pages T2–T5).

- Look at each unit and lesson title. Read the doctrinal summary statements below each lesson title and the corresponding FAAHP materials. Note whether there is an *Our Catholic Identity* reference.

Introductory Lesson

(See text pages 7–12.)

- The introductory lesson welcomes the children to the grade 2 program.
- Use this lesson to help the children get to know each other and to establish a sense of belonging.

Core Lessons

(See pages 13–42. Turn to Lesson 1 on text page 13.)

Each core lesson opens with a focusing prayer. The four teaching pages are structured according to the Shared Christian Praxis approach. Each lesson has:

- A **Beginning:** The beginning leads the children into the lesson theme through *Our Life* and *Sharing Life.*
- A **Middle:** *Our Catholic Faith* presents the important doctrines, Scripture, and teachings of our Catholic Church and their meaning for our lives. *Our Catholic Identity* pages enrich the child's understanding of Catholic traditions and practices.
- An **End:** The ending of each lesson, *Coming to Faith* and *Practicing Faith,* helps the children internalize and practice their faith in the home and in the parish.

Liturgy Lessons

(See text pages 43–48.)

Liturgy lessons appear at the end of each unit. Use these lessons at appropriate times during the year.

Review

(See text pages 55–56.)

Unit Review/Unit Test

A review and a test follow each unit in grades 1–6. Use them to help you and the families assess the progress of the children in internalizing the Catholic faith presented in the KEYSTONE EDITION of *Coming to Faith.*

In the kindergarten text, the activities on the FAAHP pages review the lesson content.

Faith Alive at Home and in the Parish (FAAHP)

(See text pages 17–18.)

Each lesson concludes with two FAAHP pages. These pages contain:

- Family Faith Background—updates families on the faith learned in each lesson;
- *Faith Summary*—contains key Church teaching to be learned by heart;
- Family Activities—a variety of activities to choose from to help families work together to deepen their faith;
- *Review*—an opportunity to recall key ideas presented in the lesson.
- *Family Scripture Moment*—special new feature for families to listen to, study, reflect on, and share God's word from the Bible.

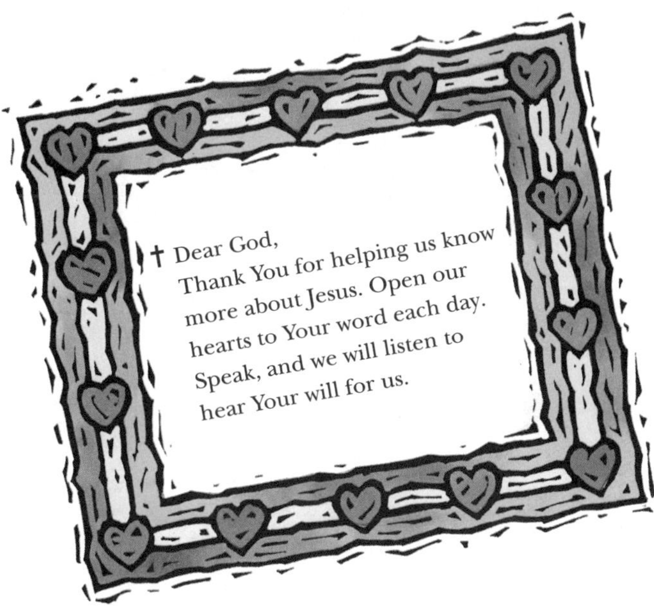

Everything you need to prepare, plan, and present your lesson

End-of-Book Resources

- *My Mass Book* is designed to help the children participate in the Sunday liturgy.
- *My Catholic Faith Book* outlines what the child has learned and is expected to understand.
- The *Prayers* section is designed to help the child learn important prayers presented in the text.
- *We Practice Our Catholic Faith* helps the children recall various Catholic practices.
- *Saints Cards* will help the children remember the saints that they will learn about this year.
- The *Glossary* includes religious words, pictures, and definitions contained in the text.
- The *Blackline Masters* in the back of the guide are correlated to specific liturgy lessons and provide a creative way to enhance those lessons.
- *Our Catholic Identity* Section is a supplement to fifteen of the class lessons. The content list on page 201 indicates the chapters suggested for their use.

GUIDE

For the Catechist: Spiritual and Catechetical Development

(See pages 7A–7B.)

These pages, which are found at the beginning of every lesson:

- provide an opportunity to deepen your own spirituality by using the Shared Christian Praxis learning/teaching process yourself;
- provide theological and scriptural background and resources for your understanding of the lesson and for enriching the children's liturgical practices and justice/peace experiences;
- provide a reference to the *Catechism of the Catholic Church* for your knowledge of Catholic teaching.

You might wish to meet occasionally with two or three other catechists to prepare your lessons and share your own faith responses.

Teaching Resources

(See page 7C.)

The page headed *Teaching Resources* contains important helps for you in the preparation of your lesson:

- *Overview of the Lesson*, which outlines the objective of each Shared Christian Praxis movement;
- *Teaching Hints*, which contain practical tips for teaching the lesson;
- *Faith Alive at Home and in the Parish*, which states the purpose of the FAAHP pages;
- *The Special-Needs Child*, which gives recommendations for helping children with visual, auditory, or motor-tactile needs;
- *Supplementary Resources*, which suggests optional materials to enrich your lesson, if time allows.

Lesson Plan Pages

(See pages 7–12.)

Each lesson plan is designed to help you to teach the lesson found in the text according to the Shared Christian Praxis approach. In order to teach your lesson, remember these steps:

1 Know your *Objectives*—they contain the purpose of the lesson.

2 Prepare the *Focusing Prayer*—this will draw the children into the lesson theme through prayer.

3 Choose your learning activities—these activities are integral to the lesson and will involve the children in the actual learning process.

4 Gather your materials—they are listed after each activity.

5 Read the annotations—they are printed in red on reduced text pages. Use them to highlight specific points in the lesson.

6 Remember to *Evaluate Your Lesson*—this is an opportunity to assess the overall effect of the lesson.

7 Use your *Enrichment* activities—these may be used to deepen the content of the lesson.

8 Select *Optional Activities*—they can be used as creative ways of extending the lesson.

9 Look at the *Faith Alive at Home and in the Parish* pages—encourage the children to bring these pages home to their families or complete them while they are with you.

10 Notice whether the lesson calls for the use of a page from the new *Our Catholic Identity* Section found in the back of the book.

Reminder:

Before you begin teaching the program, read the children's text from cover to cover, and browse through your Parish Annotated Guide.

Lesson Planning for Different Learning Styles

Reflective Questions to Assist You in Presenting Your Lesson

Lesson Plan: Beginning

- Do you welcome the children and gain their full attention before you begin the lesson?
- Do you show by your actions and expression that you are happy to be with the children?
- Do you make a point of calling each child by name during the lesson?

Lesson Plan: Middle

- Do you sit with the children when you are telling a story?
- Do you move from child to child or group to group when they are involved in learning activities?
- Do you take time to encourage or help each child?
- Do you use different tones of voice when storytelling, reading scripture, asking questions, and giving directions?

Lesson Plan: End

- Do you give the children quiet time to think about what they have learned?
- Do you send the children forth to know and practice their faith?

Presenting the *Beginning*, *Middle*, and *End* of Your Lesson

Evaluating Your Lesson

A successful catechetical program includes regular opportunities for assessment. Assessment is both measurement and evaluation, as well as a means of enrichment.

Ways to Evaluate Learning

- Invite the children to respond orally to a variety of questions.
- Have the children recite the *Faith Summary* statements of each lesson. These are indicated by the "Learn-by-Heart" symbol on the FAAHP pages.
- Have the children retell the doctrinal stories orally, in a drawing, or by role-playing.
- Have the children act out Scripture stories.
- Use word games to evaluate the children's religious literacy.
- Use the *Faith Words* from the lessons to help develop a religious vocabulary.
- Have the children write a letter to someone telling about what they have learned.
- Use the reviews and tests provided at the end of each unit.
- Have the children make up their own questions and answers on the content of faith.

Ways to Evaluate Your Teaching

- Are you using the *Catechist Resource* pages to prepare yourself for each lesson?
- Are you choosing activities that engage the children?
- Are you using the *Evaluating Your Lesson* section to assess your teaching and the children's participation?
- Is prayer an integral part of each lesson?

Use this page to review the effectiveness of your lessons.

Congratulations, Catechist! You truly are a minister of the word!

How TO CREATE A CATECHETICAL ATMOSPHERE

A catechetical atmosphere is created when children experience true Christian community in their families, their neighborhood, and their cultures. This community is formed through study, prayer, worship, and shared faith experiences. Here are its components:

KNOWING ABOUT THE FAMILIES AND NEIGHBORHOOD OF THE CHILDREN

From the very beginning of the child's life, the parents have been the primary catechists. You are a partner with the parents. The environment and practices in the home and neighborhood have had, and continue to have, a powerful influence on the faith development of the children in your group. To encourage and strengthen family involvement:

◆ Review the information your parish has given you regarding each child.

◆ Become familiar with where and with whom each child lives and who has legal custody of the child.

◆ Make sure you are aware of children who may be neglected or who come from homes that appear to be unhappy.

◆ Be mindful of and sensitive to the language spoken in the home and the religious affiliation of parent(s) or guardians.

◆ Be alert to the general health and well-being of the child.

◆ Be sensitive to the concerns of the local community.

You can, by your care and concern, guide the children to God's unconditional love. The experience of affirmation and support that you provide may indeed change a child's life.

Family Involvement

GETTING FAMILIES INVOLVED

It is essential to involve the family in the catechetical process. Regular family conversation about God and religion has a tremendous positive effect on a child's lifelong faith attitudes and practices.

Welcome the families at the beginning of the year. Explain the catechetical program and invite their participation.

◆ Introduce them to the children's text. The *Table of Contents* provides an excellent overview of what the children will be expected to learn about our Catholic faith over the course of the year.

◆ Explain how to use the *Faith Alive at Home and in the Parish* pages.

◆ Encourage a conversation about the *Faith Summary* statements. The symbol reminds families to help the children learn these by heart.

◆ Talk about the *Family Scripture Moment*, which is designed to encourage families to spend time each week using Scripture for study and prayer.

◆ Purchased stickers can be used to affirm the child. Parents may encourage the child to place a sticker on a completed review page, activity or near the *Faith Summary* they have learned.

◆ Be attentive to ways in which you can express joy or sympathy to families of the children in your group when someone is born, is hospitalized, dies, celebrates a sacrament for the first time, or experiences some other special event.

INVOLVING CHILDREN AND FAMILIES IN PARISH LIFE

The parish is an integral part of the faith life of the child. It is within the parish that the child celebrates the major events of life from birth to death.

◆ Invite the children and families to attend Mass on Sunday.

◆ Invite the whole parish community to take part in the celebration of sacraments.

◆ Encourage families to pray for one another and all the members of the parish.

◆ Begin the practice of sending greeting cards to the elderly, to the sick, and to families of those who have died.

◆ Encourage families to participate at Mass by singing, proclaiming as a lector, and in bringing up the gifts.

DEVELOPING MULTICULTURAL AWARENESS

True Christian community takes place within the context of the cultural heritage and the identity of the children we teach.

◆ Be aware of and sensitive to ethnic and cultural diversity.

◆ Encourage the children to express their cultural uniqueness through art, music, dance, food, and dress.

◆ Send communications home in the languages of the families, if possible.

◆ Invite families to share their cultural symbols and food at celebrations.

Ways to Build a Compassionate Community

PERSONAL INTERACTION

A true catechetical atmosphere is rooted in the personal interaction of the catechist, the child, and the family. You can play a vital role in creating a compassionate community by treating each child as a child of God. You do this by:

◆ being hospitable; making sure each child feels welcomed, accepted, and safe;

◆ knowing and calling each child by name often;

◆ showing kindness, love, and forgiveness to each child;

◆ sharing your thoughts, beliefs, and hopes with the children; giving them the same opportunity;

◆ being aware of and sensitive to the feelings and emotions of each child.

How to Create a Comfortable Atmosphere for Learning and Teaching

COMFORTABLE ENVIRONMENT

A suitable and comfortable environment is important for your catechetical undertakings. Such an atmosphere promotes a heightened sense of respect for the parish's catechetical mission. To help children and families feel comfortable:

◆ enhance your lesson by arranging the physical environment in as comfortable a manner as possible;

◆ wherever possible, set aside a special place for prayer. A prayer corner may be created by covering a small table with a cloth and placing a Bible and candle on the table.

MAKING DISCIPLINE POSITIVE

The word *discipline* comes from the root word *disciple*. Discipline means not only correcting misbehavior but also forming attitudes and responses that lead to good behavior. To create and maintain good discipline:

◆ use positive affirmation; acknowledge the children and remember to praise and affirm good behavior;

◆ involve the children in setting a few rules that are easy to remember, and explain why they are for the benefit of all;

◆ provide activities to build self-esteem and help children to feel good about themselves;

◆ respect the children's thoughts and ideas, and expect them to do the same with their peers;

◆ provide activities that challenge the children to cooperate with one another;

◆ deal with children who act inappropriately in a way that will calm them; set aside a space ("time out") where they can think quietly about their actions and the consequences of them.

HINTS FOR CREATIVE CATECHESIS

Here are some creative ways to make your lessons come alive.

Knowing How to Ask Questions

Ask direct, clear, and concise questions.

Give the children time to think about their responses.

Encourage the children to use their imaginations when responding to questions.

Encourage a variety of thoughtful, imaginative responses.

Being a Good Storyteller

Set the scene and identify the characters.

Look at the children. Keeping eye contact adds to the story's excitement.

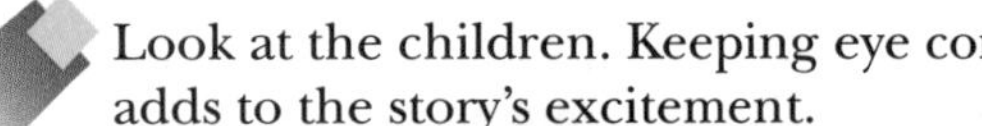

Be dramatic in voice and gesture.

Pause for dramatic effect or to ask questions.

Encourage the children's participation in the story. Invite them to add to it or finish it.

Whenever possible use text pictures to illustrate the story.

Using Silence

Children are very busy people. Silence can be both calming and enjoyable. Use short periods of silence (15–20 seconds):

before and after prayer time;

after asking a thought–provoking question;

for "time out";

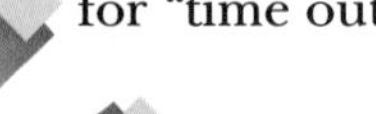
as personal reflection time;

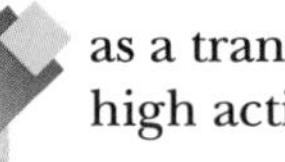
as a transition between periods of high activity and quiet time.

Memorization: Learning by Heart

Learning by heart enables children to know and recall their faith. Knowing their Catholic faith enables the children to live and practice faith.

 Singing, questioning, oral recitation, word games, and storytelling are all ways of helping children to memorize.

 Remember to help the children to understand their faith before they memorize it.

 Memorization is aided by the "Learn-by-Heart" *Faith Summaries* in every lesson.

Acting and Role-Playing

Acting out a story or scene is a natural and dramatic way for children to express themselves and learn.

 Invite the children to act out some of the stories in their text.

 Encourage the children to tell a story as other children act it out.

 Have the children role-play various situations to enter into the story and characters.

 Feel free yourself to act out or pantomime a particular story, inviting the children to provide the sound effects.

Music

Music unites cultures, languages, and customs and provides a common voice to praise God. Use music:

 to celebrate;

 to set a calm and prayerful tone;

 to reiterate the theme of the lesson;

 to relate lesson themes to contemporary songs, when appropriate;

 to encourage children to use dance to express themselves.

Photos/Illustrations

Photographs and illustrations are an integral part of each lesson.

 Point out and discuss the photos and illustrations on the text pages.

 Have the children use or refer to the art and/or photos on the text pages to retell stories.

 Have the children imagine themselves in the text pictures.

HOW TO TEACH THINKING SKILLS FOR DISCIPLESHIP

TODAY'S WORLD DEMANDS "CRITICAL THINKERS." What does being a critical thinker mean to you?

As catechists, our goal is to help young people become disciples of Jesus Christ.

Disciples of Jesus Christ act as "critical thinkers." They apply the teachings of the Church as presented in Scripture and Tradition to the real world in which they live.

Here are a few suggestions to help the young people develop critical-thinking skills in your lessons.

- Pray about contemporary events with the children.
- Help the children to distinguish between unfavorable events and those that are examples of the presence of God with us.
- When telling Scripture or faith stories, encourage the children to recall events and apply the message to their own lives.

In the learning/teaching process of Shared Christian Praxis, children develop critical thinking. At all times encourage the children to think and act as Jesus did.

T > I > M > E > L > I > N > E

Shaping Our Catechetical Heritage over the Ages

From the beginning of Christianity, the followers of Jesus Christ have turned to important documents of the Church for guidance. Sources such as those cited here are a valuable part of our Catholic teaching, tradition, and history. No attempt is being made to present an exhaustive list, but rather to show the role that documents such as those listed have played in our catechetical heritage through the ages.

The Didache 1st Century

The *Didache,* or *Teaching of the Apostles,* included early Church instruction for those preparing for Baptism.

Early Catechisms 5th–14th Centuries

An important faith summary was written by Saint Augustine in the 5th century. Other faith summaries appeared in the 9th and 14th centuries.

The Roman Catechism 1566

The landmark *Roman Catechism,* called for by the Council of Trent, was written to help priests in teaching Catholic people after the Protestant Reformation. The *Roman Catechism* was the last major catechism of the Church until the *Catechism of the Catholic Church,* promulgated in 1992.

The Second Vatican Council 1962-1965

The Council documents urged and outlined renewal throughout all phases of Church life.

The General Catechetical Directory 1971

The Second Vatican Council called for a renewal of catechesis. In response, *the General Catechetical Directory* presented guidelines for catechesis in the Church.

To Teach as Jesus Did 1972

A pastoral message on Catholic education that promoted message, community, and service as three critical elements for Catholic education.

Basic Teachings for Catholic Religious Education 1973

Doctrinal principles to guide the faith formation of Catholic people.

On Evangelization in the Modern World 1975

A turning point in the Church's understanding of the relationship between culture and the faith message.

On Catechesis in Our Time 1979

Important apostolic exhortation of Pope John Paul II on catechesis for today. Especially significant for identifying the aim and purpose of catechesis.

Sharing the Light of Faith: National Catechetical Directory 1979

A key resource for catechesis on all levels and the many dimensions of catechetical ministry. A description of and guidelines for catechesis and catechetical planning in the United States.

The Challenge of Adolescent Catechesis 1986

Addresses the foundations and ministry of adolescent catechesis, indicates a framework for such catechesis, and incorporates leadership dimensions.

Rite of Christian Initiation of Adults 1988

Restored the catechumenate for initiation into the Church, with important implications for the entire process of conversion, liturgy, catechesis, and the faith community.

Adult Catechesis in the Christian Community 1990

Focuses on and promotes the importance of adult catechesis in the faith community.

Catechism of the Catholic Church 1992

A major catechism and reference resource for bishops, priests, catechetical leaders, publishers of catechetical materials, and Catholic people.

"And so we shall all come together to that oneness in our faith and in our knowledge of the Son of God." **Ephesians 4:13**

CATECHIST'S WORKSHOP

Catechist Resources

PRIMARY GRADES

BOOKS FOR THE CATECHIST

Catechism of the Catholic Church
New York: William H. Sadlier, 1992 (1-800-221-5175)

Groome, Thomas H.
Sharing Faith
San Francisco: Harper Collins, 1991 (1-800-328-1991)

Hubbard, Most Rev. Howard J.
I Am Bread Broken
New York: Crossroads, 1996 (1-800-395–0690)

PERIODICALS FOR THE CATECHIST

The following periodicals contain articles that respond to the practical and enrichment needs of catechists and religion teachers:

Catechist
Peter Li, Inc., Dayton, OH (1-800-543-4383)

Religion Teacher's Journal
Twenty-Third Publications, Mystic, CT (1-800-321-0411)

The Catechist's Connection
The National Catholic Reporter Publishing Co., Inc., Kansas City, MO (1-800-444-8910)

BOOKS TO READ TO CHILDREN

Spier, Peter
People
New York: Doubleday, 1980 (1–800–323–9872)

Snyder, Bernadette McCarver
Have You Ever Seen an Elephant Sneeze?
Notre Dame, IN: Ave Maria Press, 1996 (1–800–282–1865)

Szaj, Kathleen C.
I Hate Goodbyes!
New York: Paulist Press, 1993 (1–800–218–1903)

DRAMAS, CRAFTS, ACTIVITIES FOR CHILDREN

Langdon, Harry
Children Celebrate: 39 Plays for Feasts
Cincinnati, OH: St. Anthony Messenger Press, 1993

MacClennan, Carole
Learning by Doing: 150 Activities to Enrich Religion Classes for Young Children
Mystic, CT: Twenty-Third Publications, 1993

—When Jesus Was Young: Stories, Crafts, and Activities for Children
Mystic, CT: Twenty-Third Publications, 1991

Mathson, Patricia
Creativities: 101 Creative Activities for Children to Celebrate God's Love
Notre Dame, IN: Ave Maria Press, 1992

RETREATS FOR CHILDREN

Hakowski, Maryann
Growing with Jesus: Sixteen half-day, full-day and overnight retreats that help children celebrate and share the light of Christ
Notre Dame, IN: Ave Maria Press, 1993

CATECHIST'S WORKSHOP

A PLANNING GUIDE

*Look for *Our Catholic Identity*, page 201.

Liturgical chapters (6, 7, 13, 14, 20, 21, 27) may be used as scheduling needs demand.

We Learn to Follow Jesus

For the Catechist: Spiritual and Catechetical Development

Adult Background

Our Life

There's an old story about a teacher in ancient China who had hundreds of students. The emperor came to visit and was impressed with the number of students. The emperor asked the old teacher, "Exactly how many disciples do you have living here?" And the teacher answered, "Oh, five or six at the very most."

Ask yourself:

- What makes this story humorous?
- For me, what does being a disciple mean?

Sharing Life

What hopes do you have about helping the children in your group to become young disciples of Jesus?

In what ways might they help you to grow or change as a disciple of Jesus?

Our Catholic Faith

In the Gospel of John we find the endearing story of how Jesus attracted His first two disciples simply by walking by. As followers of John the Baptist, Andrew and John were quick to follow their prophetic leader's cue. "There is the Lamb of God!" said the Baptist, pointing at Jesus. And the disciples immediately fell into step behind the unknown Rabbi from Nazareth. "What are you looking for?" Jesus asked. The two wondered where He lived, and He responded "Come and see" (John 1:35–39).

As catechists, we have been commissioned by the Church to extend this same invitation to the children with whom we will share *Coming to Faith.* We invite them to "Come and see" where Jesus lives and to discover what He requires of His would-be disciples. We help them to understand that a disciple is one who is so attracted to Jesus that he or she is willing to set aside other things in order to follow Him. In the process of following, the disciple learns who Jesus is and how to follow His way of love. (The word *disciple* is derived from the Latin *discipulus,* meaning "a learner." It is helpful to recall that the word *discipline* comes from the same root.)

As adults, we become increasingly aware that discipleship requires us to live as our best selves. In reflecting on the story of Jesus and the rich young man (Matthew 19:16–26), Pope John Paul II observes that even the disciples themselves were startled by Jesus' call to discipleship because the demands of following Him were so great.

Like Andrew and John when they accepted the invitation to "Come and see," we do not face the demands of discipleship on our own. What is impossible for us is fully possible with God. We have Jesus' word for it.

Coming to Faith

Describe your vision of a contemporary disciple of Jesus.

In what ways might you fulfill that vision in your own life?

Practicing Faith

How will you encourage in the children in your group a desire to follow Jesus?

The Theme of This Chapter Corresponds with Paragraph 443

LITURGICAL RESOURCES

To make the invitation of Jesus more immediate and personal for the children, create a prayer space where all can gather. A large rug or mats placed in a circle around an open Bible with a candle will serve well. Have two children, one on either side of the room, act out the part of Jesus. Each goes to invite two children at a time to "Come, follow me." When all have been gathered, hold the Bible and tell the "follow me" story in Mark 1:16–20.

JUSTICE AND PEACE RESOURCES

Invite the children to play a simple game called "What Do You Think?" Display mounted illustrations of the following or similar situations. As each is displayed, ask: "What do you think a disciple of Jesus would do if he or she saw . . ."

- a child crying in school or on the playground;
- an elderly person carrying heavy packages;
- a poor family with nothing to eat;
- a sick person who is lonely?

Teaching Resources

Overview of the Lesson

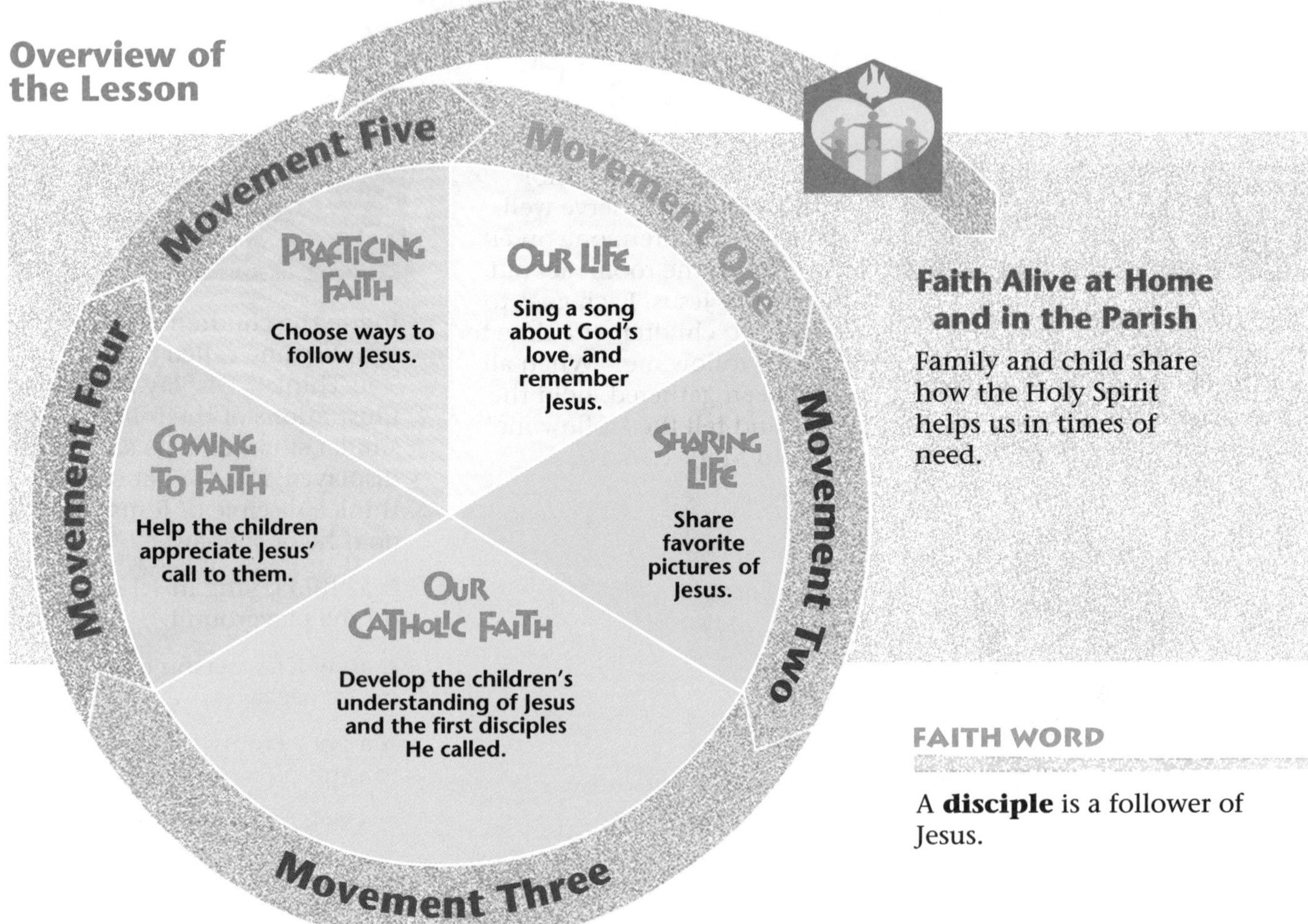

Faith Alive at Home and in the Parish

Family and child share how the Holy Spirit helps us in times of need.

FAITH WORD

A **disciple** is a follower of Jesus.

Teaching Hints

The purpose of this lesson is to give the children an opportunity to become acquainted with one another and to introduce them to the person of Jesus. It is important to create a comfortable and loving atmosphere in which the children will feel free to express themselves. Let them look through their books and notice the pictures of Jesus in them. Point out that they will be learning many more wonderful things about Jesus during the year.

Special-Needs Child

Orient the children who are visually impaired with a tour of the room. If you rearrange your room, be sure to inform these children.

Visual Needs

- large, full-color picture of Jesus with children

Auditory Needs

- headphones, recording of song and scripture from *Our Catholic Faith*

Tactile-Motor Needs

- peer helpers for creative projects

Supplemental Resources

NOTE: Resources listed throughout the guide were available at the time of publication but ongoing availability cannot be guaranteed.

My Stories About Jesus (book)
by Sarah Fletcher
Concordia Publishing House
3558 South Jefferson Ave.
St. Louis, MO 63118-3968
(1-800-325-3040)

Jesus the Leader (video)
God's Story series
Mass Media Ministries
2116 North Charles Street
Baltimore, MD 21218
(1-800-288-8825)

Objectives

To help the children

- know that Jesus is with them;
- appreciate their call to follow Jesus;
- recognize their need to learn more about Jesus.

Focusing Prayer

Greet each child warmly and take a few minutes for the children to learn each others' names. Then have them join hands and say together the prayer at the top of page 7.

Our Life

A "Together" Song

Invite the children to sit in a circle with their hands joined. Teach the song "God's Love Joins Us" on page 7 and then sing it with the children. Allow them to stand and swing their hands back and forth as they sing it. You may wish to use Sadlier's grade 2 *Coming to Jesus in Song* cassette.

Remembering Jesus

Have the children close their eyes and picture in their minds someone special they have learned about in religion class. Tell them to "hold" the picture in their minds as you ask: "Does His name begin with A? B? C?" and so forth. Have them raise their hands when you get to the correct letter. Ask the children to remember and share what they learned about Jesus.

Sharing Life

A Picture Search

Give each child a copy of the new book: *Coming to Jesus.* Read the title together and invite comments about the front cover. Read the rest of page 7 and have the children share their favorite pictures.

Enrichment

Making A Poster

Have the children examine the picture on page 7 and note the poster with the letters of Jesus' name. Let each child make a similar poster and decorate it with flowers, hearts, or other designs.

Materials needed: construction paper; markers; decorating supplies

We Learn to Follow Jesus

O God, Your love brings us together. Help us to share our faith.

Our Life

Sit quietly in a circle.
Join hands and sing.
(To the tune of "Go Round and Round")

♫ God's love joins us together (3x)
As we begin this year. ♫

Jesus our friend is with us as we begin this year. Share some things you already know about Jesus. Take turns sharing your thoughts. (1)

(1) Possible responses: He is our friend; He loves all people; etc.

Sharing Life

Look in this book.
Share the pictures you like best with your friends. Tell why you like them.

What would you like to learn about Jesus this year? Accept reasonable responses.

7

Lesson Plan: Middle

Our Catholic Faith

Listening to a Story

Hold up a Bible and see if the children can recognize it. Remind them that it is God's word, and that the Bible helps us learn more about Jesus.

Have them examine the picture on pages 8 and 9 and comment on it. Then ask them to listen quietly as you read to them the story of the picture, very dramatically, using gestures as you go along. Help the children enter into the story by pretending that they are standing or sitting on the shore near the disciples.

Faith Word

Display the Faith Word *disciple.* Have the children repeat it after you. Read the definition together with them. Point out that this year they will be learning many more wonderful things about Jesus; in order to become a follower or disciple of Jesus, we must get to know Him very well. Talk with the children about the fact that they will also get to know more about Jesus' other disciples and friends, with whom we have so much in common.

Sharing with Jesus' Friends

Talk with the children about the fact that friends and family members share many things with one another. As members

Come Follow Jesus
This year we will learn many new things about God's love.

We will grow in our Catholic faith as we read and listen to stories from the Bible.

Listen carefully to a Bible story about Jesus inviting people to follow Him.

One day Jesus was walking along the shore. He saw two fishermen, Peter and Andrew, catching fish. Jesus walked toward them and said, "Come, follow Me."

Peter and Andrew said yes. They left their fishing boats and followed Jesus.
From Mark 1:16–18

8

You might wish to have the children role-play the Scripture story.

of God's family and as special friends of Jesus, they will be sharing in some of the special gifts that Jesus left to us: the sacraments of Reconciliation and Eucharist. (Post flash cards of these two words.) Explain that these sacraments help us share in the love and forgiveness of Jesus' followers.

A Mathematical Verse

Read with the children the verse at the bottom of page 9. Invite them, as they recite it, to "draw" with their hands the plus, minus, and multiplication signs and then to add a cross for Jesus when reciting the last line.

Faith Summary

Have the children turn to the Faith Summary on page 11. Use the annotations to see if the children can express in their own words what they have learned.

FAITH WORD

A **disciple** is a follower of Jesus.

This year we will learn more about following Jesus. We will also share with all Jesus' followers, or disciples, in a special way. We will prepare to celebrate the sacraments of Reconciliation and Eucharist with the Church community. Some of us may also celebrate the sacrament of Confirmation.

Together, read how we can join with everyone who follows Jesus.

We will...

add (+) other friends with
whom we will share.
subtract (−) selfish ways and
show we care.
multiply (×) ways to help
and pray.
Jesus, our teacher, shows
us the way.

9

ENRICHMENT

A Dramatization

Invite the children to dramatize simply the story of the call of Peter and Andrew. Let one child act as narrator and tell the story in his or her own words as the others act it out. Let some children act as additional fishermen and others as passersby on the shore.

You may wish to use pages 13 and 14 of Sadlier's *Celebrating Our Seasons and Saints,* Level 2.

Lesson Plan: End

Coming to Faith

Sharing Jesus' Call

Read together the paragraph at the top of page 10. Give the children a few moments to share what they "heard" Jesus say to them. Suggest some responses of your own. Then have the children print their names on the shells in their books to show that they will respond to Jesus' message to them.

Practicing Faith

Helping One Another

Have the children reread the poem on page 9 as directed. Let them repeat the gestures they used previously. Take time to have each child contribute an example of what she or he will do to help others.

A "Come and Follow Jesus" Song

Teach the song "Come and Follow Jesus" on page 10. Then, holding a picture of Jesus in your hand, lead the children in a procession around the room.

You may wish to use Sadlier's grade 2 *Coming to Jesus in Song* cassette.

Evaluating Your Lesson

- Do you feel the children know Jesus is with them?
- Do they appreciate their call to follow Jesus?
- Have they decided to learn more about Jesus?

Enrichment

Adding to the Song

Write the words *pray, say, day, stay,* and *play* on the chalkboard. Ask the children to make up new lines to the song they have learned, using some of these words, for example: "He teaches us to pray"; "Each and every day"; "Close to Him we'll stay"; "At work or at play."

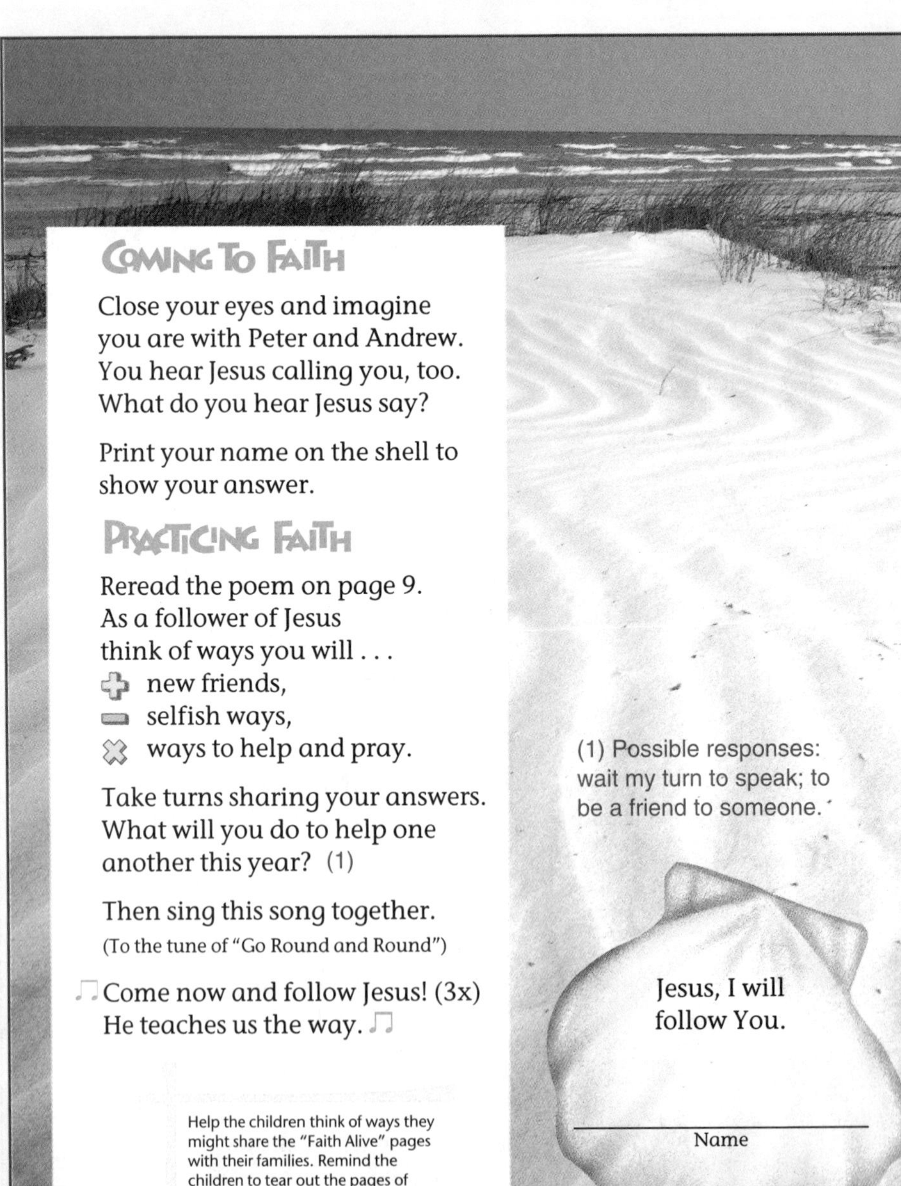

Friends of Jesus (for use with page 7)

Place a picture of Jesus in the center of a large piece of posterboard. Print under the picture "We are trying to be friends of Jesus." Explain that during this year the children will be learning more about what it means to be a friend of Jesus. If they are willing to listen carefully to learn about being a friend of Jesus, invite them to sign their name to the poster. Place the poster on the floor so that several children can write at the same time.

Have each child trace and color boy and girl patterns. Have them paste the "boys" and "girls" toward the outside of the poster with hands joining. At the bottom of the poster write "Friends of Jesus help one another."

Materials needed: picture of Jesus; posterboard or cardboard; patterns for tracing; paper; pencils; glue; scissors

Writing Some Questions (for use with page 8)

Have the children brainstorm ideas for questions they would like to ask Jesus. Write them on the chalkboard or newsprint. Give each child a piece of paper. Then have the children write the three most important questions they would like to ask. Have them fold up their questions and write their names on the blank side of the paper. Place all of the questions in a box. Seal it with tape. Write on the tape "To be opened on (date)" (the last day you will see the children).

Explain to the children that on the last day of the year, they will get their questions back. Each will have a chance to ask his or her questions and see if someone in the group can answer them.

Materials needed: paper; pencils; box; tape

Follow the Leader (for use with page 9)

Cut yellow construction paper in the shape of five flat stones. Paste the stones on a large sheet of posterboard to create a path from the bottom to the top of the board. Label the space at the top "God's Kingdom"; at the bottom write "Road to God's Kingdom."

Ask the children to think about what are the most important rules they should follow to reach the Kingdom of God. Then help them decide which five are the most important. Label the five stones with the ideas the children came up with. You might want to show this poster to the children from time to time to see if their ideas have changed.

Materials needed: yellow construction paper; posterboard; markers

Litany to Jesus (for use with page 10)

Gather the children around the prayer table and distribute parts for their special litany to Jesus.

Leader: Jesus, You are our friend.
Your love brings us together.

All: Help us to listen to Your story.

Child 1: Jesus, You call us to follow You.

Child 2: Jesus, help us to add other friends with whom we will share.

Child 3: Jesus, help us to subtract selfish ways and to show we care.

Child 4: Jesus, help us multiply ways to help and pray.

Leader: Let us pray. Our Father . . .

FAITH ALIVE AT HOME AND IN THE PARISH

In this opening lesson your child was welcomed to second grade—both as an individual and as a member of a Catholic community.

It is important that you help your child to continue to feel part of your parish community as we prepare together this year for the celebration of the sacraments of Reconciliation, Eucharist, and, in some parishes, Confirmation. One very important way to do this is to take your child to Mass each Saturday evening or Sunday.

Here are some additional ways you can continue to help your child grow in faith.

- Talk about each lesson together, including the pictures and artwork, which are important to an understanding of the lesson.
- Invite your child to share with you any songs, poems, or experiences of prayer that have been learned or shared. Even before truths of our Catholic faith are fully understood, they may be more easily absorbed through a song or prayer.
- Use the *Faith Alive at Home and in the Parish* pages to expand your child's catechesis through the experience of the community of faith in your family and in the parish family. You are encouraged to do one or two of the activities with your child if time permits. Have a conversation about the *Faith Summary* statements that summarize each lesson. Your child will be encouraged to learn certain ones by heart. "Learning by heart" means much more than simply memorizing. It means making these convictions one's own, a part of one's heart. It is much more important for your child to have the truth in the heart than to be able to repeat it exactly.

Family Scripture Moment is offered as a unique opportunity for the family to share faith by "breaking open" God's word together. The "moment" can be as brief or as long as you wish. Here is a simple outline of how to use this time.

- **Gather** together as a family. All can participate from the youngest to the oldest.
- **Listen** to God's word as it is read slowly and expressively by a family member.
- **Share** what you hear from the reading that touches your own life. Give time for each one to do this.
- **Consider** the points suggested in the text as a way for the whole family to come to a deeper understanding of God's word in the Bible.
- **Reflect** on and then share any new understandings among you.
- **Decide** as a family how you will try to live this word of God.

This year, selections from the Gospel of Matthew will be the focus of this Family Scripture Moment.

(2) What sacraments will you prepare to celebrate?

Show Jesus how happy you are to be His follower. Decorate the word *yes*.

Learn by heart **Faith Summary**

(1) • Jesus invites us to follow Him.
(1) Who invites us to follow Him?

(2) • We will prepare to celebrate the sacraments of Reconciliation and Eucharist.

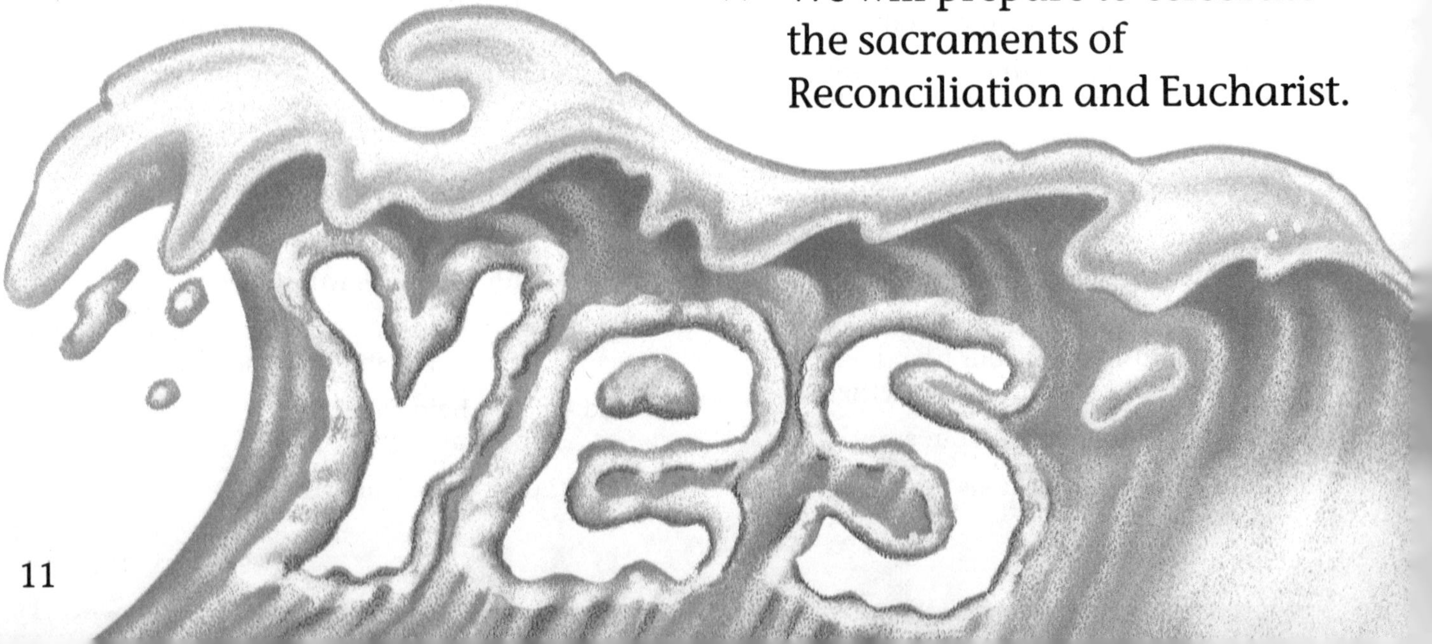

Review

When you and your child have worked together on the *Faith Summary* and any of these family activities, invite your child to choose a sticker and place it at the top of this page. Do this for every *Faith Alive* page that follows.

sticker

Tell Jesus something you want to learn about Him this year.

Family Suggestion: You may wish to provide your child with a variety of stickers that can be used on the review page throughout the year.

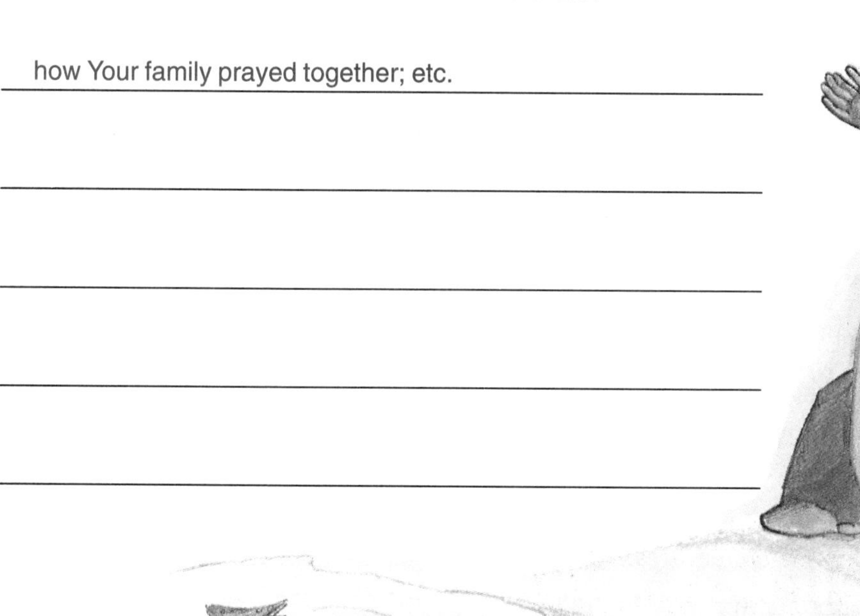

JESUS,
I want to learn about...

how Your family prayed together; etc.

Encourage the children to gather with their families to share the *Family Scripture Moment.*

FAMILY SCRIPTURE MOMENT

As you **Gather** for the first time this year to listen to Matthew's Gospel, imagine that you are in the crowd waiting to hear Jesus. **Listen** to these words.

Jesus used parables to tell the crowds many things. He did this to make come true what the prophet had said, "I will use parables when I speak to them; I will tell them things unknown since the creation of the world." Then Jesus told them this parable: "The kingdom of heaven is like this. A man is looking for fine pearls, and when he finds one that is unusually fine, he goes and sells everything he has, and buys that pearl."

From Matthew 13:34–35, 45–46

Share Why do you think Jesus compares the kingdom of God to a fine pearl?

Consider for family enrichment:

- Jesus captured people's imagination by using parables—brief stories based on ordinary life situations.
- Telling parables was a powerful way to get Jesus' listeners to think about their faith and to put the kingdom of God first in their lives, like the pearl in this parable.

Reflect and **Decide** What can our family do to show we have heard Jesus' message of God's kingdom?

For the Catechist: Spiritual and Catechetical Development

ADULT BACKGROUND

Our Life

On a brilliant April afternoon a busload of American pilgrims found themselves on a steeply winding road. They had come to the shrine at Lourdes to seek healing. But now they were on an excursion into the French Pyrenees.

When the bus pulled up at a hostel, everyone piled out to take in the view. Suddenly all chatter and laughter died away. Stunned by the majesty arrayed before them, the pilgrims broke into song. They sang of the "awesome wonder" before them, praising God with the refrain "How great Thou art!"

While the others gazed at the snow-clad peaks, the chaplain scanned their uplifted faces. Many were ravaged by illness. But all were intensely beautiful. "Truly," he whispered, "how great Thou art!"

Ask yourself:

- Have I ever been thrilled by creation? When? Why?

Sharing Life

What sometimes prevents you from appreciating the Creator's work?

Describe the relationship you would like to have with our Creator.

Our Catholic Faith

We begin to understand the revelation of God's self-expression by observing the beauty of creation. The grandeur of the sky, the richness of the earth, and the magnificence of the seas speak of God's generosity, life-giving nature, and incredible imagination. But humanity itself is the greatest manifestation of God's creative hand. As Saint Teresa of Avila says, "The Creator must be sought through the creatures."

Our understanding of God's revelation extends beyond wonder and awe in the face of the physical, however, and includes mysteries that cannot be comprehended simply by human reason.

The Trinity is not an obscure doctrine to be quickly taught and forgotten. The Trinity is a reality in our lives. In the Nicene Creed we profess this faith. God the Father is the Creator, the source of being for all that is seen and unseen. Jesus Christ is the only Son of God. He became one of us and by His death and resurrection redeemed us. The Holy Spirit is the Giver of Life, who unites all people in love, and the Sanctifier who gathers all of creation in Christ and offers it up to the Father.

We have been created in the image of God, who is a community of Persons, and who calls us into relationship with Himself. We are called to live in relationship with each other and with the Trinity. We share in the life of the Trinity through our Baptism.

Coming to Faith

How do you experience the three Persons of the Trinity in your life?

How does being made in the image of God, who is Triune, affect the way you know and love others?

Practicing Faith

How will you, as an image of the Trinity, try to live in communion with others?

How will you help your children to grow in loving God who is Father, Son, and Holy Spirit?

The Theme of This Chapter Corresponds with Paragraph 237

LITURGICAL RESOURCES

Trinitarian prayer runs like a compelling refrain throughout our liturgical and personal prayer. In the Glory to God, we praise in turn the Father, the Son, and the Holy Spirit. In the Creed, we affirm our belief in God our Father and Creator, Jesus the Savior, and the Holy Spirit Who gives us life.

Invite the children to join you in composing a litany of Trinity prayers to which the response each time is: "Holy, holy, holy!"

- God the Father, You made people very good . . .
- God the Son, You came to save us . . .
- God the Spirit, You pray in us . . .

JUSTICE AND PEACE RESOURCES

Pope John XXIII once said, "We are not on earth as museum keepers, but to cultivate a flourishing garden of life." Jesus' parable of the man who buried his talents echoes a similar lesson. The gifts we have been given are to be nurtured, to be allowed to grow. Respect for creation implies respect for all that lives: plants, animals, and persons. Respect for what lives is an acknowledgment that life will grow and change. The Christian's love for all that lives is a commitment to ensure its growth.

As you teach the children about the Trinity, help them to choose one way that they will care for creation, love as Jesus loved, or live a holy life. Have the children draw or paste pictures from magazines on a sheet of paper to show what they have chosen. Display these where the group meets.

Teaching Resources

Overview of the Lesson

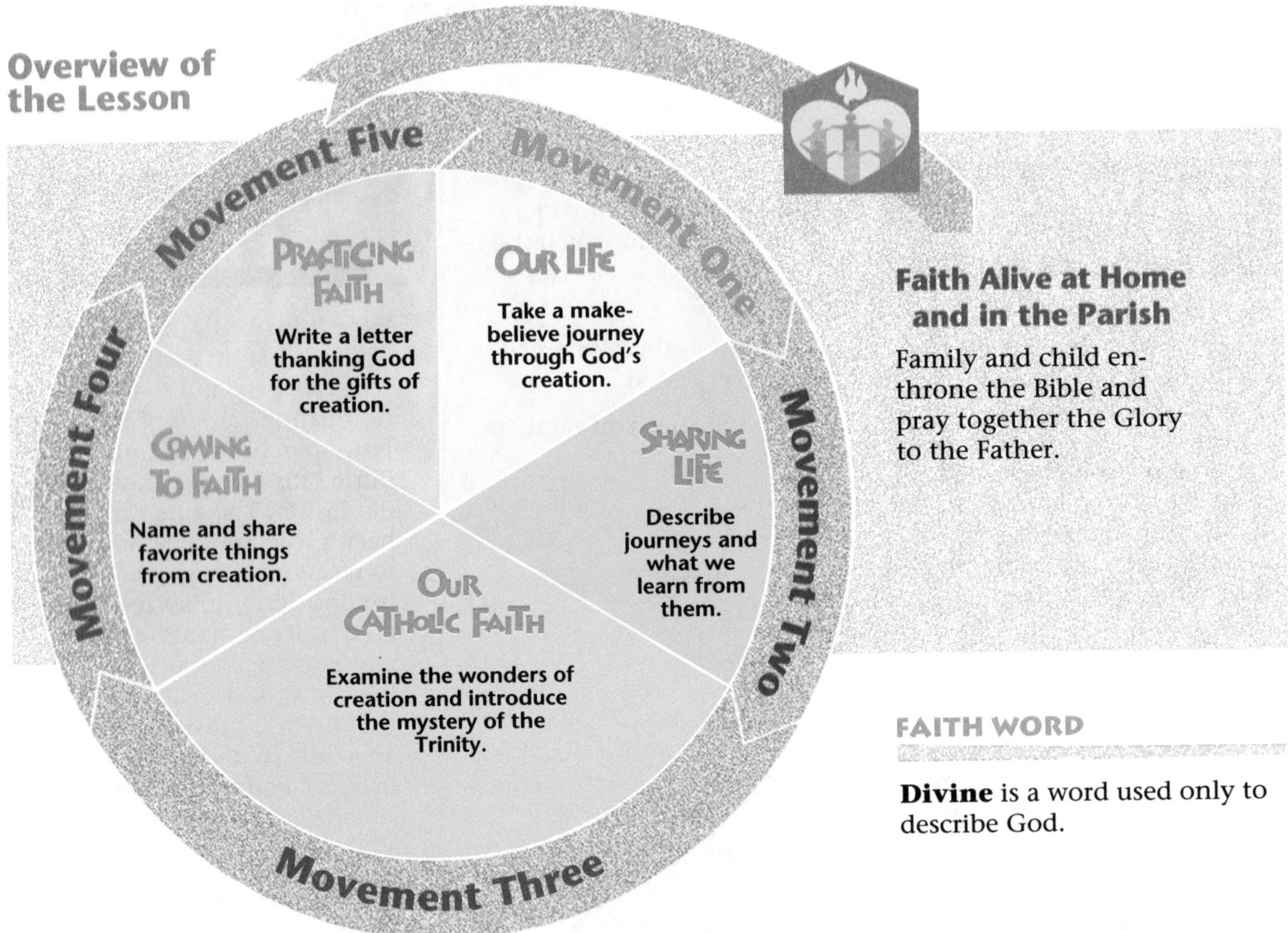

Faith Alive at Home and in the Parish

Family and child enthrone the Bible and pray together the Glory to the Father.

FAITH WORD

Divine is a word used only to describe God.

Teaching Hints

This lesson introduces the children to the wonders of God's creation. Encourage them to see that each gift of creation is an expression of God's personal love for them.

When introducing the topic of the Blessed Trinity, point out that because God is so great, we can't understand everything about Him, but we know God's great love for us by the special things that each Person does for us.

Special-Needs Child

When teaching children with special needs, keep in mind that their disabilities often make group activities physically demanding. It is important to look for signs of fatigue or frustration.

Visual Needs

- large, colorful photos of nature scenes

Auditory Needs

- headphones, instrumental recordings

Tactile-Motor Needs

- large crayons

Supplemental Resources

The Kingdom Series (video)
1. Why The Son Came
2. How The King Forgives
3. Why The Spirit Was Sent

Ikonographics
P.O. Box 600
Croton-on-Hudson, NY 10520
(1-800-944-1505)

Glory to the Father (book)
by Piera Paltro
St. Paul Books and Media
50 St. Paul's Avenue
Boston, MA 02130
(1-800-876-4463)

Lesson Plan: Beginning

Objectives

To help the children

- know the three Persons in God;
- appreciate the goodness and beauty of creation;
- recognize their call to respond in love to God.

Focusing Prayer

If possible, gather at a window and point out the beauties of creation as you lead the children in the prayer at the top of page 13.

Our Life

A Make-Believe Trip

Invite the children to open their books and look at the picture on page 13. Read aloud the first two paragraphs and then have the children tell which trip they would like to take and why. Share with the children what your own choice would be and why. Then have them close their eyes and imagine they are on their trip as you reread the choices. Use the annotation.

Multicultural Awareness

Have the children note the vastness and variety of creation as represented in the picture. Point out to the children that God made this great and beautiful world for all of us to share equally.

Sharing Life

Describing Our Journeys

Invite the children to take turns describing their journeys by answering the questions at the bottom of page 13. Be sure each child contributes at least one fact about her or his journey. See the annotation.

1 We Believe in God

Thank You, God, for the wonders of Your creation!

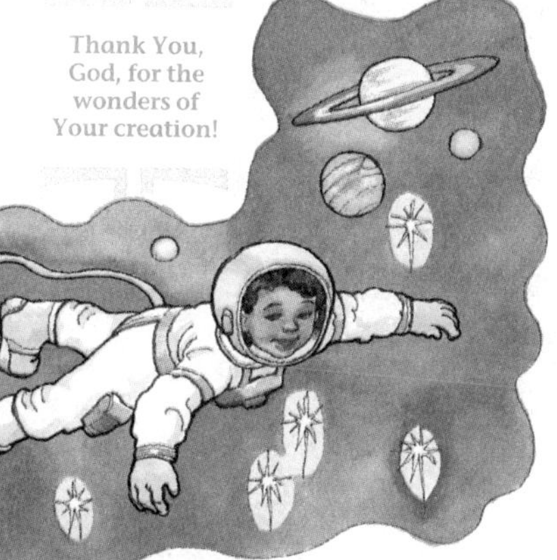

Our Life

Here are three make-believe journeys through the wonders of God's creation. Choose one.

You can soar among the sun and moon and stars. Or you can talk with the animals and birds and learn their secrets. Or you can swim underwater with fish and explore the depths of the sea.

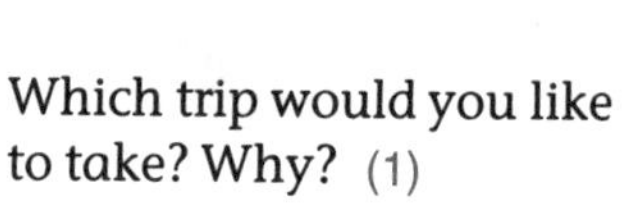

Which trip would you like to take? Why? (1)

(1) Encourage all the children to tell why they chose the one they did.

Sharing Life

What do you think you would see and hear and do on your journey? Tell about it.
Encourage acting out their trips.

What do you imagine you would learn?
Accept reasonable responses.

13

Enrichment

Creating Murals

Divide the children into three groups, depending on which "trip" they took. Give each group a large piece of cardboard and some play dough. Invite them to create a scene depicting their part of God's world. Have them share their scenes with the other groups.

Materials needed: cardboard; play dough

Lesson Plan: Middle

Our Catholic Faith

A Look at God's World

Give the children a few minutes to study the pictures of the children observing nature on page 14. Ask them to imagine they are in one of the pictures observing a part of nature. Call on volunteers to tell what they "see." Then read the four paragraphs on page 14. Impress on the children the beauty and awesomeness of God's creation and how loving God is to make us such a beautiful world.

A Happy Ending

Ask the children if they like to read stories with happy endings or sad endings. Hold up a Bible and explain that the Bible tells us the story of God's creation of the world of nature and the story of God's creation of people. Ask them to listen as you continue the story about the creation of people, to see if it has a sad or a happy ending.

Read the next three paragraphs and then talk with the children about the ending. Point out that if the story had ended after Adam and Eve's sins, (they were the first people), it would have been a sad ending. But God turned it into something happy.

Continue reading the rest of the material on page 15.

Lesson Plan: Middle

Emphasize God's total love in giving us everything we need, sending Jesus and the Holy Spirit to help us, so that each of our lives might have a happy ending. Use the annotations.

Materials needed: Bible

Our Great and Wonderful God

On the chalkboard, write the names of the three Persons in God, then have the children repeat them after you. Explain that we call the three Persons in God the Blessed Trinity. Show a flash card with the words *Blessed Trinity.*

Our Catholic Identity

Use page 1 of the *Our Catholic Identity* section in the back of the book. Talk with the children about how difficult it is to understand this wonderful mystery about three Persons in one God.

Remind them that because the three Persons in God are so important in our lives, we begin our prayers by using their names in the Sign of the Cross. Make the sign of the cross reverently with the children.

Faith Word

Display the Faith Word *divine.* Have the children repeat the word after you. Explain that it is a word used only when we are referring to God, because it describes Someone who is far above any created person or thing. Have the children find the word *divine* on the page. Then have them underline it and read the sentence that uses the word.

Faith Summary

Turn to the *Faith Summary* on page 17. Use the annotations to see if the children can express in their own words what they have learned.

You may also wish to use pages 5–6 in the activity book for *Coming to Jesus.*

FAITH WORD

Divine is a word used only to describe God.

The first people God made turned away from His love. They sinned.

God the Father did not stop loving them. He promised to send someone to save them and to show them how to love God again.

Play a telephone-whisper game. Form a circle and have each child whisper to the next, "God never stops loving us."

Stress the underlined text.

Many years later God sent Jesus, the Son of God. Jesus came to save us from sin. Jesus came to teach us how to love God, others, and ourselves. Jesus Christ is God's greatest gift to us.

Jesus knew we would need a Helper. So Jesus sent us the Holy Spirit to help us to love God, to love others, and to love ourselves.

We believe in one God. We believe that there are three Persons in one God, the Father, the Son, and the Holy Spirit. We call these three divine Persons the Blessed Trinity.

Because we are baptized we share in the life of the Blessed Trinity. We are God's own children.

Enrichment

A Trinity Mobile

Prepare cutout letters to spell the words *Father, Son,* and *Holy Spirit.* Give one letter to each child and have her or him decorate it by pasting on beads or glitter. Attach each letter, in order, to a piece of string and hang the words from a branch or a long piece of wood to make a Trinity mobile. Hang it at the center of the room to show that you are inviting the blessing of God the Father, Son, and Holy Spirit on all the children. See the annotation.

Materials needed: cutout letters; beads or glitter; paste; piece of wood; string

Lesson Plan: End

Coming to Faith

Drawing Our Favorite Things

Give each child a sheet of drawing paper and some crayons or markers. Ask the children to draw some of their favorite things from creation. Then have them share their drawings with one another.

Ask the questions listed on page 16 and give each child the opportunity to answer at least one.

Materials needed: drawing paper; crayons or markers

Practicing Faith

A Letter to God

Have the children close their eyes. Read to them the directions on page 16. Then invite them to complete their letters to God. Place these on a table with a crucifix and lead the group in a reverent Sign of the Cross.

Evaluating Your Lesson

- Do you feel the children know there are three Persons in God?
- Do they appreciate the goodness of creation?
- Have they decided to respond in love to God?

Coming to Faith

Name some of your favorite things God created. How can we show that we are glad to be alive in God's wonderful world? care for the earth; recycle; etc.

What does Jesus, the Son of God, teach us about the way we should live? to love God; others; and ourselves

What does the Holy Spirit help us to do? to love as Jesus taught

Practicing Faith

Close your eyes. Think about what God has done for you since you woke up today. Think of something good you will do for someone today because you love God. Then finish this letter.

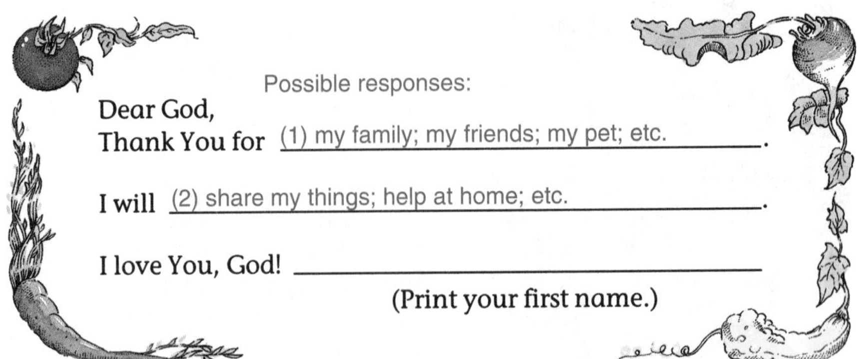

Possible responses:

Dear God,
Thank You for (1) my family; my friends; my pet; etc.

I will (2) share my things; help at home; etc.

I love You, God! ______________________
(Print your first name.)

Now let us pray together the Sign of the Cross, one of our prayers to the Blessed Trinity.

Talk to the children about ways they and their families might use the "Faith Alive" pages. Suggest that they show their families how reverently they make the sign of the cross.

Enrichment

Planting Seeds

Have available a bag of potting soil. Distribute seeds of a fast-growing herb, a plastic container, and a spoon to each child. Guide them in planting a few seeds. Talk with the children about God's goodness in giving plants the ability to make seeds so that their life could continue. Let the children be responsible for caring for the plants as they grow.

Materials needed: potting soil; seeds; plastic container; spoon

"G-MEW" Hanging Display **(for use with page 13)**

Provide cardboard patterns for a sun, star, cloud, and crescent-shaped moon. Let the children each trace one pattern on drawing paper and cut it out. On one side ask them to print "G-MEW" (God Made Everything Wonderful). On the other side have them draw or paste a picture of something God made for which they are thankful. When finished, invite the children to show and tell. Then help them attach string to the top of each shape. Hang the shapes from the ceiling or arrange them on a wall or a bulletin board.

Materials needed: cardboard patterns for tracing; drawing paper, one sheet per child; scissors; pencils; crayons; picture magazines; glue; string; tape or tacks

Blessed Trinity Crosses **(for use with page 14)**

Draw a cross outline large enough to fill a sheet of $8\frac{1}{2}$" x 11" paper. Each beam should be 2" wide. At the top of the upright beam print "Father." In the center of the transverse beam print "Son." Print "Holy" and "Spirit" on the left and right transverse beams respectively. Make a copy for each child.

Let the children decorate the crosses with small paper shapes to create "cut paper" designs. Have them cut out the crosses and hang them at home. Explain that if they stand facing the cross, it will help them remember where to place their hands when they make the sign of the cross. Conduct a demonstration.

Materials needed: cross outlines, one per child; colored paper; pencils; scissors; glue

"WHAT-DO-YOU-KNOW" Game **(for use with page 15)**

Print the following terms on index cards: *God Our Father, Jesus, Holy Spirit, Blessed Trinity,* and *Sign of the Cross*. Stack the cards face down. Have a volunteer pick up the top card and give it to you. Ask the child, "What do you know about (term on the card)?" The child then tells what he or she knows about that term. When all the cards have been used, shuffle them and repeat the game.

Materials needed: five index cards; marker

A Closing Prayer **(for use with page 16)**

Gather the children around the prayer table where the Bible is displayed. Have them sing "They are good" to the scale do-re-mi after each line of the following prayer:

God made night and day;
God made the sun and moon;
God made millions of stars;
God made fish in the sea;
God made the plants and the animals.

Walk among the children, stopping to place both hands on each one's shoulders, and say: "God created (Child's Name)." Ask the children to respond: "(Child's Name) is very good."

FAITH ALIVE AT HOME AND IN THE PARISH

In this lesson your child recalled the gifts of God our creator and the promise of hope that God gave at the very beginning of human history. This promise was fulfilled in our Savior, Jesus Christ. Your child also learned about the Blessed Trinity: the Father, the Son, and the Holy Spirit. The Blessed Trinity is a central dogma of our Catholic faith.

All of us have been created in the image and likeness of God. Just as we believe that God is a Trinity of love, so we are called to live in loving relationship with the Trinity and with one another. In Baptism we were given a share in the divine life. Through that life we are called to share in God's creative (Father), redeeming (Son), and sanctifying (Holy Spirit) work—first in our family, then in our parish, and finally in our world.

You might ask yourself:

- *How does my belief that all people are made in the image of God affect the way I treat others?*
- *How will I help my child to live and grow as a child of God?*

The Bible

Show your child the family Bible. Put it in a special place in your home. Read it and pray from it daily.

Learn by heart

Faith Summary

Who created everyone and everything good?

- God the Father created everyone and everything good.
- The Blessed Trinity means the three Persons in one God, the Father, the Son, and the Holy Spirit.
- Through Baptism we share in God's own life.

What does "Blessed Trinity" mean?

Glory to the Father

Close your eyes.
Imagine you are in your favorite
place in God's world.
Praise and thank God for all His gifts.

† Glory to the Father, and to the Son, and to
the Holy Spirit: as it was in the
beginning, is now, and will be for ever.
Amen.

You might wish to have the children pray this prayer activity at the end of the session. Then encourage them to think of at least one person they will do this with at home.

Review

Go over the *Faith Summary* together before your child completes the *Review.* The answers for questions 1–4 appear on page 200. The response to number 5 will help you see in a wonderful way how your child is trying to live as a follower of Jesus. When the *Review* is completed, have your child place a sticker on this page.

sticker

Write the correct answer on each line.

Father   Holy Spirit   Jesus   three

1. God the Father __________ created us.

2. Jesus __________ is God's own Son.

3. The Holy __________ Spirit __________ helps the friends of Jesus.

4. There are three __________ Persons in one God.

5. What does Jesus teach us to do? How will you show that you listen to Jesus?

To love God; others; and ourselves.

Possible response: I will pray; be kind to others; eat good food.

Encourage the children to gather with their families to share the *Family Scripture Moment*.

As you **Gather** ask each one to share what they love most about Jesus. Then **Listen** to what Matthew's Gospel says about Jesus.

At that time Jesus arrived from Galilee and came to John at the Jordan to be baptized by him. As soon as Jesus was baptized, He came up out of the water. Then heaven was opened to Him and He saw the Spirit of God coming down like a dove and lighting on Him. Then a voice said from heaven, "This is My own dear Son, with whom I am pleased."

From Matthew 3:13, 16–17

Share How do you know that God loves you?

Consider for family enrichment:

- We know that this gospel passage is not about our sacrament of Baptism. Jesus accepts John's baptism of repentance because Jesus wanted to be one with us sinners, even though He was sinless.
- Jesus, our Messiah, was anointed for His ministry by the Holy Spirit and identified as the beloved Son of God. The word *Messiah* means "anointed of God."

Reflect and **Decide** Ask: How do you think Jesus felt at the beginning of His public ministry? As a family, how will we try to follow His loving example this week?

2 Jesus Christ Is God's Son

For the Catechist: Spiritual and Catechetical Development

Adult Background

Our Life

Mary and Ed had high hopes for their daughter Rosa. She had just graduated from college, had several job offers, and her steady boyfriend already seemed like a son to them.

Although they did not try to push Rosa into getting married, they often talked of the "fabulous wedding" they would provide when the time came.

It came as a complete shock to Mary and Ed when Rosa decided to commit herself to a five-year lay missionary program in Central America. "I just don't get it," Ed complained. "Whatever possessed her to do such a thing?"

Ask yourself:

- What faith decision(s) have I made that others found hard to accept?
- How did my decision(s) change me?

Sharing Life

What "possesses" Christians who do God's work at some cost to themselves?

How might our teaching encourage such choices?

Our Catholic Faith

When we reflect on the reality of God's Son becoming human, we are confronted with the total gift of Jesus' being. We realize, "This is what love is: it is not that we have loved God, but that he loved us and sent his Son to be the means by which our sins are forgiven" (1 John 4:10).

Jesus is Emmanuel, God-with-us. By His life and death, He modeled for us the meaning of Christian ministry. Once, when His disciples were urging Him to have something to eat, Jesus responded by giving them some food for thought. He told them, "My food is to obey the will of the one who sent me and to finish the work he gave me to do" (from John 4:34). In that mature faith commitment, we hear the echo of an adolescent voice in the Temple saying, "Didn't you know that I had to do my Father's work?" (from Luke 2:49).

At the beginning of His public ministry, Jesus defined His mission by quoting from the prophet Isaiah:

> The Sovereign Lord has filled me with his spirit.
> He has chosen me and sent me
> To bring good news to the poor,
> To heal the broken-hearted,
> To announce release to captives
> And freedom to those in prison.
> (Isaiah 61:1)

Jesus makes it clear that what possesses those who choose to do God's work is the Spirit of the Sovereign Lord.

Coming to Faith

Envision yourself (or your parish) as one nourished by the food of which Jesus speaks. What do you see?

How might you prepare to do God's will in a new way?

Practicing Faith

How will you get to know Jesus better?

How will you listen and respond to the needs of the children during this coming week?

The Theme of This Chapter Corresponds with Paragraph 444

LITURGICAL RESOURCES

As a devoted Jew, Jesus loved the Temple. He called it His Father's house and a house of prayer. When the money-changers showed a lack of respect for the Temple, Jesus drove them out in righteous anger. The chief priests criticized Him for making Himself so at home in God's house.

Encourage the children to become familiar with their parish church so that they, like Jesus, can make themselves at home there. Conduct a guided tour. Then gather around the altar and invite them to re-tell the story of the boy Jesus in the Temple. Sing a simple song of faith.

JUSTICE AND PEACE RESOURCES

Helen Keller urged people to join the great company of those who make the barren places of life fruitful with kindness. The prayer of Saint Francis could be said to be a map that indicates these barren places of life—where there is hatred; where there is injury; where there is doubt; where there is despair; where there is sadness.

From an early age children can be encouraged to love each other as Jesus loves us. Have them consider what Jesus, at their age, might have done for the following:

- a child whom others have treated unkindly;
- someone who has been hurt;
- a family member who is sad;
- a child who is lonely.

Teaching Resources

Overview of the Lesson

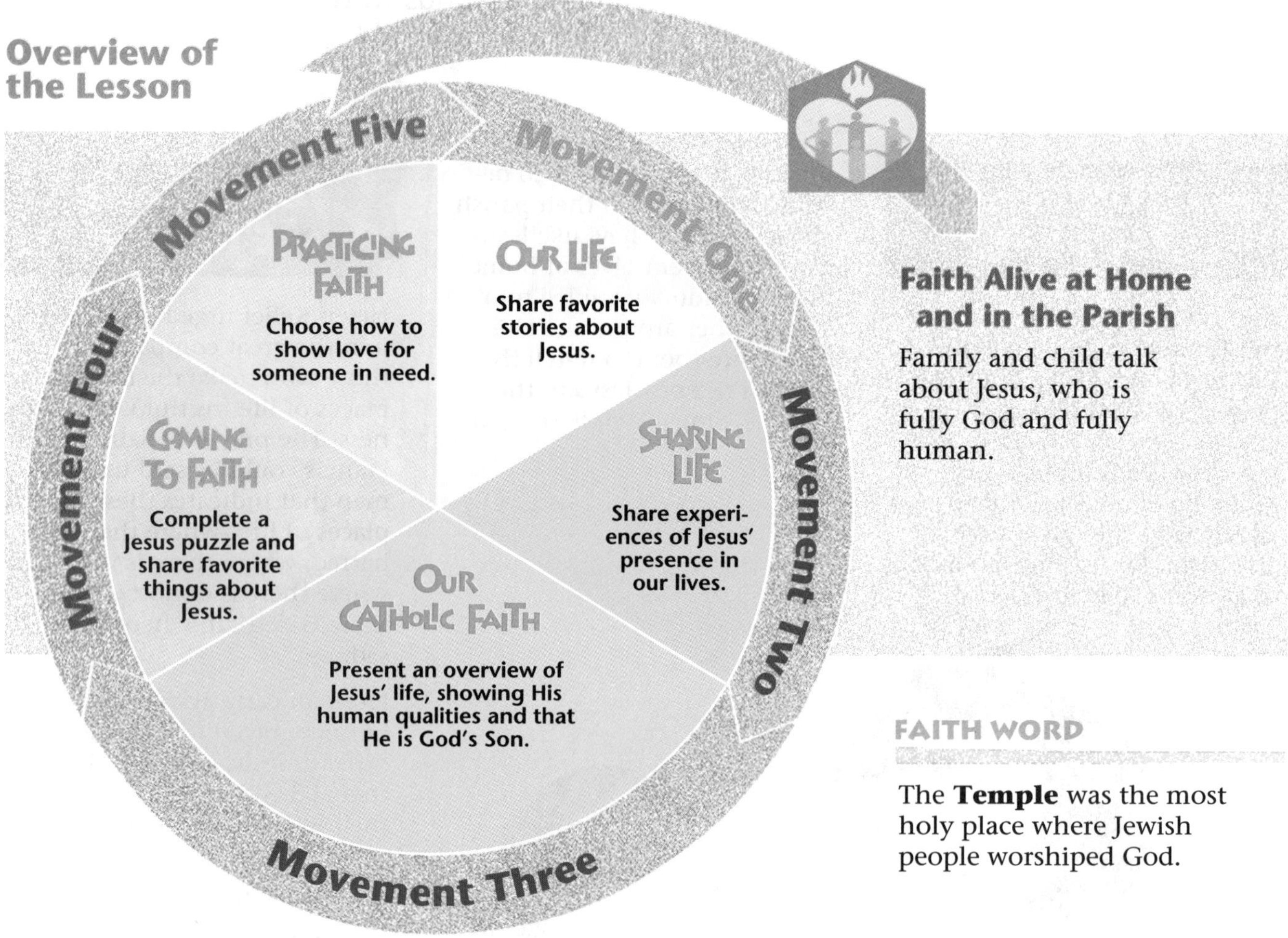

Faith Alive at Home and in the Parish

Family and child talk about Jesus, who is fully God and fully human.

FAITH WORD

The **Temple** was the most holy place where Jewish people worshiped God.

Teaching Hints

Children of this age are open and ready to enter into a child-like relationship with Jesus. The lesson will present them with an overview of Jesus' life. Be sure to spend some time talking to them about the story of Jesus in the Temple so that they can identify with Jesus as a young boy close to their own age.

This lesson introduces the children to the divine nature of Jesus; but be sure to help them see that Jesus' divine powers were always used, not to impress others, but to help those in need.

Special-Needs Child

Mainstreaming children means involving them as participating members of the group. Involve visually-impaired children in all activities.

Visual Needs

- clay to form the faith word *Temple*

Auditory Needs

- headphones, recording of story of Jesus in the Temple

Tactile-Motor Needs

- large crayons and peer tutors for drawing activities

Supplemental Resources

The God's Story series (video)
Mass Media Ministries
2116 North Charles Street
Baltimore, MD 21218
(1-800-828-8825)

The Life of Jesus (video)
Brown-ROA
2460 Kerper Blvd. P.O. Box 539
Dubuque, IA 52004-0539
(1-800-922-7696)

Jesus Promises (video)
Ikonographics
P.O. Box 600
Croton-on-Hudson, NY 10520
(1-800-944-1505)

Lesson Plan: Beginning

OBJECTIVES

To help the children

- know that Jesus is truly God's Son;
- appreciate the new life Jesus won for us;
- recognize their call to love others.

Focusing Prayer

Recall from the introductory lesson that we are all called to be followers of Jesus. Then lead the children in the prayer at the top of page 19.

Our Life

Sharing Stories About Jesus

Give the children time to examine the illustration on page 19 and to identify Jesus. Then invite them to share a favorite story about Jesus.

Telling Who Jesus Is

Ask the question at the top of the page about who Jesus is. As the children respond, print on the chalkboard, under a picture of Jesus, any key words they suggest.

Materials needed: picture of Jesus

Sharing Life

Experiences of Jesus

Call on each child to tell what she or he likes best about Jesus. Next, share with them a time when you experienced Jesus being with you in a special way. Call on several children to share any similar experiences of Jesus. Then, ask the next question.

Working with Partners

Designate a partner for each child and have them carry out the activity at the bottom of page 19. You may want to suggest a few words to help them respond, for example: *kindness, prayer, honesty, sharing,* and so forth.

ENRICHMENT

Silent Stories

Divide the children into groups of four or five. Choose a favorite story about Jesus and let one group dramatize it without using words. Ask the others to give a name to the story and tell in their own words what is happening.

Lesson Plan: Middle

Our Catholic Faith

Finger-painting Our Feelings

Ask the children if any of them have ever experienced being lost. Let them describe what happened, how they felt, and how their parents felt.

Give each child a large sheet of drawing paper and finger paints. Ask them to paint on one side of the sheet a picture of how they felt when they were lost and on the other side how they felt when they were finally found. Let those who wish share their paintings with the group.

Materials needed: finger paints; large sheets of drawing paper

Faith Word

Display the Faith Word *Temple.* Have the children read together the definition on page 21. Explain that Jewish people in the time of Jesus visited this holy place of worship on special feast days and that this is what Jesus, Mary, and Joseph were doing when Jesus, too, got lost.

Ask if the children know what city the Temple was in. If they do, write the word *Jerusalem* on the chalkboard; if not, tell them to listen for the name of the city and to raise their hand

God's Own Son

When Jesus was twelve years old, the Holy Family—Jesus, Mary, and Joseph—traveled to Jerusalem for a great celebration in the Temple.

Afterward, Mary and Joseph started back to Nazareth. They thought Jesus was with their friends. When they found out that He was not, they hurried back to look for Him. They found Jesus in the Temple, talking with the great teachers.

Mary said to Jesus, "Son, why didn't You come home with us?" Jesus answered, "Didn't you know that I had to stay in the Temple to do My Father's work?" (1)

From Luke 2:41–49 (1) Ask: Who is the Father Jesus speaks of?

Jesus was beginning to show people that He was God's own Son.

20

Lesson Plan: Middle

when they hear it in the story you are about to read to them. Tell them that Jesus was lost in the Temple there.

Listening to a Story

Ask the children to notice the picture on pages 20 and 21 and to listen carefully as you read to them the story about what happened that day. Post flash cards with the words *Nazareth, Jerusalem,* and *Temple* when you come to them in the story on page 20.

Pause after the second paragraph and refer again to the Faith Word definition of the Temple. After completing the story, emphasize the fact that Jesus was beginning to show people that he was God's own Son. Have the children underline this in their texts.

Jesus Shows His Love

Read dramatically the first paragraph on page 21, emphasizing how much Jesus cared for people. Recall some of the favorite stories about Jesus that the children mentioned previously and comment on Jesus' great love, especially for the poor and helpless.

Continue reading the rest of page 21. Point out that we call the day Jesus died Good Friday, not because it was a good thing that Jesus was nailed to the cross, but because He offered His death as a gift to God, His Father, for love of us and to free us from sin. Use the annotation. Stress the wonder of the fact that Jesus didn't stay dead but rose again three days later and won new life for us, too.

You may also wish to use pages 7–8 in the activity book for *Coming to Jesus.*

FAITH WORD

The **Temple** was the most holy place where Jewish people worshiped God.

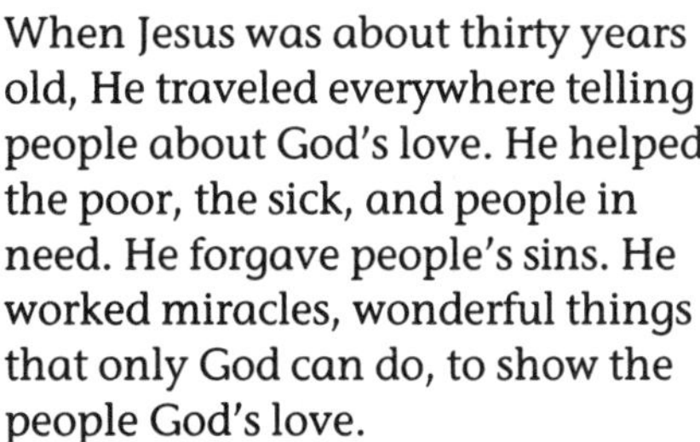

When Jesus was about thirty years old, He traveled everywhere telling people about God's love. He helped the poor, the sick, and people in need. He forgave people's sins. He worked miracles, wonderful things that only God can do, to show the people God's love.

Some people did not believe that Jesus was God's Son. Some people even wanted to kill Jesus.

One day, Jesus was arrested. Then He was nailed to a cross. His mother, Mary, and some of His friends were there. We call the day Jesus died Good Friday.

Ask: What happened on Easter Sunday?

Three days later, on Easter Sunday, something wonderful happened. Jesus rose from the dead!

How wonderful Jesus is! Because He was human, Jesus showed us how we should live. Because He was the Son of God, He saved us from sin and brought us new life.

21

Enrichment

Speaking to Jesus

Gather the children around a large crucifix. Ask them to pretend that they are there at the foot of the cross on Good Friday and that Jesus wants to speak to them. Have the children suggest what they think Jesus might say to them. Then give each child the opportunity to respond to Jesus in some way, either in words or with a gesture.

Materials needed: large crucifix

Lesson Plan: End

Coming to Faith

Completing a Puzzle

Explain the hidden-word puzzle on page 22. Complete the first sentence with the children and allow time for them to fill in the remaining words. Offer assistance to anyone who needs it. When everyone has finished, read together the completed sentences. Use the annotation.

Sharing Favorite Things

Share with the children your own favorite thing about Jesus taught in today's lesson. Then invite the children to share their favorite things.

Faith Summary

Turn to the *Faith Summary* on page 23. Use the annotations to see if the children can express in their own words what they have learned.

Practicing Faith

Loving Those in Need

Show pictures or newspaper articles that illustrate persons in need of love: a lonely person; a child crying; someone who is homeless; and so forth. Have the children suggest ways they might show love to each of these persons. Have them do the circle activity on page 22. Then lead them in the prayer at the bottom of the page.

Evaluating Your Lesson

- Do the children know that Jesus is God's Son?
- Do they appreciate the new life Jesus gives us?
- Have they decided to love others?

Enrichment

Jesus Balloons

Inflate several balloons. Ask the children to print very carefully on the balloons favorite things they learned about Jesus—for example: *Jesus is God's Son; Jesus died for us; Jesus rose.* Let them decorate the balloons, tie them with colored bows, and hang them around the room.

Materials needed: balloons; markers; colored bows

Coming To Faith

Complete the sentences from the words below to find the hidden word.

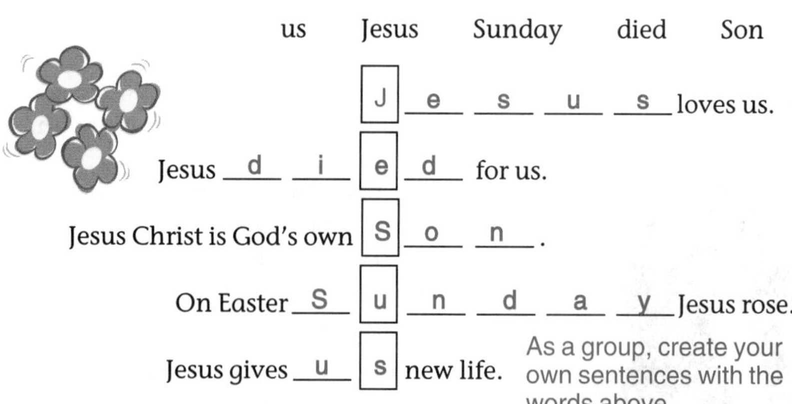

As a group, create your own sentences with the words above.

What was your favorite thing you learned about Jesus in this lesson? Tell why. Answers will vary.

Practicing Faith

Think of someone who needs your love today.

Circle how you will show your love.

- give a smile or a hug
- visit someone who is lonely
- give something to a needy person

† Now pray together: Jesus, help us to show our love by ______________. (Take turns.)

Talk to the children about ways they and their families might use the "Faith Alive" pages. Point out especially the *Family Prayer* on page 23.

22

Jairus' Daughter (for use with page 19)

Invite the children to listen as you read the following Bible story of the raising of Jairus' daughter.

Jesus was at the lakeside with a large crowd gathered around him. Jairus, an important Jewish man, threw himself down at Jesus' feet and begged him earnestly, "My little daughter is very sick. Please come and place your hands on her, so that she will get well and live!" As Jesus started off with Jairus, some messengers came from Jairus' house and told him, "Your daughter has died. Why bother the Teacher any longer?" Jesus paid no attention to what they said, but told Jairus, "Don't be afraid, only believe." When they arrived at Jairus' house, Jesus saw the confusion and heard all the loud crying and wailing. He went in and said, "Why all this confusion? Why are you crying? The child is not dead—she is only sleeping!" Jesus went into the room where the child was lying. He took her by the hand and said to her, "Little girl, I tell you to get up!"

The little girl got up at once and started walking around. (She was twelve years old.) When this happened, everyone was amazed. But Jesus gave strict orders not to tell anyone, and He said, "Give her something to eat." (from Mark 5:21–24, 35–43).

A Bible Story Play (for use with page 20)

Read the Bible story about Jesus lost in the Temple (Luke 2:41–49) to the children. Have them retell the story in their own words. When they are comfortable, lead some of them into a pantomime of the story. As one child tells the story, have others role-play Jesus, Mary, Joseph, and the teachers. Use simple signs identifying each character.

Materials needed: signs

Paper Plate Signs (for use with page 21)

Distribute large paper plates and markers or crayons. Divide the children into three groups. Invite one group to create signs reminding everyone that Jesus died for us. Have another group create colorful signs showing that Jesus rose from the dead on Easter Sunday. The third group can create signs that show how we share the new life of Jesus with others. The children may use the text to find any key words or signs they would like to use. Display the completed signs around a picture of Jesus.

Materials needed: paper plates; crayons; picture of Jesus

Missing Words (for use with page 22)

Print these words on the chalkboard or on newsprint: *new, life, Jesus, Temple.*

Then read the following incomplete statements aloud, and call on volunteers to name the missing words.

______ is God's own Son.

Mary and Joseph found the boy Jesus in the ______.

Jesus gives us ______.

Reminder: If you are going to make the "Baptismal Chart" (see page 28A), have the children bring in their baptismal dates.

FAITH ALIVE AT HOME AND IN THE PARISH

In this lesson your child learned about Jesus Christ, who is fully God and fully human. Jesus is the human face of God, eternally turned toward us with unconditional love. Jesus came among us to show us God's mercy, compassion, and love. At the very beginning of His ministry Jesus announced that He had come "to bring good news to the poor, to proclaim liberty to captives, and freedom to the oppressed" (from Luke 4:18). Whatever human feelings we feel, Jesus also felt; whatever human pain we experience, our God has known it before us.

You might ask yourself:

■ *How will I try to deepen my personal relationship with Jesus?*

■ *How will I try to listen and respond to the needs of my child this week?*

† Family Prayer

Jesus, help our family to live and share Your new life together!

Celebrating Life

Here is a project the whole family might enjoy. Create a family poster or booklet called "Our Family Celebrates Life." Fill it with family photos, especially of sacramental celebrations, drawings, old birthday and special occasion cards, vacation mementos, and other family treasures. Display your creation for all to see and enjoy.

A Daffodil Card

A daffodil is a sign of new life. Trace and color this daffodil onto the front of a card. Inside print a simple message, such as, "Jesus loves you." Give the card to someone you love.

Learn by heart

Faith Summary

Who is Jesus?

- Jesus Christ is the Son of God.

What does Jesus give us?

- Jesus gives us new life.

Show the children how to trace the daffodil on the front part of a folded 8 1/2″ x 11″ piece of paper.

Review

First go over the *Faith Summary* together before your child completes the *Review.* The answers for questions 1–3 appear on page 200. The response to number 4 will help you see whether your child understands the difference Jesus should make in our lives. When the *Review* is completed, have your child place a sticker on this page.

sticker

Circle the correct answer.

1. Jesus' new life helps us to love only our friends. Yes (No)

2. Jesus died on the cross. (Yes) No

3. Jesus rose from the dead on Easter. (Yes) No

4. How will you try to live as a follower of Jesus?

Possible responses: by giving something to a needy person;

visit someone who is lonely; etc.

Encourage the children to gather with their families to share the *Family Scripture Moment.*

As you **Gather** ask family members to recall times when they have been aware of God's presence. Then **Listen** to this gospel story.

Jesus took with Him Peter and the brothers James and John and led them up a high mountain. As they looked on, a change came over Jesus: His face was shining like the sun, and His clothes were dazzling white. Then the three disciples saw Moses and Elijah talking with Jesus. So Peter spoke up and said to Jesus, "Lord, how good it is that we are here!" While he was talking, a shining cloud came over them, and a voice from the cloud said, "This is My own dear Son, with whom I am pleased—listen to Him!"

From Matthew 17:1-5

Share How does God want you to listen to Jesus? What do you expect to hear?

Consider for family enrichment:

- The transfiguration of Jesus, like His baptism, confirms that He is the Son of God whom we will one day see in His glory.
- Here the great Old Testament figures—Moses the lawgiver and Elijah the prophet—stand and bear witness to the Son of God, who fulfills both the Law and the prophets.

Reflect and **Decide** How will we as a family follow the way of Jesus this week?

3 The Holy Spirit Is Our Helper

For the Catechist: Spiritual and Catechetical Development

Adult Background

Our Life

What devoted parent has not hovered behind the birthday child, ready to come to the rescue if the blazing candles are not all extinguished in one fell swoop? In the child's excitement, he or she may run out of breath before the task is finished. Or the child's aim may be scattershot, leaving a few candles untouched.

With great gusto, the parent adds energy and focus to the child's efforts and the mission is accomplished.

In time, the child reaches the independent years of "I can do it by myself." Later, as the candles multiply, the birthday celebrant may once again plead, "Can you help me? I can't seem to do it alone."

Ask yourself:

- What significant adults contributed energy and focus to my childhood years?
- Whom do I turn to when I "can't seem to do it alone"?

Sharing Life

How have you experienced your faith as a source of energy and direction?

How do you see the Church as a source of assistance?

Our Catholic Faith

The Holy Spirit, the third Person of the Blessed Trinity, is the One sent to us by Jesus Christ to be our advocate and our helper. In the Gospel of John we read Jesus' promise about the Holy Spirit: "The Helper, the Holy Spirit, whom the Father will send in my name, will teach you everything and make you remember all that I have told you" (John 14:26). Jesus knew that we could not live the gospel values without help. For years we cannot do it alone because we are children. Later in life there are times when we cannot do it alone because we are weary or disillusioned. At every stage of life, we need the energy and direction of the Spirit.

Since the "birthday of the Church" on Pentecost, the coming of the Spirit has been identified as a community event. In his Second Letter to Timothy, Paul writes, "For the Spirit that God has given us does not make us timid; instead, his Spirit fills us with power, love, and self-control" (2 Timothy 1:7).

Tradition recognizes seven gifts of the Holy Spirit: wisdom, understanding, fortitude, counsel, knowledge, piety (reverence), and fear of the Lord (wonder and awe). These gifts are found in people of faith and in their relationships with others. Paul writes in his First Letter to the Corinthians: "The Spirit's presence is shown in some way in each person for the good of all" (1 Corinthians 12:7). The Spirit is given to us, not for our personal gain, but precisely because we belong to the community.

Coming to Faith

Which gifts of the Spirit do you find strongest within yourself?

How are the gifts of the Spirit made manifest in your parish community?

Practicing Faith

How will you use your gifts for the common good today?

How will you affirm the gifts of the Spirit that you recognize, perhaps only in embryonic form, in your group of children?

Catechism of the Catholic Church

The Theme of This Chapter Corresponds with Paragraph 731

Liturgical Resources

Before Jesus began His public ministry, "the Spirit led Jesus into the desert to be tempted by the Devil" (Matthew 4:1). If we allow the Spirit to guide and energize us, to help us when we just can't do it alone anymore, we may sometimes find ourselves where we would rather not be led. Yet it is also the Spirit who, Paul says, "prays for us when we cannot find the words," and prayer is the lifeline of our relationship with God.

Help the children understand that the Holy Spirit first came to them in the sacrament of Baptism. If possible, take them to the baptismal font in church. Explain to them that it is through water and the Holy Spirit that we became children of God. Have each child approach the baptismal font or receptacle for holy water and bless himself or herself individually. Remind the children that each time they bless themselves with holy water they are remembering their Baptism.

Justice and Peace Resources

If we use the gifts of the Spirit for the good of all people, then the fruits of the Spirit are evident in our lives. Scripture tells us:

> . . . the Spirit produces love, joy, peace, patience, kindness, goodness, faithfulness, humility, and self-control.
> (Galatians 5:22–23)

To help the children grasp how these fruits of the Spirit make a difference in our lives, invite them to name persons who show them what it means to be loving, joyful, peaceful, and so on. Ask:

- Do you know someone who is kind? How do you know he or she is kind? How might you try to be like this person?

As children exhibit various fruits of the Spirit, quietly commend them and thank them for reminding you and the others what it means to have self-control, patience, or humility.

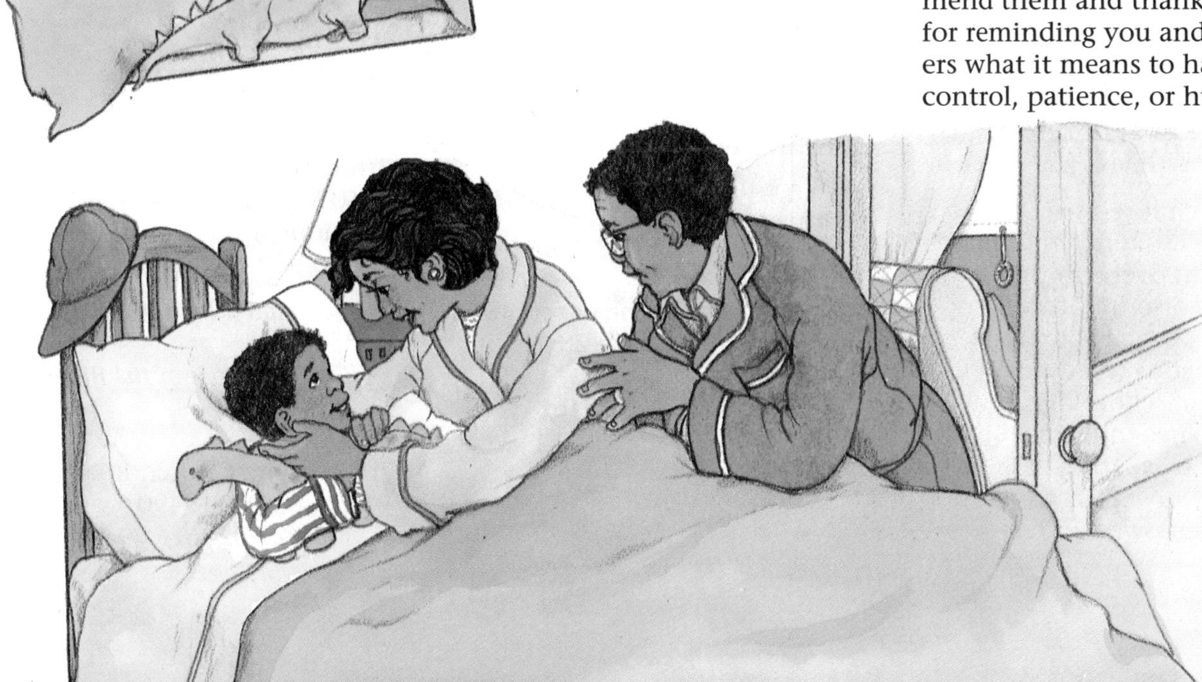

Teaching Resources

Overview of the Lesson

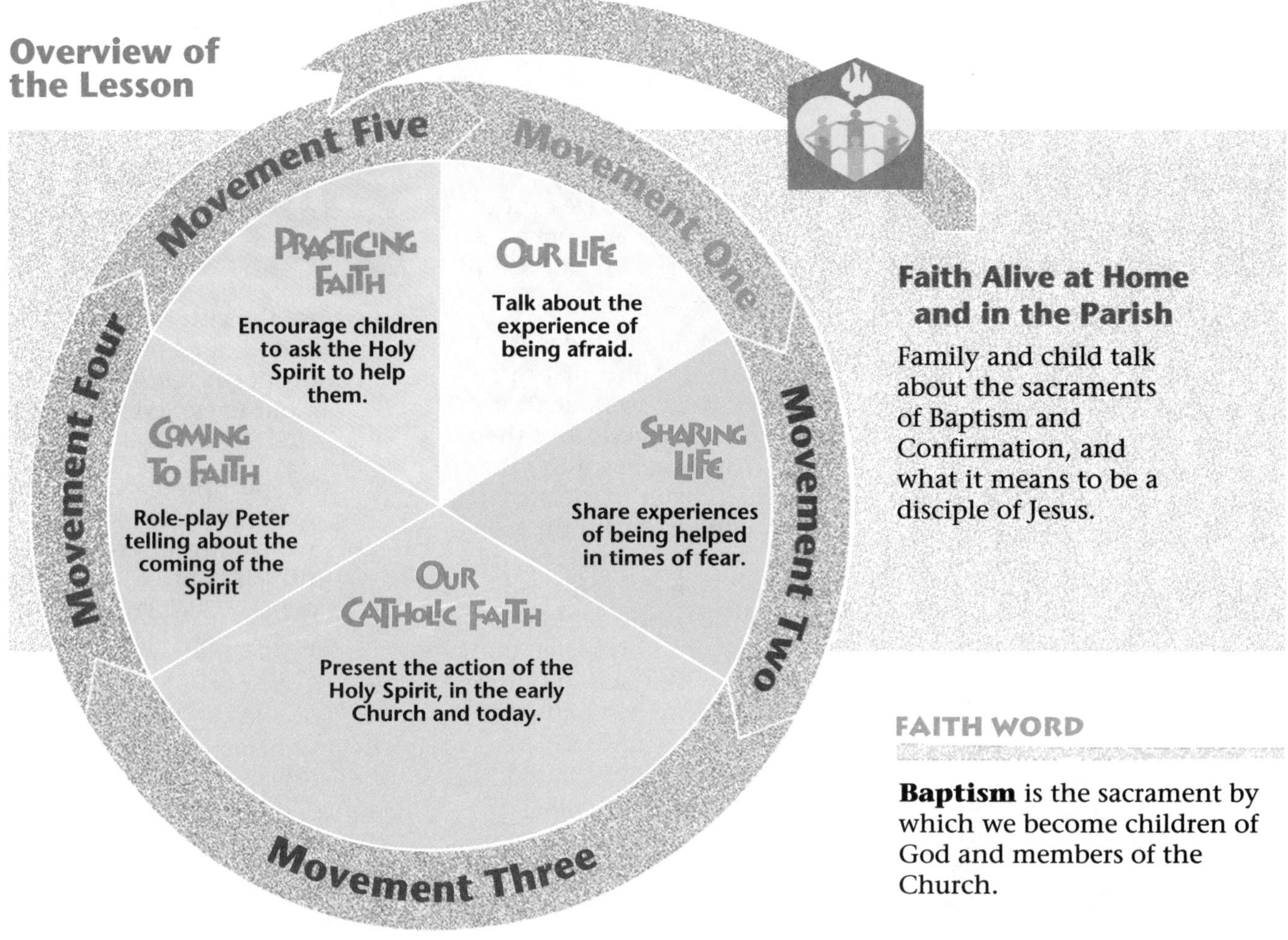

Faith Alive at Home and in the Parish

Family and child talk about the sacraments of Baptism and Confirmation, and what it means to be a disciple of Jesus.

FAITH WORD

Baptism is the sacrament by which we become children of God and members of the Church.

Teaching Hints

Because young children think so concretely, this lesson will present the Holy Spirit by showing the Spirit's *action* in the Church's beginnings and in our lives today.

Help the children see that God has given us family and friends to aid us in overcoming our fears, and also the Holy Spirit, who gives us the courage we need to live as Jesus taught us. Lead them to develop a sense of confidence in the action of the Spirit by sharing with them how the Holy Spirit has done this in your own life.

Special-Needs Child

When a new person begins to speak, subtly direct the attention of the hearing-impaired child toward that person.

Visual Needs

- large-print flash card for the faith word *Baptism*

Auditory Needs

- audiotape and headphones for the song on page 28

Tactile-Motor Needs

- peer helpers to assist with motion activities

Supplemental Resources

Welcome to Jesus' Family (video)
Jesus Signs: Baptism and Eucharist for Primary Children series
Brown-ROA
2460 Kerper Blvd. P.O. Box 539
Dubuque, IA 52004-0539
(1-800-922-7696)

The Apostles and the Early Church (video)
Children's Heroes of the Bible series
Vision Video
2030 Wentz Church Road
Worcester, PA 19490
(1-800-523-0226)

Lesson Plan: Beginning

Objectives

To help the children

- know the Holy Spirit is our Helper in the Church;
- appreciate how the Holy Spirit helps us;
- choose to follow the Holy Spirit's guidance.

Focusing Prayer

Recall for the children what they learned in Chapter 1—that the Holy Spirit is one of the three Persons in the Blessed Trinity. Then lead them in the prayer at the top of page 25.

Our Life

A Poem About Fear

Have the children note the picture of the boy in the darkened room on page 25. Ask how they think the boy might feel. Point out that at some time in each of our lives, we are afraid of something; but we don't have to face fear alone. Ask them to notice in the second picture who helped the young boy overcome his fear. Then have the children join you in reading the poem on page 25, and ask the questions following it. List their responses on the chalkboard. See the annotation.

Sharing Life

Talking About Fear

Invite the children to close their eyes and think quietly for a few minutes about a time when they were frightened. Ask the first question in the *Sharing Life* section on page 25. Have the children tell about how they were helped. Ask the last two questions on the page and share with them a time when God helped you, or someone you know, in a frightening situation. See the annotation.

3 The Holy Spirit Is Our Helper

Holy Spirit,
help us to
know and
follow Jesus.

Our Life

Sometimes I am afraid
Of scary dreams at night.
My mother hears me crying
And turns on the bedroom light.

"It's just a dream," she whispers,
And gently pats my cheek.
And soon—before I know it,
I feel safe and fall asleep.

What things make you afraid?
dreams, storms, the dark, etc.
Who helps you get over your fears?
Emphasize that it is okay to have fears and good to talk about them with a caring adult.

Sharing Life

Think of a time when you were very scared. Did someone help you? Tell about it.
Be sensitive to those who prefer not to talk.
Then talk together about this. Does God help us when we are afraid? How?
God gives us parents and teachers to help us.

25

Enrichment

Drawing a Picture

Distribute drawing paper and markers. Invite children to draw a picture of an imaginary fear they used to have. Then invite them to tell how they came to realize it was imaginary. Did someone help them to see it was imaginary?

Materials needed: paper; markers

Lesson Plan: Middle

Our Catholic Faith

A Special Promise

Remind the children again that at times, even adults can become frightened. Show a picture of the Last Supper. Tell the children this was the meal Jesus had with His followers the night before He died. Explain that Jesus knew that when He was gone, even His followers would be afraid. So Jesus made a special promise to them. He promised to send the Holy Spirit to help them when they were frightened. The Holy Spirit would give them the courage they needed. Impress on the children the great love Jesus showed in sending us the gift of the Holy Spirit.

Materials needed: picture of the Last Supper

Jesus Keeps His Promise

Give the children a few minutes to examine the picture on pages 26 and 27. Tell them that Jesus kept His promise on a special feast day we call Pentecost. Write the name of the feast on the chalkboard.

Then ask the children to listen quietly as you read to them the story of how Jesus kept His promise. Use gestures for emphasis in reading the story. Have the children notice in the picture the expressions on the faces of Jesus' followers. Let them ask questions or comment on the story.

The Story of Jesus' Church

Read aloud the first two paragraphs on page 27. Have the children underline the important words: Peter—*first leader; Holy Father, the pope.* Talk with them briefly about our present pope, John Paul II, and some things he has done as leader of the Church. Explain that the Holy Spirit helps him to do all these things for the Church.

Stress the underlined text.

The Holy Spirit Comes

It was time for Jesus to return to His Father. Jesus knew His friends would be afraid without Him so He promised to send them a Helper, the Holy Spirit. The day the Holy Spirit came is called Pentecost.

Jesus' followers were gathered in a large room. They were afraid. Suddenly a strong wind filled the house. Then what looked like tiny flames of fire settled over each of them. Jesus' friends knew this was a sign that the Holy Spirit had come to help them.

From Acts 2:1–12

Jesus' friends no longer felt afraid. The Holy Spirit had given them new courage to follow Jesus. They ran out to tell everyone the good news of Jesus.

Peter, their leader, said, "Each one of you must be baptized in the name of Jesus Christ. The Holy Spirit will help you to know and follow Jesus."

26

Lesson Plan: Middle

Faith Word

Read the third paragraph, about Baptism. Have the children read the Faith Word *Baptism* and repeat the definition after you. Let any of the children who have witnessed a Baptism tell what they recall about their experience.

Our "Pentecost"

Read the last paragraph on the page. Write the word *Confirmation* on the chalkboard or a large piece of paper. Show a picture of the bishop administering the sacrament. Explain that the Holy Spirit comes to us in a very special way in this sacrament to help us—not only to follow Jesus, but to share our faith with others courageously, as Peter did on the first Pentecost.

Our Catholic Identity

Use page 2 of the *Our Catholic Identity* section in the back of the book. Explain to the children that God the Father and God the Holy Spirit cannot be seen with our eyes, because they did not become human as the Son did.

Materials needed: picture of a bishop administering the sacrament of Confirmation

You may also wish to use pages 9–10 in the activity book for *Coming to Jesus*.

FAITH WORD

Baptism is the sacrament by which we become children of God and members of the Church.

That day three thousand people were baptized. They became Christians, followers of Jesus Christ.
From Acts 2:38–42

Our Church Begins

These Christians were the first members of Jesus' Church. Peter became the first leader of the Church. Today our Holy Father, the pope, is the leader of the Catholic Church.

The Holy Spirit is still with our Church today. At Baptism we received the Holy Spirit and became sharers in God's life and members of the Church. We are Christians, followers of Jesus Christ.

The Holy Spirit comes to us in a special way in the sacrament of Confirmation. The Holy Spirit helps us to follow Jesus and share our faith in Him with others.

27

Enrichment

Holy Spirit Badges

Give each child a piece of posterboard cut in the shape of a flame. Recall for them the symbol of fire they read about in the story of Pentecost. Have the children print on the flame: The Holy Spirit Is with Me. Then have them color the flame. Let them pin or tape these badges to their clothing and suggest that they use them to explain to their families and friends what they learned about the Holy Spirit in today's lesson.

Materials needed: posterboard cut in the shape of a flame; markers; pins or tape

Lesson Plan: End

Coming to Faith

A Pretend Game

Have the children take turns pretending they are Peter. Ask them to consider what they might say to the crowds who have gathered to listen. Let them share ideas about what they would say. Call on volunteers to role-play Peter before the crowd.

Faith Summary

Turn to the *Faith Summary* on page 29. Use the annotations to see if the children can express in their own words what they have learned.

Practicing Faith

Making a Holy Spirit Shield

Have the children note the picture of the shield on page 28. Read the first paragraph in the *Practicing Faith* section and give the children a few minutes to write what they will ask the Holy Spirit. Let them share their responses with the group.

A Sung Prayer

Gather the children in a circle and lead them in singing the "Come, Holy Spirit" song at the bottom of page 28.

You may wish to use Sadlier's grade 2 *Coming to Jesus in Song* cassette.

You may also wish to use pages 37–38 of Sadlier's *Celebrating Our Seasons and Saints,* Level 2.

Evaluating Your Lesson

- Do the children know the Holy Spirit is our Helper in Church?
- Do they appreciate how the Holy Spirit helps us?
- Have they decided to follow the Holy Spirit's guidance?

Enrichment

Caring for the Earth

Take time to encourage the children to recycle any materials that can be recycled. Go over the rules and regulations for your area. You might like to have the children make posters to hang up at home to remind others to recycle.

Materials needed: construction paper; markers

Coming to Faith

Pretend you are Peter talking to the crowd of people on the first Pentecost. Tell them about the coming of the Holy Spirit. Tell them how they can follow Jesus.

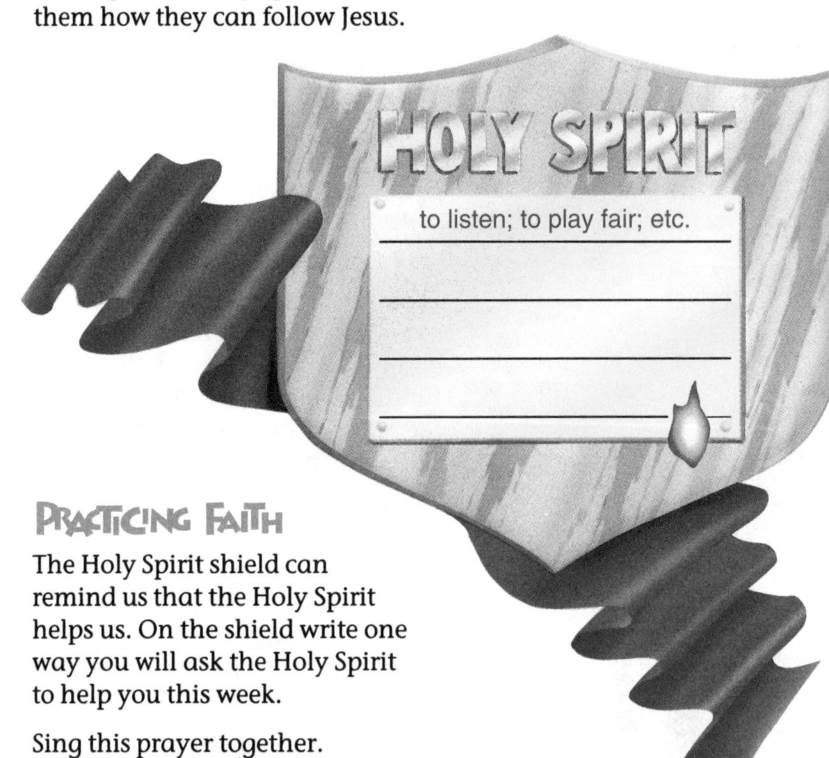

Practicing Faith

The Holy Spirit shield can remind us that the Holy Spirit helps us. On the shield write one way you will ask the Holy Spirit to help you this week.

Sing this prayer together.
(To the tune of "Come, Holy Ghost")

♫ Come, Holy Spirit, show us the way.
Help us be friends of Jesus today.
Help us be fair, peacemakers, too,
Care for God's earth as we
should do. (2 x) ♫

Talk to the children about ways they and their families might work together on the "Faith Alive" pages. Encourage them to do the "Sharing Good News Stories" activity.

Name the Worries (for use with page 25)

Prepare large, illustrated flash cards. You might wish to use pictures from magazines. Show the following situations:

- a small child looking frightened;
- a teenager looking upset;
- a small child looking unhappy.

Display each card and invite the children to name the worries the person might have had. Ask the children to tell who might help the person in each picture. Conclude by encouraging the children to be sure to talk to someone whenever they have a problem and to pray to the Holy Spirit for help.

Materials needed: large flashcards; picture magazines

Spirit Symbols (for use with page 26)

To set a prayerful mood, play a recording of the Spirit song, "Come Holy Spirit." You might wish to use Sadlier's grade 2 *Coming to Jesus in Song* cassette. Divide the children into three or four groups. Assign each group to a "painting corner" that has finger paints and water available. Encourage the children to do one of the following:

- paint large Spirit flames in any combination of red, orange, and yellow;
- paint a large dove on a bright background;
- paint how the coming of the Holy Spirit made the friends of Jesus feel.

Have the children stand in their groups around each of their paintings and sing "Come Holy Spirit" while you play the cassette.

Then ask them to be quiet for a moment and to pray to the Holy Spirit to help them.

Materials needed: finger paints; water; heavy paper; tape player (optional)

Baptism Chart (for use with page 27)

Create a Baptism chart listing the children's names and baptismal dates. In the top center of the chart print the title "The Holy Spirit Came." At the top left, above the children's names, write "To" and at the top right, above their baptismal dates, write "On."

If any children do not know the exact date, have them approximate a date two or three weeks after their birthday.

Materials needed: posterboard; markers

Spirit Shields (for use with page 28)

Provide the children with an outline of a large shield. Have the children print their baptismal name in the center of the shield and decorate the shield with things that show how they will live as friends of Jesus. Ideas (drawn or from a magazine): picture of a child planting a tree, with a motto such as "I care for God's world"; words that describe friends of Jesus, such as *loving, caring, courageous,* and so on. Have the children take their shields home to remind them to live as friends of Jesus.

Materials needed: shield outline; crayons; magazines; scissors; glue

FAITH ALIVE AT HOME AND IN THE PARISH

Your child has learned that at Pentecost the Holy Spirit came to guide the Church. Talk to your child about the sacraments of Baptism and Confirmation and what it means to share in God's own life and to be a follower of Jesus. Remind him or her that the Holy Spirit gives us the courage to live the way Jesus taught and showed us. Share memories of your own Confirmation when you were sealed with the Gift of the Holy Spirit.

You might ask yourself:

- *When do I ask the Holy Spirit to help me?*
- *How can I help my family become more courageous followers of Jesus?*

†Family Prayer

Thank You, God, for our faith.
Thank You, Jesus, for making us members of Your Church.

My Baptism

To help your child appreciate that by Baptism he or she became a sharer in God's own life and member of Jesus' Church, talk about his or her Baptism. Use this activity and any pictures you have of the christening to help you.

I was baptized on

____

My godparents are

____

____

Sharing Good News Stories

Peter and the early Christians traveled far and wide to spread the good news (gospel) of Jesus. Have a "Good News Headlines" session at home. Share highlights of your favorite Jesus stories or sayings with one another.

GOOD NEWS

Jesus said ...

Possible responses: Love one another as I have loved you.

____

Faith Summary

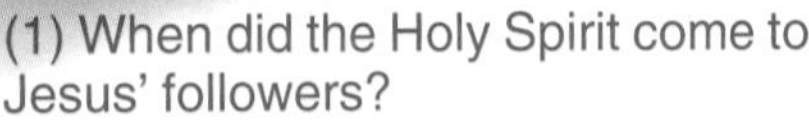

(1) When did the Holy Spirit come to Jesus' followers?

(2) How does the Holy Spirit help us?

(1) • The Holy Spirit came to the followers of Jesus Christ on Pentecost.

(2) • The Holy Spirit helps us to believe in Jesus and to live as Jesus shows us.

Review

Go over the *Faith Summary* together before your child completes the *Review.* The answers for questions 1–3 appear on page 200. The response to number 4 will help you see whether your child is growing in his or her understanding that the Holy Spirit helps us. When the *Review* is completed, have your child place a sticker on this page.

sticker

Choose the correct word.

Baptism   Pentecost   Confirmation

1. The Holy Spirit came on the first Pentecost ______________.

2. By Baptism ______________ we became sharers in God's life and members of the Church.

3. In Confirmation ______________ the Holy Spirit comes to us in a special way.

4. Tell how you will ask the Holy Spirit to help you today.

Possible responses: I will ask the Holy Spirit to help us follow Jesus

and to share our faith in Him with others.

____

Encourage the children to gather with their families to share the *Family Scripture Moment.*

FAMILY SCRIPTURE MOMENT

Gather and ask one another how we share our faith with others. Then **Listen** as Jesus speaks to us.

Jesus drew near and said to the eleven disciples, "I have been given all authority in heaven and on earth. Go, then, to all peoples everywhere and make them My disciples: baptize them in the name of the Father, the Son, and the Holy Spirit, and teach them to obey everything I have commanded you. And I will be with you always, to the end of the age."

From Matthew 28:18–20

Share What is Jesus saying to us here?

Consider for family enrichment:

- These are the final verses in Matthew's Gospel. Jesus commissions His disciples to baptize all people and teach them the Christian faith.
- The Catholic Church teaches us that we are to "bring our Christian faith into every area and level of our lives" *(Evangelization of Peoples).*

Reflect and **Decide** Read the words of Jesus aloud together. What will we do as a family to share our faith this week? With whom? How?

4 We Belong to the Catholic Church

For the Catechist: Spiritual and Catechetical Development

Adult Background

Our Life

If fifty Catholics were asked, "Name your favorite image of the Church," they might well provide fifty different answers. The Church is many things to many people. To Archbishop Guilford Young of Hobart, Tasmania, for instance, it is "the Caravan of God."

The archbishop envisions the caravan wending its way through deserts and farmlands, inner cities and far-off missions. Although the path is not always clear, the People of God know that the Driver is always with them. Some members of the caravan rush on ahead, while others drag their feet, and still others keep to the middle. But always the caravan moves forward toward its final goal.

Ask yourself:

- What is my favorite image of the Church?
- How do I relate to the caravan image?

Sharing Life

How does your image of the Church affect your faith life?

What image of the Church do you hope the children in your group will embrace when they are adults?

Our Catholic Faith

As Catholics we realize that the Church is a mystery that can be expressed in a variety of imperfect images. The Scriptures describe different aspects of the Church. Two examples are Jesus' words to Peter, and Jesus' farewell discourse.

> And so I tell you, Peter: you are a rock, and on this rock foundation I will build my church, and not even death will ever be able to overcome it. I will give you the keys of the Kingdom of heaven; what you prohibit on earth will be prohibited in heaven, and what you permit on earth will be permitted in heaven. (Matthew 16:18–19)

> And now I give you a new commandment: love one another. As I have loved you, so you must love one another. If you have love for one another, then everyone will know that you are my disciples. (John 13:34–35)

Acts of the Apostles describes the Pentecost event and confirms the mission of the disciples to proclaim the good news. Acts also defines the early Christian community in terms of its activities: "They spent their time in learning from the apostles, taking part in the fellowship, and sharing in the fellowship meals and the prayers" (Acts 2:42).

In the Church, the community of Jesus Christ becomes a visible reality. It is an outward sign given to us by Jesus Christ, by which we share in God's own life. In this sense, the Church itself is a sacrament.

Reflecting on the nature of the Church, Karl Rahner observes that "she is the community which proclaims God's salvation for others, for everybody." In other words, the Church exists not just for itself but for the whole world. The caravan is a sign of hope and invitation to all people everywhere.

Coming to Faith

How might the scriptural and traditional images of the Church affect your own image?

How will you help to make the Church a sign of salvation and hope?

Practicing Faith

What will you do to strengthen the community of Jesus?

Choose one way in which you will help the children feel belonging in and acceptance by the Church.

The Theme of This Chapter Corresponds with Paragraph 737

LITURGICAL RESOURCES

Children often associate the word *Church* simply with the parish church building. You can help them to grow beyond this limited concept by presenting several images of the Church for them to act out or draw.

For example:

- A caravan or pilgrimage: Form a procession and go around the room to the prayer space. Have each child carry a box or container marked with a gift he or she shares with others (kindness, prayer, patience, talents, and so forth). Present the gifts to Jesus, join hands, and pray: "We are the People of God on the move. We are the Church. Help us to be holy."
- Vine and branches; sheep and shepherd; the family or household of God; God's vineyard or garden.

JUSTICE AND PEACE RESOURCES

In his apostolic exhortation, "The Lay Faithful," Pope John Paul II speaks of the People of God as "laborers in the vineyard." He reminds us that Jesus says to us, "You also go and work in the vineyard" (Matthew 20:4). By its many works of justice and peace, the Church prepares the way for the full realization of God's reign.

Invite a parish minister of justice and peace to describe briefly and simply to the children how he or she is working in God's vineyard. Plan one specific way in which the children can contribute to this ministry. (For example: preparing a Peace Art exhibit for the church; praying for racial harmony; visiting the sick; collecting clothing for the poor.)

Teaching Resources

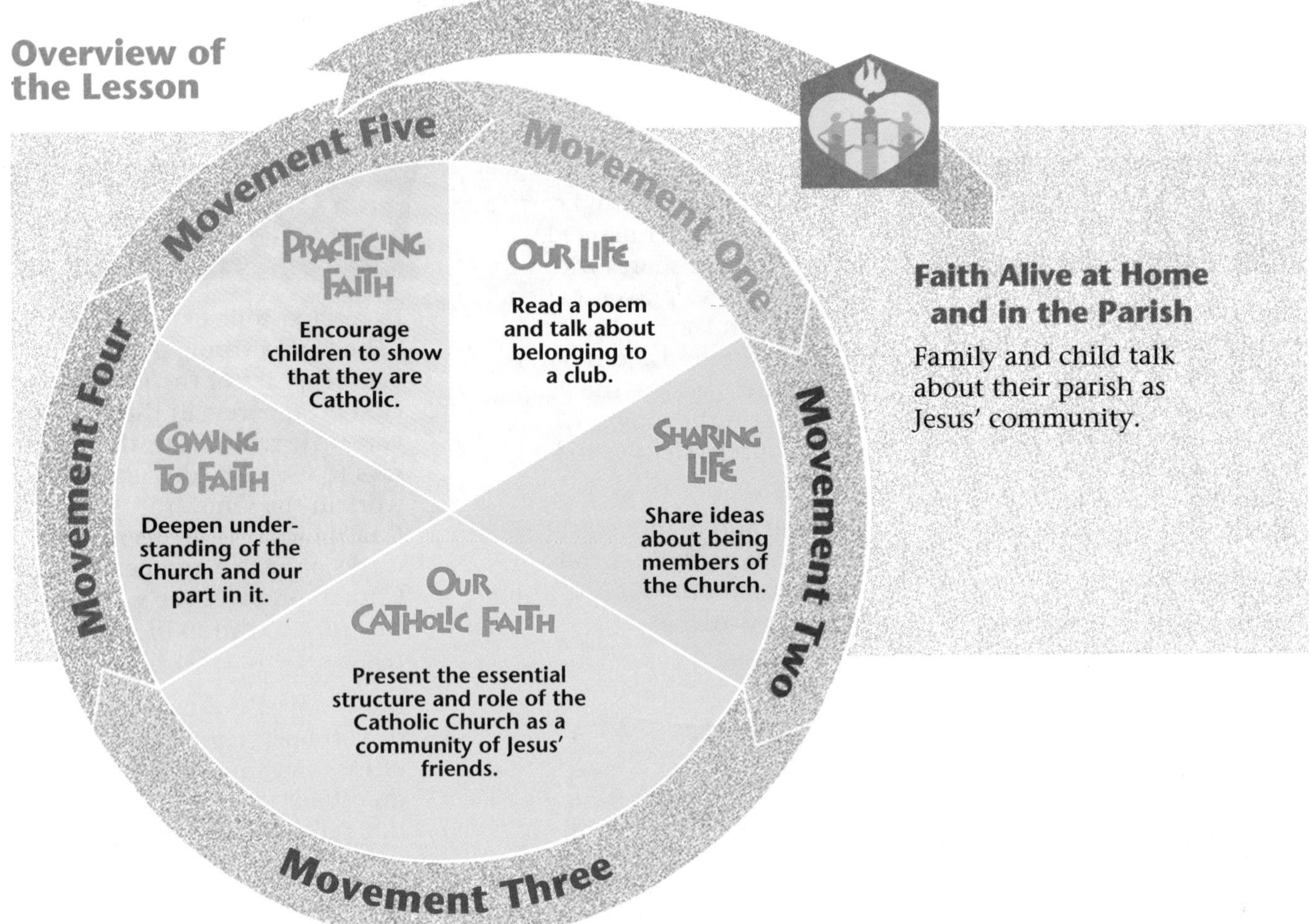

Teaching Hints

In order to develop the concept that our Catholic Church is the community of Jesus' friends, the children should be encouraged to work and pray together. Point out that they are showing what it means to belong to the community of Jesus' friends, the Church.

Be sure that in addition to understanding the role of our Church leaders, the children realize their important place as members of Jesus' Church. Show how we all serve one another by carrying out Jesus' Law of Love.

Special-Needs Child

Encourage physical activity. Let the special-needs child participate fully in skits and role-playing. This provides practice in mobility and makes him or her feel like part of the class.

Visual Needs

- picture of parish church

Auditory Needs

- audiotape and headphones for the club story

Tactile-Motor Needs

- sandpaper cross taped to desk

Supplemental Resources

Jesus Teaches and Calls Disciples (video)
Children's Heroes of the Bible series
Vision Video, Inc.
2030 Wentz Church Road
Worcester, PA 19490
(1-800-523-0226)

Lesson Plan: Beginning

Objectives

To help the children

- know they belong to the Catholic Church;
- appreciate how the Church helps them;
- choose to be good members of the Church.

Focusing Prayer

Recall how Baptism made each of us members of Jesus' Church. Then lead the children in the prayer at the top of page 31.

Our Life

Reading a Poem

Divide the children into two groups. Have each group join you in reading one verse of the poem on page 31.

Multicultural Awareness

Point out the different children in the picture. Comment on the fun they are having playing together. Explain that Jesus invites all people to be happy in His Church.

Finding a Hidden Message

Have the children find in the poem the word that tells how each child in the picture feels (*welcome*). Explain that the artwork contains a hidden message with this word in it. Give them time to find it and to write it in their books. Have them respond to the questions. See the annotation.

Sharing Life

Members of the Church

Ask the first question in the *Sharing Life* section on page 31. Have the children find the words *Catholic Church* in the title of the lesson and spell them out loud with you. Explain that the Church is called Catholic because Jesus wants all people to be a part of His Church. Have them respond to the last question on the page.

4 We Belong to the Catholic Church

Dear Jesus, help us to be good members of Your Church.

Our Life

Here with our club friends
Where we like to be,
Everyone's welcome,
Especially you and me.

Everyone's welcome—
No one's turned away.
Won't you come join us?
Come by us and play!

Find the hidden message in the picture. Write it here.

You are welcome.

Would you like to belong to this club? Why or why not?
Answers will vary.

What kind of a member would you be? Discuss helping and sharing in a group situation.

Sharing Life

To what special group do you belong with Jesus?
the Catholic Church

What kind of member does Jesus want you to be?
loving, helping, sharing

Enrichment

Making a Welcome Mat

Give each child a piece of posterboard and some markers. Guide them in printing the word *welcome*, and have them decorate it to make a welcome mat.

Materials needed: posterboard; markers

Lesson Plan: Middle

Our Catholic Faith

The Beginning of the Church

Have the children compare the picture of the children playing together on page 31 with the pictures of people on pages 32 and 33. Lead them to see that even though these groups are doing different things, each one is together for a reason.

Then tell the children to listen as you read to see if they can find the reason why Jesus' followers joined together and what we call this group of Jesus' followers. Read the first paragraph on page 32 slowly, emphasizing these two points, then have the children tell what they heard.

Our Church Leaders Help Us

Read the next three paragraphs on page 32. See if the children can identify the pope in the picture and tell what his name is. Emphasize the fact that Jesus wants all people to feel welcome in the Church. See the annotation.

Describing Photos

Give the children a few minutes to study again the pictures on pages 32 and 33. Tell them to pretend they are putting the pictures in an album. Ask what they would write under each picture.

OUR CATHOLIC FAITH

Ask the children the names of the pope and their bishop. Write them in a prominent place.

Our Catholic Church

Jesus invited His followers to form a special group, or community. Jesus wanted them to know about God's great love and to share it with all people. The community of Jesus' followers is called the Church.

Jesus chose leaders for His Church. The first leaders were called apostles. Peter was the leader of the apostles.

Today our pope and bishops continue the work of Peter and the apostles. They are our leaders in the Catholic Church. They teach us how to live our Catholic faith and to carry on the work of Jesus.

The Catholic Church is all over the world. At Baptism, we become children of God and members of Jesus' community, the Church.

32

Lesson Plan: Middle

Learning to Be Good Members

Refer again to the group of children playing together, illustrated on page 31. Have the children note that it is because the children in the picture are working *together* that they are having so much fun. Talk about the fact that when some members in a group don't do their part to work together with others, it affects the whole group badly.

We Work Together as Jesus Asks

Explain that this is true of the Church as well. Read aloud page 33 and talk with the children about some of the loving things Jesus asks us to do as good members of His Church. Compare them with the loving things Jesus did, listed at the bottom of page 33. Ask if the persons in the pictures are acting as good members of the Church.

You may also wish to use pages 11–12 in the activity book for *Coming to Jesus*.

Our Catholic Identity

Use page 3 of the *Our Catholic Identity* section in the back of the book. Ask the children if they have ever heard the priest praying for our Holy Father the Pope at Mass. If not, suggest that they listen for it next Sunday. Ask why they think the pope needs our prayers.

We Serve and Pray

Jesus taught us how to be good members of His Church. Jesus said, "Love one another as I have loved you. This is how people will know that you are My followers."
From John 13:34–35

Jesus asks the members of His Church to love and serve one another and all people. He asks us to pray and worship God together.

Today in the Catholic Church, we worship God together at Mass. We also try to show the world, by our love and care for others, that we are followers of Jesus.

Here are some loving things that Jesus did:

- Jesus loved children very much.
- Jesus cared for everyone, especially the poor and needy.
- Jesus showed people how to treat others fairly and with justice.
- Jesus showed people how to pray.

Enrichment

A Love Banner

Work with the children to make a large banner with Jesus' command *Love One Another as I Have Loved You.* Use felt as the background, with a large heart, cut out of a different color felt, pasted in the middle. Paste a picture of Jesus in the center of the heart and let the children cut the words from construction paper and paste them around the heart. Fold the top of the felt over a narrow piece of wood and attach yarn as a hanger. Post the banner in a prominent place as a sign that we are Jesus' followers.

Materials needed: felt; construction paper; scissors; picture of Jesus; paste; yarn

Lesson Plan: End

Coming to Faith

Decoding Messages

Explain the decoding activity on page 34. Move among the children as they work, offering assistance to anyone who needs it. Invite volunteers to read their sentences.

Multicultural Awareness

Share with the children that you admire the Church for its openness to people of all cultures and walks of life. Have the children note the various examples in the pictures on page 32 and 33. Then have each of them share what they like best about belonging to the Church.

Faith Summary

Turn to the *Faith Summary* on page 35. Use the annotations to see if the children can express in their own words what they have learned.

Enrichment

Making "I Am a Catholic" Cards

Tell the children that many Catholics carry an identification card so that in case of an accident, people will know to call a priest to come and bless them.

Give each child an index card and guide them in making an identification card. Have them print their names and draw a cross at the top of it.

Materials needed: index cards; pencils

Practicing Faith

Belonging to the Church

Talk with the children about how proud they should be to belong to this wonderful Church that Jesus gave us. Have them write their names in the space on page 34. Talk about ways they can show they are good members of the Catholic Church. Then lead them in the prayer at the bottom of page 34.

Evaluating Your Lesson

- Do you feel the children know they belong to the Catholic Church?
- Do they appreciate how the Church helps them?
- Have they decided to be good members?

Coming To Faith

This can be done as a group activity.

Use this code to complete the sentences below.

A	B	E	I	L	M	O	P	R	S	T	V
1	2	3	4	5	6	7	8	9	10	11	12

1. In B A P T I S M (2 1 8 11 4 10 6) we become members of the Church.

2. The pope and bishops continue the work of the A P O S T L E S (1 8 7 10 11 5 3 10)

3. Members of Jesus' Church are to L O V E (5 7 12 3) one another.

What do you like best about belonging to Jesus' community, the Church?
helping others; going to Mass; etc.

Practicing Faith

Write your name in the church. Then gather in a circle. Take turns telling what you will do to show that you are a Catholic.
See page 33 for ideas.
Pray for one another.

______ belongs to the Catholic Church.

† Jesus, help us to follow You. Help us to be good members of Your Church. Amen.

Take time to talk to the children about ways they and their families can work together on the "Faith Alive" pages. Ask them to find out the name of the pope, and the name of the bishop of their diocese.

34

Won't You Join Us? (for use with page 31)

Tell the children that the classroom will be like a club this year . . . a club for Christians. Have the children give their club a name—for example: A Club for Jesus; The Everyone Is Welcome Club; Friends of Jesus Club. Then have the children think of a few rules for the club—for example: Any new children joining our group will be welcome; we will try to be fair to one another; when we play, we will not exclude anyone. Then have them think of a motto for their group—for example, We Welcome All People. Have the children think of and draw a special sign they can use.

"Jesus Brings Us In" Game (for use with page 32)

A child playing Jesus stands in the center of the circle and, using gestures and following the music of "The Farmer In the Dell," selects each child until all are chosen.

Jesus brings us in
Jesus brings us in
Jesus brings us into His family
Jesus brings us in.
And Jesus chooses (name)
And Jesus chooses (name)
Jesus brings to God's family
And Jesus chooses (name).

At the end all stay in the circle and sing:

We all belong together
We all belong together
In God's great family
We all belong together.

Though Many We Are One (for use with page 33)

To demonstrate that we belong to a special family, the Catholic Church, have a large circle traced onto cardboard and cut into jigsaw pieces (one piece for each child in the group). Distribute a piece to each child. Have each child write his or her name on the piece. Put a large piece of cardboard on a table. Have them fit the pieces together to see that we all make up a part of the whole.

Materials needed: cardboard; scissors; pencils

Club Buttons (for use with page 34)

Draw circles for buttons, one per child, about two or three inches in diameter. Invite the children to draw their special Club sign on their buttons. Encourage them to print the name of their special Christian Club on the buttons and to cut them out. They may choose to wear the buttons themselves or give them to other Christians.

Materials needed: cardboard; scissors; crayons or markers; safety pins or yarn

FAITH ALIVE AT HOME AND IN THE PARISH

Your child is learning how wonderful it is to be a member of Jesus' Church. The Second Vatican Council reminded Catholics that by our Baptism all of us must participate as active members in the life of the Church—both in prayer and in service. All Christians must help carry on the mission and ministry that now belongs to all the people of God, the Church.

You might ask yourself:

- *How do I help my family worship well together, especially at Mass?*
- *Do I give my family a sense of pride in being Catholic? What will I do this week?*

The Mass

Ask your child to draw a picture of Jesus' community gathered together at Mass. Encourage your child to pray, sing, and be attentive at Mass.

†Family Prayer

Jesus, help us to live our Catholic faith.

In Appreciation

Help your child make a certificate to show appreciation for someone who serves a leadership role in your parish community: pastor, parish minister, music minister, catechist. Use the poem written below or create your own thank-you message.

Have a suggestion to introduce the home activity to the children. Invite the children to name the people they would like to thank.

Learn by heart

Faith Summary

(1) • The Catholic Church is all over the world.

(2) • As Christians we try to live as Jesus taught us.

(1) What is our home in the Christian family?

(2) How do we try to live as Christians?

For a Parish Leader

Write this thank-you message on a piece of paper.

Roll it up and tie it with a special ribbon.
Present it to someone who has helped you feel welcome in your parish community.

Review

Go over the *Faith Summary* together before your child completes the *Review.* The answers for questions 1–4 appear on page 200. The response to number 5 will help you see whether your child understands that being Catholic means loving and serving others, as well as praying and worshiping together. When the *Review* is completed, have your child place a sticker on this page.

sticker

Use these words to complete each sentence.

peacemakers Catholics fairly world

1. Catholics are baptized and are to live as followers of Jesus.

2. Jesus shows us how to be peacemakers.

3. Our Catholic Church is all over the world.

4. Jesus' followers try to treat people fairly.

5. Tell some ways you will try to live as Jesus taught.

I will pray and worship God at Mass.

I will show love and care for others.

Encourage family involvement.

FAMILY SCRIPTURE MOMENT

Gather and ask: How does our membership in the Church help us come closer to God and make important decisions? Then **Listen** to Jesus' words to Peter.

I tell you, Peter: you are a rock, and on this rock foundation I will build My church, and not even death will ever be able to overcome it. I will give you the keys of the kingdom of heaven; what you prohibit on earth will be prohibited in heaven, and what you permit on earth will be permitted in heaven.

From Matthew 16:18–19

Share What do you hear Jesus saying to Peter? To you?

Consider for family enrichment:

- Jesus gathers His disciples who, like a building, have Peter for their foundation. Peter (which means "rock") is given authority in the Church that is confirmed in heaven.
- We thank God for our membership in the Church founded by Jesus and which nothing can overcome.

Reflect and **Decide** How are we encouraged by Jesus' words to Peter? What contribution will our family make to our parish this week?

5 We Belong to Our Parish

For the Catechist: Spiritual and Catechetical Development

Adult Background

Our Life

In the well-known story *The Little Prince* by Antoine de Saint-Exupéry, the fox begs the prince to tame him. "If you tame me," says the fox, "then we will establish ties. No matter where you go, you will always know that I belong to you and you belong to me." Each of us longs to belong to someone who knows and cares for us. We want to establish ties with others.

Ask yourself:

- With whom have I established ties?
- What kinds of ties do I usually establish with those I like?

Sharing Life

How would you explain this process of "taming," "belonging," or "establishing ties"?

How do you establish ties with others?

Our Catholic Faith

Pope John Paul II wrote:

Being "members" of the Church takes nothing away from the fact that each Christian as an individual is "unique and irrepeatable". On the contrary, this belonging guarantees and fosters the profound sense of that uniqueness and irrepeatability, in so far as these very qualities are the source of variety and richness for the whole Church. Therefore, God calls the individual in Jesus Christ, each one personally by name. In this sense, the Lord's words "You go into my vineyard too," directed to the Church as a whole, come specially addressed to each member individually.

Because of each member's unique and irrepeatable character, that is, one's identity and actions as a person, each individual is placed at the service of the growth of the ecclesial community while, at the same time, singularly receiving and sharing in the common richness of all the Church. This is the "Communion of Saints" which we profess in the Creed. *The good of all becomes the good of each one and the good of each one becomes the good of all.* "In the Holy Church," writes Saint Gregory the Great, "all are nourished by each one and each one is nourished by all." (*The Vocation and the Mission of the Lay Faithful in the Church and in the World,* 28, December 30, 1988)

If the Pope's words do not describe the reality of our parishes, hopefully they will serve to focus our vision of what parish life should and can become.

In the early Church, Christians gathered together in a particular city under the leadership of a bishop. This assembly was called the *paroikia. Paroikia* is a Greek word meaning "a temporary dwelling place." The first Christians were very conscious of themselves as a pilgrim people. They regarded this earthly dwelling place as temporary and looked forward to the coming of Christ in glory when ". . . God may be all in all" (1 Corinthians 15:28). Over time, *paroikia* became the parish, the center both of religious life and village or town life. Parishes were considered to be part of a territory that had a church building in which groups of the faithful attended Mass.

Since Vatican II, the Church has emphasized the idea of parish as a communion of persons united in Christ rather than simply as persons in a geographical territory. We have become increasingly aware of Jesus' vision for God's reign with which our parishes have been entrusted. These are challenging times for parishes. We are called to listen to the Spirit as we discern the needs of our parishes.

Coming to Faith

What is a parish? What is its mission?

How does your participation in your parish enable it to carry on its mission?

Practicing Faith

How will you take part in your parish life?

How will you help your group of children to feel that they are a part of parish life?

The Theme of This Chapter Corresponds with Paragraph 752

LITURGICAL RESOURCES

In his novel *Anna Karenina,* Leo Tolstoy observed that "All happy families resemble each other." The same might be said of happy parishes. And the primary way in which they resemble each other is evident in their liturgical celebrations. Are the worshipers made welcome? Do they connect with one another? With the celebrant? The liturgical ministers?

Encourage the children in your group to see themselves as Jesus' connection-makers at the Mass. They might greet people at the entrance, smile at and speak to those who are alone, offer the sign of peace to the elderly. They can help to make their parish a happy family.

JUSTICE AND PEACE RESOURCES

The Church continues the mission of Jesus Christ. Jesus invites all persons to be united: "I pray that they may all be one, Father! May they be in us, just as you are in me and I am in you" (John 17:21). In continuing His mission on earth, our parishes should be home for the outcasts, the poor, and all sinners. If the only criterion for acceptance in our parish were the question "Would Jesus welcome this person?" no one would be excluded.

Involve the children and their families in a welcoming project. Have each family invite to a particular liturgy someone who has been "left out": an aged or disabled person who needs help; a widow or single person who doesn't like to come alone; a guest at a soup kitchen or shelter. If possible, share coffee and doughnuts after the Mass.

Teaching Resources

Overview of the Lesson

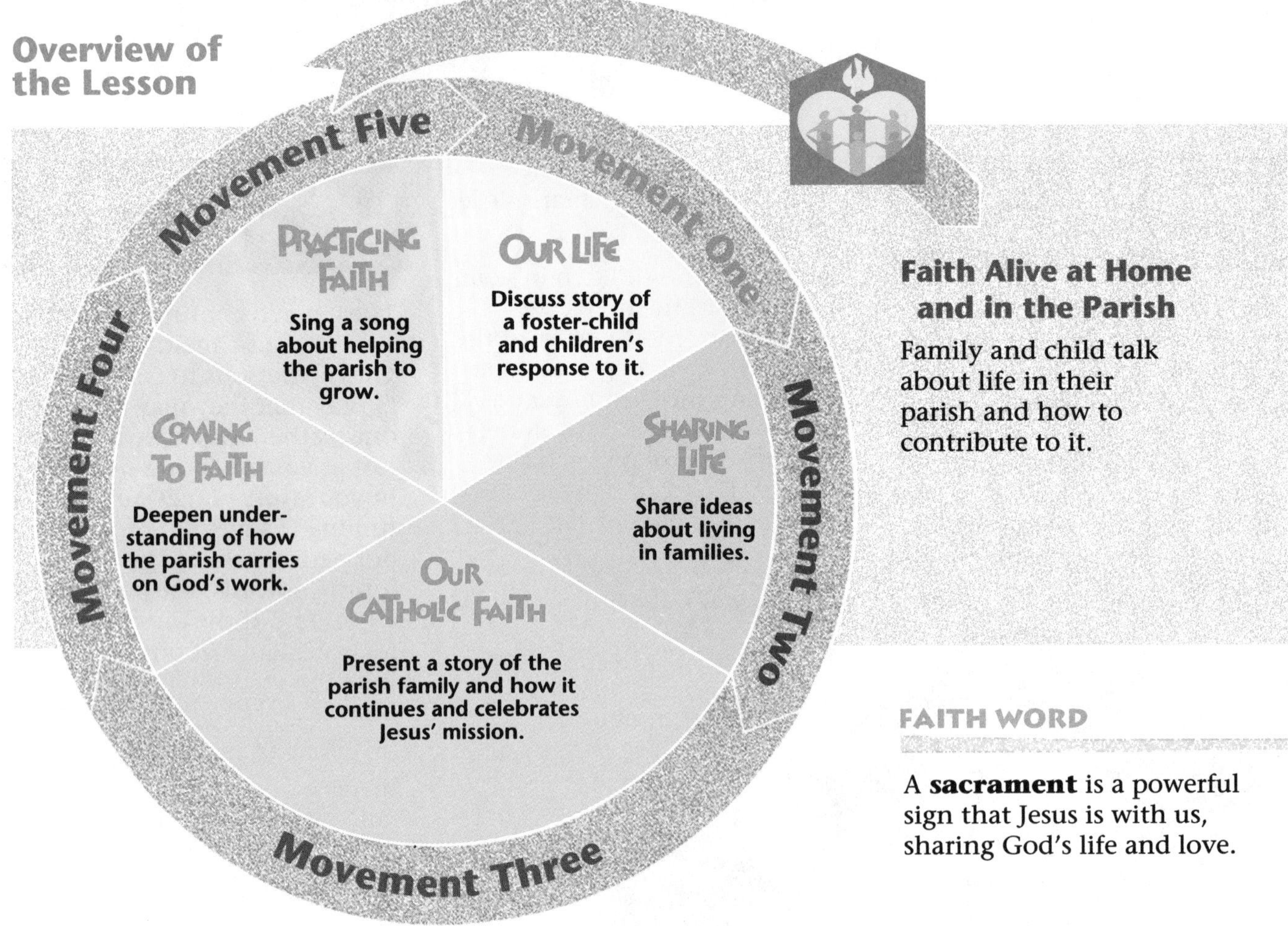

Faith Alive at Home and in the Parish

Family and child talk about life in their parish and how to contribute to it.

FAITH WORD

A **sacrament** is a powerful sign that Jesus is with us, sharing God's life and love.

Teaching Hints

In this lesson you will introduce the children to their own parish, and to the sacraments they will soon receive. Allow the children to share freely their own experiences of parish life.

If possible, invite those involved in various ministries in the parish—priests, deacons, lectors, and so forth—to speak to the children about their work. Share with the children something about your work as a catechist.

Special-Needs Child

Always face the hearing-impaired children whenever you are addressing them.

Visual Needs

- large, color picture of Jesus

Auditory Needs

- audiotape and headphones for the story of the Catholic Church

Tactile-Motor Needs

- peer helpers to assist with art activities

Supplemental Resources

Growing Up with Jesus' Family (video)
Jesus Signs: Baptism and Eucharist for Primary Children series
Brown-ROA
2460 Kerper Blvd. P.O. Box 539
Dubuque, IA 52004-0539
(1-800-922-7696)

My Father's House (video)
St. Anthony Messenger/
Franciscan Communications
1615 Republic Street
Cincinnati, OH 45210
(1-800-488-0488)
(1-800-989-3600)

Lesson Plan: Beginning

Objectives

To help the children

- know their parish is their special home in the Catholic Church;
- appreciate how their parish helps them;
- decide to contribute to the parish.

Focusing Prayer

Lead the children in the prayer at the top of page 37. Explain to them that today they will learn more about the parish, their special home in God's family.

Our Life

Responding to a Story

Have the children look at the illustration on page 37 and guess what the boys might be talking about. Read the story aloud to the children as they follow along in their texts. Then ask the follow-up questions, and encourage volunteers to share their feelings about the story and about families.

Sharing Life

Sharing Ideas About Families

Encourage awareness that God wants everyone to have a family so that all of us can have a sense of belonging, of being loved and cared for. Share your own ideas about the importance of family life. Then have the children respond to the *Sharing Life* directive and question. Invite responses from as many as possible.

Enrichment

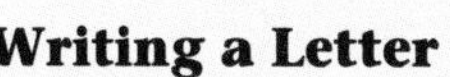

Writing a Letter

Distribute sheets of writing paper and suggest that the children write a letter, either to Dave, about his brother, or to Ed, to encourage and support him in regard to his family. Let the children illustrate the letters with pictures if they wish.

Materials needed: writing paper; pencils or pens

5 We Belong to Our Parish

Jesus, help us to follow You in our parish family.

Our Life

Dave was telling Ed about what a terrible little brother he had.

"I used to say that about my little brother, too," Ed said. "But I'd do anything to have my whole family back together again. My brother and I were split up after my parents died. I'm in a foster home now. My aunt is trying to get us together, but so far she hasn't been able."

How do you think Ed felt about not being with his family anymore? (1)

How do you think Dave felt about Ed's story? How do you feel about it? (2)

Does a family member ever make you feel happy? sad? angry?

(1) sad, lonely, missing them, angry, frustrated

(2) sad, upset, want to help

Sharing Life

Tell what is best about having a family. doing things together, loving each other, not being alone

How does God want us to live in our parish family? with love and care for others

37

Lesson Plan: Middle

Our Catholic Faith

Learning About Our Parish

Show the children a globe or map of the world. Explain that there are millions of Catholics who live all over the world. We belong to this great family. But God gives us a special family all our own within this large Church. We call it our parish family. Post a flash card with the word *parish* on it and have the children repeat it after you.

See if the children can give you the name of their parish church and write this on the chalkboard, or show them a church bulletin or church envelope with the parish name printed on it. If you know anything about the parish patron or the history of the parish, you might want to share some of this with the children.

Our Catholic Identity

If your parish is named after Mary, write its title on the board and refer to it as you introduce page 4 of the *Our Catholic Faith* section in the back of the book. Otherwise, have the children look at the picture of Mary and the children. Explain that Mary, the mother of Jesus, is a very important person in our Church. Share with the children some of your own love for Mary or tell of times when you have prayed to her.

Materials needed: globe or world map; flash card; church bulletin or envelope

Tell them you will read to them about their parish family, and invite them to follow along and to underline the word *parish* each time it appears.

Read aloud pages 38 and 39 slowly, pausing to emphasize and repeat the important points as you go along.

Faith Word

Display the word *sacrament*. Have the children repeat it

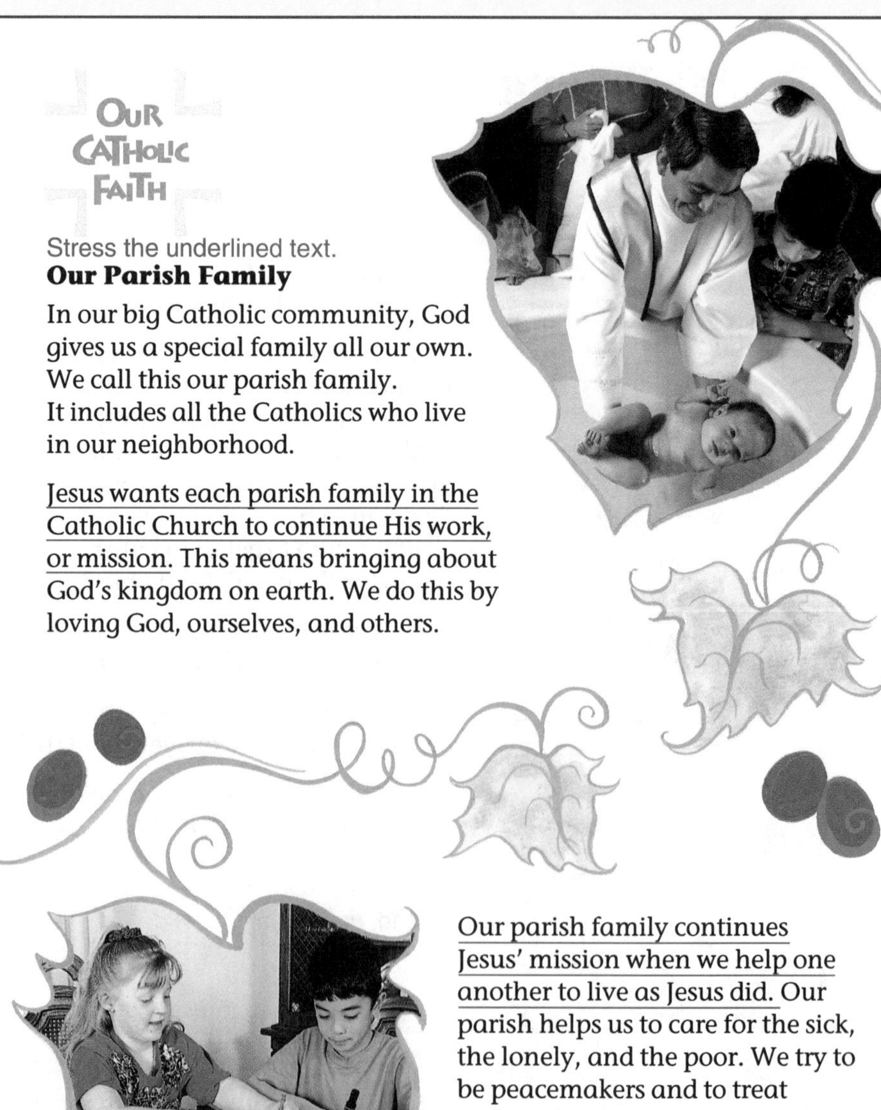
OUR CATHOLIC FAITH

Stress the underlined text.

Our Parish Family

In our big Catholic community, God gives us a special family all our own. We call this our parish family. It includes all the Catholics who live in our neighborhood.

Jesus wants each parish family in the Catholic Church to continue His work, or mission. This means bringing about God's kingdom on earth. We do this by loving God, ourselves, and others.

Our parish family continues Jesus' mission when we help one another to live as Jesus did. Our parish helps us to care for the sick, the lonely, and the poor. We try to be peacemakers and to treat everyone fairly.

38

Lesson Plan: Middle

after you, then read the definition together with them.Talk about what a joy it is to know that Jesus is always with us in so many ways.

A Picture-Search Game

Play a picture-search game with the children. Tell them you will describe something that is happening and they are to find the picture that corresponds to it and raise their hands when they do. Take time to comment on each picture and how it corresponds to the description:

- someone is being made a child of God and a member of our Catholic community;
- someone is celebrating God's forgiveness and our forgiveness of others;
- someone is receiving the sacrament of the Eucharist during Mass;
- someone is working to carry on Jesus' mission.

You may also wish to use pages 13–14 in the activity book for *Coming to Jesus.*

FAITH WORD

A **sacrament** is a powerful sign that Jesus is with us, sharing God's life and love.

We pray and worship God together in our parish church. We gather there for Mass and to celebrate the sacraments.

Here are some sacraments we celebrate in our parish church:

Baptism In this sacrament we become children of God and members of the Christian community.

Confirmation In this sacrament the Holy Spirit comes to us in a special way to help us live our faith.

Eucharist In this sacrament we remember and celebrate that Jesus saved us by His life, death, and resurrection.

Reconciliation In this sacrament the priest forgives our sins in the name of Jesus.

39

Enrichment

Celebrating Confirmation

Have a young person who is preparing to receive the sacrament of Confirmation talk to the children about what the sacrament means to him or her.

Lesson Plan: End

Coming to Faith

Talking About Our Parish

Read aloud each question in the *Coming to Faith* section on page 40. Allow the children to share their ideas.

Multicultural Awareness

Have the children take note of the variety of persons illustrated in the picture on page 40. Emphasize the great gifts that come to the Church because of the various cultures it includes.

Faith Summary

Turn to the *Faith Summary* on page 41. Use the annotations to see if the children can express in their own words what they have learned.

Practicing Faith

A Helping Song

Have the children think of something they might do to help their parish family grow as a community of Jesus' followers. Tell them to be prepared to share what they have decided to do. Remind the children that when they say "You're so welcome!" it means even the people we might not like. Everyone is welcome in Jesus' Church.

Then teach the song "This Is Our Church" on page 40. Allow time for the children to share what they will do. See the annotation.

You may wish to use Sadlier's grade 2 *Coming to Jesus in Song* cassette.

Evaluating Your Lesson

- Do you feel the children know their parish is their special family?
- Do they appreciate what they receive from the parish?
- Have they decided to contribute to the parish?

Enrichment

Hearing from Parish Members

Invite someone who has been a member of the parish for many years to come and speak to the children about what the parish has meant to her or him and what that person's special contribution to parish life has been. This is a wonderful opportunity to establish relationships with some of the older members of the parish.

Coming to Faith

Let's decide: what do you like best about our parish? Why?
Answers will vary.
How does our parish celebrate?
Mass, the sacraments, etc.
Tell how these different people in th parish can help bring about the kingdom of God in our neighborhoc

My Family Pastor Catechist

Name other persons who help in your parish.

Tell what we can do in our parish family. make a card for a sick person; take part in mass; learn about God; be kind and fair

Practicing Faith

Stop for a minute. Think quietly of a way you will help your parish family grow as a community of Jesus' followers this week.
Be ready to give your answer during our singing game.
(To the tune of "London Bridge")

This is our Church, please come in,
Please come in, please come in.
This is our Church, please come in—
You're so welcome!

How will we show we're Jesus' friend
Jesus' friends, Jesus' friends?
How will we show we're Jesus' friend
Will you tell us?
(Tell what you will do.) Encourage the children to think of a specific action.

Take time to talk to the children about ways they and their families can work together on the "Faith Alive" pages. Encourage them to share the "Communion Prayer" with a family member.

40

Creating Family Collages (for use with page 37)

Distribute magazines, scissors, glue, and large sheets of cardboard. Have the children work in small groups to create collages of things families do together. Encourage each group to show at least four or five different things families do together. When finished, invite volunteers from each group to explain their collages to the whole group. When they have finished, gather the children in the prayer corner. Ask them to place their collages on the prayer table and then to pray together "Jesus, bless all families."

Materials needed: magazines; scissors; glue; large pieces of cardboard

Members of God's Family (for use with page 39)

Have each child bring in four large index cards. Have the children write on each of their cards three or four questions they would like to ask a parishioner. Distribute them to members of the parish in whatever way seems easiest. "Returns" can be placed in a decorated box accessible to the parish members. Share the questions and the responses with the children.

Materials needed: large index cards; decorated box

What Time Is It? (for use with page 39)

Do a simple parish time line with the students. Information on important parish dates can be obtained from the parish secretary: for example, when the parish was started; when the church was built; year the present pastor came to the parish; year most of the children were baptized; and the year the children will receive the sacraments of Reconciliation and Eucharist.

Place a piece of colored tape in the middle of a sheet of posterboard. Use a different colored marker to write in the dates. Then use a regular pen to write what the dates mean.

Materials needed: colored tape; posterboard; markers

In the News (for use with page 40)

Obtain a copy of the parish bulletin to find ways in which the parish serves the friends of Jesus.

Draw an outline of a large church on posterboard. Underneath it print "Our Parish Members Serve One Another." List on the posterboard the various organizations that serve the people of your parish. Have the children decorate the poster around the church to express what the organizations do for the parish; for example, the St. Vincent de Paul Society might be represented by cans of food; lectors might be represented by a symbol of a book. Be sure the children understand what each symbol means.

Materials needed: posterboard; crayons; parish bulletin

FAITH ALIVE AT HOME AND IN THE PARISH

As Catholics we belong to the Church throughout the world and to the local Church of the diocese of which your parish is a part. This week your child has learned that the parish is where the family lives out its call to bring about the kingdom, or reign, of God on earth. We do this in our parish by praying and worshiping together and by reaching out to love and serve others, especially those in need.

Some people may think that the work of the parish is the sole responsibility of its parish leaders. But, as Vatican II reminds us, we are the people of God, the Church. We need to teach our children that all of us are the parish.

You might ask yourself:

- *How will we help our parish to be a real community of Jesus' disciples?*
- *How will we support our parish leaders this week?*

The Parish Family

Tell your child all you can about the story of your parish. Include what each of your parish leaders does and how your family contributes to parish life. If possible, involve the entire family in this discussion.

†Communion Prayer

Do the activity below with your child to build enthusiasm for being Catholic and to help anticipate receiving Jesus in Holy Communion.

Put your right hand over your heart as you pray.

Learn by heart **Faith Summary**

- Our parish is our special family in the Catholic Church.
  What is our parish?
- Our parish helps us live together as a community of Jesus' friends.
  What does our parish help us to do?

Encourage the children to say this prayer at Communion time.

Review

Go over the *Faith Summary* together before your child completes the *Review*. The answers for questions 1–3 appear on page 200. The response to number 4 will help you see whether your child understands your parish as more than just a building but, more importantly, as a community of faith. When the *Review* is completed, have your child place a sticker on this page.

sticker

Write the correct word on the line.

Eucharist parish baptized worship

1. In our parish we w orship together.

2. We are b aptized in our parish church.

3. We celebrate the sacrament of the E ucharist.

4. How can you take part in your parish?

Possible responses:

I can attend Mass. I can celebrate the sacraments with the priest and my parish.

Encourage family involvement.

FAMILY SCRIPTURE MOMENT

Gather and ask: Where do we seek help with our daily burdens? Now **Listen** to Jesus' words.

Come to Me, all of you who are tired from carrying heavy loads, and I will give you rest. Take My yoke and put it on you, and learn from Me, because I am gentle and humble in spirit; and you will find rest. For the yoke I will give you is easy, and the load I will put on you is light.

From Matthew 11:28–30

Share Ask: What do you hear Jesus saying about the heavy burdens in your life?

Consider for family enrichment:

- In the time of Jesus, farmers used oxen teams hitched together by yokes, or harness frames, to do heavy plowing. Jesus invites us to put on the light yoke of being His disciples.
- Every day we have to respond to Jesus' invitation "Come to Me." He will always be gentle with us.

Reflect and **Decide** Listen again to the words of Jesus. How will we help one another to trust in Jesus, especially in hard times?

6 PRAYER

The Theme of This Chapter Corresponds with Paragraph 2567

For the Catechist: Spiritual and Catechetical Development

Our Life

Aiming at the heart of the matter, C.S. Lewis advises that whenever we pray we begin with this prayer: "May it be the real I who speaks. May it be the real Thou that I speak to." *(Letters to Malcolm: Chiefly on Prayer)*

Ask yourself:

- Am I my true self when I pray? Why or why not?
- What is my image of the One I pray to?

Sharing Life

How do I hope to become "more real" in prayer?

Our Catholic Faith

If we wish to become the saints God intends us to be, prayer is the path we must follow. Scripture and Church tradition show us the way. The Holy Spirit, abiding within, stirs up the desire and the need to pray—even when we feel that prayer is impossible.

> For we do not know how we ought to pray; the Spirit himself pleads with God for us in groans that words cannot express. (Romans 8:26)

It is the Spirit of God who enables us to lift up our minds in prayer. Prayer may be a dialogue or a listening; an asking or an offering; a solitary silence or a liturgical celebration. But whether prayer is vocal or mental, personal or communal, it is always an expression of our relationship with God. Saint Augustine characterizes that relationship in his maxim: "True, whole prayer is nothing but love."

Coming to Faith

What form of prayer do you most need to grow in?

How will you seek that growth?

Practicing Faith

How will you try to instill a love for prayer in the children in your group?

What opportunities will you give them to experience prayer?

Teaching Resources

Teaching Hints

It is important for children, especially today, to feel that God is always present to them and for them. Try to develop this sense of awareness in the children. Help them learn to pray in a natural, comfortable way. Use the pictures in their books to illustrate different body gestures they might use in prayer. Be sure they understand that if God says "no" to something we ask in prayer, the response is motivated by God's love. Share with the children how prayer has enriched your own life.

Special-Needs Child

If you have rearranged your meeting place for this liturgy lesson, take time to re-orient any visually-impaired children.

Visual Needs

- enlarged pictures of children praying

Auditory Needs

- headphones, tape recording of prayer service

Tactile-Motor Needs

- copy of prayer service taped to desk

Supplemental Resources

Prayer Is For Children (book)
by Julie Kelemen
Liguori Publications
One Liguori Drive
Liguori, MO 63057-9999
(1-800-325-9521)

Let Us Pray…
For Young People (video)
Ikonographics
P.O. Box 600
Croton-on-Hudson, N.Y. 10520
(1-800-944-1505)

Lesson Plan: Beginning

Objectives

To help the children

- know the meaning of prayer;
- appreciate the many ways we can pray;
- choose to speak and listen to God in their lives.

Focusing Prayer

Recall for the children that Jesus came to teach us what we need to do to love God and others. Then lead them in the prayer at the top of page 43.

Our Life

Keeping in Touch

Ask the children if they have ever heard someone say, "Keep in touch," and if they know what this means. Explain that when a person is going away or saying goodbye, he or she wants to remind you not to forget him or her, but to call on the phone or write a letter.

Have the children study the illustration on page 43 and tell what is happening. Let them interpret the picture for you. Then suggest that perhaps Rosa's grandmother asked her to keep in touch, so Rosa is writing to her.

Read aloud the first two paragraphs on the page. Then have the children complete Rosa's letter. Give them time to name someone with whom they would like to talk, then have them share something they might tell that person.

Sharing Life

Talking with God

Write the word *God* on the chalkboard. Ask the children if they can see God. Ask if they think God wants us to "keep in touch." Then have them respond to each of the questions in the *Sharing Life* section. Give each child an opportunity to speak.

6 Prayer

Jesus, teach us to pray!

Our Life

Just because we don't see people doesn't mean we can't talk to them.

Rosa's grandmother lives far away. But Rosa can talk to her on the phone or write her a letter.

Help Rosa finish this letter.

Dear Grandma,
How are you? I am fine.
I ________________
____
____
____
Love,
Rosa

Think of someone with whom you would like to talk. What would you say?
Possible responses: I miss you; it is fun to be with you, etc.

Sharing Life

Can we talk to God any time we want? How?
Yes; by praying
What do you think God wants us to say?
our needs; what is in our hearts; etc.

43

Lesson Plan: Middle

Our Catholic Faith

Faith Word

Write the word *prayer* on the chalkboard or show it on a flash card. Pronounce the word for the children, and have them repeat it. Tell them to listen for this word as you read.

Understanding Prayer

Have the children turn to page 44. Read aloud the first paragraph to them and have them underline the definition for prayer. Emphasize the fact that prayer is listening as well as talking, but explain that this does not mean we "hear" God in the same way we hear others speak to us.

The Prayer of Jesus

If possible, show a picture of Jesus praying. Explain to the children that Jesus often prayed when He was with the apostles. Ask the children if they think the apostles enjoyed watching Jesus pray, and why or why not. Let them pretend that they are watching Jesus as He prays. Ask what they notice. Lead them to an awareness that Jesus prayed with few words but with great love and attention to His Father in heaven. Encourage the children to pray in the same way.

How We Pray

Read aloud the rest of page 44 and the top of page 45. Use the annotations. Have the children notice the different prayer po-

Stress the underlined text.

We Can Pray

When we love people, we talk and listen to them. We share what is in our hearts. We can talk and listen to God, too. Prayer is talking and listening to God. God's grace in us helps us to pray.

Jesus showed His followers how to pray. When we pray, we tell God what is in our hearts.

- We can praise God, who made us.
- We can tell God we are sorry for something we have done wrong.
- We can ask God's help for all people.
- We can ask God's help for our own needs.
- We can thank God for God's love and care.

Ask: How can we pray?

We can pray by ourselves. We can pray with our friends, our families, and our parish family. We can pray quietly in our hearts using our own words. We can pray special prayers like the Our Father or the Hail Mary.

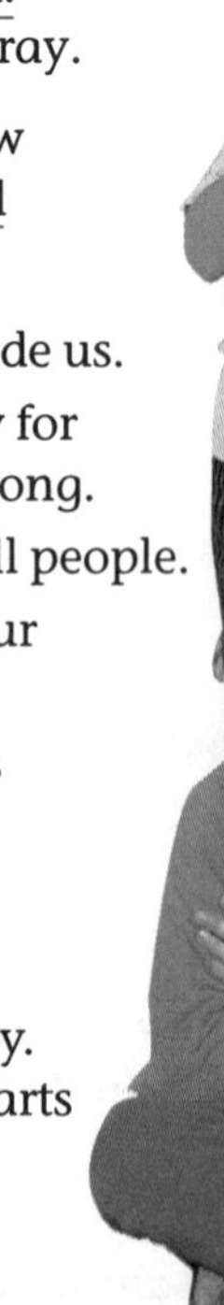

44

Enrichment

Writing a Letter

Give each child a sheet of notepaper. Let them each write a short note to someone they would like to keep in touch with them: a grandparent; a brother, a sister, or a friend who is away from home; a favorite aunt. Suggest that they pray for this person and tell her or him about it in the note. Let them draw pictures or decorate the note as they wish. Remind them to send the note in the mail.

sitions of the children in the picture. Ask the follow-up questions. You may also wish to use pages 15–16 in the activity book for *Coming to Jesus*.

You may wish to use pages 43–44 of the *Celebrating Our Seasons and Saints* level 2 book from William H. Sadlier, Inc.

Coming to Faith

Our Own Prayer

Have the children respond to the questions in the *Coming to Faith* section. Then have them make up a brief prayer of their own and write it inside the heart. See the annotation.

Faith Summary

Turn to the *Faith Summary* on page 47. Use the annotations to see if the children can express in their own words what they have learned today.

Practicing Faith

Finding a Prayer

Read the directives in the *Practicing Faith* section, one at a time. Give the children sufficient time to look through the prayers. Each child should select one and share his or her choice with the group.

FAITH WORD

Prayer is talking and listening to God.

We can even sing or act out what we want to say to God.

When will you talk to God? What will you say?

Coming to Faith

What are some ways we can pray? What is your favorite way to pray?

Answers will vary.

Make up a prayer of your own now. Tell God what is in your heart. Write your prayer here.

Practicing Faith

Look through your *Coming to Jesus* book. Look at "A Doorway to Prayer" in the back of the book. Find a prayer you will pray this week.

Enrichment

Reasons to Pray

Post a large sheet of posterboard on the wall. Write on it the following headings, leaving space underneath to complete each one: We praise God; We tell God we are sorry; We ask God's help for others; We ask God's help for ourselves; We thank God. Have the children suggest something to pray for as an example of each one. Write these on the chart, or have the children write them. Let them copy these intentions on a sheet of notepaper to take home. Suggest that they pray for one of these intentions each day of the coming week.

Materials needed: posterboard

Lesson Plan: End

Prayer Service

Before conducting the prayer service, be sure to go over the words of the service and the singing of the *Our Father.* (You may wish to use the grade 2 *Coming to Jesus in Song* cassette from William H. Sadlier, Inc.)

Read the words of the prayer service and have the children read the "All" parts. Then play the *Our Father* once for the children to listen to the melody. Play it a second time and have the children join in singing the hymn.

When you feel the children are prepared, conduct the prayer service. See the annotation. Ask the children to close their eyes, be very still, and think about a picture of Jesus. After a second or two, have the children open their eyes and begin the prayer service.

Evaluating Your Lesson

- Do the children know the meaning of prayer?
- Do they appreciate the many ways we can pray?
- Have they chosen to talk and listen to God in prayer?

† **Prayer Service**

Leader: We can talk to God whenever we want.
Let us each silently tell Him how we feel right now. . . .
God, You are great and wonderful. You made the world and everything in it.

All: O God, we praise You.

Leader: Loving God, help us to be better followers of Your Son, Jesus.
God, we pray especially for. . . .

All: (Add your own prayer here.)

Some children may not wish to speak aloud.

Leader: Loving God, we are sorry for all the times that we have been unkind to others.

All: O God, forgive us!

Leader: Loving God, thank You for taking care of us.

All: O God, we thank You.

Leader: Let's stand and join hands. We will pray as Jesus taught us.

All: (Pray or sing) Our Father . . . .

Encourage the children to take time to do the "Faith Alive" pages with their families. The family might want to choose a special time to pray together.

A Liturgy Activity

Prayer, like a conversation with a person we love, is essential to the growth of our relationship with God. Times of prayer with others can encourage our faith, even as we may be a source of encouragement to others in their efforts in prayer.

Plan a group prayer service with your children. As much as possible, incorporate their suggestions, prayers and songs with which you know they are already familiar. Be sure to include a variety of prayer activities, such as a Gospel story of Jesus and an action-prayer with body movements or mime.

A Justice and Peace Activity

There is a saying about prayer that goes: "Be careful what you pray for. You think you are asking God to handle something, but God thinks you're volunteering." Would we pray for the same things if we believed we were volunteering?

Help the children to understand our need to pray like Jesus in words and actions. Give examples: Pray for a sick person and visit him or her. Pray for the poor and help to feed them.

Do It Yourself

Use this space to create your own prayer service.

FAITH ALIVE AT HOME AND IN THE PARISH

In this lesson your child was drawn into a deeper understanding of the meaning and value of prayer and was introduced to different forms of prayer. To be a Christian is to be a person who prays frequently. We can use the formal prayers of our Church or we can pray in our own words. We can pray alone or with others. Prayer, however, is not simply a matter of talking to God. In prayer we listen to God with our hearts, with our entire selves. In all forms of prayer we come to God, who loves us more than we love ourselves.

You might ask yourself:

- *How do I pray? When do I pray?*
- *How can I help my child to pray?*

†Family Prayer

Set aside a special time for prayer together. This could be at your child's bedtime, before a meal, or at the *Family Scripture Moment*. Help your child learn the traditional prayers of our Catholic faith such as the Our Father, the Hail Mary, the Sign of the Cross, Glory to the Father, prayers before and after meals. You will find these prayers on pages 189–192. Also encourage spontaneous prayer that comes from the heart and the experiences of your child's life.

Learn by heart

Faith Summary

What is prayer?

- Prayer is talking and listening to God.
- We can pray in many ways.

How can we pray?

Our Family's Letter to God

What would your family like to say to God? Write it here.

Dear God,

Here is a suggestion to introduce the family letter activity to the children.

Have the children write a group letter to God.

Review

Go over the *Faith Summary* together before your child completes the *Review.* The answers for questions 1–4 appear on page 200. The response to number 5 will show how comfortable your child is with prayer. When the *Review* is completed, have your child place a sticker on this page.

sticker

Circle the correct answer.

1. Prayer is talking and listening to God. (Yes) No

2. We can tell God what is in our hearts. (Yes) No

3. Jesus taught His followers how to pray. (Yes) No

4. We should always pray out loud. Yes (No)

5. Tell how you like to pray.

Possible responses:
I like to sing; talk to God in my own words; etc.

Encourage the children to gather with their families to share the *Family Scripture Moment.*

Gather and ask each person: When and how do you like to pray? **Listen** as Jesus speaks to us of prayer.

Ask, and you will receive; seek, and you will find; knock, and the door will be opened to you. For everyone who asks will receive, and anyone who seeks will find, and the door will be opened to the person who knocks. You know how to give good things to your children. How much more, then, will your Father in heaven give good things to those who ask!

From Matthew 7:7–8, 11

Share Ask: What is Jesus saying to you in this reading about prayer?

Consider for family enrichment:

- How often the gospels picture Jesus at prayer. Prayer was so much a part of His life. Here He makes some amazing promises to those who persist in prayer.
- When we persist in praying for good things, and trust in God, He will always answer in our best interest.

Reflect and **Decide** Ask what it means for each family member to ask, seek, and knock. How will we show that as a family we have heard Jesus' message about prayer?

THE BIBLE

The Theme of This Chapter Corresponds with Paragraph 104

For the Catechist: Spiritual and Catechetical Development

Our Life

Many people today are engrossed in research about their family trees. We find it fascinating to investigate our ancestors and find some connection with them in our interests and our abilities.

Ask yourself:

- What stories do I know about my ancestors?
- Do I feel connected to my family's past? How?

Sharing Life

How can a sense of connection with the past be both anchoring and freeing?

How does knowing about the past help to inform the present and shape the future?

Our Catholic Faith

The Scriptures are our history as the people of God. The stories root us in relationship with God from creation and invite us to live out the covenant relationship renewed by Jesus. The Second Vatican Council encouraged easy access to the Bible for all Catholics.

When we read Scripture today, awareness of cultures, time periods, and literary forms can bring alive the personalities and issues of the Israelites of the Old Testament and the Christian community of the New Testament. In these pages, we see the response of individuals to God's call throughout history. In addition to connecting us to this past, our past, the Bible is meant for us now. It is the living word of God and through it God speaks to us today.

Coming to Faith

Why should we be aware of the cultures and literary forms presented in the Bible?

How do you hope to become more familiar with the Bible?

Practicing Faith

How will you try to listen more attentively to the readings during the Liturgy of the Word?

How will you make the Bible appealing to the children in your group?

Teaching Resources

Teaching Hints

The best way to instill in the children a love and reverence for the Bible is by your own example. Let the children see you holding the Bible with reverence. Give the Bible a place of honor in the room by placing it on a stand with an unlit candle or flowers next to it. Invite the children occasionally to read from a children's Bible. Suggest that they read a portion of the Bible each day or have their parents read stories from the Bible to them.

Special-Needs Child

When writing for children with limited vision, use felt-tip pens or thick lead pencils.

Visual Needs

- letters for faith word cut from rough fabric

Auditory Needs

- preferential positions for the procession

Tactile-Motor Needs

- preferential positions for the procession

Supplemental Resources

Children's Heroes of the Bible series (videos)
Vision Video
2030 Wentz Church Road
Worcester, PA 19490
(1-800-523-0226)

Lesson Plan: Beginning

OBJECTIVES

To help the children

- know the meaning of the Bible;
- appreciate the importance of the Bible;
- decide to learn and live what the Bible teaches.

Focusing Prayer

Hold up a Bible and see if the children can identify it. Then lead them in the prayer at the top of page 49.

Our Life

A Guessing Game

Divide the children into three groups and have each group read one of the verses of the rhyme on page 49. Pause at the end of each verse to respond to the questions. See the annotation. Let the children use the pictures as "clues" to help them answer. Then let them share some of the things they are learning.

Sharing Life

Learning in a Pretend World

Let the children imagine they have traveled to a pretend land. Let them give it a name. Have them sit in a circle with you to talk about what life is like in this land. Tell them to imagine that there is no one in this country to help them learn and there are no books to read. Point out how difficult it would be for them to learn new things here.

Then have them respond to the directive at the bottom of page 49. List their responses on the chalkboard or a large sheet of paper.

7 The Bible

Dear God, help us to hear Your word in the Bible.

Some children might want to answer the poem's questions by citing specific people.

OUR LIFE

Let's play a guessing game.

When you were a baby, you
could not walk.
Who helped you to walk?
Who helped you to talk?

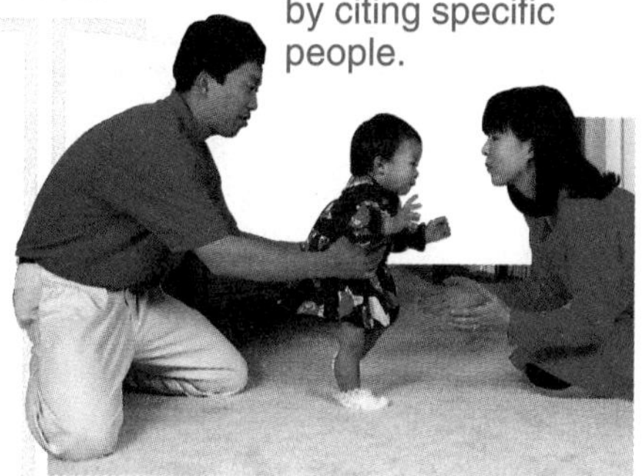

As you got bigger, you learned
many things.
Who taught you to count?
make letters? and sing?

You are still learning and
growing each day.
Who helps you to learn?
Who shows you the way?

Tell some new things you know.
How did you learn about them?
Answers will vary.

SHARING LIFE

How would you learn new things if there were no one to help you and no books to read? Possible responses: by the experience of living

Name some ways that we learn about God. from our experiences; from others; from the bible; etc.

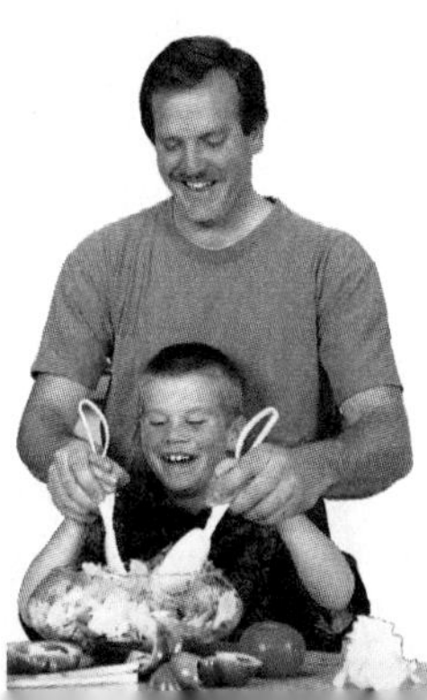

Lesson Plan: Middle

Our Catholic Faith

Learning from Pictures

Have the children study the three pictures on pages 50 and 51. Call on volunteers to tell the story of each one. Then ask them where they learned the story they just told. If they say they learned it from their parents, ask how their parents knew about it. Continue going back until you can demonstrate that the story came first from the Bible and then from those who passed it on to us.

Faith Word

Direct the children's attention to the faith word at the top of page 51. Read the definition of the word *Bible* together. Have the children close their eyes and see if they can say the definition without looking at the book.

What We Learn from the Bible

Read aloud the first paragraph on page 50. Then draw two columns on the chalkboard or a large sheet of paper and write the heading *We learn…* Ask the children to come up, one at a time, and write in either column one thing we learn from the Bible.

Read aloud the second paragraph on page 50. Let the children share other stories they have learned from the Bible. Read the rest of the page. See if the children can recall anything they remember hearing from the Bible at Sunday Mass. Explain that many of the Mass prayers are taken from the Bible. Try to instill in the children a sense of gratitude for the fact that we have such easy access to God's word, and what a blessing it is in our lives.

Enrichment

A Bible Scene

Have the children choose a favorite story about Jesus or one story that He told. Suggest that they create a Bible scene of this story, using play dough and construction paper. One child might make background trees or mountains out of construction paper; others might make the figures in the story out of the play dough. When they are finished, invite a volunteer to tell the story, using the Bible scene.

Materials needed: play dough; construction paper; scissors; markers; tape or glue

The Bible Helps Us Grow

From the Bible we learn about God and how God wants us to live.

The Bible has many stories about how much God loves us. These stories help us to learn about God's plan for the world and how to live as His people.

The Bible is the most important book for Jesus' followers. It tells us stories about God, and about Jesus and His good news for us. From these stories we learn how to live as followers of Jesus.

Every time we go to Mass, we hear God's word read to us from the Bible. We thank and praise God for giving us the Bible to help us live as His people.

The Story of Christmas

50

Lesson Plan: Middle

You may also wish to use pages 17–18 in the activity book.

Coming to Faith

Putting on Our Thinking Caps

Give each child a "thinking cap" (a piece of construction paper that you have twisted into a cone shape and taped or stapled together). Have them put on their "thinking caps" after you ask each of the questions in the *Coming to Faith* section. Try to elicit at least one response from each child.

Materials needed: construction paper; tape or stapler

Faith Summary

Turn to the *Faith Summary* on page 52. Use the annotations to see if the children can express in their own words what they have learned today.

Practicing Faith

Sharing Stories

Read aloud the directions in the *Practicing Faith* section. Give each child the opportunity either to tell a story or act one out. Remind the children that God wants us to learn lessons from the Bible that will help us live as God intends. Elicit examples from the stories they told or acted out.

FAITH WORD

The **Bible** is the book in which we read the word of God.

The Story of the Lost Son

COMING TO FAITH

What kinds of stories are in the Bible? stories of God, Jesus, Mary, the apostles, the church, people, etc.

What can you learn from the stories in the Bible? how God loves us and how God wants us to live

PRACTICING FAITH

Name a Bible story you know. Tell this story, or act it out with some of your friends.

The Story of Palm Sunday

51

Lesson Plan: End

Enthroning the Bible

Go over the prayer service with the children ahead of time. Then have a simple Bible enthronement. Prepare a table, covered with a cloth. Place a Bible stand in the middle of the table and an unlit candle on each side. Decorate the table with flowers or greens.

Have the children march in procession to the prayer table. Invite one of the children to lead the procession, carrying the Bible, and conduct the service suggested on page 52.

Materials needed: Bible; cloth-covered table; candles; flowers or greens

Evaluating Your Lesson

- Do the children know what the Bible is?
- Do they appreciate the importance of the Bible?
- Have they decided to learn God's word and live it?

Enrichment

Examining the Bible

Hold up a children's Bible. Explain to the children that there are two parts to our Bible: one that tells about the time before Jesus came, and one that tells about Jesus' life, death, and resurrection and what happened later in the Church. Show some of the pictures in the Bible and comment on them, answering any questions the children may have. Let each child examine the Bible. It is not necessary for them to know yet how to find various books in the Bible. It may be helpful for them, however, to see that the name of each book is found at the top of every page.

Materials needed: a children's Bible

† Bible Prayer Service

Leader: O God, we will put the Bible in a special place of honor because it is Your word. Let us walk quietly to our special place.
All: Praise be to God!

Leader: Listen to this Bible reading from the Book of Psalms:
God, Your word is a lamp to guide me and a light for my path.
From Psalm 119:105
The word of the Lord.
All: Thanks be to God.

Leader: Jesus speaks to us in this reading from the Gospel of John:
Whoever hears My words and believes in God who sent Me will have life forever with God.
From John 5:24
The gospel of the Lord.
All: Praise to you, Lord Jesus Christ.

Leader: Help us, God, to hear and understand Your word from the Bible. Help us to follow Your word always.
All: Amen.

Prepare a bible corner ahead of time, with a children's Bible.

Talk to the children about ways they and their families might work together on the "Faith Alive" pages. Suggest that they ask a family member to read a favorite Bible story with them.

A Liturgy Activity

The Liturgy of the Word provides us with an opportunity to hear and reflect upon the word of God. We should take the time to absorb the message, take it to heart, and allow it to change our lives.

Choose an upcoming Gospel reading to which your group can relate. Tell the story in advance of the weekend liturgies. Ask the children to listen attentively during Mass and to remember one important thing God says to us in this Bible story. Share their thoughts during the following sessions.

A Justice and Peace Activity

The bishops of the United States remind us in their pastoral letter "Brothers and Sisters to Us" that God's word proclaims the oneness of the human family. God's word announces that *all* men and women are created in God's image.

Help your group to understand that the Bible belongs to all people by displaying in the room copies of the Bible in different languages. Teach them a few names of God in a language they do not know. Pray together for missioners who carry God's word to people who hunger for it.

Materials needed: copies of the Bible in different languages

Do It Yourself

Use this space to plan biblical readings.

FAITH ALIVE AT HOME AND IN THE PARISH

In this lesson, your child learned that we hear the word of God read to us from the Bible. As the Second Vatican Council teaches us, the Bible is the word of God in human language. Centuries ago, Saint Jerome told us that "ignorance of the Scriptures is ignorance of Christ." At Mass we hear readings from both the Old and New Testament. They root us in our relationship with God, and they move us to live out that relationship in Jesus Christ. Each week your family has a special opportunity to share the word of God together in the *Family Scripture Moment* at the end of each lesson.

You might ask yourself:

- *How can I listen better to God's word in the Bible?*
- *Can our family be more faithful in listening to, reading, and sharing God's word?*

Response to God's Word

Remind your child to listen closely to God's word as it is read at Mass. Help your child remember to respond "Thanks be to God" after the first two readings and "Praise to you, Lord Jesus Christ" after the gospel is proclaimed.

Learn by heart

Faith Summary

- The Bible is the word of God.
  What is the Bible?
- The Bible helps us to live as followers of Jesus.
  What does the Bible help us to do?

A Favorite Bible Story

Choose a favorite Bible story. Think of the part of the story you like best. Draw it here.

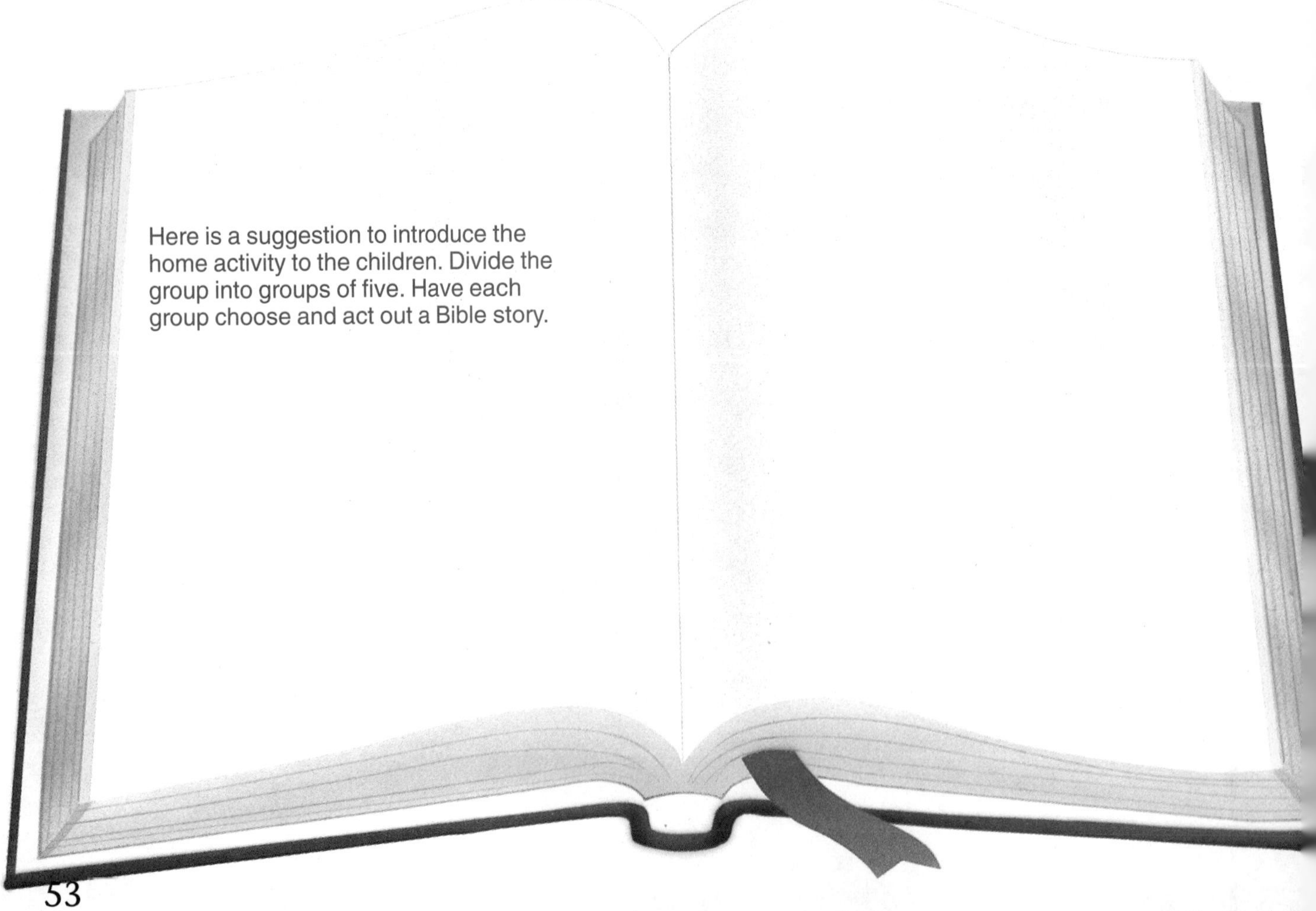

Here is a suggestion to introduce the home activity to the children. Divide the group into groups of five. Have each group choose and act out a Bible story.

Review

Go over the *Faith Summary* together before your child completes the *Review.* The answers for questions 1–4 appear on page 200. The response to number 5 will show you if your child has learned something from the Bible. When the *Review* is completed, invite your child to choose a sticker for this page.

sticker

Circle the correct answer.

1. The Bible is the word of God. (Yes) No

2. We hear God's word only at Mass. Yes (No)

3. The Bible tells of God's love for us. (Yes) No

4. The Bible shows us how to live as followers of Jesus Christ. (Yes) No

5. Tell something you have learned from the Bible.

Possible responses:

God loves us; God's plan for the world and how to live as God's people.

Encourage the children to gather with their families to share the *Family Scripture Moment.*

Gather and ask: What part does the Bible play in our lives? **Listen** well to Jesus' words.

Do not think that I have come to do away with the Law of Moses and the teachings of the prophets. I have not come to do away with them, but to make their teachings come true. So then, whoever disobeys even the least important of the commandments and teaches others to do the same, will be least in the kingdom of heaven. On the other hand, whoever obeys the Law and teaches others to do the same, will be great in the kingdom of heaven.

From Matthew 5:17, 19

Share How are we trying to be "great" in the kingdom of God?

Consider for family enrichment:

- Jesus honors and fulfills God's word in the Old Testament. By His life and teaching, Jesus shows us how the spirit of God's law is to be fulfilled.
- When we, by word or example, teach others to live by the word of God, Jesus promises that we will be "great" in God's kingdom.

Reflect and **Decide** What does it mean for us to fulfill the spirit of God's law? How will we as a family show this week that we are guided by God's word?

UNIT 1 • REVIEW

Use the annotations on this page to review the major points of Unit 1.

We Believe in God

Ask: What do we believe about God?

We believe in one God. We believe that there are three Persons in one God, the Father, the Son, and the Holy Spirit. We call these three divine Persons the Blessed Trinity.

Jesus Christ Is God's Son

Ask: What do we believe about Jesus?

Jesus Christ is the Son of God. Jesus is also human, as we are. Jesus died and rose from the dead to give us new life.

The Holy Spirit Is Our Helper

Ask: What happened on Pentecost?

The Holy Spirit came to the friends of Jesus on Pentecost. The Holy Spirit gave them courage to live and tell everyone the good news of Jesus. The Holy Spirit helps us today.

We Belong to the Catholic Church

Ask: What is the community of Jesus' followers?

The community of Jesus' followers, or disciples, is the Church. We become children of God and members of the Catholic Church.

We Belong to Our Parish

Ask: What do we do in our parish church?

Our parish church is the place where Catholics in our neighborhood gather together to pray and worship God.

UNIT 1 • TEST

Use these words to finish the sentences below.

Church Trinity Son Holy Spirit

1. We call God, Father, Son, and Holy Spirit, the Blessed ___Trinity___.

2. Jesus Christ is God's ___Son___.

3. The ___Holy___ ___Spirit___ gives us the courage to live as Jesus' followers.

4. The ___Church___ is the community of Jesus' followers.

5. How will you show that you belong to the Catholic Church?

   Possible responses: I will be kind and fair.
   I will attend Mass on Sunday.

Child's name ____________________________________

Your child has just completed Unit 1. Have your child bring this paper to the catechist. It will help you and the catechist know better how to help your child grow in the faith.

____ My child needs help with the part of the Review/Summary I have underlined.

____ My child understands what has been taught in this unit.

____ I would like to speak with you. My phone number is ____________.

(Signature) ____________________________

8 God Loves Us Always

For the Catechist: Spiritual and Catechetical Development

Adult Background

Our Life

The best-selling eyeglass frames at the vision center are made of titanium, a metal used in equipment for space exploration, and they are guaranteed to be noncorrosive, scratch-proof, and practically indestructible. The purchaser of these wonder-frames is assured that they are worth the exorbitant price since "the frames will probably outlast you!"

We all search for things that will last, whether it's a new pair of shoes or a friendship. One of the greatest condemnations we can level at a thing or a relationship is to say, "It will never last!"

Ask yourself:

- When did I invest money, time, or myself in something I hoped would last?
- What do I consider to be lasting in my life now?

Sharing Life

How do you determine how you will invest money, time, or yourself?

What do you mean by "lasting"?

Our Catholic Faith

There were creation stories long before Genesis was written. The idea of a creator was familiar to ancient people, but the idea of a *caring* creator was unique. Other tribes had gods who they believed were responsible for their existence, but only the Israelites had a God who remained personally involved in their lives and history:

> Can a woman forget her own baby
> and not love the child she bore?
> Even if a mother should forget her child,
> I will never forget you.
> Jerusalem, I can never forget you!
> I have written your name on the palms of my hands.
> (Isaiah 49:15–16)

The God of the Israelites was not content to care for them from the heavens. God became Emmanuel, God-with-us. In Jesus Christ, all of humankind is united. By His death and resurrection, Jesus Christ has made us sharers of God's own life and love.

Despite our sins, our limitations, our finitude, God has chosen to love us forever. It is the Holy Spirit within us who urges us and enables us to live the Law of Love that Jesus taught us:

> Love the Lord your God with all your heart, with all your soul, with all your mind, and with all your strength.... Love your neighbor as you love yourself.
> (Mark 12:30–31)

When we cooperate with the Holy Spirit's promptings, we become effective heralds of God's reign. The good news becomes enfleshed in us as we teach and tend, heal and console, pray and proclaim, do justice and make peace.

Coming to Faith

How do you demonstrate in your life that God's love is lasting?

How do you cooperate with the Holy Spirit's promptings?

Practicing Faith

How will you live the Law of Love more completely in your life?

Choose to be an image of God's faithfulness by creating an emotionally safe and nurturing environment for your group of children.

The Theme of This Chapter Corresponds with Paragraph 2052

LITURGICAL RESOURCES

In *The Spiritual Life of Children,* Robert Coles shares many beautiful and often profound insights provided by the young people he interviewed. Among them was a nine-year-old named Tommy who envisioned the Holy Ghost as an immense rainbow arched protectively above the earth.

After talking about the Holy Spirit with your group, invite the children to draw the third Person of the Trinity. Have them share their images and invite the group to respond to each drawing with an original prayer. Examples might be:

- Holy Spirit, help us choose!
- Holy Spirit, You make us brave.
- Holy Spirit, You are beautiful!

JUSTICE AND PEACE RESOURCES

Justice and peace are the universally desirable offspring of love. If we hope to achieve the former, we must become more spiritually skilled at the latter. If we truly love someone or some group, says Saint Paul, we will never do them any harm. (See Romans 13:10.)

Let the children know that they can become champion justice- and peacemakers if they begin now by exercising their ability to love others. Each day, give them one simple exercise to do, such as:

- Share something that belongs to you.
- Do not argue at home today.
- Be kind to a child who is not kind to you.

Teaching Resources

Overview of the Lesson

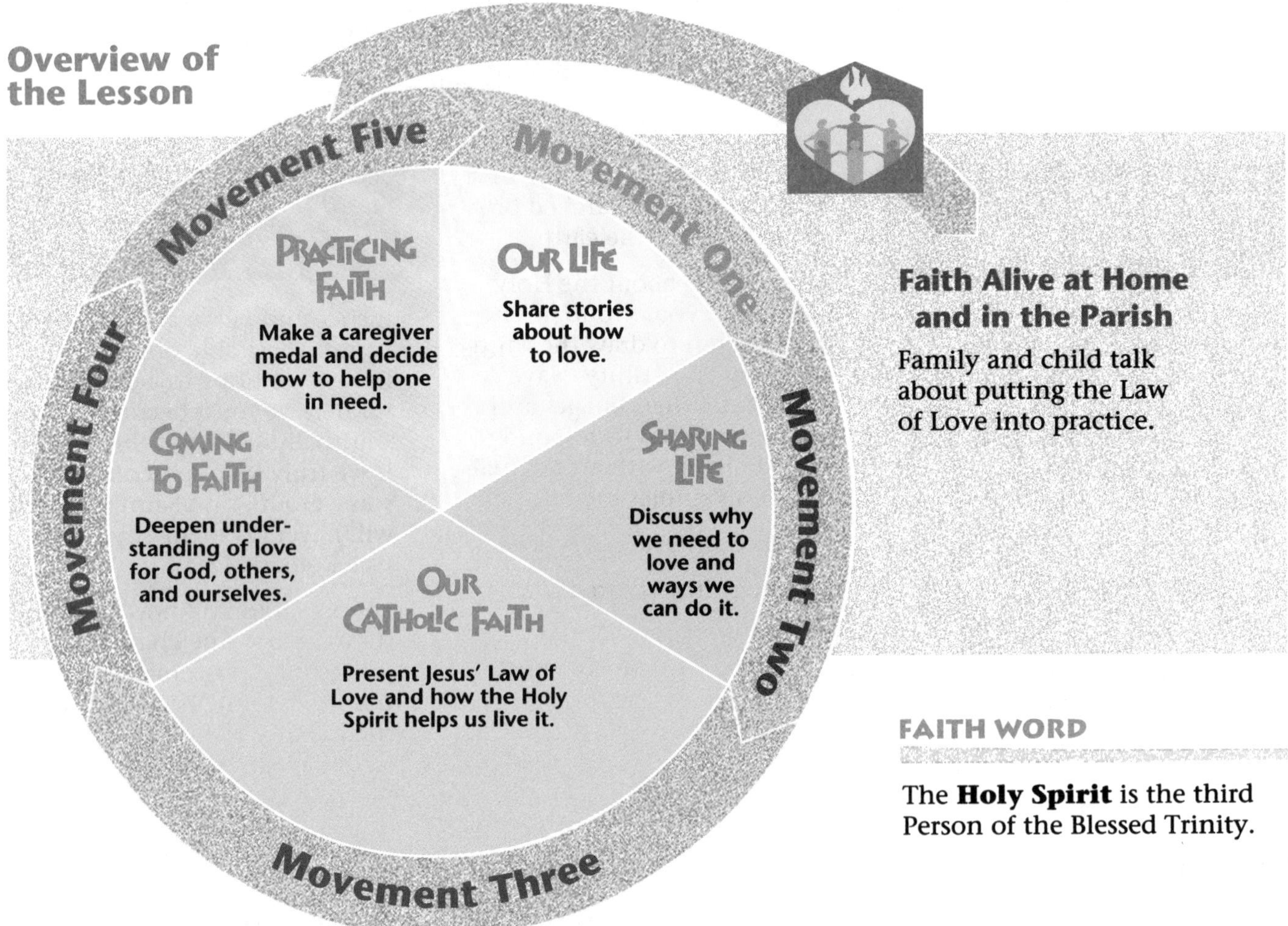

Faith Alive at Home and in the Parish

Family and child talk about putting the Law of Love into practice.

FAITH WORD

The **Holy Spirit** is the third Person of the Blessed Trinity.

Teaching Hints

Children need to be more aware of how the Law of Love applies to their lives in a practical way. Use examples from their own home, school life, and play to show them that Jesus wants us to love all people. Emphasize the fact that even when it might be difficult to do this, the Holy Spirit is always there to help them. Be sure they understand Jesus' message that loving others, whom we can see, is a way we show our love for God, whom we cannot see.

Special-Needs Child

Treat mainstreamed children the same as other children. Expect the same standards of behavior.

Visual Needs

- faith word *Holy Spirit* in sandpaper letters
- a raised picture of Jesus

Auditory Needs

- directly face child when reading text

Tactile-Motor Needs

- copy of caregiver medal taped to the child's desk

Supplemental Resources

Just Being There (video)
Harmony Park series
Brown-ROA
2460 Kerper Blvd.
P.O. Box 539
Dubuque, IA 52004-0539
(1-800-922-7696)

Sammy, the Good Neighbor (video)
The Parables for Children series, Vol. 2
Mass Media Ministries
2116 North Charles Street
Baltimore, MD 21218
(1-800-828-8825)

Lesson Plan: Beginning

Objectives

To help the children

- know that God loves them;
- appreciate God's love and care for all people;
- feel motivated to love others as they are loved.

Focusing Prayer

Recall from previous sessions God's love shown in creation and in sending Jesus to us. Then lead the children in the prayer at the top of page 57.

Our Life

Picture Storytime

Have the children examine each of the pictures on page 57. Ask them to notice how each person is showing love. Invite volunteers to tell a story about each picture, explaining how the persons in it are showing love.

Have the children respond to the question and final directive in the *Our Life* section.

Sharing Life

Answer Sentences

Read the questions in the *Sharing Life* section with the children. Give them a few minutes to think of their answers. Then turn each question into a statement for them to complete, for example: "We know someone loves us when . . ." Have them write what you dictate and then make a complete sentence out of it. Let them share their sentences.

8 God Loves Us Always

God, thank You for always loving us.

Our Life (1) Parents; grandparents; brothers; sisters; God; Jesus; etc.

Look at the pictures. Each one tells you something about love.

Make up a story about each picture. Tell how each person is showing love.

Possible responses:

Whom do you love? (1)

Tell what it means really to love someone. care for them; help them; etc.

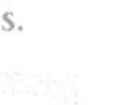

Sharing Life Possible responses:

How do we know when someone loves us? She (he) helps me; takes care of me when I am sick; etc.

Why do we need to love other people? To help them; God wants me to; etc.

How can you grow as a loving person? Do loving things; pray and ask God to help me; etc.

57

Enrichment

A Secret-Friend Note

Ask the children to think of someone in their school or neighborhood who is not very well-liked by others. Give each child a sheet of $5\frac{1}{2}'' \times 11''$ paper, and markers. Have them fold the paper in half. Suggest that they write "secret-friend" notes to these persons, telling them that God loves them and that they do, too. Challenge the children to do what they can to become friends with these persons and to make them feel more loved.

Materials needed: $5\frac{1}{2}'' \times 11''$ paper; markers

Lesson Plan: Middle

Our Catholic Faith

Drawing the Law of Love

Have the children note the first title on page 58. Ask them to read it together, then write the words *Law of Love* on the chalkboard or newsprint.

Read aloud the first sentence at the top of the page and the story from Mark following it. See the first annotation. Then pass out drawing paper and markers to each child. Tell them to divide the paper into three parts. Have them draw a picture in each part to show whom this law tells us to love.

Materials needed: drawing paper; markers

Jesus, Our Leader

Talk with the children about different leaders they admire. Discuss how important it is for a leader not only to *tell* us what we should do but to *show* us by his or her example.

Then have the children study the picture on pages 58–59. Ask how they can tell from the picture that Jesus is a good Leader (He welcomes all people; He is helping the woman who is sick). Read and discuss the next two paragraphs on page 58. Emphasize Jesus' great understanding and His compassion for all people, no matter who they were. Use the annotation.

Our Catholic Identity

Use the *Our Catholic Identity* page for this chapter (page 5). Talk to the children about why Jesus called Himself the Good Shepherd. You might want to have the children trace the picture of Jesus carrying the lamb.

Multicultural Awareness

Point out to the children that there are persons who are kind and loving toward some people but not toward others. Ask if they think these persons keep the Law of Love. Explain that Jesus showed us how to love people no matter what color their skin is, where they come from, or how rich or poor they might be. God wants us to treat all people with love.

Stress the underlined text.

The Law of Love

Jesus came to show us how we are to love God, ourselves, and others.

One day a man came to Jesus with a question. "What is the most important thing God wants us to do?" he asked. <u>Jesus said, "Love God with all your heart. Love others as you love yourself."</u>
From Mark 12:28–31

<u>Jesus spent His whole life showing us how to live this Law of Love.</u> Many sick and lonely people came to Jesus to be healed. He did not send them away, even when He was very tired. Jesus showed them God's love and healed them.

Jesus fed people who were hungry to show them God's love. When Jesus met people who had cheated and lied and stolen, He forgave their sins. He helped them to change and lead better lives.

Ask: What does Jesus tell us is the most important thing God wants us to do?

58

Lesson Plan: Middle

Working for the Kingdom

Continue by reading the first two paragraphs on page 59. Use pictures to illustrate helping the sick, hungry, and lonely, and forgiving others. Help the children to see that these are specific ways they can keep the Law of Love.

Materials needed: pictures to illustrate helping the sick, hungry, and lonely, and forgiving others

Making Right Choices

Have the children try to think back to the time when they were infants. Ask if they were able to make choices for themselves as infants. Point out that their parents had to make decisions for them about what to eat, what to wear, and so forth. Instill in them a sense of pride in the fact that now they are old enough to make choices of their own, and emphasize that it is important that they make the right choices.

Read the first paragraph about the Holy Spirit on page 59. Help the children understand that it is difficult even for adults to make right choices, and so God has given us Someone who can help. Only when we have the courage to do the right thing can we be truly happy.

Faith Word

Direct the children's attention to the faith word *Holy Spirit.* Read the definition with them. Explain that the Holy Spirit is the very special Helper God has given us. Then continue by reading the last two paragraphs on the page. Use the annotation.

You may wish to use pages 37–38 of Sadlier's *Celebrating Our Seasons and Saints,* Level 2.

You may also wish to use pages 19–20 in the activity book for *Coming to Jesus.*

FAITH WORD

The **Holy Spirit** is the third Person of the Blessed Trinity.

We need to love others as Jesus did. Jesus wants us to help people who are sick, hungry, or lonely. He wants us to forgive others and to be fair with everyone.

Each time we help others as Jesus did, we show that we love God with all our hearts and that we love others as ourselves. This is the way we work for the kingdom of God.

The Holy Spirit

Every day we can choose to do things that are right or things that are wrong. We need to ask ourselves, "Will this choice help me to be a better person? Will it hurt or harm someone else? Does it respect the rights of others?"

It is not always easy to choose to do the right thing. Jesus knew this, so He gave us the Holy Spirit to be our Helper. Ask: How does the Holy Spirit help us?

The Holy Spirit helps us know and do what is right. The Holy Spirit gives us the courage to live the Law of Love.

59

Enrichment

Making a Love Chain

Give each child a pencil and a strip of construction paper. Tell them they will be making a love chain to show that the Holy Spirit is helping them make the right choices. Help them write on the strips one right choice they have already made to love God, themselves, or others as Jesus taught us. When they have finished, staple the strips together to make a love chain. Attach it to the bulletin board.

Materials needed: strips of construction paper; pencils

Lesson Plan: End

Coming to Faith

Explaining How to Love

Guide the children in responding to the first directive in the *Coming to Faith* section on page 60. Have them use the drawings they made at the beginning of the session to help them. Then let them complete the circling activity, and have them respond together to the final question.

Faith Summary

Turn to the *Faith Summary* on page 61. Use the annotations to see if the children can express in their own words what they have learned today.

Practicing Faith

Making a Caregiver Medal

Guide the children in making caregiver medals described on page 60 and have each one write her or his name on it.

Acting Out How to Help

Read aloud the three situations described in this section, and have volunteers act out how they would help these persons.

Read the final paragraph. Encourage the children to do the activity.

Evaluating Your Lesson

- Do you feel the children know that God loves them?
- Do they appreciate God's love for all people?
- Have they decided to love others as they are loved?

Coming To Faith

Explain how we are to love God, others, and ourselves.

Think of someone who is being treated unfairly. Then circle what you can do.

- I can walk away
- I can be mean
- I can be kind

Who can help you to love other people and treat them fairly?
Parents, teachers, parish ministers, etc.

Practicing Faith

Make a caregiver medal. Write your name on it.

Practice how you will help someone in need this week by acting out one of these stories together.

- A child has no one to play with at recess
- A classmate is sick at home
- Someone you know is very sad

Find someone who needs you this week at home, in school, or in your neighborhood. Decide with your family how you will help that person.

60

Discuss with the children ways they and their families might use the "Faith Alive" pages together. Suggest they ask for the help they might need from a family member to do the *Practicing Faith* activity at home.

Enrichment

A Story About Choices

Read the story of Pinocchio, or a comparable child's story that illustrates the consequences of choices made.

Let the children comment on the good and bad choices Pinocchio made, and tell who in the story helped him to decide what was right and wrong.

Stories of Love (for use with page 57)

Have the children join together to write a story about love. Help them get started by giving the first sentence. For example, "Once upon a time there was a brother and sister named John and Alice." Then ask the children, one at a time, to share a sentence to add to the group story of love. You might like to record the story on a large sheet of newsprint or on the chalkboard. After the story is completed, use the following questions for discussion:

■ Who showed love in the story? How?

■ Can you tell a story of someone who showed love for you?

■ Who can tell a story of a time they showed love for someone else?

■ Does God ever stop loving us?

Materials needed: newsprint; marker

Living the Law of Love (for use with page 58)

Give each child two pieces of brown and one piece of red construction paper. Have them cut out a tree trunk from one piece and a number of tree branches from the second piece of brown paper. Then have them cut a large heart from the red paper, print the words *Living the Law of Love* on it, and paste it in the center of the tree trunk.

Encourage the children to take the tree trunk and the branches home and to glue a branch to the tree each time they see someone (or they themselves) show love for God, others, or themselves. Be sure to remind the children to print on the branch the name of the person (themselves or a friend) they saw living the Law of Love.

Materials needed: brown and red construction paper; glue; scissors

Jesus Lived the Law of Love (for use with page 59)

Use the following Scripture story to show the children how Jesus lived the Law of Love.

Encourage the children's participation by inviting them to mime the story. Begin by having the group listen as you read "Jesus Cures Bartimaeus" (Mark 10:46–52). Then invite volunteers to mime the story as you reread it.

Explain the idea that because Jesus was God He could perform miracles. He could help the blind man to see. Then have the children think about how they could live the Law of Love if they met a blind person.

Please Don't Break My Heart! (for use with page 60)

Distribute two hearts to the children: one whole heart and one "broken" heart. Invite the children to respond to the following situations by holding up the appropriate heart.

■ Paul wants his little brother Steve's baseball. Paul takes Steve's baseball from his room when Steve is not there.

■ Olivia takes the new girl Sharon to lunch and invites me to join them.

■ Miss Ogden gives a math test. When she isn't looking, Michael looks in his book for an answer.

Materials needed: paper hearts

FAITH ALIVE AT HOME AND IN THE PARISH

Your child is being taught the Law of Love. Sometimes it is hard for a child to think about what God wants when choices have to be made. As parents you have a responsibility to help your second grader make good choices. By Baptism we are always called to live and make choices according to the Law of Love. For Christians everyone is our neighbor, especially those most in need.

Find time to talk over any problems your child might have in making choices according to the Law of Love. Remind your child that God will forgive us even when we make bad choices. Teach your child to tell both God and the person hurt that he or she is sorry.

The Good Shepherd

To help your child understand that God always loves us, read the story of the Good Shepherd (Luke 15:1–6) to your family. Talk about times when Jesus has been your Good Shepherd. Who mirrors this Good Shepherd for you in your parish? To whom can you or your child be a "good shepherd" this week?

Living the Law of Love

This week encourage your child to put the Law of Love into practice by being more considerate of the needs of others, even when this is hard to do.

Help your child plan to do one of the following: share toys; keep belongings in their place; let others choose the TV show; help others with chores.

Learn by heart

Faith Summary

(1) • We must love God with our whole heart. We must love others as ourselves.

(2) • The Holy Spirit helps us to make good choices.

(2) Who helps us to make good choices?

(1) How should we love God and others?

Talk with your family about ways you can care for each other as Jesus, the Good Shepherd, cares for you. Pray the Thank You praye

Here is a suggestion to help the children do this activity at home: Take a few minutes to talk about how wonderful the world would be if everyone cared for one another.

Thank You, Jesus,
for showing us
how to love.
Your friend,

____

Review

Go over the *Faith Summary* together before your child completes the *Review.* The answers for questions 1–4 appear on page 200. The response to number 5 will show you whether your child is growing in practicing the Law of Love. When the *Review* is completed, have your child place a sticker on this page.

sticker

Circle the correct answer.

1. We must love God with our whole heart. (Yes) No

2. It is all right to be mean to others. Yes (No)

3. The Holy Spirit will always help us make good choices. (Yes) No

4. It is always easy to make good choices. Yes (No)

5. How will you show love for others this week?

Possible responses: I will be fair to my friends. I forgive people who hurt me.

Encourage the children to gather with their families to share the *Family Scripture Moment.*

FAMILY SCRIPTURE MOMENT

As you **Gather,** invite family members to explain what it means to be "great" in following Jesus. Then **Listen** to Jesus' words.

The disciples came to Jesus, asking, "Who is the greatest in the kingdom of heaven?" So Jesus called a child, had this child stand in front of them, and said, "I assure you that unless you change and become like children, you will never enter the kingdom of heaven. The greatest in the kingdom of heaven are those who humble themselves and become like this child. And whoever welcomes in My name one such child as this, welcomes Me."

From Matthew 18:1–5

Share Ask: To what greatness is Jesus calling us this week?

Consider for family enrichment:

- Jesus is telling His disciples how they should relate to one another. He warns them not to seek power over others or to be self-serving.
- Jesus invites us to adopt a humble attitude so that we might have a childlike openness to faith.

Reflect and **Decide** Think of some people in our parish who have taken Jesus' message to heart. How will we show our support for them?

9 WE MAKE CHOICES

For the Catechist: Spiritual and Catechetical Development

ADULT BACKGROUND

Our Life

A student's parents make an appointment to see the school principal. The student received a failing grade on his last test, but otherwise has been making acceptable progress. His parents complain to the principal of unfair treatment. The next day, the principal scolds the teacher for failing the student and suggests that the student be retested. In class, the teacher overhears the student boasting that his parents fixed things so that he will never fail again.

Ask yourself:

- How do I think the teacher feels about the student's parents? The principal? The student's response?
- When has someone behaved insensitively toward me?

Sharing Life

What motivates us to sometimes treat others unfairly?

Why are we sometimes unaware of these motivations?

Our Catholic Faith

All persons are created in the image of God, who is perfect goodness. Yet people do bad things. We were made to love, but we are free to choose to love or not to love. In every choice, whether we are conscious of it or not, we decide who we are and whether or not we will love. Choosing to do something that is against God's Law of Love is sin. Sin damages or destroys the good persons we were meant to be. Sin alienates us from God and others.

Although Jesus Christ has overcome sin and won for us our place in God's life, we still experience sin and its effects, the disorder and disorientation of being alienated from God. In order to make better choices, we can follow the Scriptures and the teachings of God and the Church.

The Ten Commandments remain the touchstone of morality for most Christians. In the Decalogue, our relationships to God and others are outlined. The first three commandments deal specifically with our relationship to God, while the remaining seven speak to our relationship with others. In His teaching, Jesus does not dismiss the Ten Commandments. Rather, He presents the overriding vision that encompasses all of them. The key to good choices is a right understanding of love:

> "Teacher," [a lawyer once asked Jesus] "which is the greatest commandment in the Law?" Jesus answered, " 'Love the Lord your God with all your heart, with all your soul, and with all your mind.' This is the greatest and the most important commandment. The second most important commandment is like it: 'Love your neighbor as you love yourself.' "
> (Matthew 22:36–39)

Jesus' whole life was a definition of love: His acceptance of all people, His healings, His forgiveness. Whether He was praying, teaching, or washing feet, Jesus' love of God and neighbor was constantly evident.

Coming to Faith

What guidelines do you follow in moral decision-making?

What is sin and how does it affect you?

Practicing Faith

How will you be guided by the Ten Commandments and the Law of Love in a new way?

How will you help the children in your group to see the consequences of sin?

The Theme of This Chapter Corresponds with Paragraph 2054

LITURGICAL RESOURCES

Considering our God-given limitations as human beings, a life of love would be impossible were it not for the fact that we were given God's Spirit to help us. When we face difficult moral decisions, the Holy Spirit guides us through prayer, Scripture, tradition, and the wisdom of people in the faith community. When our decisions include insights and strength from these sources, we can be sure we have chosen lovingly.

Share with your group an adaptation of the Penitential Rite from the Mass as a way of expressing sorrow for all the times we and others have not chosen to do God's will. Gather at the prayer table and invite the children to respond consecutively "Lord, have mercy," "Christ, have mercy," "Lord, have mercy," to petitions like these:

- Jesus, forgive all sinners.
- Jesus, help us to choose to do God's will.
- Jesus, help us to love.

JUSTICE AND PEACE RESOURCES

Hailing the "splendor of truth," Pope John Paul II observes, "But no darkness of error or of sin can totally take away from man the light of God the Creator" (*Veritatis Splendor,* August 6, 1993, Introduction). The Holy Father insists that a "yearning for absolute truth" burns constantly in human hearts.

You might choose to apply this spiritual insight on the Inextinguishable Light to a dramatization of the *Our Life* story on page 63. Invite three children at a time to act out the story of Dana, Justin, and Huan. Have each wear a yellow candle flame symbol. When the first two choose wrongly, turn out the lights as a sign that they are in the dark. Then have them choose rightly and hold a large paper sun over their heads. Announce, "God's light is always burning in us."

Teaching Resources

Overview of the Lesson

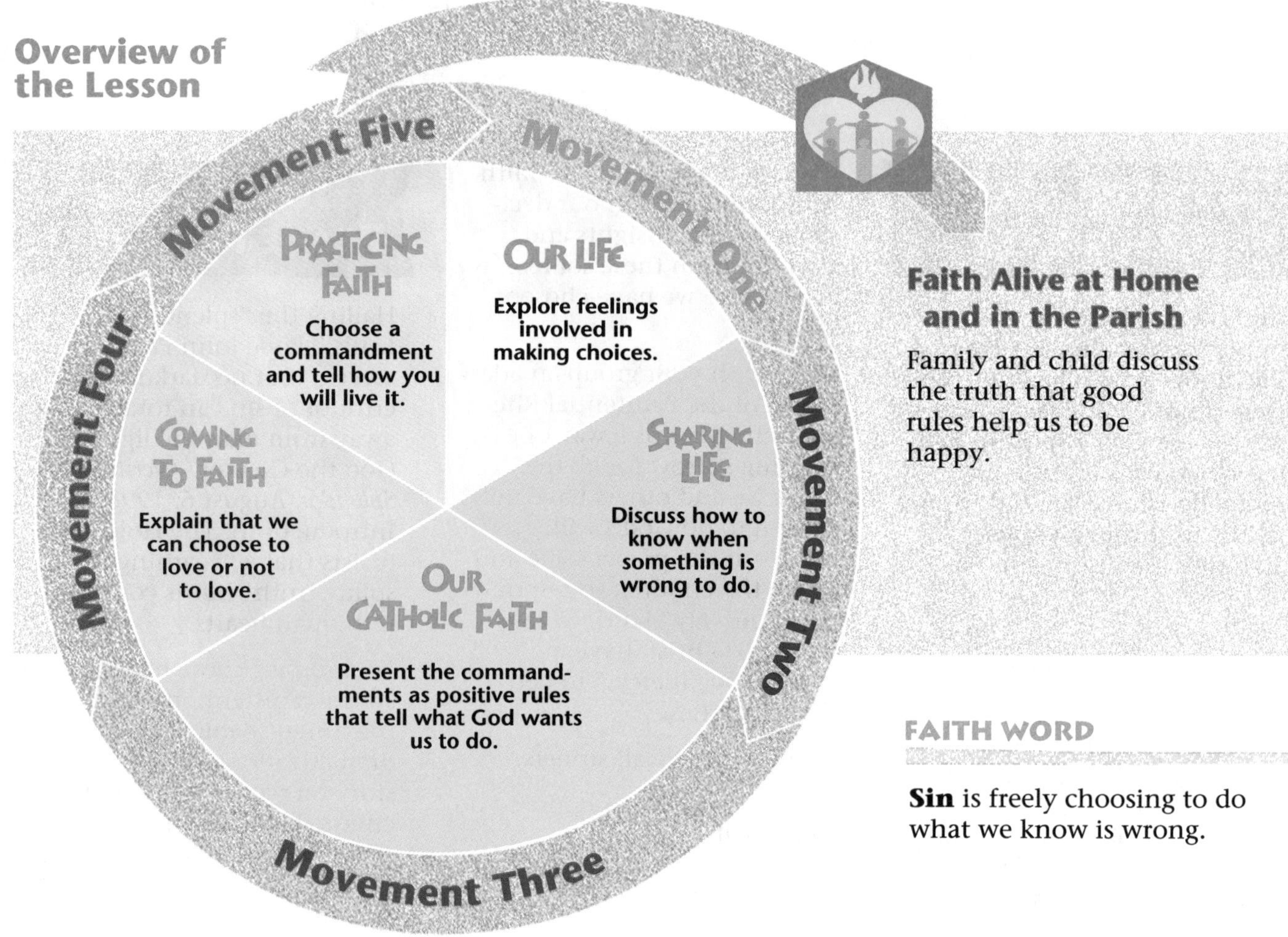

Faith Alive at Home and in the Parish

Family and child discuss the truth that good rules help us to be happy.

FAITH WORD

Sin is freely choosing to do what we know is wrong.

Teaching Hints

In this lesson, the children will be presented with the challenge of making right choices.

The commandments will be taught as positive rules which guide them in making right choices. Help the children to discern specific ways of carrying out these commandments in their own lives. While encouraging them to make right decisions, be sure they understand that God never stops loving them, even when they have made bad choices.

Special-Needs Child

Provide an atmosphere of acceptance in which all the children can realize how special they are.

Visual Needs

- the Ten Commandments in large letters

Auditory Needs

- audiotape and headphones for the Ten Commandments

Tactile-Motor Needs

- large thick markers for drawing activity

Supplemental Resources

The Burning Bush (video)
In the Beginning series
Vision Video
2030 Wentz Church Road
Worcester, PA 19490
(1-800-523-0226)

God's Rules For Me (video)
St. Paul Books and Media
50 St. Paul's Avenue
Boston, MA 02130
(1-800-876-4463)

Lesson Plan: Beginning

Objectives

To help the children

- know the importance of making right choices;
- appreciate God's forgiveness;
- decide to love as God commands.

Focusing Prayer

Recall for the children that Jesus, our Leader, shows us how to make right choices. Then lead them in the prayer at the top of page 63.

Our Life

Acting Out a Story

Call the children's attention to the title of the lesson. Ask them to look at the illustration on page 63 as you read the story. Then invite three children to act out the parts silently as you read the story a second time. Tell the children that one thing good actors try to do is to feel what the persons they portray are feeling. Invite those who are observing to try to imagine especially what Huan is feeling. After the second reading, ask the children to respond to the follow-up questions.

Sharing Life

Thinking About Choices

Have the children respond to the questions in the *Sharing Life* section.

9 We Make Choices

Jesus, help us to make good choices.

OUR LIFE

Dana and Justin were whispering in a corner of the field. They were pointing at a new boy, Huan, and were making fun of him. Huan was from Vietnam. He did not speak English very well yet.

Why were Dana and Justin making fun of Huan? He didn't speak English well; to be funny; etc.

How do you think Huan felt? sad; lonely; hurt; etc.

How do you feel when you do (1)something wrong? (2)something right?
(1) ashamed; sorry; afraid; etc. (2) proud; happy; good about myself; etc.

SHARING LIFE Possible responses:

How do you feel about what Dana and Justin did? Why? sad, angry Because they hurt Huan's feelings

How do you know when it is wrong to do something? I feel sorry; upset; etc.

Imagine what Jesus would say to Dana and Justin about their choice. Share your thoughts. "Are you being loving?"

63

Enrichment

Expressing Our Feelings

Explain that sometimes we can tell how persons feel by their body language—the way they look, or how they walk or talk. Invite each child to express in looks, gestures, or words how they think Huan felt when Dana and Justin made fun of him, and then to express how they would like to have made Huan feel.

Lesson Plan: Middle

Our Catholic Faith

Making Right Choices

Recall from the previous lesson why Jesus came: to show us how to love God, ourselves, and others. Talk with the children about how this can be difficult to do at times, but that God gives us the help we need to make right choices.

Read aloud and comment on the first two paragraphs on page 64 in the children's texts.

Faith Word

Write the faith word *sin* on the chalkboard. Have the children share their understanding of sin. Then read the definition together.

An Unhappy Word

Ask the children if they think *sin* is a happy or unhappy word. Have them tell why. Explain that sin is the opposite of doing God's will and that it brings unhappiness into our lives. Read the rest of page 64 to the children. Use the annotations. Let the children talk freely about their understanding of sin, and be sure to dispel any exaggerated ideas they may have. Use the pictures on page 64 to emphasize the fact that mistakes and accidents are not sins and that no matter what we do wrong, God *always* forgives us when we are sorry.

Stress the underlined text.

Choosing Love

We can choose to love God, others, and ourselves, or we can choose not to love. When we obey the Law of Love, we do God's will.

Sometimes people are selfish and mean. They fight and treat others unfairly. They turn away from God's love on purpose. They sin.

Sin is freely choosing to do what we know is wrong. We sin when we disobey God's law on purpose. We turn away from His love.

Sin is not doing God's will. All sins are wrong. Sin offends God. It upsets the peace that Jesus wants us to have in our hearts, families, neighborhood, parish Church, and world.

Sometimes we make mistakes or cause an accident. We do something wrong, but we do not mean to do it. Mistakes are not sins. Ask: How do the pictures show the difference?

Remember, God never stops loving us, even when we choose to sin. He always forgives us when we are sorry.

64

Lesson Plan: Middle

The Ten Commandments

Explain to the children that one way God gives us to live the Law of Love is to ask us to keep the Ten Commandments. Read aloud the first paragraph on page 65. Then read the rest of the material on page 65 together with the children. Point out how the Ten Commandments are ways in which we can keep the Law of Love: The first three tell us how to love God, and the other seven tell us how to love ourselves and others. After reading the Ten Commandments, ask the children to tell one way they can live each of the commandments. Use the annotation.

Multicultural Awareness

Talk with the children about how Jesus gave His life for all people, no matter what color their skin is or what country they came from, and that Jesus wants us to love all people as He does. Ask the children if they think Dana and Justin were doing this when they treated Huan the way they did. Lead them to see that Dana and Justin did not use God's help to make a right choice in this situation and that this always leads to unhappiness.

You may wish to use pages 21–22 in the activity book for *Coming to Jesus.*

FAITH WORD

Sin is freely choosing to do what we know is wrong.

Doing What God Wants

The Ten Commandments tell us what God wants us to do. They help us obey the Law of Love and live for God's kingdom. If we follow them, we will know we are making good choices.

Note: The children need not commit the commandments to memory at this time.

The first three commandments show us how to love God.

1. We try to put God first in our lives.
2. We use God's name only with love and respect.
3. We keep Sunday as God's special day of prayer and rest.

The other commandments show us how to love ourselves and others.

4. We listen to and obey those who care for us.
5. We care for all living things.
6. We care for our bodies and respect others.
7. We do not steal; we are fair to everyone.
8. We are truthful in what we say and do.
9. We are faithful to those we love.
10. We help people to have what they need to live.

Enrichment

A Ten Commandments Game

Give each child a sheet of drawing paper and markers and a folded slip of paper with a number from one to ten written on it. Invite them to draw a picture of someone obeying the commandment that corresponds to the number they received. When all are finished, call on volunteers to hold up their pictures, one at a time, and see if the group can guess which commandment is portrayed. Let them read together from their texts each commandment as it is guessed.

Materials needed: drawing paper; markers; slips of paper

Lesson Plan: End

Coming to Faith

Loving and Unloving Choices

Ask the children to listen carefully to the examples you read from page 66 and to picture themselves in each situation. Give them time to designate with a smile or sad face what kind of choice they think each one is. Have them tell why they thought the act was loving or unloving.

Faith Summary

Turn to the *Faith Summary* on page 67. Use the annotations to see if the children can express in their own words what they have learned today.

Practicing Faith

Writing Decisions

Follow the first directive in this section. Use the annotation. Then have each child choose a commandment he or she finds hard to follow. Ask who Jesus gave us to help us in making right choices. Write the words *Holy Spirit* on the chalkboard or newsprint. Invite the children to do the activity in their books. Let them decorate the page as they wish.

Evaluating Your Lesson

- Do the children know the importance of making right choices?
- Do they appreciate that God always forgives us?
- Have they chosen to love as God commands?

Enrichment

Commandment Cutouts

Divide the children into ten groups. Prepare large outlines of the numbers one through ten on separate sheets of paper, then give one number to each group to cut out. Have each group look up the words of the commandment that corresponds to its number, print the words on the number, and decorate it. Join the numbers together with ribbon or strips of paper and hang the banner across the chalkboard.

Materials needed: large outlines of numbers 1 through 10; ribbon or strips of paper; markers

Coming to Faith

Draw a ☺ in the box beside each loving choice.

Draw a ☹ in the box beside each unloving choice.

☹ You start a fight with a friend.

☺ You talk to a classmate who seems lonely.

☺ You want to stay in bed on Sunday, but you get up and go to Mass.

☹ You call someone a name and hurt that person's feelings.

Practicing Faith

(1) Encourage discussion of each commandment and how we can live it.

With your friends, talk about what the Ten Commandments teach us. (1) Choose a commandment you find hard to follow. Write what you will do this week to show you really want to live it.

Talk to the children about ways they and their families can work together on the "Faith Alive" pages. Encourage them to talk with their families about the fact that the Ten Commandments help us make good choices.

Making Choices **(for use with page 63)**

Read aloud the following incomplete stories. Divide the children into three groups. Have each group make up a cartoon strip to illustrate an ending to one of the stories. You might wish to assign a different story to each group.

After supper each night, Michael goes to his bedroom to finish his homework. One night Michael sees his video game nearby...

■ What do you think Michael will do?

Ashley was running in the living room and bumped into a table, knocking down and breaking Mom's new lamp. When Mom came into the room, Ashley...

■ What do you think Ashley will tell her mom?

Craig and Lisa were standing by the candy counter. An older boy near them whispered, "Hey, take some candy bars. Nobody's looking. I do it all the time." Craig and Lisa...

■ What do you think Craig and Lisa will do?

Each group takes a turn presenting their cartoon to the whole group. The group then decides if the best choice was made and why they think so.

A Commandment Booklet **(for use with pages 64–65)**

Have each child fold a piece of paper in half and cut along the fold; have them make a booklet by placing the half-pages inside one another. Then have them write and decorate the title "Living the Commandments" on the cover.

List four or five commandments on the chalkboard or large sheet of paper. For example, "Keep God first; Keep Sunday holy; Do not steal," etc.

Ask the children to choose and write one commandment on the first left-hand page and to draw a picture of themselves keeping that commandment on the right-hand page. Ask the children to write under their drawings the name of a person who they think can help them live that commandment. Then ask them to do the same for two other commandments.

Materials needed: paper; scissors; crayons or markers; stapler

Stepping Stones **(for use with page 65)**

Using heavy cardboard, cut out ten "stones" large enough to write one of the commandments on each stone. See page 65 for the listing of the Ten Commandments. Place the "stones" in random order on the floor. Call for a volunteer to find and jump next to the first commandment. Let those in their seats use their books to read the first commandment. If the volunteer has jumped to the correct commandment, he or she calls on another child to jump to the second commandment, and so on.

When all ten commandments have been found, the children should pick up their stones and stand in front of the room holding the commandments from one to ten. Encourage the children to read the commandments in order.

FAITH ALIVE AT HOME AND IN THE PARISH

Your child is learning how to know right from wrong. He or she has been taught what sin is and that the Ten Commandments help us to make good choices. But this is not enough. Your child also needs to live in a family that shows by its actions how to choose to do God's will. The Church reminds us that the family is a crucial place for moral formation.

Your child needs private time with you regularly to talk over the good, the bad, and the seemingly unimportant things that make up each day. Doing this will help your child get into the habit of seeking help before making serious choices.

To help your child understand how the Ten Commandments help us to make good choices, talk about times when you and other family members made good choices in following the commandments. Discuss how these choices showed love.

Help your child to decorate the sign below, which shows how important the commandments are.

Sharing Family Rules

Help your child to see that good rules make us happy. Make a list of your family's rules. Talk about them to see whether each is a good rule. Help your child to see why we obey rules. Also explain that God gave us the commandments out of love.

† Family Prayer

The laws of God are right,
and those who obey them are happy.
The commandments of God are always fair.

From Psalm 19:8

Learn by heart Faith Summary

What is sin?

- Sin is freely choosing to do what we know is wrong.

What do the Ten Commandments show us?

- The Ten Commandments show us how to love God, others, and ourselves.

Decorate this sign.

You may want to introduce the home activity to the group. Ask the children to share what the sign means.

Review

Go over the *Faith Summary* together before your child completes the *Review*. The answers for questions 1–4 appear on page 200. The response to number 5 will help you see whether your child is learning to think and act less selfishly. When the *Review* is completed, have your child place a sticker on this page.

sticker

Circle the correct answer.

1. When we obey the Law of Love we do (wrong, God's will).

2. (Sin, A mistake) is freely choosing to do what we know to be wrong.

3. You will know you are making good choices if you obey (the Ten Commandments, strangers).

4. We should choose (always, sometimes) to do God's will.

5. How will you try to love God and others this week?

Possible responses:

I will say my morning and night prayers.
I will do one kind act for someone each day.

Encourage the children to gather with their families to share the *Family Scripture Moment*.

Gather and recall some choices we have had to make because of our faith. Then **Listen** as Jesus says what we must do to gain eternal life.

Jesus said, "Keep the commandments if you want to enter life. Do not commit murder; do not commit adultery; do not steal; do not accuse anyone falsely; respect your father and your mother; and love your neighbor as you love yourself." The young man replied, "I have obeyed all these commandments. What else do I need to do?" Jesus said to him, "If you want to be perfect, go and sell all you have and give the money to the poor, and you will have riches in heaven; then come and follow Me."

From Matthew 19:17–21

Share what each person hears Jesus saying here.

Consider for family enrichment:

- Keeping the commandments is the first requirement of being a disciple of Jesus.
- Jesus challenges us to go beyond the minimum, to share with the poor and needy and to keep God at the center of our lives.

Reflect and **Decide** How will our family help someone who is poor, sick, or lonely this week?

10 God Forgives Us

For the Catechist: Spiritual and Catechetical Development

Adult Background

Our Life

Molly slams the door and yowls for her Mom. The seven-year-old's knees are bleeding. She can't wait to tell her tale of woe in which her older sister Peg is the obvious villain.

"It was all her fault!" Molly begins, as Mom applies first-aid cream. After hearing the entire story, Mom proceeds with the caution of a diplomat. Through a series of gentle questions, she helps Molly to accept her share of the blame for the hurt knees.

Ask yourself:

- What stories of being hurt have I shared recently?

Sharing Life

How does telling these stories help you?

Who do you turn to when you hope to be healed?

Our Catholic Faith

Jesus was not dispatched from the heavens as a commander of condemnation to catch human beings in their weaknesses and punish their failures in the Father's name. The Son of God was sent because God fully understands us, in our goodness and our sinfulness, and God knew how difficult it would be for us to accept the reality of God's forgiveness. Jesus not only proclaimed forgiveness, He was forgiveness and love incarnate.

We celebrate God's loving forgiveness in the sacrament of Reconciliation. The process of preparing for and experiencing Reconciliation allows us to "own our faults" and discern how to avoid them in the future. In this sacrament we experience the forgiveness of God and are reconciled to God and one another. The word *reconcile* means "to bring together." We celebrate that God wants to bring us back to Him always. In this sacrament, we are enabled to heal the divisions that have separated us from others and to heal the divisions in our own hearts.

Forgiveness, the healing of persons and relationships, the restoration of wholeness to human existence, is the day-by-day work of the Christian. We, as Church, reach out to those who are wounded physically and spiritually. We continue Jesus' ministry to make things whole.

Coming to Faith

How do you experience God's forgiveness through the Church?

How does your faith call you to be a reconciler?

Practicing Faith

What will you do to be a healer in your parish?

How will you be a reconciler with and among the children in your group?

The Theme of This Chapter Corresponds with Paragraph 1446

LITURGICAL RESOURCES

We all need help when it comes to mending relationships. We need a loving God who assures us that we have been forgiven and have the capacity to forgive. We need our God, who enables us to overcome our fear, shyness, shame, pride, or inability to make the first move.

Gather the children around the prayer table. Invite them to pray these lines adapted from the Our Father:

- Our Father, forgive us. (Raise arms high, bow deeply.)
- Our Father, teach us to forgive as You forgive. (Raise arms high, fold hands, bow.)
- Our Father, we will be Your peacemakers! (Raise arms, offer a sign of peace.)

JUSTICE AND PEACE RESOURCES

Plan one or more simple "living justly" prayer services on the theme of forgiveness and mending broken relationships. Each service might combine a familiar faith song, a gospel story in which Jesus forgives someone, a "Be still and listen to your heart" time for remembering things we are sorry for, a prayer of contrition and/or the Our Father.

Among the Gospel stories which might be mimed by children wearing expressive masks or basic costume pieces are:

- Luke 15:3–7, The Lost Sheep;
- Luke 15:11–24, The Lost Son;
- Luke 19:1–10, Jesus and Zacchaeus.

Teaching Resources

Overview of the Lesson

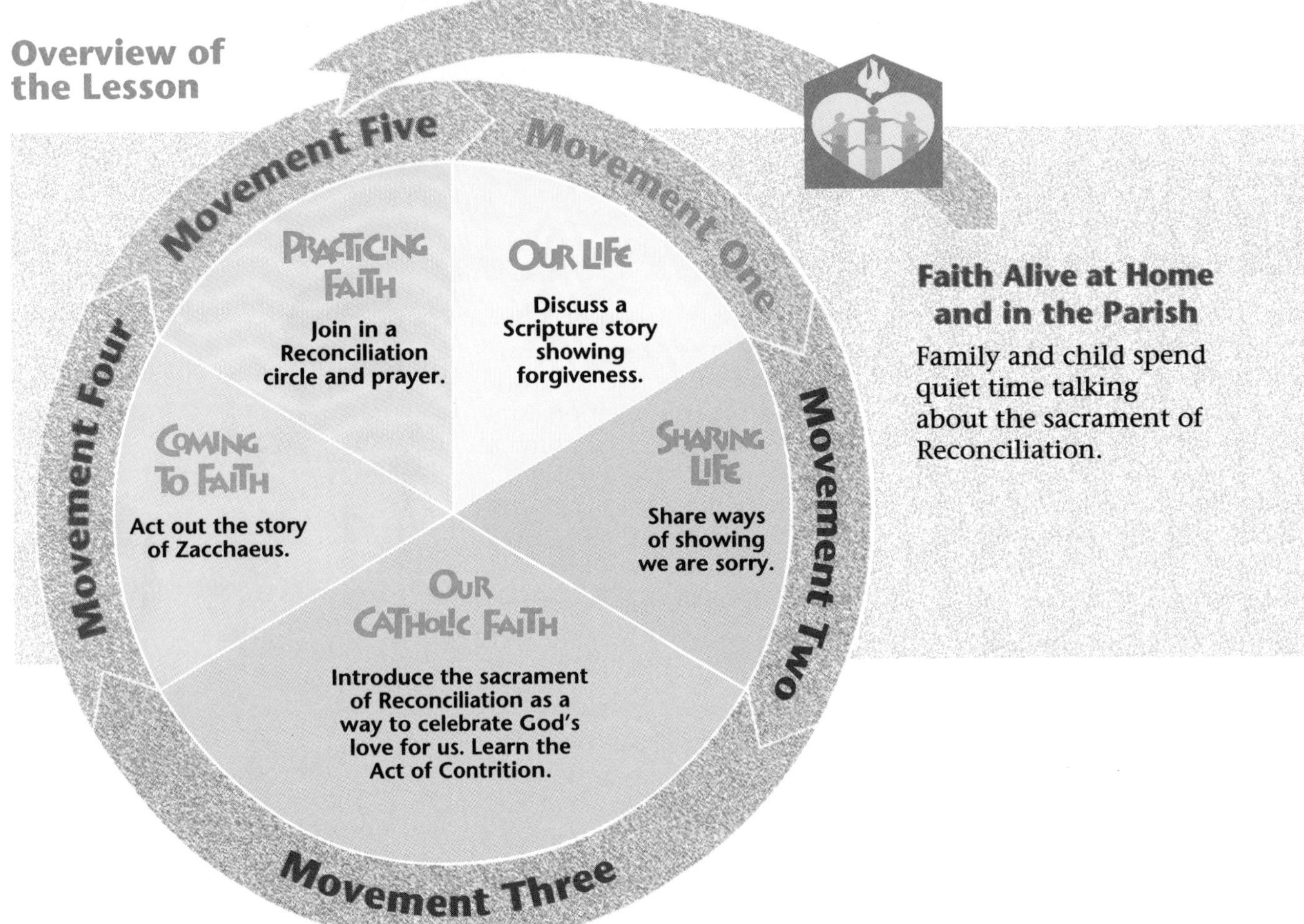

Faith Alive at Home and in the Parish

Family and child spend quiet time talking about the sacrament of Reconciliation.

Teaching Hints

This lesson focuses on the importance of expressing sorrow for our sins, to God and to those whom our sins have hurt. Some children may find it more difficult than others to express sorrow. Encourage them with the use of the suggested puppets and the dramatization of the Zacchaeus story. Have them draw pictures to express ways of saying "I'm sorry." Lead the children to see that expressing sorrow for something we have done wrong brings us peace.

Special-Needs Child

When teaching visually-impaired children, encourage oral interaction and response.

Visual Needs

- recordings of Scripture story and Act of Contrition

Auditory Needs

- preferential seating

Tactile-Motor Needs

- words of Act of Contrition taped to desk
- peer helpers for projects

Supplemental Resources

Joey (video)
St. Paul Books and Media
50 St. Paul's Avenue
Boston, MA 02130
(1-800-876-4463)

Jesus Heals (video)
Jesus Stories series
EcuFilm
810 Twelfth Ave. So.
Nashville, TN 37203
(1-615-242-6277)

Lesson Plan: Beginning

Objectives

To help the children

- understand the sacrament of Reconciliation;
- appreciate the gift of God's forgiveness;
- desire to forgive and be forgiven.

Focusing Prayer

Remind the children that we all sometimes make wrong choices and need to ask God's forgiveness. Today we will say a prayer asking God to have mercy on us, which is another way of saying, "God, please forgive us." Then lead them in the prayer at the top of page 69.

Our Life

Listening to a Bible Story

Before reading the story on page 69, have the children look at the picture for a few minutes. Invite them to tell what they think is happening in the picture. Then ask them to listen carefully as you read the story to them. Have them share responses to the follow-up questions. Use the annotation.

Sharing Life

Thinking About Making Up

Explain to the children that when we are sorry for having done something wrong, we show it by trying to do something to make up. Ask the first question in the *Sharing Life* section. Invite responses to the second question. Then ask how Zacchaeus showed he was sorry.

10 God Forgives Us

Lord, have mercy on us.

Our Life

One day a crowd followed Jesus. Zacchaeus, a dishonest tax collector, was there. He could not see over people's heads. So he climbed a tree to see Jesus. Jesus came to the tree and said, "Hurry down, Zacchaeus. I must stay with you tonight."

Zacchaeus was so happy that Jesus wanted to come to his house. He said to Jesus, "Lord, I will give half of all I have to the poor. If I have cheated anyone, I'll give back four times what I owe."

Jesus knew Zacchaeus was sorry for having cheated people.
Jesus forgave him.

From Luke 19:1–10 Ask: Why did Zacchaeus need to be forgiven?

How do you think Zacchaeus felt when Jesus spoke to him?
surprised, happy, sorry

Why did Jesus forgive Zacchaeus?
Because he was sorry for cheating people.

Sharing Life

Was it easy for Zacchaeus to give back what he had stolen?
Accept reasonable responses.

What does Jesus want us to do when we have done something wrong?
Say and show we are sorry; etc.

69

Paper Bag Puppets

Have the children make paper bag puppets to act out the story of Jesus and Zacchaeus. Form pairs. Give each pair two lunch bags and crayons. Have them draw a face on each bag to represent Jesus and Zacchaeus. Then help the children tie the bags around their wrists, using string.

Materials needed: paper bags; crayons; string

Lesson Plan: Middle

Our Catholic Faith

Display the word *Reconciliation.* Have the children repeat it after you. Explain that reconciliation is what happens when two people have hurt each other in some way and then make up again. Tell the children that today they will learn why the Church chose this name for a wonderful sacrament that Jesus has given us.

Focusing on Reconciliation

Read the first paragraph on page 70. Emphasize the fact that God always forgives us when we are sorry. Have the children underline the word *reconciled.*

Read the next paragraph. Have them examine the picture on page 70 and tell what they see happening in it.

Continue reading the rest of the page. See the annotation. Emphasize the wonder of God's goodness in giving us this sacrament. When we receive it as we should, we know that our sins are forgiven and that everything is all right again—with God, with ourselves, and with others.

A Special Prayer of the Church

Talk with the children about how there are many ways of saying, "I'm sorry." Sometimes we can say it by giving a gift to someone we have hurt. Sometimes we say it by shaking hands. But most often we say it in words. Tell the children that the Church has given us a very special prayer to use when we want to tell God we are sorry for sinning. Ask the children to

Stress the underlined text.

The Sacrament of Reconciliation

God always forgives us when we are sorry. We try not to sin again. We must also try to make up, or be reconciled, with those we have hurt.

In the Catholic Church we celebrate God's forgiveness in the sacrament of Reconciliation, or Penance. In this sacrament we praise God. We thank Him for loving and forgiving us.

<u>In this sacrament we tell God that we are sorry for our sins. We promise not to sin again. We try to make up for what we have done wrong.</u>

The sacrament of Reconciliation is a great celebration because we celebrate God the Father's love for us. It is a sacrament for everyone in our parish.

We celebrate the sacrament of Reconciliation in our parish church. The priest forgives our sins in God's name and in the name of the Church. We know that our sins are forgiven. <u>The priest will never tell anyone what we said to him in this sacrament.</u>

70

Lesson Plan: Middle

find the name of the prayer on page 71.

Display the word *contrition.* Explain that it means sorrow. Go over each part of the Act of Contrition with the children. Have them note in the right-hand column the important point to stress in each part. Divide the children into three groups and have them alternate saying the parts of the prayer. Then say it several times together. See the annotation.

Our Catholic Identity

The *Our Catholic Identity* for this chapter, page 6, provides instruction about the priests' vestments. If possible, take the children to the vesting sacristy in church to show them a stole and alb, or have the items on display in the classroom. Let the children examine them closely.

You may also wish to use pages 23–24 in the activity book for *Coming to Jesus.*

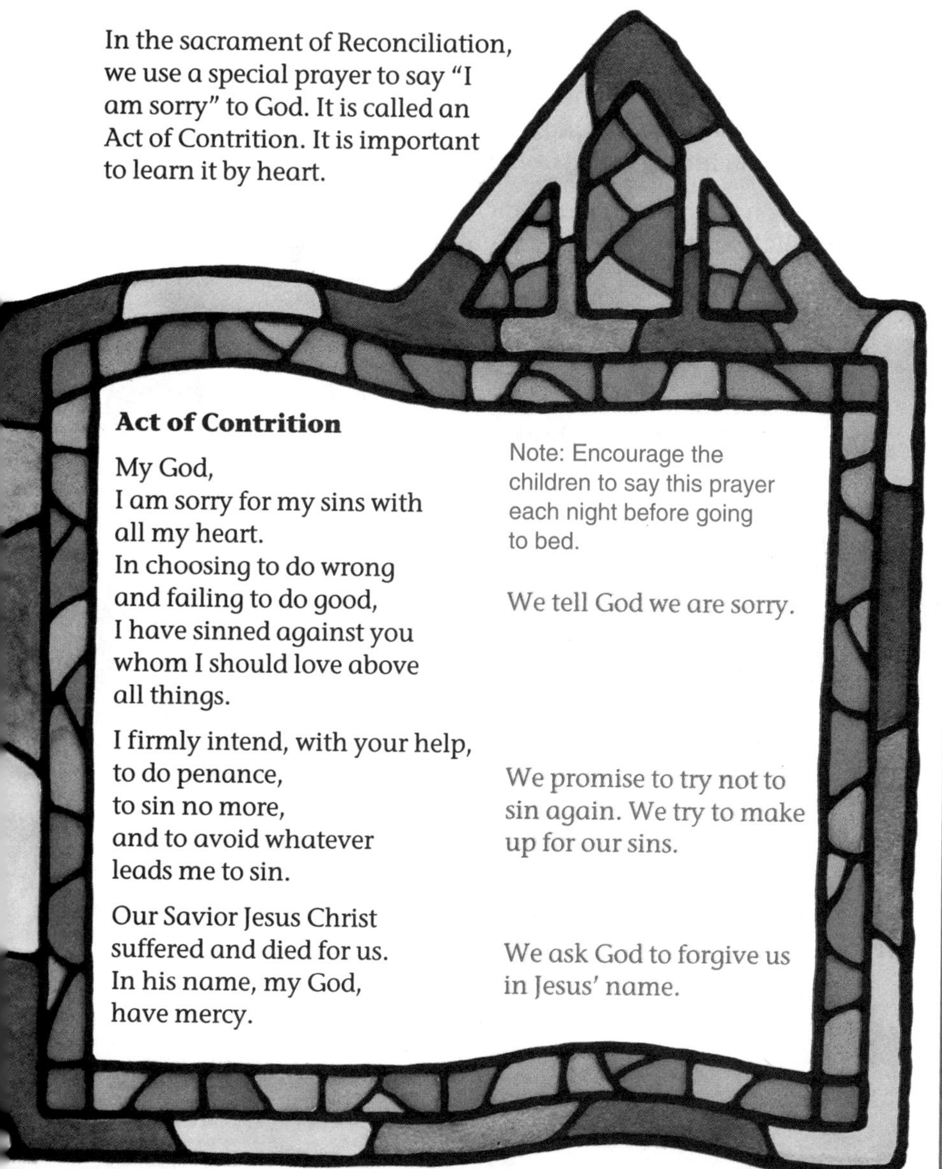

In the sacrament of Reconciliation, we use a special prayer to say "I am sorry" to God. It is called an Act of Contrition. It is important to learn it by heart.

Act of Contrition

My God,
I am sorry for my sins with all my heart.
In choosing to do wrong and failing to do good,
I have sinned against you whom I should love above all things.

Note: Encourage the children to say this prayer each night before going to bed.

We tell God we are sorry.

I firmly intend, with your help,
to do penance,
to sin no more,
and to avoid whatever leads me to sin.

We promise to try not to sin again. We try to make up for our sins.

Our Savior Jesus Christ
suffered and died for us.
In his name, my God,
have mercy.

We ask God to forgive us in Jesus' name.

Enrichment

Prayer Screen

Make stained-glass hangings as reminders to say the Act of Contrition each evening. Give each child a printed copy of the Act of Contrition, a sheet of construction paper, and a piece of white tissue paper that is larger than the construction paper.

- Have each child paste the Act of Contrition in the center of the construction paper.
- Draw a design around the prayer. Cut it out to make openings in the construction paper. (Be careful not to cut the prayer.)
- Put tissue paper on layers of newspaper. Spray with water to make the paper damp, not wet.
- Sprinkle food coloring on the damp paper. Lift paper gently to let colors run. Let dry.
- Put a thin layer of glue on the back of the construction paper. Lay it on the tissue paper. Trim the edges.

Materials needed: copies of Act of Contrition; construction paper; white tissue paper; newspaper; spray bottle(s); food coloring; pencils; scissors; glue stick; crayons

Lesson Plan: End

Coming to Faith

Acting Out a Story

Have the children dramatize the story of Zacchaeus. Let two volunteers take the parts of Jesus and Zacchaeus, and have the others act as persons in the crowd. Prepare the children by talking about what Jesus, Zacchaeus, and the crowd must have felt.

Faith Summary

Turn to the *Faith Summary* on page 73. Use the annotations to see if the children can express in their own words what they have learned today.

Practicing Faith

A Reconciliation Circle

Have a table prepared with a crucifix, a bowl of water, and packets of sugar. Gather around the table and follow the procedure suggested in the *Practicing Faith* section on page 72.

Invite the children, one at a time, to recite the Act of Contrition, and empty a packet of sugar in the water. You might like to play quietly the song, "Sometimes It's Not Easy" (Sadlier's grade 2 *Coming to Jesus in Song* cassette).

After the peace greeting, have the children see how the sugar has dissolved. Explain that this is something like what happens when we bring our sins to Jesus in Reconciliation: Jesus "dissolves" them in His love and forgiveness.

Materials needed: crucifix; bowl of water; sugar packets

Evaluating Your Lesson

- Do the children know the meaning of reconciliation?
- Do they appreciate God's forgiveness?
- Have they decided to forgive and ask forgiveness?

Enrichment

An "I'm Sorry" Card

Distribute markers and drawing paper to each child. Have the children think of someone they may have hurt recently. Have them make cards to say they are sorry. Let them present the cards to these persons.

Materials needed: drawing paper; markers

Coming to Faith

Act out the story of Zacchaeus together.
Let people take turns playing the roles.
Tell what you have learned from the story.
God forgives us when we are sorry.
To help you celebrate the sacrament of Reconciliation, learn the Act of Contrition by heart.

Practicing Faith

Make a reconciliation circle with your friends. Be very still. Think in your heart about one thing you have done for which you are sorry. Then link arms and pray the Act of Contrition together.

Turn to the person on each side of you. Shake hands and say, "The peace of Christ be with you."

Take a few minutes to talk to the children about ways they and their families can work together on the "Faith Alive" pages. Encourage them to pray the Act of Contrition with a family member.

TV Broadcast (for use with page 69)

Dramatically read the Bible story about Zacchaeus on page 69, having the children follow along in their books. Choose volunteers to be "TV reporters," and others to be interviewed. Have the "reporters" retell the story in their own words as if it happened that day, and have them interview other children to get their reactions. Use any hand-held object as a "microphone." Encourage the children to be dramatic.

Materials needed: prop for microphone

A Handy Reminder (for use with page 70)

Distribute construction paper to the children. Let them trace an outline of one hand. On each finger let them print one of the steps in receiving the sacrament of Reconciliation:

- We praise God
- We thank God
- We tell God we are sorry
- We promise not to sin again
- We try to make up

Have the children cut their "hand" out, punch a hole at the top of the hand and tie a piece of string through it. Suggest that they tie these to the doorknob of their bedroom as a reminder for each time they receive the sacrament of Reconciliation.

Materials needed: construction paper; markers; scissors; hole punch; string

Which Doesn't Belong? (for use with page 71)

Write the following words on the chalkboard or newsprint.

Reconciliation, forgiveness, sacrament, water,

sins, sorry, confirmation, Penance,

godmother, Act of Contrition, prayer, sorry,

Zacchaeus, tree, tax collector, Peter

Call on volunteers to choose the word that doesn't belong in each group. Then ask someone else to explain why it doesn't fit with the other words. You might wish to have the children continue this game by creating other groups of words where one does not belong.

Quiz Game (for use with page 72)

Copy the following statements onto paper, making one copy per child.

- This is where Zacchaeus was when Jesus saw him.
- This is the job that Zacchaeus had when Jesus saw him.
- This is what Jesus did to Zacchaeus.
- This is the sacrament in which we celebrate God's forgiveness.
- This is another name for Reconciliation.
- This is the special prayer we use to say "I'm sorry."

Have the children work in pairs and play an oral quiz game. Call on children to give their answers.

FAITH ALIVE AT HOME AND IN THE PARISH

Your child has learned that in the sacrament of Reconciliation we celebrate God's forgiveness. He or she has learned that God will always forgive us if we are sorry for our sins, promise not to sin again, and make up for what we have done wrong.

Many adult Catholics first learned to call this sacrament *confession.* The Church now prefers to call it Reconciliation to emphasize that it is a sacrament of healing and forgiveness.

You might ask yourself:

- *Do I look upon celebrating the sacrament of Reconciliation as an opportunity to seek God's peace, love, and forgiveness?*
- *What message about the sacrament of Reconciliation do I want to give to my family?*

† Act of Contrition

Pray with your child the Act of Contrition that was learned in this lesson. (This may be a different form from the one you learned.) Help your child learn it by heart by repeating it phrase by phrase after you.

† My God,
I am sorry for my sins with all my heart.
In choosing to do wrong
and failing to do good,
I have sinned against you
whom I should love above all things.
I firmly intend, with your help,
to do penance,
to sin no more,
and to avoid whatever leads me to sin.
Our Savior Jesus Christ
suffered and died for us.
In his name, my God, have mercy.

Learn by heart

Faith Summary

(1) • The Church celebrates God's forgiveness in the sacrament of Reconciliation.

(1) What does the Church celebrate in Reconciliation?

(2) • We celebrate the sacrament of Reconciliation with our parish family.

(2) With whom do we celebrate Reconciliation?

Review

Go over the *Faith Summary* together before your child completes the *Review.* The answers for questions 1–3 appear on page 200. The response to number 4 will show whether your child understands that one way of thanking God for forgiveness is by loving and helping others. When the *Review* is completed, have your child place a sticker on this page.

sticker

Circle the correct answer.

1. God forgives us only now and then. Yes (No)

2. In the sacrament of Reconciliation we receive the forgiveness of God and the Church. (Yes) No

3. We have to make up with those we hurt. (Yes) No

4. Tell how you will show thanks for God's forgiveness.

Possible responses: I will try not to sin again.

Encourage the children to gather with their families to share the *Family Scripture Moment.*

As you **Gather,** ask: when or about what do we feel "lost"? Now **Listen** to Jesus' message of hope.

What do you think a man does who has one hundred sheep and one of them gets lost? He will leave the other ninety-nine grazing on the hillside and go and look for the lost sheep. When he finds it, I tell you, he feels far happier over this one sheep than over the ninety-nine that did not get lost. In just the same way your Father in heaven does not want any of these little ones to be lost.
Matthew 18:12–14

Share what positive messages each family member heard in this parable.

Consider for family enrichment:

- Shepherds in Jesus' time knew each of their sheep by name and would go to great lengths to find them when they wandered off from the flock.
- In this parable, Jesus portrays God as a good shepherd who seeks out the lost.

Reflect What are some of the ways that God comes "looking for us" with love and mercy?

Decide How will we be ministers of love and mercy in our family and parish this week?

11 WE PREPARE FOR RECONCILIATION

For the Catechist: Spiritual and Catechetical Development

ADULT BACKGROUND

Our Life

The mother of a Catholic school kindergartner tells this true story about an unexpected response to a rhetorical question. During a children's liturgy, the homilist recalled how Jesus had given up His life to save us from our sins. Father X then asked, "Who among us has lived our lives without sin? Who of us can say that we are perfect?"

As though on cue, the entire kindergarten class raised their hands. (Story contributed to *Catholic Digest* by Louise Norton.)

Ask yourself:

- When was the last time I admitted having done wrong, and asked another's forgiveness?
- What response did I receive?

Sharing Life

How does your faith affect your willingness to seek forgiveness?

How do you feel about being imperfect?

Our Catholic Faith

What is conscience? Where does it come from? *The Church in the Modern World,* a document of the Second Vatican Council, affirms that conscience is a person's "most secret core" and "sanctuary." It is the place where God's Law of Love is inscribed and heeded. It is the voice that whispers, "Choose love. Choose life. Do good. Shun evil."

Emphasizing the natural law, which Saint Thomas Aquinas defined as "the light of understanding infused in us by God, whereby we understand what must be done and what must be avoided," Pope John Paul II goes on to describe conscience as "the witness of God himself, whose voice and judgment penetrate the depths of man's soul, calling him...to obedience" (*Veritatis Splendor,* August 6, 1993, 58).

Following one's conscience does not mean doing whatever we want. We must act responsibly and we also have the responsibility to form a correct conscience by studying the Gospel message and applying it to everyday life. The Church, too, helps us to form our conscience correctly. The teaching authority of the Church guides and directs the faithful.

Although the goal of our lives is union with Jesus Christ, we frequently miss the mark. In the sacrament of Reconciliation, we encounter the healing presence of Jesus Christ. By taking part in the celebration of this sacrament, we renew our commitment to turn away from our sins and live the good news of the kingdom of God.

Coming to Faith

How will you define conscience?

How does the sacrament of Reconciliation deepen our union with Jesus?

Practicing Faith

What will you do to strengthen the voice of conscience in your life?

How will you help the children in your group to admit wrongdoing and forgive the wrongs of others?

Catechism of the Catholic Church

The Theme of This Chapter Corresponds with Paragraph 1456

Liturgical Resources

An examination of conscience can begin like a visit to the doctor. The first question is, "Where does it hurt?" What are the relationships in my life that are raw and wounded? What have I done to make them that way? What am I willing to do to begin the healing process? We have to be careful that an examination of conscience does not ask routine questions in the same old way. We need to ask new questions that prompt an ever-deepening process of growth in our friendship with Jesus.

Hold a prayer service in which you read the passage about Jesus telling His disciples to "Let the children come to me and do not stop them, because the Kingdom of heaven belongs to such as these" (Matthew 19:14). Call each child's name. Have him/her place a name tag on a poster that displays a picture of Jesus. Remind the children that Jesus wants to be their friend and loves them just as they are.

Justice and Peace Resources

As you prepare for Reconciliation, help the children to understand that sin has consequences for all of society. It is not something strictly between God and a person.

For example: When an entire group of people keeps a greater share of the world's resources than is rightfully theirs, they participate in the sin of greed. Because of their sin, many others are forced to live with a lesser share of the available resources. The greed and selfishness of one group leads to the poverty, hunger, and resentment of other groups.

Form groups and pass out play money. Give one child in each group very little play money. Have the children discuss their feelings about having a lot of money or not enough. Decide on one action that the children can take to share with those who do not have enough food or money.

Teaching Resources

Overview of the Lesson

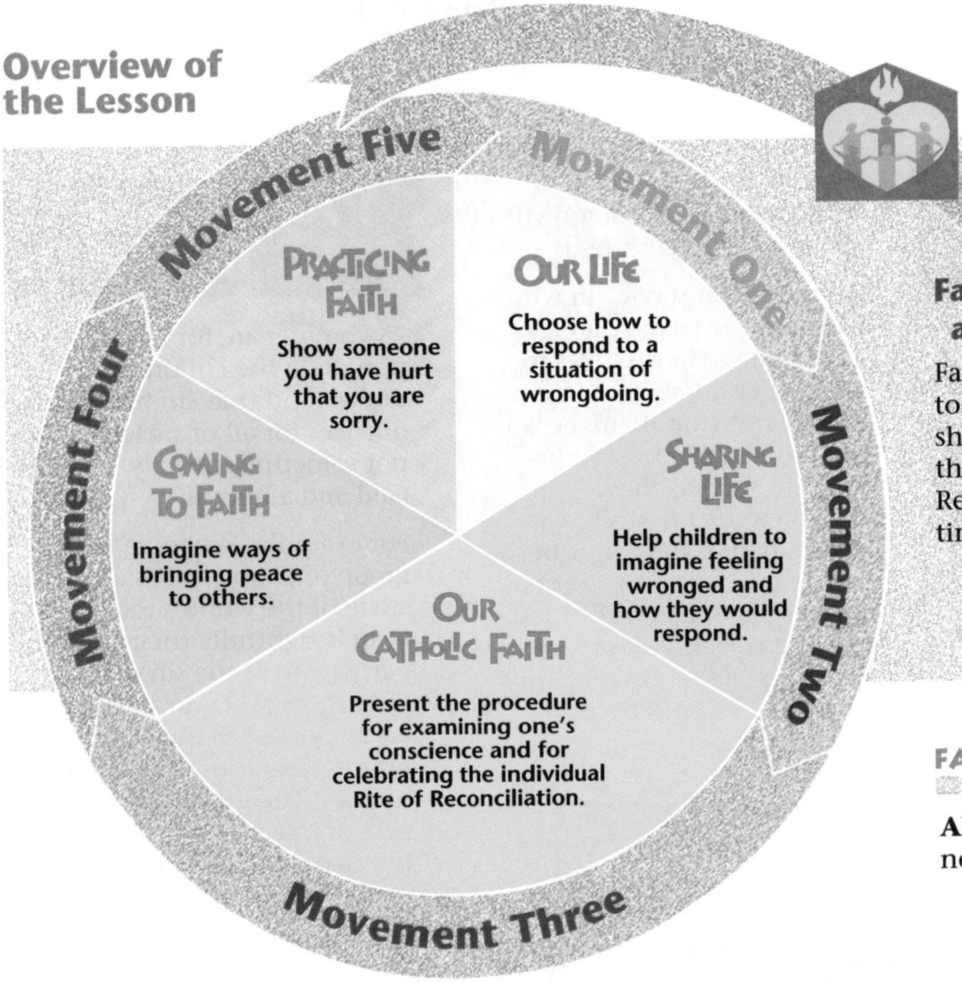

Faith Alive at Home and in the Parish

Family helps the child to decide whether he or she is ready to celebrate the sacrament of Reconciliation at this time.

FAITH WORD

Absolution is God's forgiveness of our sins.

Teaching Hints

In this lesson the children will be introduced to the individual Rite of Reconciliation. It may be helpful to list, on the chalkboard or on flashcards, the steps in preparing for the sacrament. Emphasize the importance of prayer to the Holy Spirit before examining their conscience. Have children roleplay to illustrate some sins that they might commit, and have them act out going to confession.

Special-Needs Child

When working with mainstreamed children, stress their strengths and help them to assess their limitations realistically.

Visual Needs

- faith word *absolution* in sandpaper letters

Auditory Needs

- clear, concise directions for activities

Tactile-Motor Needs

- "How to Examine My Conscience" chart taped to desk

Supplemental Resources

Skateboard (video)
Mass Media Ministries
2116 North Charles Street
Baltimore, MD 21218
(1-800-828-8825)

Lesson Plan: Beginning

Objectives

To help the children

- know how to prepare for Reconciliation;
- appreciate God's gift of forgiveness;
- recognize the importance of preparing well.

Focusing Prayer

Have the children close their eyes and think of something they have done for which they would like to ask God's forgiveness. Then lead them in the prayer at the top of page 75.

Our Life

Making Choices

Invite the children to look at the illustration in the *Our Life* section as you read the first paragraph. Recall for the children what they learned about the importance of making right choices. Then invite individuals to choose an ending that Matt and Sara might choose. Ask the follow-up questions, and discuss the children's responses. Help the children see that forgiveness often requires great courage.

Sharing Life

Thinking Things Through

Invite the children to respond to the first question in the *Sharing Life* section. Emphasize the fact that Matt and Sara were not only destroying Ryan's property, they were intentionally trying to hurt him. Recall for the children Jesus' command to love one another.

Then have the children imagine themselves in Ryan's place. Ask the final question, and have them share reasons why they would forgive.

11 We Prepare for Reconciliation

Loving God, forgive us our sins.

Our Life

Matt and Sara ripped Ryan's backpack. They did it on purpose. It was a special gift from his family.

What might Matt and Sara do? They might:

- tease Ryan and tell him to buy another bag.
- run away and later tell God they are sorry.
- tell Ryan they are sorry for doing something wrong, offer to fix the bag, then ask God to forgive them.

Possible responses:

What would be the easiest thing for Matt and Sara to do? the hardest?
1 and 2 easiest; 3 hardest

What do you think Jesus would want them to do?
Make up; say you are sorry; etc.

Have you ever had to make a choice like this? Tell what you did.
Do not force anyone to answer this question.

Sharing Life

Possible responses:

Why do you think it was wrong for Matt and Sara to rip Ryan's backpack? It did not belong to them; it hurt Ryan; etc.

Imagine that you are Ryan. If Matt and Sara told you they were sorry, would you forgive them? Tell why or why not.
God wants us to forgive others.

75

Enrichment

Role-Playing

Divide the children into small groups. Help them make up stories telling about young people being mean to one another. Then have them imagine two endings to the stories. In the first ending, have the children show how the young people became friends again; in the second, how they didn't become friends again. Invite volunteers to act out their stories.

Lesson Plan: Middle

Our Catholic Faith

Getting Ready to Celebrate

Talk with the children about the importance of preparing for events like taking an exam, going to a party, going on a trip, and so forth. Emphasize the fact that often the success of the event depends on how well they have prepared.

Point out also that there are often persons who help us to prepare: parents, friends, and so forth.

Then read aloud the first three paragraphs on page 76. Use the annotation. Recall for the children what they learned about the Holy Spirit. Lead them to see that besides giving us the courage to do what is right, the Holy Spirit also helps us know what is right or wrong to do.

Examining Our Conscience

Have the children underline the words *examine our conscience*. Explain that our conscience is a special gift from God. It is like the voice of the Holy Spirit inside of us, telling us what God wants us to do in a particular situation. Talk with the children about how sometimes people will try to guide them in directions other than what God wants, but there is something within us that helps us to know right from wrong. We call that our conscience.

Explain that when we examine something, we look at it carefully; when we examine our conscience, we think about our choices; we ask ourselves if we made right or wrong choices.

Take time to go over the examination of conscience on page 79, answering any questions the children may have.

Ask: How do we get ready for Reconciliation? (Numbers 1–5)

Celebrating Reconciliation by Ourselves with a Priest

(1) We get ready to celebrate the sacrament of Reconciliation by asking the Holy Spirit to help us remember our sins.

(2) We think about the times we made bad choices or did the wrong thing. Remember, mistakes are not sins.

(3) We ask ourselves if we have been living as Jesus wants. We do this when we examine our conscience. (See page 79.)

(4) Then we tell God we are sorry for our sins. (5) We promise to tell or show those we have hurt that we are sorry.

We can celebrate the sacrament of Reconciliation with our parish family and a priest or by ourselves with a priest.

Celebrating by ourselves with the priest (1–9)

When we celebrate by ourselves, (1) we meet with the priest. (2) He greets us in God's name and in the name of the Church.

76

Lesson Plan: Middle

Celebrating the Sacrament

Continue reading the rest of pages 76 and 77, taking time to explain carefully each step in the reception of the sacrament. Refer to the illustrations as you go along. Review the Act of Contrition, which the children learned in the previous session. Emphasize the wonder of the great gift Jesus has given us and how easy God makes it for us to receive forgiveness. Slowly and clearly, read aloud once again the steps for taking part in the sacrament of Reconciliation by ourselves with the priest. (The annotated numbers may help you in presenting the steps.)

If the children will be celebrating the sacrament in the near future, you may wish to reinforce their understanding of the ritual by taking the priest's role and having a few children take turns "going through the motions" with you.

Faith Word

Display the faith word *absolution*. Have the children repeat it after you and read together the explanation in the last three paragraphs on page 77. Point out the wonderful gift that this is and what peace it can bring to us when we have sinned.

You may wish to use pages 25–26 in the activity book for *Coming to Jesus*.

FAITH WORD

Absolution is God's forgiveness of our sins.

(3) We make the sign of the cross together.(4)The priest may read from the Bible about God's forgiveness.

(5) We confess our sins to God by telling them to the priest. We call this making our confession. The priest never tells anyone what we say in confession.(6)After telling our sins, we can talk with the priest. He will help us to live as followers of Jesus.

(7) Then the priest gives us a penance. A penance is something good we can do or prayers we can say to show we are sorry.

(8)We say an Act of Contrition.(9)Then the priest says the words of absolution, telling us that God has forgiven us.

We are reconciled with God and one another. The priest says:
"Through the ministry of the Church may God give you pardon and peace, and I absolve you from your sins in the name of the Father, and of the Son, † and of the Holy Spirit."

This sacrament brings us God's peace and helps us grow as forgiving people.

Enrichment

The Reconciliation Room

Take the children to visit the Reconciliation Room in your church (and/or the confessional, if one is still used in your parish). Show the children the stole that the priest wears when celebrating the sacrament of Reconciliation. Explain that it is a symbol of the power he has to forgive our sins. Let the children comment freely and ask questions.

Lesson Plan: End

Coming to Faith

Sharing Ideas

Recall for the children the meaning of the examination of conscience. Then discuss the children's responses to the question and directives in the *Coming to Faith* section. Share with them some of your own ideas for bringing God's peace to others. Let them share their ideas as well.

Faith Summary

Turn to the *Faith Summary* on page 79. Use the annotations to see if the children can express in their own words what they have learned today.

Practicing Faith

A "Healing Heart" Activity

Give the children a few minutes to think about someone they may have hurt. Then invite them to complete the "healing heart" activity. End with the Act of Contrition.

Evaluating Your Lesson

- Do the children know how to prepare for Reconciliation?
- Do they appreciate God's gift of forgiveness?
- Have they decided to prepare well for the sacrament of Reconciliation?

Enrichment

Forgiving Others

Ask the children if they recall any words in the Our Father that speak of forgiveness. Have them pray together: "Forgive us our trespasses as we forgive those who trespass against us." Ask if they have ever seen a NO TRESPASSING sign, and talk about what it means.

Give each child a sheet of construction paper with one of the words from the Our Father phrase. Have them cut around their words in "cloud" shapes. Other children can cut empty "clouds" for spaces. Then have them paste together the phrase on a long strip of posterboard, and hang it above the chalkboard or on a bulletin board.

Materials needed: construction paper; scissors; posterboard; paste

Coming to Faith Possible responses:

What should we ask ourselves when we examine our conscience? If we have been living as Jesus wants; etc.

Imagine ways you can bring God's peace to others. Forgive those who hurt us; etc.

Share your ideas with your friends. Encourage the children to share specific examples.

Practicing Faith

Think of someone you have hurt. Draw a picture of that person in this "healing heart" letter.

What can you do or say to show this person you are sorry? Write it in the letter.

Will you do what you have promised? Pray the Act of Contrition together.

78

Talk to the children about ways they and their families might use the "Faith Alive" pages. Encourage them to ask someone at home to go over the examination of conscience with them.

Deciding to Show Sorrow (for use with page 75)

Write the following stories on the chalkboard or newspring.

- If I hurt someone's feelings, what should I do?
- If I blamed someone for something she (he) did not do, what should I do?
- If I told the teacher a lie about someone, what should I do?

Form pairs to decide what should be done. Let several share their solutions.

Then have volunteers make up additional stories, and have the children discuss them.

Celebrating Reconciliation (for use with page 76)

Give each child a list of the steps involved in celebrating the individual rite of the sacrament of Reconciliation.

1. We ask the Holy Spirit to help us remember our sins.
2. We think about the times we made bad choices.
3. We examine our conscience.
4. We tell God we are sorry for our sins.
5. We make the sign of the cross with the priest.
6. We confess our sins to the priest.
7. We talk to the priest.
8. We receive a penance.
9. We say an Act of Contrition.
10. The priest absolves us.

Encourage the children to decorate the page with symbols that express what Reconciliation means to them. Have them glue the page to a piece of cardboard.

Encourage them to take their cards to church whenever they celebrate the sacrament of Reconciliation.

Materials needed: copies of the steps for Reconciliation; crayons; cardboard; glue

Prayer for Forgiveness (for use with page 77)

Have the children name some times when we need forgiveness. Write their responses on the chalkboard or a large sheet of paper.

Then write the following on the board:

Loving God, forgive me my sins.
I will ____________________.

Have the children help you complete the prayer for each of the times written.

Word Memory (for use with page 78)

Have the children sit in a circle. Have prepared index cards with the following terms written on them, one per card: *penance, absolution, reconciliation, confession, examination of conscience, act of contrition*. Stack the cards face down in the center of the group. Have the children take turns picking a card and telling what they know about the term written on it.

Materials needed: index cards

FAITH ALIVE AT HOME AND IN THE PARISH

Your child is learning how to celebrate the sacrament of Reconciliation. You can help your child decide when he or she is ready to celebrate this sacrament for the first time. One way to teach your child how to prepare for this celebration is by examining your own conscience. You might ask yourself:

- *Have I hurt any members of my family?*
- *What can I do to show them I am sorry?*

Help your child learn to examine his or her conscience. Show your child how to use the questions below to think about the times he or she may have made bad choices or done the wrong thing. Be sure that your child does not confuse a mistake with a sin.

†Family Prayer

Forgive us, God, for all our sins.
Help us to forgive those who hurt us!

How to Examine My Conscience

Go over the examination with the children before they use it at home.

1. When I make choices, do I sometimes forget to think first about what God wants me to do? Have I done what God wants?
2. Have I used God's name in a bad way?
3. Have I forgotten to worship God on Sunday? Did I try to share in the Mass?
4. Have I disobeyed the grown-ups who take care of me?
5. Have I forgotten to give my body the good food and sleep it needs?
6. Have I forgotten to show respect for myself and others?
7. Have I taken anything that is not mine or treated others unfairly?
8. Have I always told the truth?
9. Have I hurt someone by what I have said or done?
10. Have I refused to help people who are in need?

Learn by heart

Faith Summary

- We examine our conscience to remember our sins.
  Why do we examine our conscience?
- We confess our sins to a priest and receive God's forgiveness.
  What happens in the sacrament of Reconciliation?

Review

Go over the *Faith Summary* together before your child completes the *Review*. The answers to questions 1–3 appear on page 200. The response to number 4 will show whether your child understands how to use the examination of conscience to prepare for the sacrament of Reconciliation. When the *Review* is completed, have your child place a sticker on this page.

sticker

Circle the letter next to the correct answer.

1. When we tell our sins to the priest we are

a. examining our conscience. (b.) confessing our sins.

2. The priest asks us to say or do something to show we are sorry. This is called

(a.) penance. b. examining our conscience.

3. When the priest says the words that tell us we are forgiven, we receive

(a.) absolution. b. Baptism.

4. Tell how you will get ready to celebrate the sacrament of Reconciliation.

I will examine my conscience.

Encourage the children to gather with their families to share the *Family Scripture Moment*.

Gather and ask what it means to be a forgiving person. Then **Listen** to God's word.

Some people brought to Jesus a paralyzed man, lying on a bed. When Jesus saw how much faith they had, He said to the paralyzed man, "Courage, My son! Your sins are forgiven." Then some teachers of the Law said to themselves, "This man is speaking blasphemy!" Jesus perceived what they were thinking, and so He said, "Is it easier to say, 'Your sins are forgiven,' or to say, 'Get up and walk'? I will prove to you, then, that the Son of Man has authority on earth to forgive sins." So He said to the paralyzed man, "Get up, pick up your bed, and go home!" The man got up and went home.

From Matthew 9:1–6

Share what you heard for your life today.

Consider for family enrichment:

- Jesus first heals the paralyzed man's spirit by forgiving his sins. He then heals the man's physical illness.
- As Catholics our celebration of the sacrament of Reconciliation should reflect a whole life of mercy and forgiveness.

Reflect and **Decide** What reconciliation do we need in our family? How will we celebrate this?

12 We Celebrate Reconciliation

For the Catechist: Spiritual and Catechetical Development

Adult Background

Our Life

We all have people in our lives—parents, teachers, mentors, and role models—who have required us to do "impossible" things. By their faith in our ability to do it—change, grow, achieve—they gave us a boost over self-imposed limits. Like the great Sherlock Holmes himself, we discover that in "eliminating the impossible," we arrive at the truth.

There is One whose faith in us exceeds that of all the others. And the most "impossible thing" He requires us to do is to forgive our enemies. When we do, we arrive not only at truth but joy and healing as well.

Ask yourself:

- Is there (or has there been) someone I cannot forgive? Why?

Sharing Life

How does your faith help you to achieve the "impossible" feat of forgiveness?

In what way does sacramental Reconciliation help you to arrive at the truth?

Our Catholic Faith

Jesus' life and His teachings were filled with seemingly irreconcilable differences. He spoke from His humanity and His divinity. His teachings speak of losing life to be alive and of embracing poverty to find the Kingdom. Jesus Christ took the opposites of life and wove them together. He reconciled human beings with God and reconciled outcasts with the community. With Jesus there are no "irreconcilable differences."

In the sacrament of Reconciliation, we celebrate this reconciliation between God and humanity. The Rite of Reconciliation itself helps us to understand the relation of Reconciliation to the whole community and emphasizes our joy and thanksgiving for the gift of God's forgiveness.

The primary acts of the Rite of Reconciliation are contrition, confession, act of penance, and absolution. Contrition is so very important, for Jesus Christ asks us to experience a change of heart: "Turn away from your sins, because the Kingdom of heaven is near!" (Matthew 4:17). The reading of the word of God calls us to conversion and to recognize our sins. Confession of sins is more than listing our offenses to the priest. We show our desire to "begin a new life" by accepting the penance that the priest gives us. The act of penance may be a prayer, self-denial, or especially service to one's neighbor, because sin and forgiveness always affect others. Lastly, the priest gives us God's pardon through the sign of absolution. While we may celebrate the sacrament by ourselves with the priest, we actually do it in union with the whole Church. We ask forgiveness realizing that our sins have not only damaged us but have weakened the whole body of Christ. We look forward to the future with renewed hope and trust in God and in ourselves.

Coming to Faith

How would you describe the process of Reconciliation?

What have your positive experiences of the sacrament of Reconciliation been?

Practicing Faith

How will you practice your ability to forgive this week?

How will you prepare your group to be reconciled with God and others in the sacrament of Reconciliation?

The Theme of This Chapter Corresponds with Paragraph 1480

LITURGICAL RESOURCES

Reconciliation is both a call to conversion and a celebration of conversion that has already taken place. To be reconciled with others and with our God means we are willing to change, to seek growth. Part of an ability to change requires that we establish new ways of relating, new patterns of behaving. Our prayers of reconciliation should be prayers for patience with ourselves and others; pleas to see the possibilities for growth and change; and prayers of gratitude for the hope that our experiences of being reconciled give us for our future.

Invite the children in your group to offer this Reconciliation Prayer.

All respond: "Jesus, help us."

- To forgive ourselves when we have done wrong...
- To forgive others who have done wrong...
- To be patient with ourselves and others...

In the name of the Father...

JUSTICE AND PEACE RESOURCES

There is need for reconciliation at all levels of life; intrapersonal, interracial, intercultural, international. Our ministry of reconciliation, as a Church and as individuals, has to reach to all levels. Such a commitment to reconciliation, encompassing the world and requiring mutual respect, understanding, dialogue, and trust, can tend to overwhelm and even paralyze our best intentions. Yet it is possible to simplify the multitude of complex issues surrounding global reconciliation to the original message of the Gospel. We can act as reconcilers by loving others as ourselves and by being willing to forgive "seventy times seven" times.

Invite the children to join the "Peace Force." Give each a gold star badge to wear as a reminder that members of the Force do the following:

- avoid arguing and name calling;
- make friends with children who have been left out;
- say "I'm sorry" and shake hands when they need to ask for forgiveness.

Teaching Resources

Overview of the Lesson

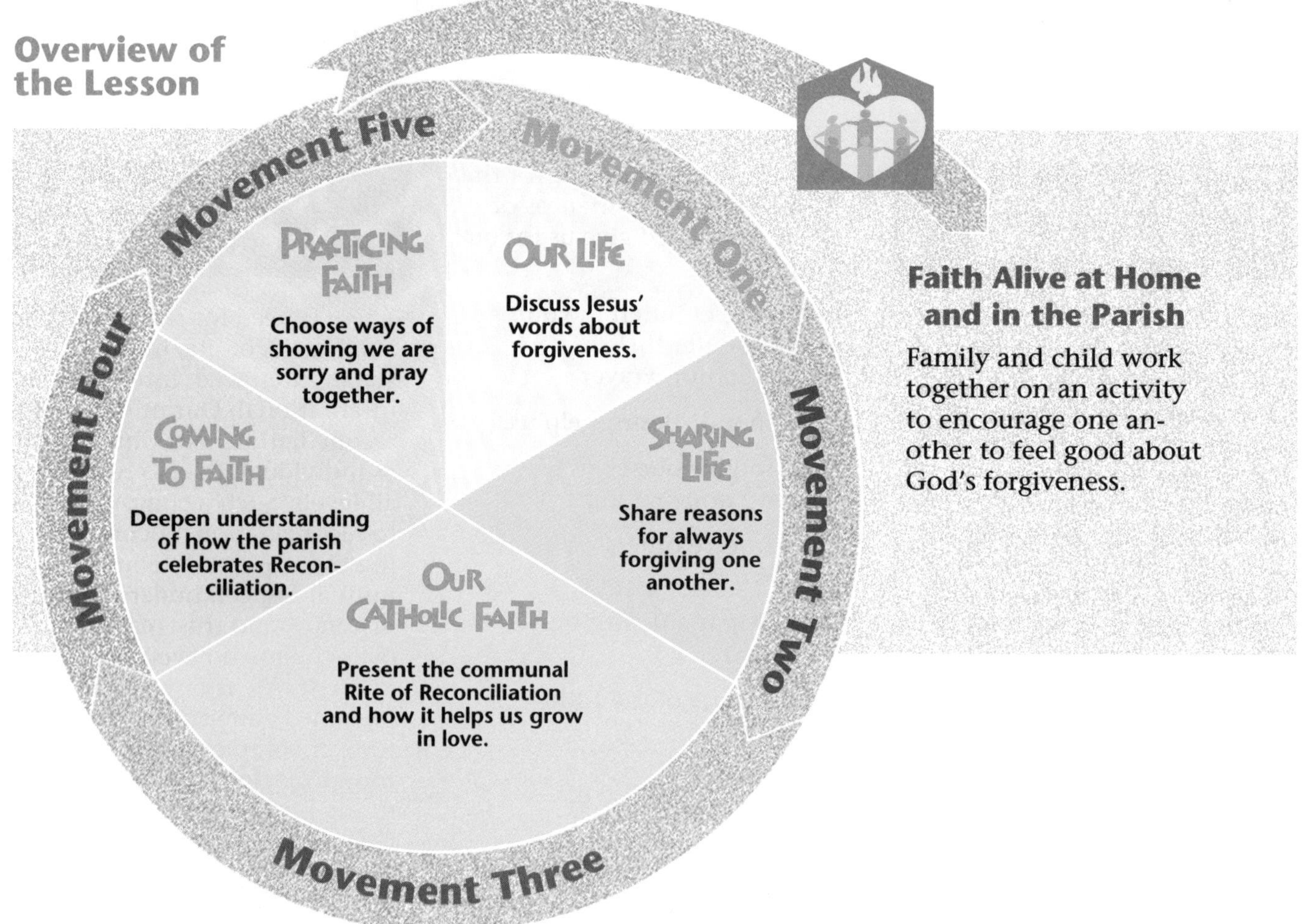

Teaching Hints

Focus again on the importance of belonging to the parish family in presenting the communal Rite of Reconciliation. You may wish to invite a priest to take them through a simple, short communal celebration in the church. Engage the children as much as possible in song and prayer during the service. Let the children enter the Reconciliation room with the priest or deacon so that they have a sense of familiarity with the environment.

Special-Needs Child

When writing for children with limited vision, use a felt-tipped pen or thick lead pencils. Use wide-lined paper.

Visual Needs

- *70 x 7 means always* in sandpaper letters

Auditory Needs

- audiotape and headphones for the communal Rite of Reconciliation

Tactile-Motor Needs

- peer helper for the circle activity

Supplemental Resources

First Reconciliation (video)
The Stray (video)
St. Anthony Messenger/
Franciscan Communications
1615 Republic Street
Cincinnati, OH 45210
(1-800-488-0488)
(1-800-989-3600)

Lesson Plan: Beginning

Objectives

To help the children

- know how Reconciliation is celebrated in the parish;
- appreciate the experience of celebrating together;
- recognize the importance of forgiveness.

Focusing Prayer

Remind the children of the marvel of God's continuing forgiveness in our lives. Then lead them in the prayer at the top of page 81.

Our Life

A Story About Forgiveness

Set the scene for the Scripture story on page 81.

The apostles were probably walking along with Jesus as He taught them. He had been talking to them about forgiveness and how to help those who had sinned. Peter listened to what Jesus said about forgiveness, but he had a question to ask. Let us hear what it was and how Jesus answered it.

Read aloud with expression the story from Matthew. Then ask the questions that follow the story. Use the annotations.

Sharing Life

Walking with Jesus

Choose one child to take the role of Jesus, and let the others pretend they are apostles. Have them sit in a circle around "Jesus" and ask Him the question in the *Sharing Life* section. See the annotation. Let the child representing Jesus respond as he or she thinks Jesus might have answered. Then let the other children tell if they think Jesus would have said anything different.

12 We Celebrate Reconciliation

Loving God,
Your mercy
lasts forever.

Our Life

This is what Jesus said about forgiveness.

One day Peter asked Jesus, "Lord, how many times do I have to forgive someone? Seven times?"

"No, not seven times," answered Jesus, "but seventy times seven!" In the Bible, this means "always."

Then Jesus said that this is how God forgives us.

From Matthew 18:21–23

What do you think of Jesus' answer to Peter? Jesus wants us to forgive always.

Who always forgives you? God

Do you always forgive?
Allow time for the children to quietly reflect on this question.

Sharing Life

Possible response:

Why do you think God wants us to forgive one another always?
God always forgives us.

Share your ideas with your friends.

81

Enrichment

A Picture Story

Distribute large sheets of drawing paper. Have the children divide them into two or three frames, as in a comic strip, and draw a picture story about forgiveness in their lives. Let them share their picture stories with one another when finished.

Materials needed: drawing paper; crayons or markers

Lesson Plan: Middle

Our Catholic Faith

Doing Things Together

Talk with the children about the fact that sometimes we enjoy doing things by ourselves, but at other times we would rather do them with others. Share with the children some things you especially like to do with others. Then have them give examples from their own lives.

Celebrating as a Family

Recall for the children what they learned about receiving the sacrament of Reconciliation individually. Explain that the Church encourages us to receive this sacrament, at times, as a family.

Help the children to see that just as when a person in a family does something wrong it affects the whole family, so too in the Church when someone sins, the whole Church family is hurt in some way. Recall that when the priest forgives our sins, he is acting in the name of God and of the Church. Let the children comment on this, and try to elicit from them the importance of the support they can receive from the presence of their parish family.

We Celebrate Together

Read pages 82 and 83 and go over the steps in the communal celebration, one at a time. See the annotation. Outline the procedure as clearly as possible, using flash cards for the following words:

We
gather
listen
examine our conscience
pray an Act of Contrition
make our confession

The Priest
gives us a penance
says words of absolution

OUR CATHOLIC FAITH

Note: The dots indicate the order of the steps that we follow in the celebration of the sacrament.

Stress the underlined text.

Celebrating with Others

We have learned how to celebrate the sacrament of Reconciliation by ourselves with the priest. At times we celebrate the sacrament of Reconciliation with the priest and with other people in our parish. Here is what we do.

- We gather with our parish family and sing a song. The priest welcomes us.
- We listen to a story from the Bible about God's mercy. The priest or deacon explains the story. He reminds us that God always loves us and forgives us when we are sorry for our sins.
- We examine our conscience. We think about the times we may not have lived as followers of Jesus.
- Together we pray an Act of Contrition and the Our Father. We ask God to help us not to sin again.
- The priest meets with us one by one. We make our confession. Remember, the priest never tells anyone what we say to him!

82

Lesson Plan: Middle

We
gather again
thank God

The Priest
blesses us

We
sing a happy song

If your parish community is dismissed after the individual confessions, do not stress the last steps (beginning with *gather again*).

Materials needed: flash cards of words listed above

- The priest gives us a penance.
- Then the priest says the words of absolution.
- After all have had a turn to meet with the priest alone for confession, we gather together again.
- We thank God for His love and forgiveness.
- The priest blesses us. He asks us to bring Jesus' peace to others.
- We sing a happy song to thank God for forgiving us.

Celebrating Reconciliation helps us to grow in our love for God, others, and ourselves. Jesus, our friend, helps us to forgive others as God forgives us.

Our Catholic Identity

Use the *Our Catholic Identity* on page 7 in the back of the book. Show the children how the priest makes the sign of the cross. Have them make the sign of the cross on themselves and answer "Amen."

Studying Pictures

Have the children examine the photos on pages 82–83 as you explain the procedure followed in the communal celebration. Let them suggest which step is illustrated in each photo.

Talk about what the persons must feel as they are confessing their sins or exchanging a greeting of peace. Help the children see what a great gift of love this sacrament is, because of the peace it brings in knowing that things are right with God, ourselves, and others.

Read the last paragraph on page 83. Emphasize how Jesus always gives us the ability to forgive others, no matter how much they may have hurt us, and that this helps our love to grow stronger.

You may wish to use pages 27–28 in the activity book for *Coming to Jesus*.

Enrichment

A Church Visit

Take the children to church. Invite a priest to explain the importance of the parish celebration of Reconciliation, and have him go through the procedure with the children. Have the children visit the Reconciliation Room again. Talk with them about why some persons might want to use the screen when confessing their sins while others might not. If time allows, let each child practice going to confession.

Lesson Plan: End

Coming to Faith

Sharing What We Learn

Have the children pretend that a new boy or girl in their class has just become a Catholic. Invite them to respond to the directive in the *Coming to Faith* section on page 84 by explaining to the newcomer the *meaning* of Reconciliation, *how* they receive it, and *why*. See the annotation.

Multicultural Awareness

Have the children note the various cultures represented in the picture on page 84. Point out the wonder of our parish family's being made up of so many different people from all parts of the world.

Faith Summary

Turn to the *Faith Summary* on page 85. Use the annotations to see if the children can express in their own words what they have learned today.

Practicing Faith

A Reconciliation Prayer

Place a crucifix and Bible on the prayer table. Have the children gather around it and hold hands. Follow the procedure suggested in the *Practicing Faith* section. See the annotation. End with an appropriate song, such as "How Good It Is." (You might use the cassette for Sadlier's *Coming to Jesus in Song*.)

Evaluating Your Lesson

- Do the children know how Reconciliation is celebrated in the parish?
- Do they appreciate its importance?
- Have they decided to be forgiving?

Enrichment

Creating a Reconciliation Room

Invite the children to help you set up a "reconciliation room" in the corner of your classroom. Section off a corner. Place there two chairs and a small table. Place a Bible and a crucifix on the table. Encourage the children to role-play going to the sacrament of Reconciliation in their "reconciliation room."

Coming to Faith

Tell how our parish family can celebrate the sacrament of Reconciliation together.
(See pages 82–83.)

Practicing Faith

Gather in a circle with your friends. Be very still. Think about something for which you are very sorry. Think of what you will do to show you are sorry. Encourage the children to act on making up for their sins.

Pray together,

† Loving God, we are sorry for all the things we have done wrong. Help us to show that we are really sorry.

Then say to the person on each side of you, "________, God loves and forgives you."

Talk to the children about ways they and their families might use the "Faith Alive" pages. Encourage them to pray the "Forgiveness Prayer" as a closing faith response.

84

A Singing Prayer (for use with page 81)

Invite one of the children to tell or read the story of what Jesus said about forgiveness on page 81.

Then have the children sing the response "seventy times seven" to the musical scale of do-re-mi. Go over it a few times to be sure the children can sing their response.

Read the following petitions and have the children sing the response "seventy times seven" after each petition.

- Lord, how many times do I have to forgive someone?...
- Lord, when my friend is mean to me, how many times must I forgive?...
- Lord, when my friend is unkind to me, how many times must I forgive?...

Reconciliation Room Diorama (for use with pages 82–83)

Have the children work in groups to create a diorama of a Reconciliation room. Use shoe boxes without lids. Cover the boxes with paper. Tell the children to refer to the pictures on pages 82 and 83 for help in knowing what is in the room. Remind them to represent the priest and a person going to confession. Have them use pipe cleaners or clay, and construction paper to make the people and objects.

Materials needed: shoe boxes; glue; tape; scissors; clay; pipe cleaners; construction paper; crayons; markers

A Forgiveness Cloth (for use with page 83)

Help the children decorate a piece of white cloth to cover the prayer table. Write the words *We Forgive Always* in the center of the cloth. Have the children go over the words with a purple magic marker. Explain that violet or purple is the color the Church uses for sorrow. Then have each child write *70 x 7* on the cloth. Use the cloth as a reminder of Jesus' words about forgiveness.

Materials needed: white cloth; purple markers

Making a Stole (for use with page 84)

Point out the stole on the priest on page 83. Explain that the stole is worn when the priest takes part in certain religious ceremonies, for example, when the priest administers the sacrament of Reconciliation. Invite the children to think of a symbol they could use to remind them that Jesus always forgives us when we are sorry. For example: two hearts; "I'm sorry" pin; two hands shaking; a smiling face; and so on.

Cut out a piece of purple fabric on felt approximately five inches wide and sixty inches long, or use construction paper. As the children finish their symbols, invite them to paste their symbols on the fabric. Display the finished stole in the Reconciliation room when the children receive the sacrament for the first time.

Materials needed: purple fabric or construction paper; drawing paper; crayons; scissors; paste

FAITH ALIVE AT HOME AND IN THE PARISH

Your child has now learned the two ways that we celebrate the sacrament of Reconciliation. Help your child to understand the things that are always part of the sacrament of Reconciliation. Then use the activity below to encourage your child to feel good about God's forgiveness.

Celebrating Reconciliation

- We examine our conscience and are sorry for our sins. We promise not to sin again.
- We confess our sins.
- We receive a penance.
- We pray an Act of Contrition.
- We receive absolution.

† Forgiveness Prayer

God, forgive our sins and give us peace. We ask this through Jesus Christ. Amen.

Forgiveness Cross

Trace, color, and wear this cross to celebrate God's forgiveness.

Learn by heart

Faith Summary

- We can celebrate Reconciliation either by ourselves with the priest or with others in our parish and the priest.
  How can we celebrate Reconciliation?
- Celebrating Reconciliation helps us to grow in our love for God, others, and ourselves.
  How does celebrating Reconciliation help us to grow?

Review

First go over the *Faith Summary* together before your child completes the *Review*. The answers for questions 1–3 appear on page 200. The response to number 4 will show you whether your child has learned to forgive as well as be forgiven. When the *Review* is completed, have your child place a sticker on this page.

sticker

Circle the correct answer.

1. In Reconciliation we celebrate that God (forgives, forgets) us.

2. We confess our sins to the (priest, deacon).

3. In the sacrament of Reconciliation, the priest gives us a (medal, penance).

4. How will you show love for those who have hurt you?

Possible responses:

pray for them; treat them fairly; be kind to them.

Encourage the children to gather with their families to share the *Family Scripture Moment*.

Gather and ask: What kind of forgiver am I? **Listen** as Jesus speaks to us about unlimited forgiveness.

Peter came to Jesus and asked, "Lord, if my brother keeps on sinning against me, how many times do I have to forgive him? Seven times?" "No, not seven times," answered Jesus, "but seventy times seven."

Matthew 18:21–22

Share When are some times you find it hard to forgive? Why?

Consider for family enrichment:

- In the Bible, seven is considered the perfect number. Jesus uses "seventy times seven" to mean "always" or "without limit."
- Every Christian family should be a place of reconciliation and forgiveness.

Reflect and **Decide** How can we learn to forgive over and over again? When will we take the opportunity to celebrate the sacrament of Reconciliation?

13 ADVENT

The Theme of This Chapter Corresponds with Paragraph 1171

For the Catechist: Spiritual and Catechetical Development

Our Life

Because this lesson opens with a play about the annunciation, it is an appropriate place to provide clear Church teaching about angels. The angel Gabriel announces to Mary that she is to be the Mother of God. Today, angels are portrayed in myriad places—on television shows, on greeting cards, as cute figurines in shop windows.

Ask yourself:

- What do Catholics really believe about angels?

Sharing Life

Has popular culture misinterpreted angels for you and young people? Have angels become nothing more than cute figurines? Have they lost their relationship to God and become nothing more than commodities to buy and sell like lapel pins or pretty pictures?

Our Catholic Faith

The Advent season begins a new liturgical year for the Church. We prepare to hear again the timeless proclamation of faith that the second Person of the Blessed Trinity took on our human nature. This marvelous reality was first announced to Mary by an angel. What are angels?

The Church's teaching, based on Scripture, is clear. The existence of angels is a truth of our faith. Angels were created by God. In the *Catechism*, 330, we read: "As purely *spiritual* creatures angels have intelligence and will: they are personal and immortal creatures, surpassing in perfection all visible creatures, as the splendor of their glory bears witness." Although angels are frequently portrayed in Scripture as messengers and servants of God, you will find a more complete understanding of angels in the *Catechism*, 328–336 .

Coming to Faith

How might you join with the angels in serving and praising God?

Practicing Faith

How will you say with Mary during this Advent season, "I will do whatever God asks of me"?

Teaching Resources

Teaching Hints

Liturgical seasons like Advent provide many opportunities for children to become involved in religious customs. Let the children make an Advent wreath to keep in the room, and open your class each week with a prayer. Try to deepen the children's sense of expectancy by "counting the days" until we celebrate the wonderful event of Jesus' birth. Help the children to see that every day can be a "Christmas" for us if we invite Jesus to be born into our hearts.

Special-Needs Child

Special-needs children may have difficulty concentrating. Involve them in helping you throughout the lesson.

Visual Needs

- peer helper to assist with writing activity

Auditory Needs

- headphones and tape recording of song

Tactile-Motor Needs

- copy of *Practicing Faith* page taped to desk

Supplemental Resources

Advent Roads (video)
Following Jesus Through the Church Year series
Twenty Third Publications
P.O. Box 180
Mystic, CT 06355
(1-800-321-0411)

The Best Gift of All (book)
by Cornelis Wilkeshuis
St. Paul Books and Media
50 St. Paul's Avenue
Boston, MA 02130
(1-800-876-4463)

Lesson Plan: Beginning

OBJECTIVES

To help the children

- know the meaning of Advent;
- appreciate the importance of preparing to celebrate Christmas;
- choose to prepare well for Christmas.

Focusing Prayer

Introduce the focusing prayer at the top of page 87 by talking with the children about the importance of letting friends know you like them to be with you. Suggest that they pray it in a welcoming spirit.

Our Life

A Play About Mary

Select children for the parts indicated in the Advent play on page 87. Give the children a few minutes to look over their lines while the other children gather in a circle around them. Turn out the lights. Have one child be prepared to turn on the lights at the end of the narrator's introduction. Then have them act out the play simply and all join in on the Hail Mary at the end. You may wish to use the grade 2 *Coming to Jesus in Song* cassette from William H. Sadlier, Inc.

Sharing Life

Focusing on Mary

Have the children study the picture of Mary on page 87. Let them suggest what she might be thinking after the angel left her. Then have them respond to the question in the *Sharing Life* section. Offer some of your own ideas. Explain to the children that God chose Mary for this important role because she always said yes to whatever God asked her to do. Suggest that they each follow Mary's example. Let them respond to the directive at the bottom of the page by suggesting ways they might say yes to God as they wait for Christmas.

13 Advent

Come, Lord Jesus, live in our hearts!

OUR LIFE

An Advent Play

Narrator: In the little town of Nazareth, a young girl named Mary is saying her prayers. Suddenly the room is full of light.

Angel: Hello, Mary, how are you?

Mary: (Frightened) Oh! Who are you?

Angel: I am God's messenger. Do not be afraid, Mary. God is with you. You are full of grace. You will have a child. You will call Him Jesus.

Mary: A child! How can this happen?

Angel: The Holy Spirit will come to you. Your child will be the Son of God.

Mary: I will do whatever God asks of me.

Narrator: And the angel left her. Nine months later, Jesus was born at Bethlehem.

Based on Luke 1:26–38

All: (Say or sing) Hail Mary . . . .

SHARING LIFE

Possible responses:

What do you think Mary will do as she waits for Jesus to be born? pray; share her joy with others; prepare for Jesus' birth

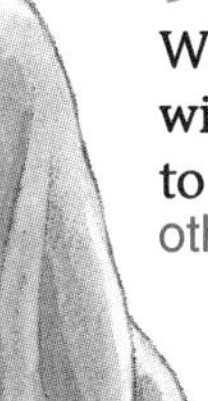

Share together what we might do as we wait for Christmas. pray; be kind to others; etc.

Lesson Plan: Middle

Our Catholic Faith

A Time of Waiting

Give each child a paper circle. Tell the children to pretend their birthday is coming soon. Have them draw a face on the circle, depicting how they would feel as they waited for their birthday to arrive. When they have finished, let them share their drawings and explain why they would feel this way. Explain that waiting can be a happy and exciting experience when we are looking forward to seeing or being with someone we love.

Materials needed: paper circles; pencils or markers

Mary Waits for Jesus

Give the children another paper circle. Tell them to draw a picture on it of how they think Mary felt while she was waiting for Jesus to be born. Then have them share their drawings and explain them.

Materials needed: paper circles; pencils or markers

Advent—Our Time of Waiting

Read aloud the first paragraph on page 88. Emphasize the fact that we prepare to celebrate Jesus' birth, which happened in the past, but we also prepare for the time Jesus will come again, when the world ends. Talk with the children about what a happy time Advent should be for us and for all of Jesus' followers who have been faithful to Him. See the annotation.

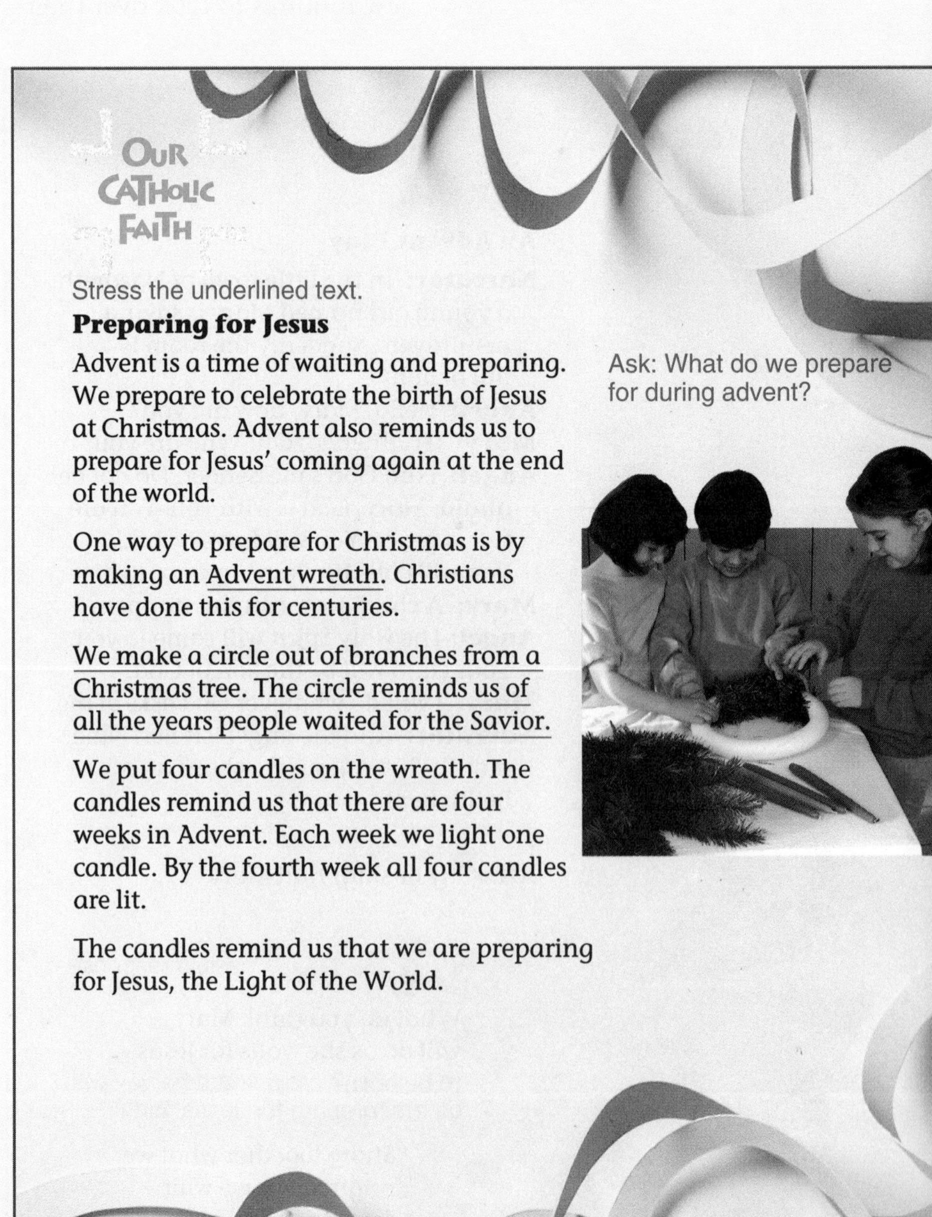

Stress the underlined text.

Preparing for Jesus

Advent is a time of waiting and preparing. We prepare to celebrate the birth of Jesus at Christmas. Advent also reminds us to prepare for Jesus' coming again at the end of the world.

Ask: What do we prepare for during advent?

One way to prepare for Christmas is by making an Advent wreath. Christians have done this for centuries.

We make a circle out of branches from a Christmas tree. The circle reminds us of all the years people waited for the Savior.

We put four candles on the wreath. The candles remind us that there are four weeks in Advent. Each week we light one candle. By the fourth week all four candles are lit.

The candles remind us that we are preparing for Jesus, the Light of the World.

88

Lesson Plan: Middle

Have the children look at the picture on page 88. Let them note the happy expressions on the faces of the children. Ask what is happening in the picture. Let them share any experiences they have had of making or using Advent wreaths. Then read the rest of page 88. You may also wish to use pages 29–30 in the activity book for *Coming to Faith.*

Coming to Faith

Preparing During Advent

Place the following pictures on your desk or on a table in the front of the room: a few pictures of children praying or doing kind deeds; a scene of spring; a Thanksgiving celebration; a picnic; a baseball game (or substitute any other activity that has nothing to do specifically with Jesus); and a picture of the birth of Christ. Turn the pictures upside down. Then read aloud the question in the *Coming to Faith* section.

Invite volunteers to choose one of the pictures and hold it up so the class can see it. Ask the group to respond with a *yes* if the picture answers the question or statement you asked or a *no* if it doesn't.

Faith Summary

Turn to the *Faith Summary* on page 91. Use the annotations to see if the children can express in their own words what they have learned today.

Enrichment

Making an Advent Wreath

Work with the children on making an Advent wreath for the classroom. Use a Styrofoam ring. Entwine branches of pine or some other type of greens around the circle. Attach three purple and one pink candle to the circle by melting some wax, pressing the candles down on it, and letting it dry. Tie a matching bow on each candle, or use white bows for each one. Recall for the children the significance of each thing as you add it. Place the Advent wreath in a prominent place in the room.

You may wish to use pages 23–24 of the *Celebrating Our Seasons and Saints* level 2 book from William H. Sadlier, Inc.

Lesson Plan: End

Practicing Faith

An Advent Prayer Service

Have the children turn to page 90 in their books. Read aloud the directives at the top of the page and give them time to complete them.

Have the children bring their books and gather around the table with the Advent wreath. Pray the Advent wreath prayer together. End with an appropriate hymn.

Evaluating Your Lesson

- Do the children know the meaning of Advent?
- Do they appreciate the importance of preparing for Jesus' coming?
- Have they decided to prepare well?

Enrichment

An Advent Bookmark

Give each child a strip of posterboard about 3″ wide and 8″ long and a small picture of Mary (these may be obtained from religious catalogs or magazines). Ask the children what they think might have been a short prayer that Mary might have said as she waited for Jesus. Write their responses on the chalkboard or a large piece of paper. An example might be: "Jesus, come and live in me." Let the children write one of these neatly on their cards and then decorate them as they wish. Have them write their name on the back of the card. Suggest they use it as a bookmark and a reminder to say the prayer each day during Advent.

Materials needed: posterboard; markers; pictures of Mary; glue

Practicing Faith

Name four things that you will do to help others during Advent. Write them on the candles. Then color the branches of the Advent wreath.

Possible responses:

I will help around the house.

I will be a peacemaker.

I will ask God to bless my family.

I will visit someone who is sick or alone.

† **Advent Wreath Prayer**

God, You gave us Your Son, Jesus, because You love us so much.

Move our hearts to reach out to people around us who are poor, sick, or lonely. Prepare our hearts to welcome Jesus, Your Son. Amen.

Ask: What can we do to help the poor, sick, or lonely?

90

A Liturgy Activity

The presence of angels and other messengers is woven throughout our Advent liturgies, prayers, and songs. Isaiah and John the Baptist urge us to "Make ready the way of the Lord!" The angel Gabriel assures us that the Child to be born of Mary is the "Son of the Most High."

Teach the children an Advent prayer or song in which angels appear. Choices include "Advent Song" by Mary Lu Walker (Paulist Press) and "Mary's Song" by C. Uehlein (Our Sunday Visitor). Invite them to draw or paint the Advent angels.

Materials needed: drawing paper, crayons or markers

A Justice and Peace Activity

When the crowds asked John the Baptist how they were to prepare a way for the Lord, he required them to turn away from their sins, to be baptized, and to "Do those things that will show that you have turned from your sins" (Luke 3:8). He then advised all who had more clothes and food than they absolutely needed to share what they had.

Invite your children and their families to particiate in a "John the Baptist Project." Each person might choose to give one good article of clothing or one delectable holiday treat to an area shelter for homeless families.

Do It Yourself

Use this space to create your own Advent activity.

FAITH ALIVE AT HOME AND IN THE PARISH

In this lesson, the season of Advent was presented as a time of waiting for Jesus' coming both at Christmas and at the end of the world. In our parish Advent liturgies we are invited to recognize the rebirth of Jesus in our lives. We are encouraged to make room for His "comings" by growing in faith and love. By accepting Jesus into our lives and by trying to follow Him in our love and care for others, we prepare for His coming in glory at the end of time. In a sense, our whole Christian life is a time to prepare for the coming of Jesus each day and at the end of our lives.

You might ask yourself:

- *How can I respond better to Jesus as He comes into my daily life?*
- *How can I help my child prepare for Christmas at home and in our parish?*

Symbol of Peace

The lion and lamb together represents peace in our hearts, in our homes and in the world. Discuss this symbol with your child. Meet with your family to plan activities, discuss schedules, and iron out small problems to prepare for a peaceful Christmas.

Faith Summary

- During Advent we prepare to celebrate the birth of Jesus at Christmas.
  What do we prepare for during Advent?
- We prepare also for Jesus' coming again at the end of the world.
  What else do we prepare for during Advent?

Trace this peace placemat.
Put it in the center of your table during Advent.
Pray these words often.

Jesus,
may Your
peace
be in our
hearts
and in our
homes.

Review

Go over the *Faith Summary* together before your child completes the *Review*. The answers to questions 1–3 appear on page 200. The response to number 4 will show ways in which your child plans to get ready spiritually to celebrate Christmas. When the *Review* is completed, have your child place a sticker on this page.

sticker

Color the ○ next to the correct response.

1. Advent comes right before

○ Easter. ● Christmas.

2. We prepare for Jesus' _______ during Advent.

● birthday ○ followers

3. Jesus will come again at the end of the

● world. ○ year.

4. Tell how you will prepare for Christmas.

Possible responses: I will help at home.

I will pray for my family.

Encourage the children to gather with their families to share the *Family Scripture Moment*.

Gather and **Listen** as Jesus gives us an urgent message.

Watch out, because you do not know what day your Lord will come. If the owner of a house knew the time when the thief would come, you can be sure the owner would stay awake and not let the thief break into the house. So then, you also must always be ready, because the Son of Man will come at an hour when you are not expecting Him.

From Matthew 24:42–44

Share What are some ways that Jesus comes to us every day?

Consider for family enrichment:

- This is one of Jesus' teachings about the end of the world and His second coming. Only by living faithfully each day can we prepare for Jesus.
- Advent is the season in which we prepare for Jesus' coming at Christmas and also for His second coming at the end of time.

Reflect Are there ways in which we as a family can be "watchful" for the coming of Jesus?

Decide As a family, choose something to do to prepare for Jesus' coming this Christmas.

CHRISTMAS

The Theme of This Chapter Corresponds with Paragraph 1172

For the Catechist: Spiritual and Catechetical Development

Our Life

It's easy to point an accusing finger at the unconverted Ebenezer Scrooge. But sometimes, without our knowing it, his "Bah! Humbug!" attitude creeps into our hearts. We get so caught up in the pre-Christmas rush and responsibilities that the holy day begins to feel more like a burden than a celebration. We actually hear ourselves saying, "Ohhhhh, I'll be so glad when it's over!"

Ask yourself:

- What things tempt me to say "Bah! Humbug!"?

Sharing Life

What is your vision of how Christmas should be celebrated?

What do you think keeps Christmas from being celebrated this way?

Our Catholic Faith

Just as Jesus' birth in Bethlehem stood in contrast to the expectations of His society, so the manger scene stands in sharp contrast to the opulence with which so many people celebrate Jesus' birth today. But as Archbishop Oscar Romero observed in a Christmas homily, only "those who need someone to come on their behalf" will truly have Emmanuel. There is always room for Him in the hearts of those who have poverty in spirit.

His Spirit today is, as it was in the stable, one of simplicity and peace. We can rediscover it for ourselves by redirecting our expectations and simplifying our celebrations.

Coming to Faith

In what way does your celebration of Christmas reflect Jesus' Spirit of simplicity and peace?

How do you experience your need for Him to come on your behalf?

Practicing Faith

What will you do to help others who have a "Bah! Humbug!" attitude?

How will you help your children to experience Emmanuel's love for them?

Teaching Resources

Teaching Hints

In this lesson, the children will be introduced to the Christian origins of symbols like the Christmas tree, the star, and candles. Involve the children in making cards or other objects with these symbols to reinforce this idea for them. Suggest that they share this knowledge with parents and friends whenever they see these symbols on cards or in store displays during this season.

Special-Needs Child

Place hearing-impaired children where they can easily see you and any illustrations.

Visual Needs

- enlargement of the *Faith Summary*

Auditory Needs

- headphones and tape for song.

Tactile-Motor Needs

- if needed, assistance in being part of the "living Christmas card"

Supplemental Resources

Jesus the Child (video)
God's Story series
The Little Brown Burro (video)
Mass Media Ministries
2116 North Charles Street
Baltimore, Maryland 21218
(1-800-828-8825)

Lesson Plan: Beginning

Objectives

To help the children

- know the story of Jesus' birth;
- appreciate the true meaning of Christmas;
- choose to share the good news of Jesus' birth.

Focusing Prayer

Talk with the children about the importance of sharing happy experiences with others. Then lead them in the prayer at the top of page 93.

Our Life

The Story of Christmas

Have the children gather around a manger scene or a picture of Jesus' birth as you read to them the Christmas story from Luke on page 93. Read the angels' song of joy with great enthusiasm. Then ask the follow-up question and call on several children for responses.

Sharing Life

Using Our Imaginations

Have the children examine the illustration of the shepherds on page 93. Then have them pretend they are one of the shepherds hurrying to see Jesus. Call on as many children as possible to respond to the questions in the *Sharing Life* section. Use the annotation.

14 Christmas

Loving God, thank You for the gift of Jesus, Your Son.

(1) Have the children close their eyes while you read the *Sharing Life* question. Then have them answer each question in turn.

Joseph and Mary traveled from Nazareth to the town of Bethlehem. It was very crowded, and there was no room at the inn. Joseph found a stable where he made a place for Mary to rest in the soft hay.

That night Mary gave birth to Jesus. She wrapped Him in a blanket and made a bed for Him in a manger.

Some shepherds were watching their sheep nearby. Suddenly an angel came to them and said, "Do not be afraid, for I bring you joyful news. This day a Savior is born. You will find Him lying in a manger."

Then the sky was filled with angels singing, "Glory to God in the highest, and peace on earth to all God's friends."

From Luke 2:4–14

What do the angels mean by "peace on earth"?

A world where people love God and love one another.

Sharing Life

Imagine you are one of the shepherds. What do you see? How do you feel? What will you do next? (1)

Lesson Plan: Middle

Our Catholic Faith

Symbols of Jesus

Show the children four Christmas cards, each of which should depict one of the following: the birth of Jesus; a star; a Christmas tree; a candle. Ask them which one they think should remind us of Jesus. Surprise the children by telling them that every one of the cards can remind us of Jesus.

Once you have their curiosity aroused, have them open their books to page 94. Read the page together, and tell them to raise their hands when they find the reason why the cards with the tree, the star, and the candle can remind us of Jesus. Have them underline the sentences that tell why.

Encourage the children to think of this whenever they see these symbols on cards or in Christmas displays.

Studying a Picture

Have the children study the winter scene on pages 94 and 95. Ask if they can find each of the symbols of Jesus in the picture. Ask them how the scene makes them feel. Emphasize again that Christmas is a time of peace and that Jesus came to teach us how to live together in a peaceful, loving way.

You may also wish to use pages 31–32 in the activity book for *Coming to Jesus*.

Stress the underlined text.

We Celebrate Christmas

Each Christmas we celebrate the birth of Jesus. Many families put up a Christmas tree and decorate it.

The Christmas tree reminds us of the new life Jesus gives us. The tree's branches are evergreen. They make us think of Jesus' new life that lasts forever.

Christmas is a time of peace. We put a star on top of the Christmas tree. It reminds us of the star that shone over Bethlehem at the birth of Jesus, the Prince of Peace.

We light candles to remind us of Jesus, who is the Light of the World.

94

Lesson Plan: Middle

Coming to Faith

Teacher for a Day

Prepare slips of paper with a child's name written on each one. Call on someone to choose one of the slips and read out the name. Tell the child whose name is called that he or she is appointed "teacher for a day." Have that child read the questions in the *Coming to Faith* section and have the teacher respond to them. Let the children add anything they wish to the responses or ask other related questions.

Materials needed: slips of paper with each child's name

Faith Summary

Turn to the *Faith Summary* on page 97. Use the annotations to see if the children can express in their own words what they have learned today.

Practicing Faith

A "Living" Christmas Card

Have the children open their books to page 95 and read the directions in the *Practicing Faith* section. Guide them in deciding who will take the different parts in the "living Christmas card."

Enrichment

A Christmas Candle

Distribute a cardboard tube to each child (paper towel or toilet-tissue rolls can be used), or make one out of white posterboard. Let each child cut a flame shape out of yellow or orange paper and attach it to the top of the tube, to make a "candle." Have them print Jesus' name and paste a small picture of Jesus on the tube. Make a stand for the "candle." Small plastic containers from the grocery store can be used for this. Turn back the bottom of the "candle" tube and staple it to the stand. Have them attach a bow to the "candle" or its stand and decorate it with holly leaves cut out of green construction paper. Encourage the children to give this candle as a gift to someone who is sick or homebound, and tell them about why the candle is a symbol of Jesus. Suggest that they pray that Jesus bring light into this person's life.

Materials needed: cardboard tubes or posterboard; small pictures of Jesus; markers; stapler; ribbon; small plastic containers; yellow, orange, and green construction paper; glue

You may wish to use pages 27–28 of the *Celebrating Our Seasons and Saints* level 2 book from William H. Sadlier, Inc.

Lesson Plan: End

Prayer Service

Before conducting the prayer service and the "living Christmas card," be sure to go over the words of the service and the singing of "O Come All Ye Faithful." (You may wish to use the grade 2 *Coming to Jesus in Song* cassette from William H. Sadlier, Inc.)

Read the words of the prayer service and have the children read the "All" parts. Then play "O Come All Ye Faithful" once for the children. Play it a second time and have the children join in singing the hymn.

When you feel the children are prepared, conduct the prayer service. Ask the children to take their places for the "living Christmas card." Have a moment of silence and then begin the prayer service.

Evaluating Your Lesson

- Do the children know the story of Jesus' birth?
- Do they appreciate the true meaning of Christmas?
- Have they decided to share the good news of Jesus' birth?

Enrichment

Making Jesus Symbols

Distribute sheets of green, white, and yellow construction paper. Invite the children to make and cut out each of the three symbols of Jesus mentioned on page 94. Have them print on the back of each one why it is a symbol of Jesus. Then let them decorate the front as they wish.

If you have a tree in the room, attach hooks to the symbols and let the children hang them on the tree. Or tie a length of yarn across the front of the room and hang the symbols from it.

Materials needed: green, yellow, and white construction paper; scissors; yarn; hooks

† **Christmas Prayer Service**

All: (Sing)

♫ O come all ye faithful,
Joyful and triumphant,
O come ye, O come ye to Bethlehem!
Come and behold Him, born the
king of angels.
O come let us adore Him, O come let us
adore Him,
O come let us adore Him, Christ the Lord! ♫

Leader: Jesus came to bring peace. Let us reach out our hands in peace to the whole world! We pray for peace.
All: Jesus, we pray for peace on earth.

Leader: Let us join hands. We pray for peace for all people.
All: Jesus, we pray for peace on earth.

Leader: Let us place our hands on our hearts. May we have peace in our homes, our parish, and our hearts.
All: Jesus, we pray for peace on earth.

Leader: As a sign of our peace, let us shake hands with one another.
All: (Sing "O Come All Ye Faithful.")

Talk to the children about ways they and their families might use the "Faith Alive" pages. Especially encourage them to visit the Christmas crib in their parish church with a family member.

96

A Liturgy Activity

The early Christians adopted the date of the pagan feast that celebrated the rebirth of the sun god for their celebration of Christmas. In this way the Christians celebrated the birth of Jesus Christ, the Son of God, as the true light of the world.

Invite your group to make large cardboard candles, suns, stars, and moons. Mount them on a dark blue fabric. Sing "Infant Jesus, You are our light" to the notes of the musical scale.

Materials needed: construction paper; scissors; dark blue fabric

A Justice and Peace Activity

In his address to teachers on September 12, 1987, in New Orleans, Pope John Paul II said, "Help your students to see themselves as members of the universal church and the world community."

During the Christmas season, have the children in your group send Christmas greetings of peace to world leaders. The children should make their own cards and choose desired recipients from a list of leaders in nations where there is war, conflict, ethnic division, or economic distress.

Materials needed: construction paper; crayons or markers

Do It Yourself

Use this space to create your own celebration of Christmas.

FAITH ALIVE AT HOME AND IN THE PARISH

In this lesson, your child heard again the story of Christmas and thought about God's gift of peace. Christmas can be a time of great stress and "busyness." Jesus wants us to come to the stable—to that place of silence, of prayer, of peace that is the quiet of our own hearts. There we can find Jesus. His Spirit guides us and encourages us to simplify our material needs this Christmas.

You might ask yourself:

- *What distracts my family from peace at Christmas?*
- *How will I help my family celebrate this Christmas in simplicity and peace?*

Learn by heart

Faith Summary

- Jesus was born in a stable in Bethehem.
  Where was Jesus born?
- He came to bring us new life and peace.
  Why did Jesus come to us?

A Special Gift

Here is a Christmas gift tag.
Trace it carefully.
Decorate it and cut it out.

Make a tag for each family member. On each tag, write a "gift" you wish for that person. For example, you could write "peace" or "happiness."

To: ....

From: ....

Review
Go over the *Faith Summary* together before your child completes the *Review*. The answers to questions 1–4 appear on page 200. The response to number 5 will show whether your child is coming to understand the real meaning of Christmas.

When the *Review* is completed, have your child place a sticker on this page.

sticker

Choose the correct answer. Write it on the line.

stable   God   shepherds   Peace

1. We call Jesus the Prince of Peace.

2. Jesus was born in a stable.

3. An angel appeared to some shepherds.

4. The angel said, "Glory to God in the highest."

5. Tell how you will celebrate Christmas with your family and parish.
I will go to Mass; etc.

Encourage the children to gather with their families to share the *Family Scripture Moment*.

Gather and have family members recall ways they have found Jesus at Christmas. **Listen** to God's word.

Jesus was born in the town of Bethlehem in Judea, during the time when Herod was king. Soon afterward, some men who studied the stars came from the East to Jerusalem and asked, "Where is the baby born to be the king of the Jews? We saw His star when it came up in the east, and we have come to worship Him." They went into the house, and when they saw the child with His mother Mary, they knelt down and worshiped Him.
From Matthew 2:1–2, 11

Share What can we do to give honor to Jesus at Christmas?

Consider for family enrichment:

- An important theme in Matthew's Gospel is the Church community. In this infancy story the Magi, who come from outside Judaism, foreshadow the expansion of Jesus' Church throughout all nations.
- The Magi can represent all of us who seek Jesus, "who came as a light to all nations."

Reflect and **Decide** What gifts might Jesus most desire from us, modern-day "magi"? How will we seek Him during the Christmas season in the poor and needy?

SUMMARY 1 • REVIEW

Use the annotations on this page to review the major points of Units 1 and 2.

Our Catholic Faith

God created everyone and everything good. Jesus is God's own Son and one of us. Jesus shows us how to love God, ourselves, and others. God the Holy Spirit is our special Helper. The Holy Spirit came on Pentecost and is with us today.

Ask: Who is Jesus?

Ask: Who is the Holy Spirit?

Ask: What happens at Baptism? at Confirmation?

At Baptism we become members of the Catholic Church. In Confirmation the Holy Spirit comes to us in a special way. We pray and worship together at Mass. Our parish is our special family in the Catholic Church.

The Sacrament of Reconciliation

The Holy Spirit helps us to make good choices. The Ten Commandments show us how to love God, ourselves, and one another. Sin is freely choosing to do what we know to be wrong. We sin when we disobey God's law on purpose.

Ask: What is sin?

The Catholic Church celebrates God's forgiveness in the sacrament of Reconciliation. We examine our conscience to get ready to celebrate this sacrament. We confess our sins to a priest. The priest forgives us in God's name and we are helped to grow in loving God, others, and ourselves.

ACTIVITY: Have the children pantomime one of the parts of celebrating Reconciliation. Write the following terms on index cards: *examine our conscience, sorrow for our sins, confess our sins, penance, Act of Contrition,* and *absolution.* Invite a child to choose a card and pantomime that part of the celebration of Reconciliation for the group. Continue until all the cards are used.

SUMMARY 1 • TEST

Circle the correct answer.

1. Jesus is God's (Father, Son).

2. God the Holy Spirit is our special (Helper, Pastor).

3. I examine my (conscience, penance) to get ready for the sacrament of Reconciliation.

4. God forgives us (sometimes, always) when we are sorry.

5. Tell how you can celebrate the sacrament of Reconciliation.

   Possible responses:

   I can celebrate by myself with the priest.
   I can celebrate with my parish family.

Child's name ______________________________

Your child has just completed Unit 2. Have your child bring this paper to the catechist. It will help you and the catechist know better how to help your child grow in the faith.

____ My child needs help with the part of the Review/Summary I have underlined.
____ My child understands what has been taught in this unit.
____ I would like to speak with you. My phone number is ____________.

(Signature) ______________________________

15

Jesus Gives Us the Mass

For the Catechist: Spiritual and Catechetical Development

Adult Background

Our Life

Kate Wallace was home with the flu. As she sat down at the table alone, nostalgia settled in beside her. "How long has it been since we all had dinner together?" she wondered. Often enough either she or Sam was working late, or one of their teens had a game.

Memories of family meals when the children were younger soon had Kate pining for those lost opportunities to share the day's events and insights.

Ask yourself:

- How would I complete this story?
- How important are meals in my life?

Sharing Life

Why do we sometimes show little respect for food and family meals?

In what ways are meals "sacred events"?

Our Catholic Faith

Jesus showed great respect for meals as occasions for fellowship and as symbols of the heavenly banquet to which all are invited. He recognized that communal meals nourish our bodies and our spirits. The gospels are replete with stories in which Jesus "feeds" His host or hostess by sharing spiritual truths. He taught Simon the Pharisee the true meaning of hospitality (Luke 7:36–47). He invited Himself to supper at the home of Zacchaeus so that the tax collector could be nourished by an experience of repentance (Luke 19:1–10).

Most importantly, Jesus knew the human hunger for God's word and thirst for knowledge of God. He spoke the fullness of His message, "I am the bread of life" (John 6:35). He prepared His disciples to receive the gift of Himself at the Last Supper.

The Mass is a call to gather in Jesus' name, to pray, and to focus on Jesus' presence in our midst. At Mass we openly offer the sacrifice of Jesus Christ and celebrate the Lord's Supper. The whole community of the faithful unites with one another and celebrates His risen presence. The introduction in *The Roman Missal,* tells us:

> In the celebration of the Mass, which perpetuates the sacrifice of the cross, Christ is really present in the assembly itself, which is gathered in His name in the person of the minister, in his word, and indeed substantially and unceasingly under the eucharistic species.

Coming to Faith

What insights into the links between family meals and communal liturgies do you have?

How can you help the children to understand the sacrifice of the Mass as a special community meal?

Practicing Faith

How will you help others to be fed physically and spiritually?

How will you share with your group the delight of celebrating with others and the joy of belonging to a community?

The Theme of This Chapter Corresponds with Paragraph 1323

LITURGICAL RESOURCES

In the beautiful Danish film *Babette's Feast*, the title character is a once-famous French chef who is now anonymously serving an impoverished religious community. The film's main event is a lavish meal at which Babette expends all her lottery winnings and her culinary arts on the aged community members. By her example, she teaches the connections between self-sacrifice and a sacred meal.

Solicit the help of parents in planning a simple meal at which the children can serve at the table. Give the children an opportunity to "wait on" their parents or family members as an act of love. Help them to see that feeding others can be a way of putting the needs of others before our own.

At the end of the meal (which may be as simple as sandwiches, a beverage, and dessert), draw the connection with the Mass as our parish family meal. Recall that the Mass is Jesus' sacrifice to God for us.

JUSTICE AND PEACE RESOURCES

Each time we celebrate the Eucharistic Liturgy we recall Jesus' request at the Last Supper: "Do this in memory of me." We fulfill His request by celebrating the Mass and thanking God for the sacrifice of God's own Son.

Invite the children to work together in small groups, painting or coloring and decorating long paper banners on which "Do this in memory of me" is printed. Alert them to listen for these words as the priest prays over the bread and wine at the Mass.

Then ask each group to suggest one good deed we can do for hungry people "in memory of Jesus." Recall that people hunger for food, for forgiveness, for friendship, and for other basic necessities of life.

Teaching Resources

Overview of the Lesson

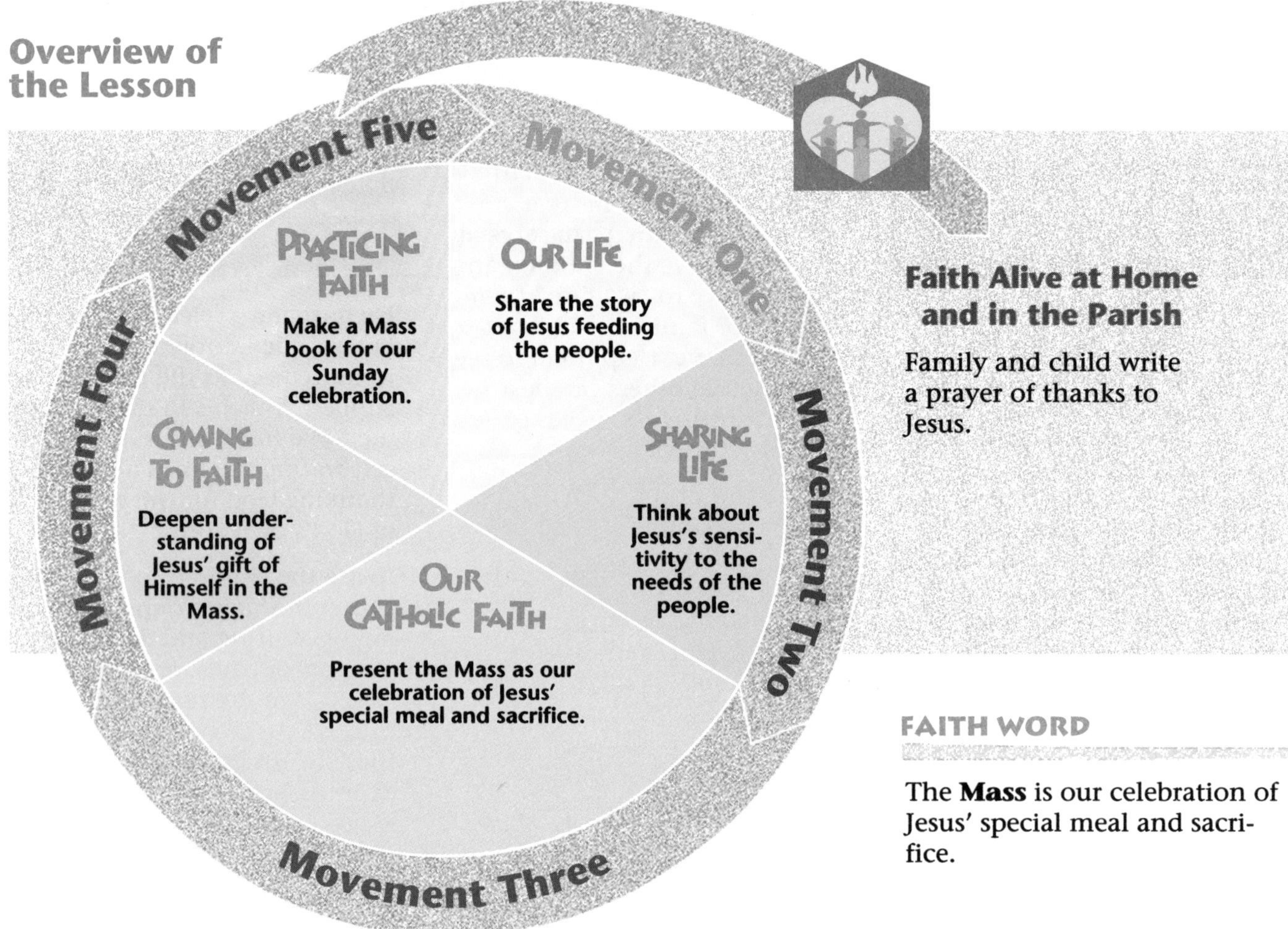

Faith Alive at Home and in the Parish

Family and child write a prayer of thanks to Jesus.

FAITH WORD

The **Mass** is our celebration of Jesus' special meal and sacrifice.

Teaching Hints

In this lesson, the Mass will be introduced through the story of Jesus feeding the people. It is important that the children see the relation of Jesus' feeding of the people to the Mass today. This will help them sense our need to be fed by the Lord so that the Mass becomes much more than an obligation. It is Jesus' gift of Himself in response to our need. Be sure to emphasize that the Mass is both a remembrance and a celebration of Jesus' life, death, and resurrection.

Special-Needs Child

Emphasize visual communication with hearing-impaired children. Increase the amount of visual information through use of pictures and overhead projectors.

Visual Needs

- preferential seating

Auditory Needs

- headphones, tape recording of the Bible reading

Tactile-Motor Needs

- helper to assist with Mass book

Supplemental Resources

Mass for Young Children: Parts I & II (video)
St. Anthony Messenger/
Franciscan Communications
1615 Republic Street
Cincinnati, OH 45210
(1-800-488-0488)
(1-800-989-3600)

Lesson Plan: Beginning

Objectives

To help the children

- know the meaning of the Mass;
- appreciate the gift of the Mass;
- choose to celebrate the Mass with their parish family.

Focusing Prayer

Have the children relate what they already know about the Mass. Then lead them in the prayer at the top of page 101.

Our Life

Listening to a Story

Gather in a circle and introduce the story on page 101 by talking with the children about experiences they have had of traveling and getting hungry. Point out that the people with Jesus were so excited about His message that they even forgot about eating. Read the story with expression, and have the children share what they liked best about it.

Sharing Life

Thinking About Jesus

Have the children examine the picture on page 101. Give them time to comment on it. Then divide them into two groups and have each group respond to one of the questions in the *Sharing Life* section. Help the children appreciate Jesus' sensitivity to the needs of the people.

15 Jesus Gives Us the Mass

Thank You, Jesus, for giving us the Mass.

Our Life

One day a large group of people followed Jesus to listen to Him. Jesus called His friends together and said, "I feel sorry for these people. They have been with me for a long time and have nothing to eat. If I send them home hungry, they will faint."

His friends said, "Where will we find food to feed so many people?"

Jesus saw they had only seven loaves of bread. He took the bread, gave thanks to God, broke the bread and gave it to the people. Everybody ate and there was still some left over!
From Mark 8:1–8

Tell what you like best about this story.

Sharing Life

Possible responses:
(1) Jesus cares for all people.
What does this story teach us about Jesus? (1)
(2) Jesus feeds us in a special way during Mass.
When does Jesus feed us in a special way? (2)

101

Enrichment

A Story "Line"

Discuss the fact that those who came to Jesus that day were ordinary people just like us. Distribute sheets of drawing paper and markers and have each child draw a picture of a girl or boy who might have been in the crowd and give their figures names. Tie a long length of yarn across the chalkboard. Attach a picture of Jesus. Invite the children, one at a time, to tell about the boy or girl they have drawn and how they might have felt being with Jesus. Let the children clip their pictures to the line.

Materials needed: picture of Jesus; yarn; paper; markers

Lesson Plan: Middle

Our Catholic Faith

Thinking About Others

Introduce the story of the Last Supper by discussing the importance of thinking about others. Explain to the children that this is an important sign of growing up. Point out how much Jesus loved His closest friends and followers, the apostles, and that He realized they would need help to go on after He died. Ask the children to suggest some things Jesus might have done to help them.

Listening to a Story

Have the children study the pictures as you read with great expression the story of the Last Supper on page 102. Have the children point to the bread and wine in the picture as you read about them.

Celebrating the Last Supper

Ask the children if they would like to have been there at the Last Supper, when Jesus gave us the loving gift of His Body and Blood. Point out that today we have a way of celebrating the Last Supper. We call it the Mass. Read aloud the last two paragraphs on page 102. Use the annotations. Encourage the children to talk about their experiences of going to Mass.

Our Catholic Identity

Use the *Our Catholic Identity* on page 8 in the back of the book. Prepare a loaf of bread and a goblet of grape juice. Read the prayer: Blessed Be God Forever. With great expression and reverence, demonstrate the gestures of the priest as he prays the blessings at Mass. Have the children respond, "Blessed be God forever," each time.

You may wish to use pages 41–42 in *Celebrating Seasons and Saints,* Level 2.

Faith Word

Display a flash card with the faith word *Mass*. Read with the children the definition given at the top of page 103. Have them

OUR CATHOLIC FAITH

Stress the underlined text.

A Special Meal

Jesus knew that all His friends would need special help to grow in love for God and others. So at the Last Supper Jesus gave us Himself to be our Bread of Life. This is what He did.

During the meal Jesus took the bread and wine that were on the table. He blessed them and gave them to His friends. He told them that the bread and wine were now His Body and Blood. He also told them to celebrate this special meal over and over again in memory of Him.

From Luke 22:14–20

Today our celebration of Jesus' Last Supper is called the Mass. We gather with our parish family every Sunday or Saturday evening to celebrate Jesus' special meal.

Ask: "What happens at Mass?"

At Mass we listen to the word of God together. At Mass the bread and wine become Jesus Himself through the words and actions of the priest. Jesus is with us as our Bread of Life.

102

Lesson Plan: Middle

share their understanding of the word *sacrifice*. Then read aloud the first paragraph on page 103.

Jesus' Gift of His Life

Show a crucifix or picture of the crucifixion to the children as you read the next paragraph on page 103. Use the annotation. Let the children touch the crucifix or picture to help them enter into the feelings of Jesus' great love for us. Explain that Jesus wanted us to remember and celebrate His life, death, and resurrection so that we would never forget His great love for us and that we do this at Mass. Read aloud the last two paragraphs on page 103.

You may also wish to use pages 35–36 in the activity book for *Coming to Jesus*.

FAITH WORD

The **Mass** is our celebration of Jesus' special meal and sacrifice.

A Special Sacrifice

A sacrifice is an offering to God of something important. A sacrifice is a special gift of love.
Ask: "What sacrifice did Jesus offer?"
The day after the Last Supper, Jesus offered a great sacrifice to God. He loved each of us so much that He gave His life for us. Jesus died on the cross. He died to save us from sin and bring us new life. Jesus is our Savior.

At Mass, the priest offers the eucharistic sacrifice in Jesus'name. We remember and celebrate Jesus' life, death, and resurrection. Jesus gives Himself to us in Holy Communion so that we may grow as children of God and become more like Him. Holy Communion helps us to grow in our Catholic faith.

Jesus wants us to celebrate the sacrifice of the Mass with our parish family every Sunday or Saturday evening.

103

Enrichment

Role-Playing

Have the children role-play the Last Supper. Take the part of Jesus yourself, and let one child represent each of the apostles. If there are more than twelve children, have the extras pretend they are the boy or girl they drew, observing what is happening. Ask the children to think of what those present must have been thinking or feeling as they watched Jesus change bread and wine into His Body and Blood. After role-playing this action of Jesus, have the children respond as they think the apostles or an observer might have. End by saying a prayer or singing a song of thanksgiving. (You might like to use *Do This in Remembrance of Me* on Sadlier's grade 2 cassette *Coming to Jesus in Song.*)

Lesson Plan: End

Coming to Faith

Finding the Hidden Word

Have the children fill in the blanks on page 104 to find an important word that tells us the name of our celebration of Jesus' death and resurrection. Then read and complete each sentence with them. If you used the enrichment activity from the preceding section, you may wish to have them recall it as they do the imagining activity. See the annotation.

Faith Summary

Turn to the *Faith Summary* on page 105. Use the annotations to see if the children can express in their own words what they have learned today.

Practicing Faith

Making a Mass Book

Read aloud the directions in the *Practicing Faith* section and have the children make their own Mass book. Review the Mass by going over each page with them. Encourage the children to use these books at Sunday Mass.

Evaluating Your Lesson

- Do the children know the meaning of the Mass?
- Do they appreciate the gift of the Mass?
- Have they decided to celebrate the Mass with their parish family?

Enrichment

A Gift of Love

Recall for the children that in the Mass, Jesus gives us the gift of Himself. Explain that this is the most wonderful gift anyone could receive.

Distribute the materials. Let the children place the picture of Jesus in the box, wrap it, and attach a bow to the top. On the gift card, have them print: To (child's name), from Jesus. Let them take the gift box home to remind them of the wonderful gift of Himself that Jesus gives us in the Mass.

Materials needed: small boxes; pictures of Jesus; bows; wrapping paper; gift tags

Coming to Faith

Use these words to find the hidden word.

Savior gives Bread meal

The Last Supper is Jesus' special m e a l.

Jesus is our B r e a d of Life.

Jesus Christ is our S a v i o r.

At Mass Jesus g i v e s us Himself.

(1) Encourage the children to share their feelings about Jesus' gift of Himself in Holy communion.

Imagine yourself at the Last Supper. What is happening? How do you feel? (1) What do you say to Jesus?

Possible responses: Thank You for Holy communion; thank You for the Mass. I love You.

Practicing Faith

Find pages 181 to 184 in your book. Follow the directions and you will make your own Mass book. After you have put your Mass book together, look through it with your friends. Talk about what each page tells you.

Will you bring your Mass book to Mass this Sunday or Saturday evening?

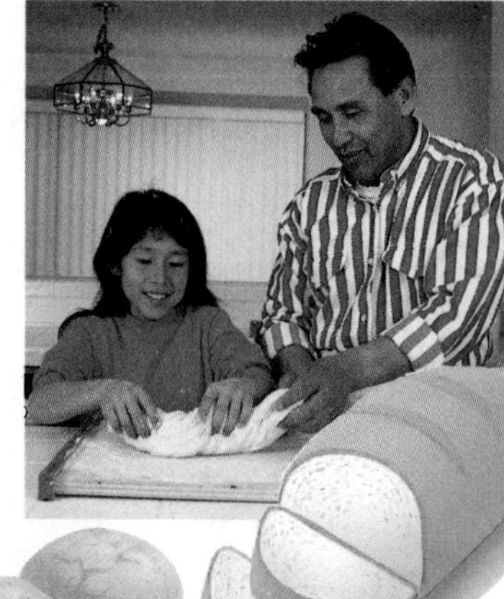

Talk to the children about ways they and their families might use the "Faith Alive" pages. Encourage them to bring their Mass books to Mass this week and to write a thank you prayer on page 105.

104

A Gospel Scene **(for use with page 101)**

Have the children draw slips of paper to see which character they will sketch from the Scripture story (Mark 8:1–8). Distribute paper and let them draw and color a picture of this person and paste it on posterboard. Have them cut it out in outline, leaving two inches at the bottom to fold back. Tape the figures to a large sheet of green posterboard. Add "grass" by cutting squares of green paper into strips and pasting these on the posterboard. Have the children use the display to retell the story.

Materials needed: slips of paper; drawing paper; markers; scissors; tape; green posterboard; green construction paper

A Mitten Puppet Story **(for use with page 102)**

Give each child two sheets of construction paper. Guide them in using their hand, with fingers together and thumb spread wide, to draw a large mitten. Have them cut out the 2 sheets together to make a front and back. Be sure they leave space at the wrist to fit their hand into. Staple around the edges of each mitten. Have them each draw a face on their mittens. Suggest that their puppets are children who lived downstairs in the home where Jesus celebrated the Last Supper with his apostles, and that they were hiding in the room during the meal. Invite volunteers to come forward and let their puppets describe what they saw.

Materials needed: construction paper; stapler; markers; scissors

I Love You This Much! **(for use with page 103)**

Show a crucifix and have the children notice Jesus' arms extended as if to say to us, "See, I love you this much!"

Distribute sheets of aluminum foil 9" x 12". Have them cut or tear it in half lengthwise. Fold each half in three sections to make two long strips. Staple these together to form a cross. Give each child a strip of construction paper the size of the crossbeam. Have them print on it: "I love you (their name) this much!" Tape these to the crossbeams. Attach ribbon to the tops of each cross and hang them as a reminder of Jesus' very great love for each of us.

Materials needed: crucifix; aluminum foil; stapler; construction paper; markers; tape; ribbon; yarn; scissors

"We Are One" Chart **(for use with page 104)**

Talk about the bread and wine Jesus used at the Last Supper, and explain that the bread, made from many grains of wheat, and the wine, made from the juice of many grapes, stand for all of us united together in Jesus.

Distribute small pieces of purple and yellow construction paper. Invite each child to draw and cut out a large grape and a stalk of wheat and to write her or his name on them. Have them take turns taping them to the chart until a bunch of grapes and a sheaf of wheat are formed. Add stems and leaves to the grapes. Print at the top: "We are One in the Eucharist."

Materials needed: construction paper; scissors; tape; markers

FAITH ALIVE AT HOME AND IN THE PARISH

The Mass is the greatest prayer of the Church. Participating regularly in the Mass is a powerful source of our identity as Catholics. In fact, the Church reminds us that it is our "Sunday obligation." Your child has learned that at Mass we remember and celebrate Jesus' life, death, and resurrection. Your child also knows that Jesus gives us Himself in Holy Communion so that we may grow to be more like Him and follow His way.

It is important to help your second grader develop a lifelong love for the Mass. To do this, your family must model an enthusiasm for participating in the Mass every weekend and for receiving Jesus, our Bread of Life, in Holy Communion.

You might ask yourself:

- *How can I help my family appreciate the Mass?*
- *What will I do this week to renew my enthusiasm for participating in the Mass? How will I share it with my family?*

Preparing for Mass

Plan a special family meal with your child. Have your child help you with food preparation. Talk about why sharing meals is important.

Use the Mass book your child made from the back of his or her book to review what happens during Mass. Help your child learn the responses so that he or she may participate more fully at Mass.

As an introduction to the home activity, you might want to make a large basket for your wall. Encourage the children to make up a group prayer to thank Jesus.

On the basket, write your prayer of thanks to Jesus:

Learn by heart Faith Summary

- The Mass is both a meal and a sacrifice.
  What is both a meal and a sacrifice?
- Jesus gives us the gift of Himself in Holy Communion.
  What gift does Jesus give us in Holy Communion?

Review

Go over the *Faith Summary* together before your child completes the *Review.* The answers for questions 1–4 appear on page 200. The response to number 5 will help you see whether your child is becoming more familiar with the celebration of Mass. When the *Review* is completed, have your child place a sticker on this page.

sticker

Choose the correct word.

Bread   died   Christ   Life   Mass

1. Our celebration of Jesus' special meal is called the M<u>ass</u>.

2. At Mass the bread and wine are changed into the Body and Blood of C<u>hrist</u>.

3. Jesus is our B<u>read</u> of L<u>ife</u>.

4. At Mass we remember that Jesus loved us so much that He d<u>ied</u> for each of us.

5. Tell what you will do at Mass this weekend.

Possible responses: I will thank Jesus for dying for us.

Encourage the children to gather with their families to share the *Family Scripture Moment.*

Gather and ask: How can sharing meals be an expression of love? **Listen** as Jesus shares His last meal with His friends.

While they were eating, Jesus took a piece of bread, gave a prayer of thanks, broke it, and gave it to His disciples. "Take and eat," He said, "this is My Body."

Then He took a cup, gave thanks to God, and gave it to them. "Drink it, all of you," He said, "this is My Blood, which seals God's covenant, My Blood poured out for many for the forgiveness of sins."

From Matthew 26:26–28

Share Imagine you are at the Last Supper. What do you hear Jesus saying?

Consider for family enrichment:

- In Matthew's Gospel, Jesus celebrates the Last Supper at a Passover meal. At this meal the offering of His Body and Blood foreshadows His coming passion and death on the cross.
- As Catholics we treasure the real presence of Jesus in the Eucharist.

Reflect and **Decide** What does the Eucharist mean for us as a family? Can we make a family meal a special time for sharing our lives and love?

16 We Prepare for Eucharist

For the Catechist: Spiritual and Catechetical Development

Adult Background

Our Life

Psalm 23, to the Lord our Shepherd, contains the consoling line, "You prepare a banquet for me" (Psalm 23:5). Who among us is not thrilled at the prospect of a bountiful feast being prepared for us? But if we want to be properly "dressed" for the banquet so that we can enjoy it to the fullest, we have to make a few preparations of our own.

Ask yourself:

- What signs has Jesus given me that He is indeed preparing a banquet for me?

Sharing Life

How have I been preparing for the banquet?

In what ways might I be unprepared right now?

Our Catholic Faith

The first Christians called the celebrations of the Eucharist the "Lord's Supper." They gathered in one another's homes to remember what Jesus had said and done, and to do what Jesus had asked them to do in His memory.

Today, the Mass is also a community celebration. Much of what we do during Mass is imbued with meaning that links us with Christian communities of the past and present.

As early as the fourth century, the use of special clothing worn at Mass came into practice. These vestments were adapted from clothing styles of the Roman Empire.

The Roman tunic and mantle gradually developed into the garments that today are known as the *alb* and the *chasuble.* The *stole* is a long band of cloth. It is worn over the left shoulder of the deacon and around the neck of the priest. The *dalmatic* is an elaborate form of the tunic. It is usually worn by the deacon in place of a chasuble.

Since New Testament times, the objects needed for the celebration of the Lord's Supper have become more formalized. The altar symbolizes both the whole Christian assembly and Christ Himself. It is a place of sacrifice, as well as the table at which the Lord's Supper was shared. The cup and plate used to hold the wine and bread became known as the *chalice* and *paten.* Other articles that came to be used at Mass are the large *altar cloth,* a *corporal,* the smaller cloth on which the sacred vessels are placed, and a *purificator* or cloth to clean the chalice. There are also a *crucifix, candles, cruets* to hold the water and wine, and a *ciborium* or container for the hosts.

In the Mass, the past, present, and future become one. We make present the sacrifice and supper of the Lord. We take part in a foretaste of that heavenly liturgy toward which we journey as pilgrims.

Coming to Faith

In what ways are we linked to the Christian communities of the past?

How can understanding the meaning of liturgical symbols and articles enhance your participation in the Mass?

Practicing Faith

How will you prepare for the eucharistic celebration this week?

How will you encourage in your group an appreciation for liturgical vestments and symbols?

GIVE THANKS GIVE THANKS GIVE THANKS GIVE THANKS GIVE THAN GIVE

The Theme of This Chapter Corresponds with Paragraph 1348

LITURGICAL RESOURCES

The Psalms are woven into the fabric of the Church's liturgy, both the Mass and the Prayer of Christians (also known as the Liturgy of the Hours). When we offer these ancient prayers, we echo our Jewish and Christian ancestors in faith.

To help the children in your group prepare for a prayerful celebration of First Eucharist, teach them the following passages from Psalm 23. (After they know the words, add the accompanying movements.)

The Lord is my shepherd;
I have everything I need.
(23:1)
(Extend right arm upward; then cup both hands together.)

You prepare a banquet for me... you welcome me as an honored guest.
(From 23:5)
(Spread both arms wide; then swing right arm forward and take a deep bow.)

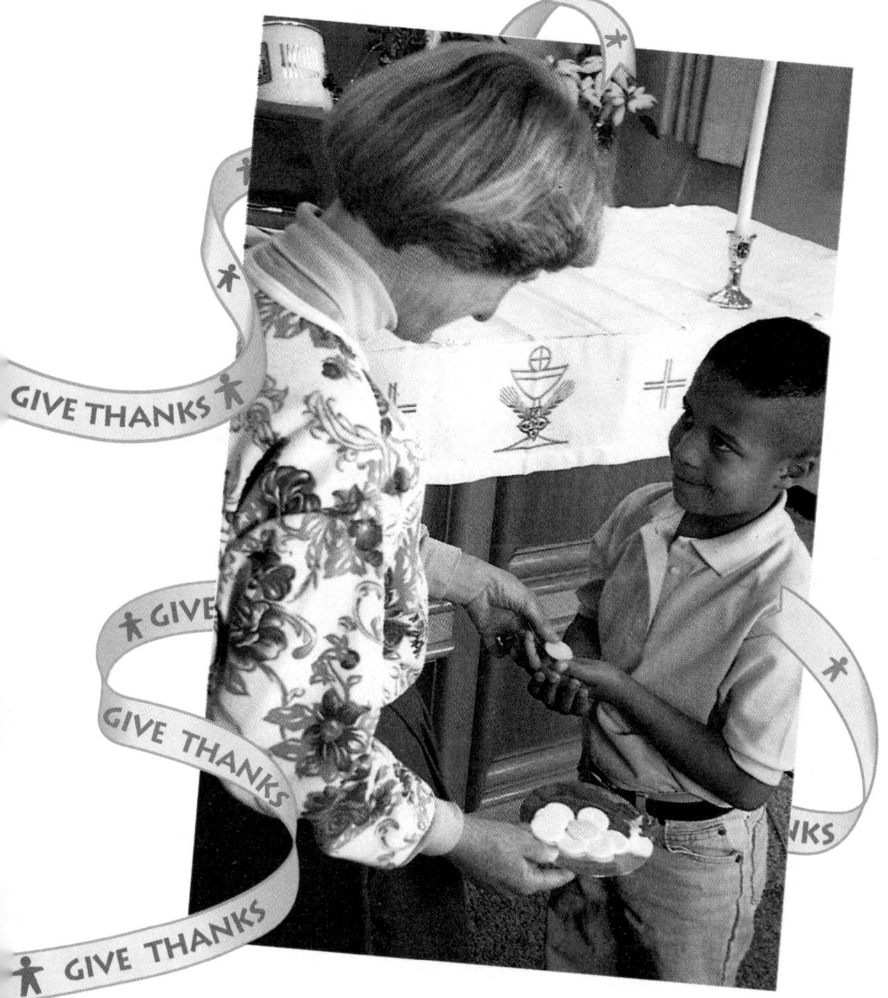

JUSTICE AND PEACE RESOURCES

Explain to your group the symbolism of the colors used during the Church's year. The color white symbolizes joy. Tell the children that when they see the color white, it will remind them that they are to bring God's joy to all people. The color purple symbolizes anticipation during Advent and penance during Lent. When they see the color purple, it should remind them to do or say something to make up for the sad things of the world. The color red is a symbol of the Holy Spirit and the blood of Christ and the martyrs. When they see the color red, it should remind them of the fire of love. Green stands for life and growth. Remind the children, when they see this color, to think about how they are growing in God's life and love.

Ask each child to choose one of these colors and to draw a picture of what that liturgical color reminds them to do. Mount the drawing on a sheet of paper using the color that the student has chosen. Make sure the sheet is larger than the drawing so that the child's work is framed by the liturgical color.

Teaching Resources

Overview of the Lesson

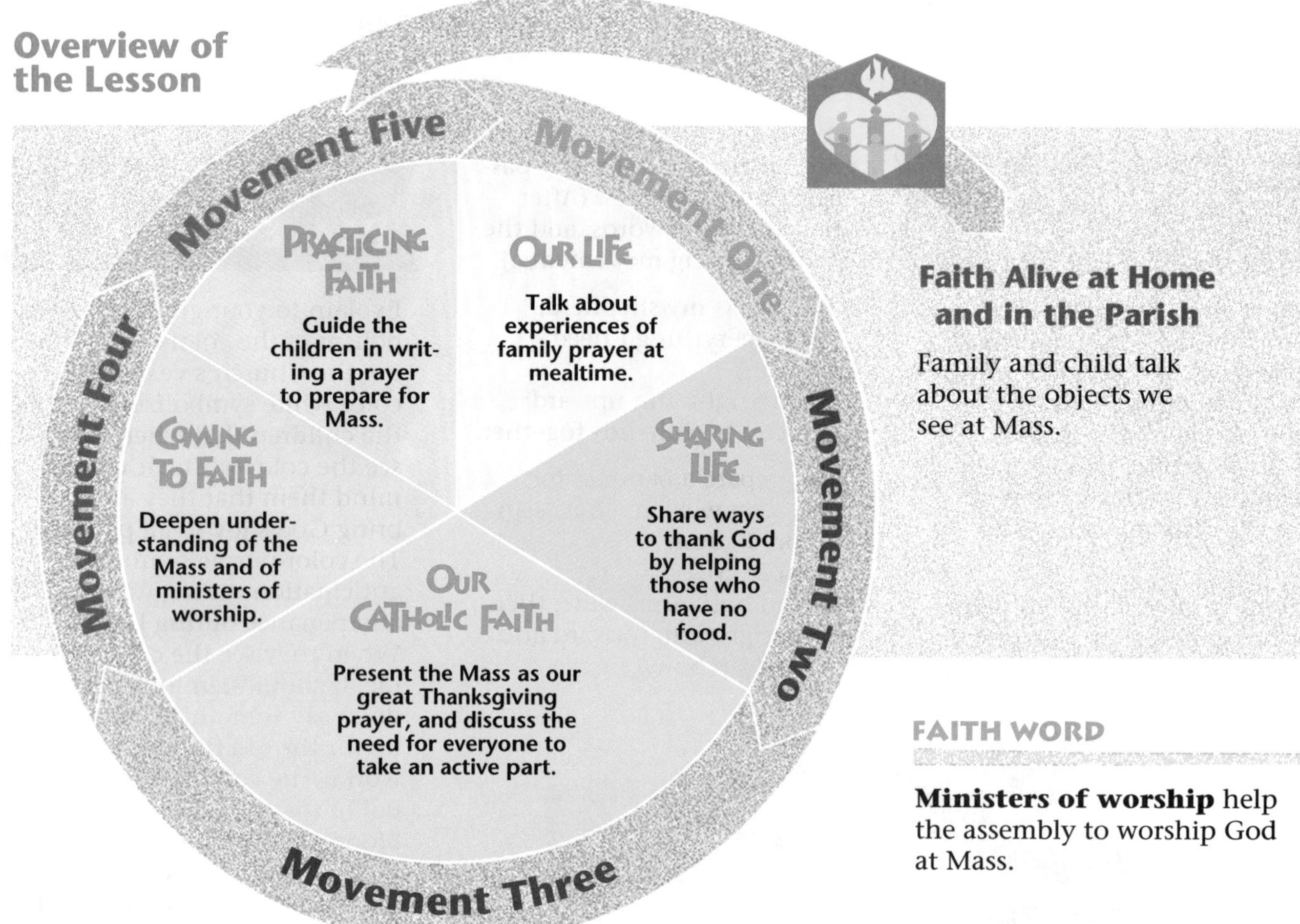

Faith Alive at Home and in the Parish

Family and child talk about the objects we see at Mass.

FAITH WORD

Ministers of worship help the assembly to worship God at Mass.

Teaching Hints

This lesson focuses on the Mass as the great thanksgiving prayer of the Church. It is important to begin developing in the children a sense of need to express their gratitude to God for the many gifts they have received. Help them to see that participating fully in the Mass through prayer and song is one of the best ways they can do this.

Special-Needs Child

A visually-impaired child cannot see a smile of approval. A pat on the arm means the same thing as a smile does to a sighted child.

Visual Needs

- letters for faith words cut from rough fabric

Auditory Needs

- headphones and tape recording of prayer

Tactile-Motor Needs

- copy of prayer taped to desk or table

Supplemental Resources

There's So Much to Do and So Many People (video)
The Marvelous Mystery series
Our Sunday Visitor
200 Noll Plaza
Huntington, IN 46750
(1-800-348-2440)

When I Go to Jesus' House (video)
Brown-ROA
2460 Kerper Blvd.,
P.O. Box 539
Dubuque, IA 52004-0539
(1-800-922-7696)

Lesson Plan: Beginning

OBJECTIVES

To help the children

- know the Mass as a thanksgiving prayer;
- appreciate the importance of worshiping together as family;
- choose to participate fully in the Mass.

Focusing Prayer

Talk with the children about the importance of preparing well for special events. Then lead them in the prayer at the top of page 107.

Our Life

A Thanksgiving Banner

Give the children some time to study the banner pictured on page 107. Have them notice the words and symbols and tell what special day they think is being celebrated. Then read the story aloud. See the annotation. Have the children respond to the follow-up questions and let the children share any prayers they might know.

Sharing Life

Sharing Our Gifts

Have the children look again at the prayer Katie offered. Ask whom she mentions in the prayer that she wants to help. Then ask the question at the bottom of page 107.

16 We Prepare for Eucharist

Jesus, help us prepare to celebrate the Eucharist.

OUR LIFE

Invite the children to imagine they are sitting next to Katie and ask them to pray the prayer silently as you read it.

It was Katie's turn to say grace before meals. As the family held hands she said,

"Oh, God, we want to thank You not
just for our food. We also thank
You for the love in our family
that makes us want to help those
who have no food,
who have no home,
who have no love like ours. Amen."

What did you like best about Katie's prayer?

What prayer would you like to say before a family meal?

(1) Possible responses: by sharing what God has given us; by sharing God's love.

SHARING LIFE

How can you thank God by helping those who have no food? (1)

ENRICHMENT

Hearing Those Who Help

Invite a member of the St. Vincent de Paul Society or some other service group to talk in general to the children about persons in need. Let the children suggest ways they might help: contributing money they have earned; collecting canned goods; and so forth.

Lesson Plan: Middle

Our Catholic Faith

Faith Words

Display flash cards with the words *Eucharist* and *ministers of worship*. Print the words *giving thanks* on the back of the *Eucharist* flash card. Pronounce the terms for the children and ask them to listen for these words as they read the lesson. Wait until they come up in the reading to define them.

Our Thanksgiving Prayer

Recall for the children what they learned in Chapter 6 about the different kinds of prayer we offer to God. If they don't remember these, have them turn back to page 44 in their books and read them together. Explain that there are many ways of saying "thank you" to God (refer again to Katie's prayer), but that the greatest thank-you prayer we have is the Mass.

Have the children read together the first paragraph on page 108. Focus on the Mass as the most special way we have of saying "thank you" for the wonderful gift of Jesus.

The Eucharist

Read aloud the next paragraph on page 108. Direct the children's attention to the flash card that says *Eucharist*. Turn it around and have them read the meaning on the back. Then

Stress the underlined text.

Celebrating Eucharist

The Mass is the great thanksgiving prayer of the Catholic Church. We thank God for His love and blessings. In a special way we thank God for the gift of Jesus, the Son of God.

Our parish celebration of Jesus' special meal, the Mass, is also called the Eucharist. The word *Eucharist* means "giving thanks."

We come together to celebrate the Eucharist. We call all who gather the *assembly*. As God's people we hear the word of God, we pray and sing, and we offer the sacrifice of the Mass together.

Our ordained ministers lead our celebration. They are our bishops, priests, and deacons. They wear special clothes for Mass called vestments.

Lesson Plan: Middle

read aloud the next paragraph on page 108 and have the children note especially the word *assembly*. Tap each child's shoulder and say: "At Mass on Sunday, (child's name) is part of the assembly."

Studying the Pictures

Have the children examine the picture of the entrance procession. Talk about the fact that the Mass, our Catholic family's thanksgiving prayer, is so important that we have special ministers of worship to help us celebrate it. Have the children read both the definition of the faith word at the top of page 109 and the last paragraph on page 108. Ask them to name their parish priest, other parish priests, and any deacons they might know. Write their names on the chalkboard.

Point out the picture of the eucharistic minister. Explain that there are many different ministers of worship who help with the celebration of Mass. Write on the chalkboard or large sheet of paper the names of each one mentioned on page 109 as you read this material to them.

Our Catholic Identity

Use the *Our Catholic Identity* on page 9 in the back of the book. Have the children practice genuflecting. If possible, plan a trip to church so that they can genuflect before the tabernacle. Point out that some people are unable to genuflect and that they are not being disrespectful. Respect is something we feel in our mind and heart and express in many different ways.

You may also wish to use pages 37–38 in the activity book for *Coming to Jesus*.

FAITH WORD

Ministers of worship help the assembly to worship God at Mass.

Other ministers of worship also help us to celebrate Mass. The eucharistic ministers help to give out Holy Communion. The lector reads some of the Bible stories to us.

The song leader leads us in singing. The altar servers help the priest at the altar. The ushers welcome people and collect the money we give to help the needy and to support our parish church.

We get ready for Mass by praying quietly to remember what we are about to celebrate. Then we join together to have a wonderful celebration.

Enrichment

Parish Ministers

Invite some of your parish ministers of worship—eucharistic ministers, lectors, ushers, or musicians—to come and speak to the children about their part in helping us celebrate the Mass.

Lesson Plan: End

Coming to Faith

Recalling the Mass

Ask the opening question in the *Coming to Faith* section, and direct the children's attention to the flash card to respond.

If some of your ministers of worship were present for your group, ask the children to name them and to recall what each one explained about her or his role in the Mass. If the ministers were unable to come, ask the children to name as many as they recall and tell what they have observed these ministers of worship doing at Mass. Then ask the concluding question.

Faith Summary

Turn to the *Faith Summary* on page 111. Use the annotations to see if the children can express in their own words what they have learned today.

Practicing Faith

Writing a Prayer

Explain the prayer activity on page 110. Give the children a few minutes to think of their responses to the question and then have them write out their prayer.

Evaluating Your Lesson

- Do the children know the Mass as a thanksgiving prayer?
- Do they appreciate worshiping together?
- Have they decided to participate fully?

Enrichment

A Thanksgiving List

Recall for the children that the Mass is the great thanksgiving prayer of the Church. Give them a few moments to think about something they would like to thank God for.

Hang a long sheet of drawing paper on the wall. At the top, print the words *We Thank You God, For....* Invite each child to come up and write on the list one thing for which he or she is thankful. Lead the children in a thank-you "litany" by praying the words at the top of the list and using their contributions as a response.

Coming to Faith

What is another name for the Mass? the Eucharist

Name some ministers of worship you have seen at Mass. How do they help us to celebrate together? song leaders help us sing; ushers welcome us; etc.

How can we participate in celebrating the Mass? sing; pray; listen to the readings and the homily; etc.

Practicing Faith

Write a prayer that you and your family can pray together before Mass this weekend.

What would you like to say to God?

____

____

____

110

Talk to the children about ways they and their families might use the "Faith Alive" pages. Suggest that they learn the names of the objects they see at Mass. Pray a favorite prayer as a closing faith response.

A "Thank You" Placemat **(for use with page 107)**

Give each child a sheet of heavy construction paper to use as a placemat. Have stencils available for the letters to spell EUCHARIST and THANK YOU. Have the children trace these letters on sheets of wallpaper, shelving paper, or gift wrap, and cut them out. Guide them in pasting the word *EUCHARIST* on one side of the placemat and *THANK YOU* on the other side. Have them draw a border around each side of the placemat with markers or crayons. They can use these whenever your group has snacks or a party.

Materials needed: construction paper; letter stencils; wallpaper, shelving paper, or gift wrap; markers; scissors

Designing Vestments **(for use with page 108)**

Use the blackline master on page T38 to make copies for each child of the priest's chasuble and stole. Talk to the children about these two vestments and about the different colors used by the Church for each season of the Church year. You may wish to take the children to the sacristy to see some of the vestments worn by the priest. Then have them finish designing the chasuble and stole on the blackline master.

Materials needed: copies of blackline master for each child; markers or crayons

An Appreciation Note **(for use with page 109)**

Give each child a folded sheet of note-size paper. On the chalkboard, list the names of your parish priests, deacons, lectors, eucharistic ministers, and any other ministers who help make the liturgy more meaningful. Let each child choose a name and write a note of appreciation to that minister, thanking him or her for making their eucharistic celebration more beautiful. Encourage them to mention a prayer or act of love that they will say or do for this person to show their gratitude. Have stencils available of a chalice, candle, cross, or church. Have the children use these to decorate the cover of their notes by holding the stencil over the cover and rubbing it with colored chalk or outlining it with markers. They can print a greeting under the symbol.

Materials needed: notepaper; pencils; stencils; colored chalk or markers

A Doorknob Reminder **(for use with page 110)**

Make a copy of the blackline master on page T39 for each child. Have the children cut out the doorknob hanger and glue it to a piece of light cardboard or oaktag cut to the same size. Then invite the children to decorate their hangers as they wish and complete the "promise." Then have the children take their cards home to hang on the doorknob of their bedroom, as a reminder to participate better in the celebration of the Eucharist.

Materials needed: blackline master; light cardboard or oaktag; markers; scissors; glue

FAITH ALIVE AT HOME AND IN THE PARISH

In this lesson your child learned why the Mass is our greatest prayer of thanksgiving. Remind your child that at Mass:

- we praise God;
- we thank God for all His blessings;
- we ask God to bless us;
- we tell God we are sorry for our sins and ask for help to be good disciples of Jesus;
- we hear the word of God;
- Jesus comes to us in Holy Communion.

Our Parish Church

On slips of paper write the names of some objects we see at Mass: for example, altar, cross, candles, lectionary with Bible readings, ambo (lectern). Before Mass, or during a separate church visit, let your child pick a slip of paper and then point to the object in church.

Talk to your child about this picture of the sanctuary. Help your child understand how each thing helps us to celebrate together at Mass.

†Family Prayer

Thank You, Jesus, for giving us the Mass.

Here is a suggestion to introduce the children to the home activity. Invite the children to name and talk about each of the items on this page.

Learn by heart

Faith Summary

- Eucharist means "giving thanks."
  What does Eucharist mean?
- Mass is the great thanksgiving prayer of the Catholic Church.
  What is the great thanksgiving prayer of the Catholic Church?

Circle the things in the picture you do not know and ask about them. Tell about the things you do know.

Review

Go over the *Faith Summary* together before your child completes the *Review.* The answers for questions 1–4 appear on page 200. The response to number 5 will help you see whether your child is beginning to understand the Mass as the great thanksgiving prayer of the Catholic Church. When the *Review* is completed, have your child place a sticker on this page.

sticker

Complete the sentences by using the words below.

thanks worship Mass assembly

1. Ministers of ___worship___ help us to take part in the Mass.

2. The ___Mass___ is our greatest prayer of thanksgiving.

3. Eucharist means giving ___thanks___.

4. The ___assembly___ is all the people gathered for Mass.

5. What will you thank God for at Mass this Sunday?

Possible responses: my family; my friends; etc.

Encourage the children to gather with their families to share the *Family Scripture Moment.*

Gather and **Listen** to the story of Jesus feeding a huge and hungry crowd.

Jesus called His disciples to Him and said, "I feel sorry for these people, because they have been with Me for three days and now have nothing to eat. I don't want to send them away without feeding them, for they might faint on their way home." So Jesus ordered the crowd to sit down on the ground. Then He took seven loaves and a few fish and gave them to the disciples; and the disciples gave them to the people. They all ate and had enough.

From Matthew 15:32, 35–37

Share Imagine you are with Jesus. What do you see Him doing? What does this teach you?

Consider for family enrichment:

- This important miracle story, told in all four gospels, presents Jesus as caring for people's physical hungers as well as their spiritual ones.
- In the Eucharist, Jesus feeds us with His own Body and Blood to sustain us in living the Christian life.

Reflect and **Decide** How does this story challenge us to share with the hungry? Pray the Lord's Prayer together, pausing at "give us this day our daily bread."

17 THE LITURGY OF THE WORD

For the Catechist: Spiritual and Catechetical Development

ADULT BACKGROUND

Our Life

Jesuit retreat master Anthony de Mello enjoys telling the story of a state governor who visited the White House and was astounded at the number of people President Calvin Coolidge could meet with each day. While the governor often had to stay in his office until late at night, the president had concluded all of his meetings by the dinner hour. "Why is that?" asked the governor. "Because you talk," replied Coolidge.

Ask yourself:

- How good a listener am I?
- What makes me think so?

Sharing Life

Why is listening such a crucial skill for the follower of Jesus?

How do I hope to improve this skill?

Our Catholic Faith

From the earliest days of the Church, the reading of Sacred Scripture has been an essential part of the liturgy. It is at the Liturgy of the Word during the celebration of the Eucharist each week that most Catholics have their principal contact with Scripture.

Throughout the liturgical year and within the cycles of the lectionary readings, Catholics hear God's word from most of the books of the Bible. Preeminent in the liturgy is the gospel reading, because the gospels are the heart of Scripture for us. As the Pontifical Biblical Commission points out, "The triple cycle of Sunday readings gives a privileged place to the Gospels, in such a way as to shed light on the mystery of Christ as principle of our salvation" (*The Interpretation of the Bible in the Church*, Origins, January 6, 1994, 522). This is also why we sing a gospel acclamation and stand for the proclamation of the gospel as we come to know the life and teachings of our Savior, Jesus Christ.

Guided by the Holy Spirit, the Church is the authentic interpreter of Sacred Scripture. The Church helps us to deepen our love for and our understanding of the word of God. Through the dedicated work of Scripture scholars, we have come to know so much more of the beauty of the Bible, the richness of its language, how it was handed on orally and in written form, and the early communities that treasured it in their midst. We know better than ever before that the Scriptures faithfully hand on to us the honest truth about Jesus.

As the Pontifical Biblical Commission reminds us, "The church, as the people of God, is aware that it is helped by the Holy Spirit in its understanding and interpretation of Scripture. The first disciples of Jesus knew that they did not have the capacity right away to understand the full reality of what they had received in all its aspects. As they persevered in their life as a community, they experienced an ever-deepening and progressive clarification of the revelation they had received. They recognized in this the influence and the action of 'the Spirit of truth,' which Christ had promised them to guide them to the fullness of the truth (Jn. 16:12–13). Likewise the church today journeys onward, sustained by the promise of Christ: 'The Paraclete, the Holy Spirit, which the Father will send in my name, will teach you all things and will make you recall all that I have said to you' (Jn. 14:26)" (*The Interpretation of the Bible in the Church,* Origins, January 6, 1994, 515).

Coming to Faith

How can you become more familiar with the Bible?

In what ways can you help your group enjoy the Bible and see it as the word of God?

Practicing Faith

How will you show that you have listened to the liturgical readings?

How will you help your group to develop listening skills?

The Theme of This Chapter Corresponds with Paragraph 1349

LITURGICAL RESOURCES

Reading the word of God is a special responsibility. In the pastoral letter on "The Use of Vernacular at Mass," the bishops of the United States remind us:

> All Scripture readings are to be proclamations, not mere recitation. Lectors and priests should approach the public reading of the Bible with full awareness that it is their honored task to render the official proclamation of the revealed Word of God to His assembled holy people. The character of this reading is such that it must convey that special reverence which is due the Sacred Scriptures above all other words.

Invite a lector to share with your group his or her love for this ministry. The lector might describe how he or she prepares to proclaim God's word, and demonstrate by offering a reading to which the children can relate. Examples include: Jonah 3:1–5, 10; 1 Kings 3:5–12, and 2 Corinthians 13:11–13. Discuss how the children can live this word of God.

JUSTICE AND PEACE RESOURCES

In his address to Catholic educators during a papal visit to the United States, Pope John Paul II said:

> Often today Catholic education takes place in changing neighborhoods; it requires respect for cultural diversity, love for those of different ethnic backgrounds, service to those in need, without discrimination. Help your students to see themselves as members of the universal church and the world community. Help them to understand the implications of justice and mercy. Foster in your students a social consciousness which will move them to meet the needs of their neighbors and to discern and seek to remove the sources of injustice in society.

Have the children find out about their ancestry. Display a map of the world in your classroom. Talk about and point out the many places from which their families came. As a group, make and decorate a banner that says, "We are the family of God." Have each child sign his or her name on the banner.

Teaching Resources

Overview of the Lesson

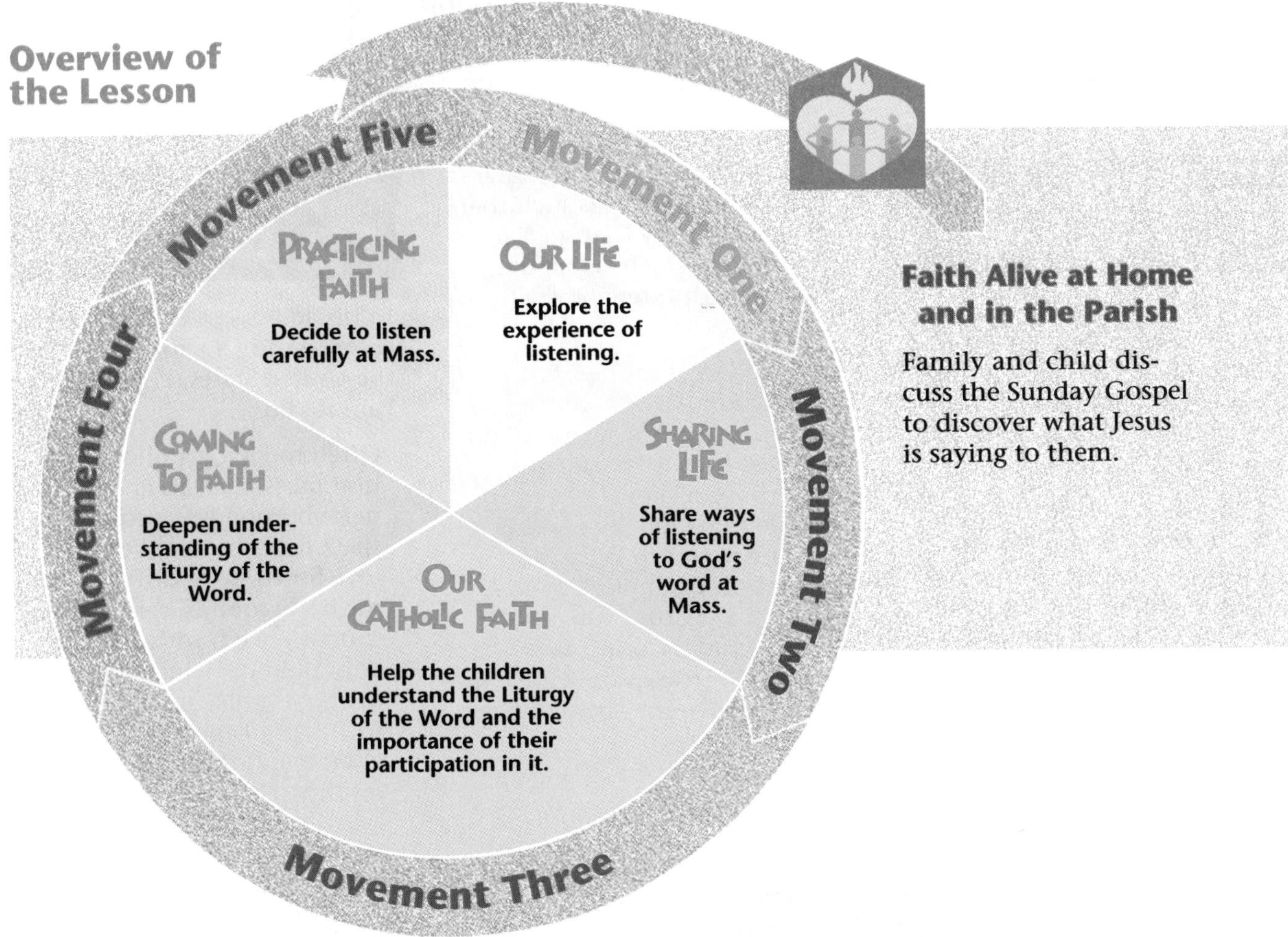

Faith Alive at Home and in the Parish

Family and child discuss the Sunday Gospel to discover what Jesus is saying to them.

Teaching Hints

This lesson focuses on the first part of the Mass: the Liturgy of the Word. Help the children develop a sense of reverence for the word of God, which we hear at Mass. If possible, give them the opportunity of planning and celebrating a simple Liturgy of the Word. Emphasize once more the importance of each person taking an active part in the Mass.

Special-Needs Child

Seat the hearing-impaired child where she/he can see as much of the group as possible. Avoid talking while facing away from the child.

Visual Needs

- child's Mass responses cut from sandpaper

Auditory Needs

- tape recording of child's Mass responses

Tactile-Motor Needs

- copy of prayer taped to desk

Supplemental Resources

Long, Long Ago and There's So Much to Do (video)
The Marvelous Mystery series
Our Sunday Visitor
200 Noll Plaza
Huntington, IN 46750
(1-800-348-2440)

We Listen to God's Word (video)
Brown-ROA
2460 Kerper Blvd.
P.O. Box 539
Dubuque, IA 52004-0539
(1-800-922-7696)

Lesson Plan: Beginning

Objectives

To help the children

- know the Liturgy of the Word;
- appreciate God's speaking to us in the Mass;
- decide to listen and respond to God's word.

Focusing Prayer

Tell the children that today's lesson will be all about listening and that you will question them later to see how well they listened. Then lead them in the prayer at the top of page 113.

Our Life

Stories About Listening

Tell a humorous story about a time when you did not listen carefully and got things mixed up. Encourage the children to share similar experiences.

A Listening Game

Have the children study the illustration on page 113. Divide the children into groups of five and designate a leader for each group. Read aloud the directions for the game. Go to the leader of each group and whisper in her or his ear: "At Mass we listen to the word of God." After the children have passed the message along, have them respond to the follow-up questions.

Sharing Life

An Imaginary Message

Read aloud the directive in the *Sharing Life* section. Suggest some examples of whom the important message might be from: the president, the pope, the principal of their school. Conclude by asking the final question.

17 The Liturgy of the Word

Jesus, speak to us. We will listen.

Our Life

Play this "listening" game. Five children stand in a line. The first child thinks of a message to whisper to the second child. The second whispers the same message to the third, and so on down the line.

The fifth child hears the message and says it out loud. Then the first child says what the first message was.

Did both say exactly the same thing? Use the children's experiences to reinforce good listening skills.

Do you think you are a good listener? Why? Yes, I pay attention; listen carefully; etc.

Sharing Life

Imagine you are going to hear a very important message. Show how you would listen.

How can you listen to God's word at Mass? I will look at the reader and try to think only about what he/she is saying; etc.

113

 Enrichment

Listening to a Poem

Challenge the children by asking them to listen carefully as you read a poem. When you are finished, divide the group into two teams to see which side can answer the most questions. "Trees," by Joyce Kilmer, would be an appropriate verse. Some questions might be: "Does the author like poems or trees better?" "How do you know?" "At whom does the tree look all day?"

Lesson Plan: Middle

Our Catholic Faith

Beginning Our Mass

Read the first paragraph on page 114 with the children. Review the meaning of the assembly and of Baptism. Read aloud the next paragraph and help the children to see that asking God and one another to forgive us is our way of getting ready to celebrate the Mass with the priest.

Continue reading the rest of page 114 and the first two paragraphs on page 115. If possible, show the children the lectionary used at your parish Mass or a Bible. Let the children take turns carrying it as illustrated in the picture on page 115. Explain that it is held reverently and proudly so that all can see it, because the word of God is so special for all of God's family. Ask the children to share any stories from the Bible they remember hearing read in the gospel or discussed in a homily.

We Tell What We Believe

Read aloud the paragraph on page 115. Write the word *Creed* on the chalkboard. Explain that the word means "I believe" and that in this prayer we name all the important things we believe about God. Have the children find in the paragraph the sentence that

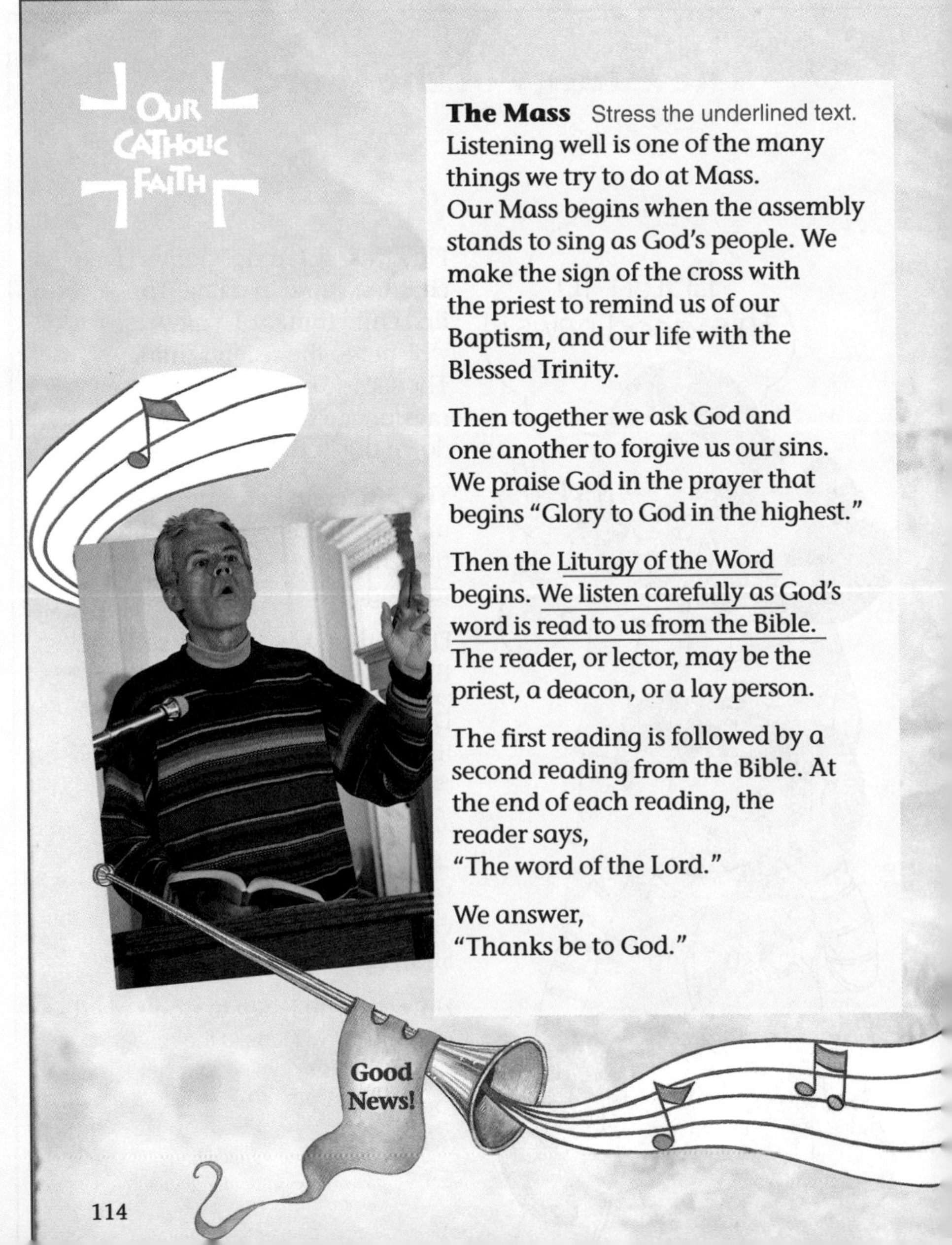

The Mass Stress the underlined text.
Listening well is one of the many things we try to do at Mass.
Our Mass begins when the assembly stands to sing as God's people. We make the sign of the cross with the priest to remind us of our Baptism, and our life with the Blessed Trinity.

Then together we ask God and one another to forgive us our sins. We praise God in the prayer that begins "Glory to God in the highest."

Then the Liturgy of the Word begins. We listen carefully as God's word is read to us from the Bible. The reader, or lector, may be the priest, a deacon, or a lay person.

The first reading is followed by a second reading from the Bible. At the end of each reading, the reader says,
"The word of the Lord."

We answer,
"Thanks be to God."

114

Lesson Plan: Middle

tells something important we believe in, and read it together.

After reading the next paragraph, ask the children to name some persons in need they might like to pray for. Then finish reading the material on page 115.

Identify Ministers of Worship

Recall for the children what they learned the previous week about ministers of worship. Give them time to study the illustrations on pages 114 and 115 to see if they can identify any of these ministers.

You may also wish to use pages 39–40 in the activity book for *Coming to Jesus.*

Then the priest or deacon reads the gospel. The gospel is the good news that Jesus Himself gave us. We listen carefully because we can hear the message of Jesus. At the end of the reading, the priest or deacon says,
"The gospel of the Lord."

We answer,
"Praise to you, Lord Jesus Christ."

Then we listen as the priest or deacon explains the readings from the Bible. This is called the homily, or sermon.

Good News!

Have the children practice their responses to the Liturgy of the Word.

After the homily we stand for the Creed. We say that we believe in God, the Father, the Son, and the Holy Spirit.

After the Creed we say the Prayer of the Faithful. We pray for the pope, our leaders, our country, our family, and all those in need.

The lector reads the prayers aloud. We listen and may respond, "Lord, hear our prayer."

The Prayer of the Faithful ends the Liturgy of the Word.

We listen well to the readings because this will help us to do what God wants.

115

Enrichment

Teacher for a Day

Have prepared flash cards with the following words and phrases: *Sign of the Cross; we ask forgiveness; Glory to God; first reading; second reading; gospel; Creed; homily.* Invite the children to take turns pretending to be a teacher. Have them come up, choose a flash card, and explain its meaning to the group.

Materials needed: flash cards

Lesson Plan: End

Coming to Faith

Making Up a Prayer

On the chalkboard or a large sheet of paper write the words *Liturgy of the Word.* Ask the children to tell what happens in this part of the Mass. Then have them turn to page 116 and complete the activity there. When they have finished, have each child read her or his petition and let the rest of the group respond.

Faith Summary

Turn to the *Faith Summary* on page 117. Use the annotations to see if the children can express in their own words what they have learned today.

Practicing Faith

Being Attentive to God's Word

Discuss with the children how they might be more attentive to God's word at Mass.

Singing a Song

Go over the melody to "Frère Jacques." Then lead the group in singing the song at the bottom of page 116. (You may wish to use the grade 2 *Coming to Faith in Song* cassette.)

Evaluating Your Lesson

- Do the children know the Liturgy of the Word?
- Do they appreciate God's speaking to us at Mass?
- Have they decided to listen and respond to God's Word in their lives?

Enrichment

Role-Playing

Choose children to take the parts of ministers of worship at Mass. Give each one a name card telling which minister of worship he or she represents. Let the remaining children act as the assembly. Choose two easy readings and a gospel. Take the part of the priest, and guide the children in acting out their parts. Have the children sit, stand, and kneel as they would during the Liturgy of the Word.

Looking Ahead

If you wish to use the *Enrichment* activity at the end of the *Our Catholic Faith* section in the next lesson, instruct each child to bring in a shoebox next week.

Coming to Faith

Tell what happens during the Liturgy of the Word.

We listen to God's Word in the readings and in the homily. We pray the Creed and the Prayer of the Faithful.

Make up your own prayer to say at the Prayer of the Faithful. Listen as each reads, "We pray for

Possible responses: __________

family; friends; peace in the world; etc. __________

__________."

Then answer: "Lord, hear our prayer."

Practicing Faith

Decide together how you will listen more carefully at Mass. Then sing this song.
(To the tune of "Frère Jacques")

Possible responses: sit quietly; pay attention to the reader; follow in my Mass book; etc.

We will listen, we will listen
To Your word, to Your word.
Speak, and we will hear You.
Jesus, give us all a
Listening heart,
listening heart.

Talk to the children about ways they and their families might use the "Faith Alive" pages. Pray a family Prayer of the Faithful as a closing faith response.

Who Can Listen Best? (for use with page 113)

Play for the children a tape of sounds, such as a hammer pounding, a bell ringing, a cat meowing, and so forth. Give each child a sheet of paper with drawings representing each of these sounds being made, but placed in random order. Ask the children to listen very quietly as you play the tape, and to number the drawings on the paper in the order that they hear the sounds. When finished, have them compare their responses. Talk with the children about the great importance of listening carefully, especially at special moments like when the word of God is read at Mass.

Materials needed: tape of sounds; cassette player; paper with drawings of sounds

A Ribbon Banner (for use with page 114)

Recall that at Mass the lector ends each scripture reading by saying "The Word of the Lord" to remind us that God speaks to us in the Bible. Have the children make a ribbon banner to attach to your Bible stand or to the wall above it. Use 3 inch-wide ribbon. Have the children use letter patterns to trace "The Word of the Lord" across the ribbon. Then have them color in the letters with gold markers or cover them with glue and sprinkle glitter on them. Have the children carry the banner and the Bible in procession to your prayer corner, ceremoniously place it on a table with candles on either side, and attach the banner. End with a short reading from one of the psalms, and let the children join you in proclaiming: "The word of the Lord."

Materials needed: 3-inch wide ribbon; markers, or glue and glitter; candles

Liturgy of the Word Steps (for use with page 114–115)

On the chalkboard, draw eight ascending steps and tape a sign underneath that says *Liturgy of the Word.* On the chalkboard ledge place, in random order, flashcards reading: SIGN OF THE CROSS; WE ASK FORGIVENESS; WE PRAISE GOD; FIRST READING; GOSPEL; HOMILY; CREED; PRAYER OF THE FAITHFUL. Invite volunteers to come forward, choose a flashcard, and tape it to the chalkboard on a "step," in the order in which it occurs in the Liturgy of the Word. Allow the children to use their books (pages 114–115) for reference. When all the "steps" are completed, read them together with the children.

Materials needed: flashcards; tape

Petition Prayer (for use with page 116)

Provide the children with a variety of pictures illustrating someone or something we might pray for at Mass—for example: a homeless person; someone who is sick; and so forth. Invite the children to choose a picture and to mount it on a sheet of construction paper. Have them write below it a petition beginning with the words: "We pray for. . . ." You may wish to give them a few examples. When finished, invite the children to come to the front of the room, show their pictures, and read the petition. Have the group respond: "Lord, hear our prayer."

Materials needed: pictures; construction paper; glue; pencils

FAITH ALIVE AT HOME AND IN THE PARISH

Your child has learned how important it is to listen carefully to the readings at Mass during the Liturgy of the Word. He or she has been taught to think about what God is saying to each of us in the Bible readings. Through the Bible, we learn how to live as the people of God.

To help your child become more attentive to God's word, discuss the Bible readings after Mass each week. Remind the family members to listen carefully during the Liturgy of the Word to prepare for this discussion.

The *Family Scripture Moment* is another valuable opportunity to share the word of God together as a family.

†Family Prayer

Take time before a meal or before your child goes to bed to pray together with your family. Have your child suggest who and what to pray for. Ask other family members to respond, "Lord, hear our prayer," as in the Prayer of the Faithful at Mass.

Learn by heart

Faith Summary

- In the Liturgy of the Word, we listen to the word of God read from the Bible.
  What do we listen to in the Liturgy of the Word?
- The gospel tells us the good news Jesus gave us.
  What does the gospel tell us?

Here is a suggestion to introduce the home activity. Encourage the children to talk with their families about the gospel reading after Mass on Sunday before doing this activity.

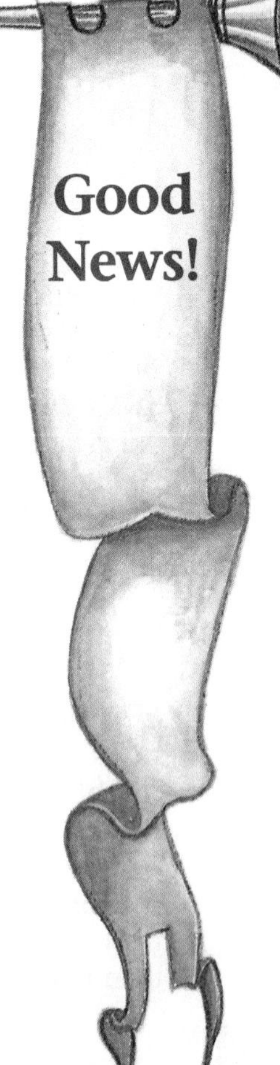

Act out or **draw** what Jesus is saying to you in this Sunday's gospel.

Review

Go over the *Faith Summary* together before your child completes the *Review.* The answers for questions 1–4 appear on page 200. The response to number 5 will help you find out how your child is learning to participate in the Mass. When the *Review* is completed, invite your child to place a sticker on this page.

sticker

Circle the correct answer.

1. One of the readings at Mass is the (gospel, homily).

2. We listen to readings from the Bible in the (Entrance Song, Liturgy of the Word).

3. We show we believe in God—Father, Son, and Holy Spirit—when we pray the (Creed, Our Father).

4. We pray to God for ourselves and others in the Prayer of the (Gospel, Faithful).

5. Tell how you will get ready to take part in the Mass this weekend.

Possible response: I will try to listen carefully to people when they speak to me.

Encourage the children to gather with their families to share the *Family Scripture Moment.*

Gather and ask: How might we be called to share our faith in Jesus? **Listen** as Jesus begins His own preaching.

When Jesus heard that John had been put in prison, He went away to Galilee. This was done to make come true what the prophet Isaiah had said, "Galilee, land of the Gentiles! The people who live in darkness will see a great light." From that time Jesus began to preach His message: "Turn away from your sins, because the kingdom of heaven is near!"

From Matthew 4:12, 14–17

Share what you hear Jesus saying here.

Consider for family enrichment:

- After the death of John the Baptist, Jesus knew that the time had come to begin preaching the kingdom of God, which was already present in Him.
- Notice that from the very beginning of His ministry, Jesus calls us to change our lives.

Reflect and **Decide** How can we as a family prepare to listen well to the readings at Mass? Is there some change we need to make as a family?

THE LITURGY OF THE EUCHARIST

For the Catechist: Spiritual and Catechetical Development

ADULT BACKGROUND

Our Life

In response to a parish survey, many parishioners complained that they did not experience "a sense of community" at St. Joseph's. A member of the parish commission then came up with a bright idea. "Let's sponsor a Heritage Potluck Supper and invite everyone to bring a dish representing their ethnic heritage," she suggested. "They might even choose to wear ethnic costumes or symbols and explain them to others at their table."

That high-voltage idea proved to be a great success. Parishioners brought every dish from polenta to Irish stew, sushi, tamales, and hominy grits. Everyone shared their food and their identity.

Ask yourself:

- If I were a member of St. Joseph's, what would I contribute to the supper?
- Why might I enjoy such a meal?

Sharing Life

How do such suppers create community?

How often do you encourage and participate in parish meals?

Our Catholic Faith

From ancient times, the concept of worship often included an element of offering the best. For example, the Old Testament recounts the gift of firstfruits or of a prized animal being offered to Yahweh. Jesus stressed a different kind of offering of the best to God:

> For this reason, when Christ was about to come into the world, he said to God: "You do not want sacrifices and offerings, but you have prepared a body for me. You are not pleased with animals burned whole on the altar or with sacrifices to take away sins. Then I said, 'Here I am, to do your will, O God, just as it is written of me in the book of the Law.'"
> (From Hebrews 10:5–7)

Jesus offered Himself and through His life and death taught us to offer ourselves. Each of us brings to the Eucharist our gift: the free offering of all that we are.

As ancient people did, we bring our best to God. Of course, our best is not an unblemished offering, but one that is shot through with human limitations and failings. Like the dish we bring to the potluck supper, however, our offering of self is the finest recipe we have to offer at this moment.

Just as the potluck supper is more wonderful than the sum of its parts, so our offerings become far more than the sum of people gathered. Jesus, already present in the community and the word of God, now becomes present in another dimension. Through the power of the Spirit, Jesus becomes the bread that nourishes us. As we offer our gifts to be changed, so now Jesus offers us Himself and empowers us to work for the Kingdom of God: "The Bread that I will give him is my flesh, which I give so that the world might live" (John 6:51).

Coming to Faith

How do you hope to offer the best of yourself to God?

Describe your vision of the eucharistic community.

Practicing Faith

What gift of self will you offer to the eucharistic community?

What gifts of self will you encourage the children to make?

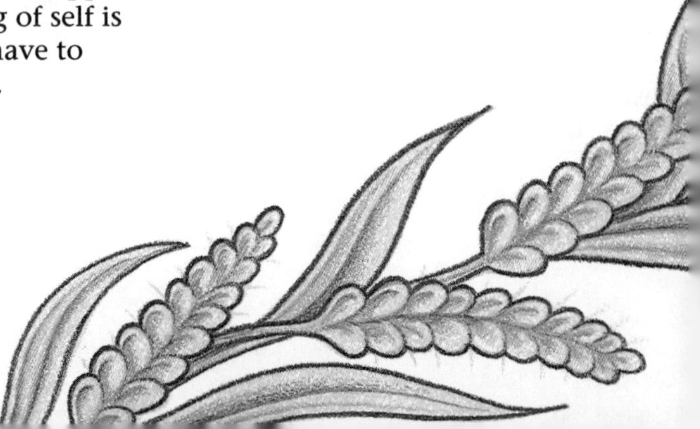

The Theme of This Chapter Corresponds with Paragraph 1352

LITURGICAL RESOURCES

There is an old story about the holy pastor Saint John Vianney, who spent long hours in the confessional of his parish church. Day after day the pastor noticed an aged peasant sitting near the tabernacle. Finally, he asked the peasant what he was doing there. "I look at Him. He looks at me. And we are happy," said the man.

Catholics revere the real presence of Christ in the Blessed Sacrament. The Blessed Sacrament is kept in a tabernacle that is usually placed on a side altar or in a special chapel. Devotion to Christ's presence in the Blessed Sacrament is a special part of many people's spirituality, and the Church continues to encourage us to pray to Jesus in the Blessed Sacrament. Give your group an opportunity to gather in front of the tabernacle and sit quietly for a few minutes.

JUSTICE AND PEACE RESOURCES

In the 1986 pastoral letter *Economic Justice for All*, our bishops remind us, "No one may claim the name Christian and be comfortable in the face of hunger, homelessness, insecurity, and injustice found in this country and the world" (27).

Hold the Bible and tell the story of how Jesus fed the hungry crowd of men, women and children (Matthew 15:32–37). Then ask:

Are there hungry children in the world today? Tell me about them.

How do you think Jesus wants us to help these hungry children?

Plan together one way the children can contribute food, save pennies, or earn money to provide food for poor children in the community or the missions.

Teaching Resources

Overview of the Lesson

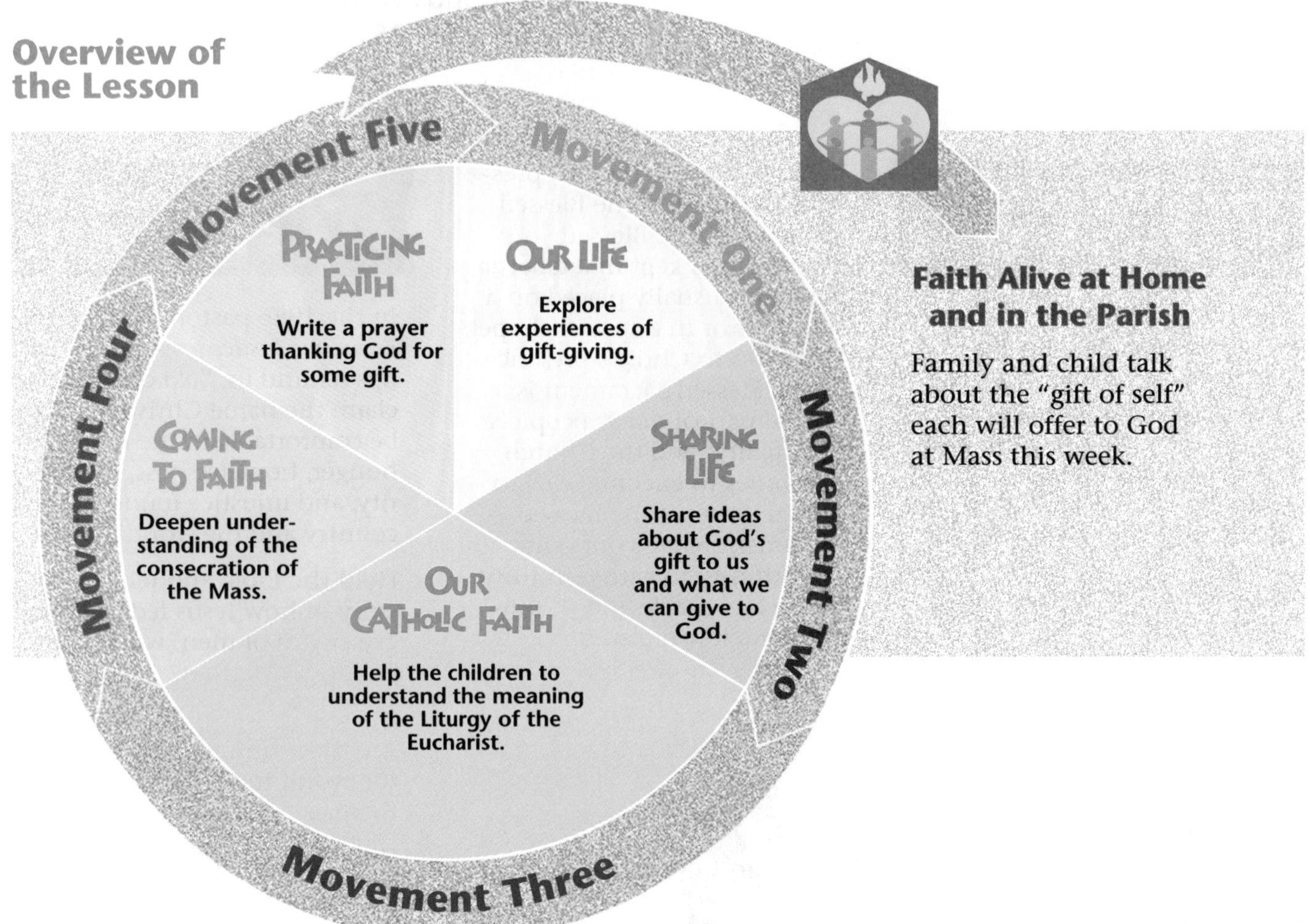

Faith Alive at Home and in the Parish

Family and child talk about the "gift of self" each will offer to God at Mass this week.

Teaching Hints

This lesson will familiarize the children with the prayers and rites of the second part of the Mass. Be sure to emphasize the gift-giving aspect of the Eucharist. Help them to see that the bread and wine are signs of the gift of ourselves to God. Talk with the children about the many grains that make up the bread and the many grapes that make up the wine. In the Eucharist they become one.

Special-Needs Child

The teacher of special-needs children must learn not to overreact to negative behavior but to patiently guide such children toward more socially acceptable behaviors.

Visual Needs

- tape recording of *Faith Summary* and Mass responses

Auditory Needs

- headphones, tape recording of Mass responses

Tactile-Motor Needs

- peer helper to assist with writing a prayer

Supplemental Resources

We Celebrate Jesus Within Our Eucharist (video)
Brown-ROA
2460 Kerper Blvd.,
P.O. Box 539
Dubuque, IA 52004-0539
(1-800-922-7696)

The Little Grain of Wheat (video)
Treehaus Communications Inc.
P.O. Box 249
Loveland, OH 45140-0249
(1-800-638-4287)

Lesson Plan: Beginning

Objectives

To help the children

- know the meaning of the Liturgy of the Eucharist;
- appreciate Jesus' gift of Himself;
- decide to participate actively in the Mass.

Focusing Prayer

Lead the children in saying the prayer at the top of page 119. Have them use gestures like uplifted arms to express their desire to receive Jesus.

Our Life

Studying Pictures

Have the children study the illustrations on page 119 and identify what is happening in each picture. Use the questions in the *Our Life* section to explore their feelings about gifts.

Sharing Life

Making Lists

Ask the children to name some gifts God has given them. List them on a sheet of newsprint. Then have the children respond to the first question in the *Sharing Life* section. Ask the children to close their eyes and to picture in their minds a gift they might offer together in thanksgiving to God. List their responses on the second sheet of newsprint.

Materials needed: two sheets of newsprint; markers

18 The Liturgy of the Eucharist

Jesus, come to us as our Bread of Life.

Our Life

Have you ever made a gift for someone you love? Tell about it. Encourage the children to share their experiences.

Have you ever given up something you wanted so that you could buy a gift for someone you love? Share your story. Yes; saved my allowance; did extra jobs; etc.

How does giving a gift to someone make you feel? Good inside; happy; glad; etc.

How do you feel when you receive a gift from someone else? Excited; happy; want to open it; etc.

Sharing Life

(1) My family; the world; myself; etc.

(1) Name some gifts God has given you. Why do you think God gave them to you? (2)

(2) To show God's love for me; etc.

Can you imagine a gift that all of us could give to God? Let's make a list!

119

Enrichment

A Gift of Love

Ask the children to each think of some person to whom they would like to give a gift of love. Guide the children in cutting red hearts out of construction paper. Suggest that they write the words *I love you* on their hearts, leaving space at the bottom for a name. Have available some small shells, buttons, or beads. Have the children form the person's name with these and paste them on the heart. Suggest that they give it to the person.

Materials needed: construction paper; small shells, buttons, or beads; paste

Lesson Plan: Middle

Our Catholic Faith

Faith Word

Display a flash card with the words *Liturgy of the Eucharist.* Pronounce the words for the children and have them repeat the phrase after you. See if the children recall the meaning of the word *Eucharist.* Ask them to listen for the meaning of *Liturgy of the Eucharist* during the reading.

Materials needed: flash card

Two Parts of the Mass

Draw a line down the middle of the chalkboard, or a large sheet of paper, to make two columns. Write the heading *Liturgy of the Word* over the first column. Help the children recall what happens in this first part of the Mass, and list this on the board. Then write *Liturgy of the Eucharist* over the second column. Ask the children to think about what we might list in this column. Ask them to pay close attention as you read aloud pages 120 and 121 to find out what happens in this part of the Mass.

The Liturgy of the Eucharist

Have available a cup of wine and some hosts for the children to see. Read aloud the first paragraph on page 120. Discuss these gifts as symbols of ourselves.

Materials needed: cup of wine; hosts

Continue reading the next two paragraphs. Use gestures to demonstrate as you read, and have the children join in on all the responses included in quotation marks.

Write the words Eucharistic Prayer on the chalkboard as you begin reading the next paragraph. Show the children that the first word is another form of the word *Eucharist.* Ask them to read the words again, substituting the word that means the same thing as Eucharist.

Doing What Jesus Did

Show a picture of the Last Supper or have the children turn back to the one on pages 102 and 103 in their books. Continue reading aloud the rest of page 120 and the first

Stress the underlined text.

OUR CATHOLIC FAITH

The Liturgy of the Eucharist

The part of the Mass following the Liturgy of the Word is called the Liturgy of the Eucharist. We bring gifts of bread and wine as signs of ourselves. This is our way of saying, "Thank You, God, for all You have given us."

The priest prays and thanks God for His gifts to us. We answer, "Blessed be God forever."

Later the priest raises his arms in prayer. With the priest we give praise to the Father through Jesus Christ. The whole assembly prays, "Holy, holy, holy Lord."

This is the beginning of the Eucharistic Prayer. It is our prayer of praise and thanks for all of God's wonderful gifts.

During this prayer, the priest says and does what Jesus did at the Last Supper.

He takes the bread and says the words of Jesus.

120

Lesson Plan: Middle

three paragraphs on page 121. Ask the children to note the pictures of the priest offering the consecrated bread and wine. Have them compare the pictures. Explain that even though the surroundings are different, the priest is doing the same thing Jesus did at the Last Supper.

Multicultural Awareness

Point out that in the Eucharist we are all united in Christ. We are one family. Emphasize the wonder of this oneness and the respect we should have for one another because of this, regardless of the color of our skin or the country we may be from.

Have the children underline the word *consecration* in their books. Emphasize the fact that even though the bread and wine may look exactly the same after the priest's words, they are different. They have truly become Jesus.

Read aloud the last three paragraphs on page 121 and have the children read the response found in quotation marks.

Our Catholic Identity

The *Our Catholic Identity* on page 10 in the back of the book is a good way to end this session. Use the page as a help to encourage the children to form the habit of speaking quietly to Jesus in their hearts after Communion. Let them share their responses to the question. Ask what they think the children in the picture might be saying to Jesus.

You may also wish to use pages 41–42 in the activity book for *Coming to the Church.*

"Take this, all of you, and eat it: this is my body which will be given up for you."

Then the priest takes the cup of wine and says, "Take this, all of you, and drink from it: this is the cup of my blood."

Through the words of the priest and the power of the Holy Spirit, the bread and wine become Jesus Himself.

This is called the consecration of the Mass. We still see what looks like bread and wine. Our faith tells us they are now the Body and Blood of Christ.

The priest then asks us to proclaim our faith. We can say,
"Christ has died,
Christ is risen,
Christ will come again."

We believe that Jesus Christ is really present with us.

121

Enrichment

Making an Altar

Invite each child to make an altar by standing a shoebox upright on one of its long sides, with the open side to the back. This will form the base of the altar. Place the cover over the other long side of the box to form the tabletop. Tape the two parts together. Give the children gold-colored construction paper. Have them cut out a chalice and paten; give them white paper and have them cut out a circle for a host. Let each one print her or his name on the side of the box. Display these around the room.

Materials needed: shoeboxes; paste or tape; gold-colored and white construction paper; scissors

Lesson Plan: End

Coming to Faith

A Pretend Class

Call on volunteers to pretend they are going to teach others who are not Catholic about the Holy Eucharist. Suggest that they use their "altars" to explain what happens to the bread and wine at Mass. Have the children respond together for the proclamation of the faith.

Faith Summary

Turn to the *Faith Summary* on page 123. Use the annotations to see if the children can express in their own words what they have learned today.

Practicing Faith

A Thanksgiving Prayer

Read aloud the directive in the *Practicing Faith* section and allow time for the children to formulate their responses. Then have them write those responses in their books.

Gather in a circle and let each child say his or her prayer out loud. End with a concluding prayer of thanks.

Evaluating Your Lesson

- Do the children know the meaning of the Liturgy of the Eucharist?
- Do they appreciate Jesus' gift of Himself?
- Have they chosen to take an active part in Mass?

Talk to the children about ways they and their families might use the "Faith Alive" pages. Pray the Mass acclamation on page 121 as a closing faith response.

Enrichment

A Visit to the Sanctuary

Take the children to church and have them gather in the sanctuary around the altar. Invite a priest or deacon to explain the important parts of the Mass to the children. If possible, show them the vestments and sacred vessels used at Mass. Allow them to ask any questions they may have.

Gifts of the Heart (for use with page 119)

Talk with the children about gifts of the heart. Offer examples, such as doing a kind act for someone in need, letting a sister or brother have her or his way when you want yours, being friendly to a lonely classmate. Explain that these are the most precious gifts we can give others.

Have the children work with you to make a "Gifts of the Heart" box. Cover a small box with white paper. Have the children cut out small red hearts. Give each child a slip of paper on which to write one suggestion for a gift of the heart they could give. Have them fold and paste these to the small red hearts and drop them into the box. Suggest that the children pick a heart and offer the gift written on it to someone.

Materials needed: cardboard box; white and red construction paper; scissors; paper; pencils

A Mass Spinner (for use with page 120)

Use the blackline master on page T40 to help the children make Mass spinners. Have the children color the pictures. Then tape two pieces of string firmly to the middle of the circle on each side. Paste one colored picture on a circle of cardboard the same size as the picture. On the reverse side of the cardboard, paste the other picture upside down. Have the children grab the strings firmly and twirl them around until the strings on each side of the circle are twisted together. Then have them slowly let go and release the string. The picture will unwind quickly and it will appear as if the boy and girl are presenting the offertory gifts to the priest.

Materials needed: blackline master; string; cardboard; heavy tape; crayons or markers

A Eucharist Puzzle (for use with page 121)

Use the blackline masters on pages T41 and T42 to make copies of the Eucharist crossword puzzle and the clues. Show the children how to work a crossword. Allow the children to use their books to find the answers. Have the children color the picture in the center and decorate the border of the puzzle.

ANSWERS TO PUZZLE

ACROSS	DOWN
1. bread	1. Body
4. Christ	2. Eucharist
5. words	3. wine
7. Supper	5. with
	6. died

Materials needed: blackline master; crayons or markers

Opposite Color Cutouts (for use with page 122)

Give each child a half-sheet of white and a whole sheet of yellow construction paper. Guide them in tracing and cutting from the white sheet the outline of a chalice and host. Have them paste the half-sheet of white on the right side of the yellow sheet, and the cutout portion on the left so that the left is white on gold, and the right is gold on white. Have the children print BEFORE at the top and BREAD AND WINE at the bottom of the left page, and AFTER at the top and JESUS at the bottom of the right page as a reminder of what happens at the Consecration.

Materials needed: white and yellow construction paper; pencils; scissors; paste

AT HOME AND IN THE PARISH

Your child has learned that during the Liturgy of the Eucharist the priest says and does what Jesus did at the Last Supper. The bread and wine become the Body and Blood of Christ. We call this the *real presence*. Your child also learned that we bring the gift of ourselves when we gather as the eucharistic assembly.

Explain to your child the importance of bringing the gift of oneself to Mass. Talk to your family about the "gift of self" each will offer to God at Mass this week. Encourage each family member to choose one special thing he or she will do.

Make a list of the family choices as a reminder to make the "gift of self" at Mass. Display the list where all can see it. Draw a bow next to each "gift of self" after it is carried out.

†Family Prayer

Pray together one of the responses we make to proclaim the mystery of faith.
Christ has died,
Christ is risen,
Christ will come again.

Learn by heart

Faith Summary

- At Mass we offer gifts of bread and wine to God.
  What gifts do we offer at Mass?
- During the Eucharistic Prayer, our gifts of bread and wine become the Body and Blood of Christ.
  What do our gifts of bread and wine become?

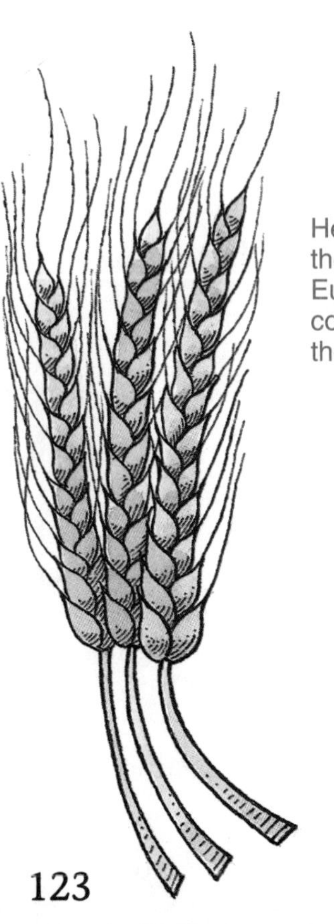

Here is a suggestion to introduce the home activity. Talk with the children about what they might see during the Liturgy of the Eucharist. You might wish to mention the importance of the congregation as well as the importance of the priest offering the Mass.

Draw one thing you see at the Liturgy of the Eucharist.

Review

Go over the *Faith Summary* together before your child completes the *Review.* The answers for questions 1–3 appear on page 200. The response to number 4 will help you find out whether your child is growing in his or her participation in the Mass. When the *Review* is completed, have your child place a sticker on this page.

sticker

Circle the correct answer.

1. The second part of the Mass is the Liturgy of the Eucharist. **(Yes)** No

2. Catholics believe that Jesus is really present in the Eucharist. **(Yes)** No

3. The priest does what Jesus did at the Last Supper. **(Yes)** No

4. Tell one gift you can give to Jesus at Mass.

Possible response: I will do one kind act for someone.

Encourage the children to gather with their families to share the *Family Scripture Moment.*

FAMILY SCRIPTURE MOMENT

Gather and ask: What are some of your thoughts when you see a crucifix? **Listen** as Matthew tells us of Jesus' great sacrifice for us.

They crucified Jesus and then divided His clothes among them by throwing dice. Above His head they put the written notice of the accusation against Him: "This is Jesus, the King of the Jews." Then they crucified two bandits with Jesus, one on His right and the other on His left. Jesus gave a loud cry and breathed His last. Then the Temple curtain was torn in two, and the earth shook. When the soldiers watching Jesus saw what happened, they were terrified and said, "He really was the Son of God! "

From Matthew 27:35, 37–38, 50–51, 54

Share What do you learn about Jesus from this story?

Consider for family enrichment:

- Out of love for us, Jesus offered His life on the cross. We remember His sacrifice to God each time we celebrate the Eucharist.
- At Mass we unite ourselves with Jesus' great act of love. We ask God to make us "a living sacrifice of praise." (Fourth Eucharistic Prayer)

Reflect and **Decide** As a family what gift will we bring to Mass next Sunday?

19 WE ARE SENT TO LOVE AND SERVE

For the Catechist: Spiritual and Catechetical Development

ADULT BACKGROUND

Our Life

People use a variety of expressions when saying goodbye to visitors and guests. An elderly German lady used to say "Come good home." An Irish priest used the expression "Safe home" as visitors left his house. Some visits end with an admonition: "Take care," Be good," or "Drive carefully." Other departures are blessed with the hope of reunion: "Hurry back!", "See you tomorrow," or "Until next time."

On occasion a visit ends tearfully, and the goodbye is a final one, perhaps a silent one. Sometimes visits end abruptly, unexpectedly, and there is no last word of farewell.

Ask yourself:

- What expression of farewell do I usually use?
- What feelings do I try to express by my farewells?

Sharing Life

How do your farewells indicate finality or hope of reunion?

For you, what is the spiritual significance of farewells?

Our Catholic Faith

The final passages of the Gospels indicate Jesus' farewell to His followers. For example, Matthew's Gospel concludes, "Go, then, to all peoples everywhere and make them my disciples: baptize them in the name of the Father, the Son, and the Holy Spirit, and teach them to obey everything I have commanded you. And I will be with you always, to the end of the age" (Matthew 28:19–20). Similar farewells are found in the other three Gospels.

Jesus' farewells contain two common elements: an indication that He would still be present with His followers, and a commissioning of His followers for a task. Clearly, Jesus' goodbyes were not an empty "See you around." His words were filled with the comfort of His continuing presence and the challenge of carrying on His mission.

The farewell at the end of the Mass echoes Jesus' own farewell to His followers. First we receive a blessing and then we are sent: "Go in peace to love and serve the Lord." The comfort of the blessing is ours, that we might share with others as others have shared with us. We pray that we may meet the challenge of proclaiming the good news through our own lives.

When this farewell is voiced, the celebrant might add "And see you next week!" Whether it is articulated or not, this invitation to reunite is always present. To it, the community responds "Thanks be to God!" Those who endeavor to live the gospel values depend on returning to the community for the nourishment and support that only fellow disciples can give.

Coming to Faith

How can you live your mission to love and serve the Lord this week?

How can you support others as they try to "go in peace to love and serve the Lord"?

Practicing Faith

What will you do this week to be a blessing for others?

How will you teach the children in your group to be peacemakers?

The Theme of This Chapter Corresponds with Paragraph 1396

LITURGICAL RESOURCES

In his book *Gratefulness, the Heart of Prayer,* Brother David Steindl-Rast told us to bless whatever there is simply because it is. He believes that that is what we are made for as human beings. The three related activities of thanksgiving, blessing, and praise are all part of our primary vocation to gratefulness, he adds.

We show that we are a eucharistic people when we go forth from the Mass to give thanks for our joys and sorrows, to bless others and be a blessing to them, and to praise God in daily prayer.

Nourish the vocation to gratefulness in the children by teaching them to:

thank God and others every day for the gifts they receive;

say "God bless you" to others in their family, school and parish;

praise God in their own words for the beauties of creation.

JUSTICE AND PEACE RESOURCES

In *The Gospel of Peace and the Danger of War,* (1978) the bishops of the United States remind us:

> The Church must be a prophetic voice for peace. In the tradition of the last three popes the Church in our land must explain the meaning of peace, . . . and stand against those forces and elements which prevent the coming of true peace.

Invite the children to sing (or sing along with a recording) a song of peace, such as the round "Dona Nobis Pacem" ("Give Us Peace"). Invite them to share their hopes and ideas about world peace. Have them draw or paint what they think peace looks like.

Display the peace drawings in the parish or send them to a world leader whose country is now involved in armed conflict. Remind the children to pray for this leader and her or his country every day.

Teaching Resources

Overview of the Lesson

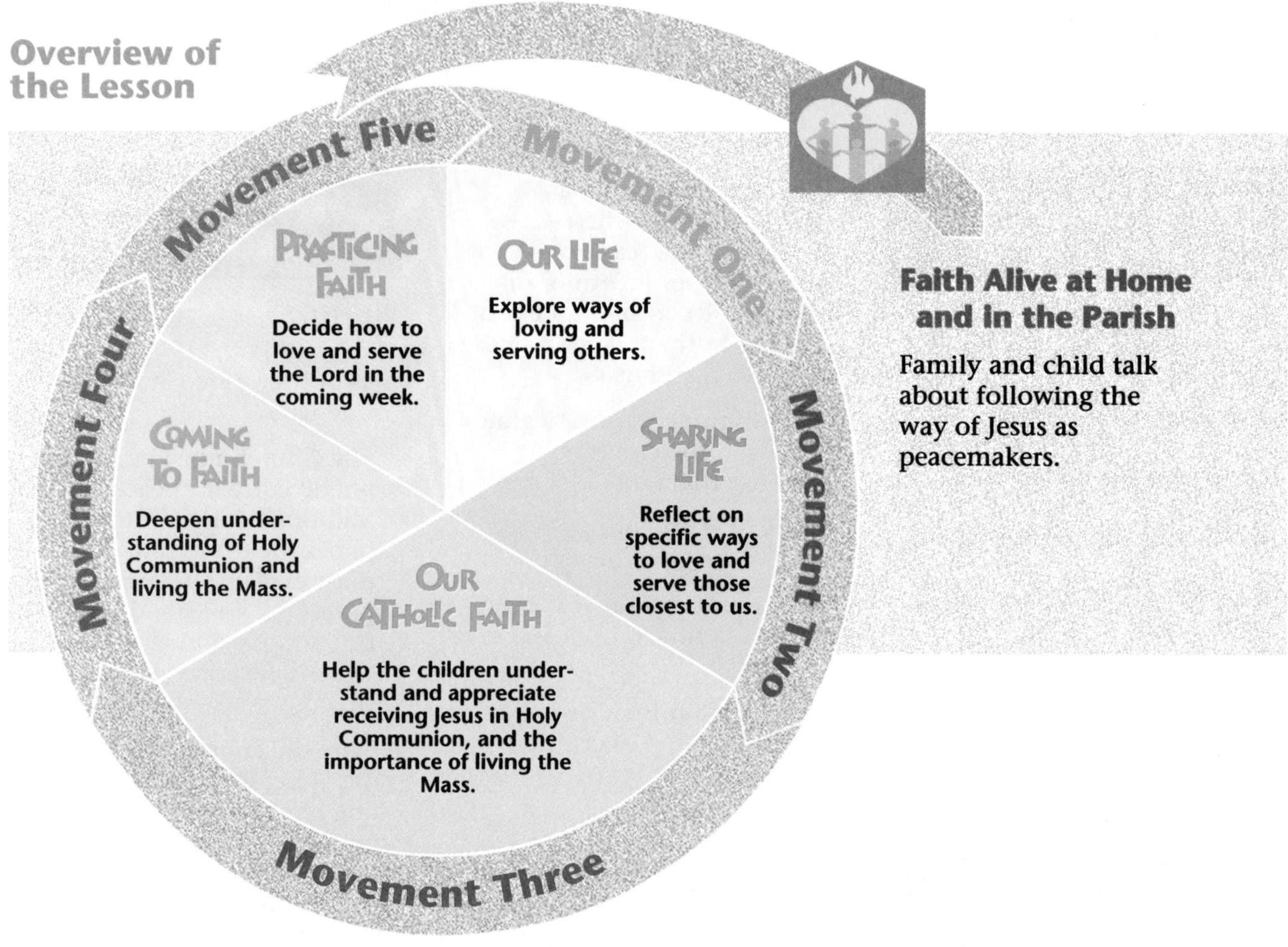

Faith Alive at Home and in the Parish

Family and child talk about following the way of Jesus as peacemakers.

Teaching Hints

This lesson will help the children discover that the Mass continues after they leave church. Encourage them to reflect often during the week on the need to live out the gift of themselves they made at Mass. It might be well to remind them of it just before they leave the classroom and to have them do an examination of conscience at the beginning of their sessions to find out what they have done during the week to live the Mass.

Special-Needs Child

Help visually-impaired children by having them use sandpaper shapes of the Mass responses.

Visual Needs

- an actual paten and host for child to feel

Auditory Needs

- tape recording of Mass responses

Tactile-Motor Needs

- assistance in drawing picture

Supplemental Resources

Jesus Comes to Us (video)
Brown-ROA
2460 Kerper Blvd.,
P.O. Box 539
Dubuque, IA 52004-0539
(1-800-922-7696)

Special Things, Special Seasons, Special Days (video)
Our Sunday Visitor
200 Noll Plaza
Huntington, IN 46750
(1-800-348-2440)

Lesson Plan: Beginning

OBJECTIVES

To help the children

- understand the concluding rites of Mass;
- appreciate their call to live the Eucharist;
- choose to love and serve others.

Focusing Prayer

Talk briefly with the children about the importance of peace in the world. Then lead them in the prayer at the top of page 125.

Our Life

Interpreting Pictures

Give the children a few minutes to examine the pictures on page 125. Invite them to respond to the first directive in the *Our Life* section. Then use the questions to guide them in their interpretation of the pictures. Give each child an opportunity to respond to the last directive.

Sharing Life

Drawing Pictures of Service

Distribute a sheet of drawing paper and crayons or markers to each child. Have them reflect quietly on the question and the thinking activity in the *Sharing Life* section. Invite them to respond by drawing a picture of something they can do to love and serve one of the groups mentioned. Let them share their drawings.

Materials needed: drawing paper; crayons or markers

19 We Are Sent to Love and Serve

Dear Jesus, let peace begin with us.

(2) Helping a younger person; feeding the hungry; helping an older person; etc.

OUR LIFE

Tell what the people in each picture are doing.
Helping others

(1) How are they showing their love for God? How are they serving others? (2)
(1) By helping others

Name one way you can show that you love God by serving others.
Possible responses: being a good friend; cheering up a sick person; collecting food for the hungry

SHARING LIFE

How does Jesus want us to serve others? Help at home; help a younger brother or sister; etc.

Close your eyes. Think quietly of ways you can love and serve some of these people:

- your family
- your friends
- your parish.

Now let us share our ideas.

ENRICHMENT

Interviewing for Service

Have each child choose a partner. Let the pairs take turns pretending they are interviewing each other in order to write an article on helping one another. Suggest some questions they might ask, such as: "Why do you think we should serve one another?" "What are some ways you can serve others at home? at school? your friends?" Call on a few volunteers to do their interview before the group, and let the others share their responses.

Lesson Plan: Middle

Our Catholic Faith

Faith Word

Write the faith word *Holy Communion* on the chalkboard or a large piece of paper. Tell the children that they will learn more about what this means in today's lesson. Ask them to listen for these words and try to learn their meaning as you read the material together.

Focus on Receiving Communion

Recall briefly for the children the parts of the Mass they have already learned. Have them turn to page 126 and listen carefully as you read aloud the first two paragraphs. Then ask them to name some of the more important words they heard read. List these on the chalkboard for later reference.

Continue reading aloud the rest of page 126. Have the children respond with *Amen* each time the words *we answer* are read.

Have the children read together with you again the first sentence in the last paragraph on page 126. Explain that the word *Communion* means "to be united with," and we call it *Holy Communion* because it is Jesus, the Son of God, with whom we are united, as well as with one another. Try to arouse a sense of appreciation in the children by your own excitement in speaking about Holy Communion.

Multicultural Awareness

Help the children understand that Jesus gave us Himself in Holy Communion because He wants us all to be united with one another no matter what color our skin, what country we or our parents are from, or whether we are men or women, adults or children. At the Last Supper Jesus prayed that we all be one in Him, just as He is one with His Father in heaven.

Our Catholic Identity

At this point, turn to the *Our Catholic Identity* on page 11 in the back of the book. After reading the title, *Lamb of God*, ask the children whether they have ever heard these words. See whether they recognize them as part of the Lamb of God prayer in the Mass. Recall for the children that John the Baptist was a cousin of Jesus and that he had tried to prepare people for Jesus' coming. He spoke these words to some of His followers.

Stress the underlined text.

Our Catholic Faith

Holy Communion

At Mass we receive Jesus in Holy Communion. Jesus, our Bread of Life, helps us love and serve others. We begin Communion time by praying the Our Father. We ask that we may be forgiven, just as we forgive others.

Then the priest prays that Jesus Christ will give us peace. We share a sign of peace with the people around us.

Those who are ready go to receive Jesus in Holy Communion.

We may receive in the hand or on the tongue. We hear,
"The body of Christ."
We answer, "Amen."

We may also receive from the cup.
We hear, "The blood of Christ."
We answer, "Amen,"
and drink from the cup.

Through Holy Communion we are united with Jesus and one another. After Communion there is a quiet time. We can talk to Jesus, who is with us in a special way.

126

Lesson Plan: Middle

Learning How to Receive

Obtain some unconsecrated hosts and a cup of grape juice. Be sure the children understand that they have not yet been blessed by the priest and changed into Jesus. Use the pictures in the book to help demonstrate the proper way to receive the host in the hand or on the tongue and how to receive from the chalice.

Go back to the list of important words you wrote down earlier in the lesson. Discuss these with the children and be sure they understand the meaning of each and why it is important.

The Mass Ends and Continues

Ask the children if they ever heard of something ending and beginning at the same time. Tell them that there is a way in which we can say this about the Mass. Ask them to listen carefully as you read page 127 to see if they can find out what this way is.

Read aloud the second and third paragraphs again. Talk to the children about the importance of carrying the Mass into their everyday lives.

You may also wish to use pages 43–44 in the activity book for *Coming to Jesus*.

Have the children practice their responses.

As the Mass ends, we hear the priest ask God to bless us.

We make the sign of the cross while the priest says,
"May almighty God bless you,
the Father, and the Son,†
and the Holy Spirit."

We answer, "Amen."

We then hear the priest or deacon say, "Go in peace to love and serve the Lord."
We answer,
"Thanks be to God."

By these words we know that the Mass is ended.

We also know that saying "thank You" to God does not end with the Mass. Each day we must find ways to love and serve others.

After Mass Jesus wants us to bring His peace to others in our family, parish, school, neighborhood.

127

Enrichment

A Before-and-After Chart

Distribute a sheet of drawing paper, a marker, and some gold and white paper to each child. Guide them in making charts to illustrate the changing of the bread and wine into Jesus. Have them draw a line down the middle of the paper on each side. On one side, let them draw a host and a chalice with the marker and write the words *bread* and *wine* under the drawings. On the other side, let them cut out a host from the white paper and a chalice from the gold paper. Have them print "Jesus" across the bottom. When they are finished, call on volunteers to use their drawings to explain what happens to the bread and wine and how it happens.

Materials needed: drawing paper; white and gold paper; markers; scissors

Lesson Plan: End

Coming to Faith

Recalling What We Learned

Have the children respond to the first directive in the *Coming to Faith* section. Then ask the question and give each child an opportunity to contribute an answer. Act out the part of the priest saying the words of dismissal, and then have the children explain the meaning.

Faith Summary

Turn to the *Faith Summary* on page 129. Use the annotations to see if the children can express in their own words what they have learned today.

Practicing Faith

Drawing Our Response

Have the children note the words of the children in the illustration on page 128. Give them a few minutes to decide what they will do to love and serve the Lord in the coming week. Then give each child some colored pencils to draw themselves into the picture and write their response. Conclude with the suggested activity.

Evaluating Your Lesson

- Do the children understand the concluding rites of the Mass?
- Do they appreciate their call to live the Mass?
- Have they decided to love and serve others?

Enrichment

Writing a Letter

Give each child a sheet of writing paper, a pencil, and some markers. Invite them to write a letter to Jesus to thank Him for the gift of Holy Communion. Suggest that they tell Jesus in the letter what they will do to show how grateful they are. Let them decorate their letters. Suggest that they share the letters with their parents.

Materials needed: pencils; markers; writing paper

Coming to Faith

Possible Responses:

Share why we want Jesus to come to us in Holy Communion.
To become united with Jesus and one another

What can we say to Jesus after receiving Holy Communion?
Thank You, Jesus, for coming to me

Tell in your own words the meaning of the last prayer at Mass, "Go in peace to love and serve the Lord." We must bring peace to others as Jesus did; etc.

Practicing Faith

Decide what you will do to love and serve the Lord this week. Put yourself and your idea in the picture.
Accept all reasonable responses.

Gather in a circle. Take turns sharing what you have decided to do.

After each one speaks, everyone says, "Go in peace to love and serve the Lord."

Talk to the children about ways they and their families might use the "Faith Alive" pages. Encourage them especially to do the peacemaker activity with a family member. Then pray the prayer for peace as a closing faith response.

Promise Notes (for use with page 125)

Give each child three standard index cards. Have them look in the *Sharing Life* section on page 125 in their books, and note the three groups of persons Jesus wants them to serve. Ask them to write and sign a "promise note" to a person in each of these groups, telling one way they will serve them in the coming week. Have them decorate the cards using stickers or flowers cut from greeting cards. Have them present these to the persons they chose.

Materials needed: index cards; pencils; scissors; paste; stickers or flowers cut from greeting cards

A Communion Banner (for use with page 126)

Have the children work together to make a large banner to display as they prepare for receiving Jesus in the Eucharist. Use burlap, felt, or some other heavy fabric for the background. Tape a large, attractive picture of Jesus in the center. Have the children cut out large letters that read: THE BODY OF CHRIST. AMEN.; THE BLOOD OF CHRIST. AMEN. Have them decorate the letters. At the top left-hand corner of the banner, tape a ciborium with hosts showing, made from gold and white paper. At the bottom left-hand corner, tape a chalice cut from gold paper. Then invite the children to come up and attach their letters to the banner with tape. Have them place the words THE BODY OF CHRIST. AMEN. next to the ciborium and THE BLOOD OF CHRIST. AMEN. next to the chalice. Use this banner from time to time to review with the children the procedure for receiving communion.

Materials needed: burlap, felt, or other heavy fabric; picture of Jesus; gold and white paper; tape; scissors

A "Helping at Home" Calendar (for use with page 127)

Distribute copies of the current calendar month. Have the children locate today's date and ask them to write near it one way they will bring peace to their family during the coming week. Suggest that they fill in some service for each week. Have the children each bring their calendar home and hang it in his or her room as a reminder of ways they can prepare to receive Jesus into their hearts.

Materials needed: copies of current calendar month; pencils

A First Communion Diary (for use with page 128)

Give each child two sheets of 8 1/2" x 11" colored paper, folded and stapled to make a small booklet. Talk to the children about how people write their most personal thoughts and feelings in a diary. Explain that this will be a one-day diary in which they can write their thoughts and feelings about their First Communion day. Suggest that they address their words to "Dear Jesus" instead of "Dear Diary." Have several small pictures of Jesus available that they can paste on the cover of their diary, or have them draw a host and chalice. Have them print on the cover: "My First Communion Diary" and decorate it.

Materials needed: colored paper; stapler; small pictures of Jesus; paste; markers

FAITH ALIVE AT HOME AND IN THE PARISH

Your child has learned that at Mass we are sent forth to be people of justice and peace, people who love and serve others. In this way we truly live the Eucharist which we have celebrated. Talk to your child about the fact that receiving Holy Communion helps us to follow the way of Jesus. Use the chart below to help your family to be Jesus' peacemakers.

Learn by heart

Faith Summary

- We receive Jesus Christ, our Bread of Life, in Holy Communion.
  Whom do we receive in Holy Communion?
- After Mass we continue to love and serve God and one another.
  What do we do after Mass?

Remember and Pray

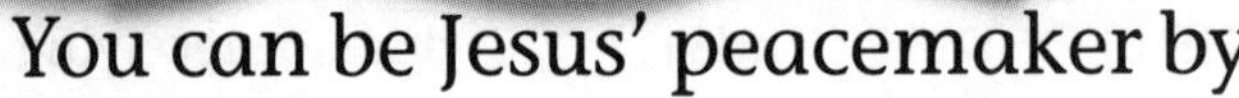

You can be Jesus' peacemaker by

- being the first to say "I am sorry" when there is a fight.
- not arguing when you are asked by your family to do something.
- telling someone how much you love him or her, especially when that person is tired, sad,or cranky.
- forgiving someone who has been unkind to you.
- praying for peace in our world.
- trying to be fair, even to those who are not fair to you or whom you do not like.

Review

Go over the *Faith Summary* together before your child completes the *Review*. The answers for questions 1–3 appear on page 200. The response to number 4 will help you see whether your second grader truly understands why taking part in the Mass is so important for a disciple of Jesus. When the *Review* is completed, have your child place a sticker on this page.

sticker

Circle the letter beside the correct answer.

1. In Holy Communion we receive
   (a.) Jesus. **b.** just bread.

2. Jesus wants us to be
   a. unfair. **(b.)** peacemakers.

3. We leave Mass to love and serve God and
   a. only our friends. **(b.)** everyone we meet.

4. Tell one thing you will do this week to be a peacemaker.

   Possible response: I will share my games with others.

Encourage the children to gather with their families to share the *Family Scripture Moment.*

As you **Gather** invite family members to recall when someone shared his or her faith with them. Then **Listen** to Jesus' words.

Do not be afraid of people. What I am telling you in the dark you must repeat in broad daylight, and what you have heard in private you must announce from the housetops. Do not be afraid of those who kill the body but cannot kill the soul. Not one sparrow falls to the ground without your Father's consent. As for you, even the hairs of your head have all been counted. So do not be afraid; you are worth more than many sparrows!

From Matthew 10:26–31

Share Ask family members what hopeful or consoling message they heard from these words of Jesus.

Consider for family enrichment:

- Jesus addresses these words to His disciples as He sends them out to preach the good news.
- Jesus assures us that God is always with us as we proclaim our faith in Him.

Reflect What image from this reading do we most want to remember?

Decide something to do as a family this week to share your Christian faith.

20 LENT

The Theme of This Chapter Corresponds with Paragraph 618

For the Catechist: Spiritual and Catechetical Development

Our Life

Imagine yourself as your favorite tree or plant. Your goal in life is to become the most beautiful full-grown Scotch pine or flowering cactus or American Beauty rose you can possibly be. Right now you can feel the juices stirring in your roots. The growing season is about to begin!

Ask yourself:

- How will I try to take full advantage of this season?

Sharing Life

In what ways will you try during Lent to grow toward maturity as one rooted in Christ?

Our Catholic Faith

Lent is a time of ongoing conversion to Jesus Christ, not only for ourselves but for those preparing for baptism.

We are marked with ashes and reminded of our mortality. We are exhorted to repent for our sins, and to make use of traditional disciplines to do so: sacrifice, prayer, and fasting. Lent is our penitential journey toward the Easter renewal of our baptismal vows. During Lent, we take stock of ourselves and reflect on our participation in the passion, death, and resurrection of Jesus Christ.

Lent is the growing season, in which we are "like trees that grow beside a stream" and "bear fruit at the right time" (from Psalm 1:3). By fasting from those things that prevent or slow our spiritual growth, we clear away the obstacles that stand between us and the Son who rises at Easter.

Coming to Faith

What is the meaning of Lent for you?

How can Lenten practices contribute to spiritual growth?

Practicing Faith

What will you do to blossom during Lent?

How will you help the children in your group to grow during Lent?

Teaching Resources

Teaching Hints

This lesson focuses on Lent as a time to grow. It is an opportune time to introduce the idea that thinking of others is an important part of "growing up" and that this often demands sacrifice. Provide a "Sacrifice Box" with suggestions of ways they might be thoughtful of others. Let the children draw one of these to do each week during Lent. Remind them that when they do these things for others, they are doing them for Jesus.

Special-Needs Child

Visually-impaired children often need to touch felt or sandpaper shapes before making objects themselves.

Visual Needs

- letters for faith word cut from rough fabric

Auditory Needs

- headphones, tape recording of the prayer service

Tactile-Motor Needs

- enlarged copy of fountain art taped to desk

Supplemental Resources

The Promise (video)
St. Anthony Messenger/
Franciscan Communications
1615 Republic Street
Cincinnati, OH 45210
(1-800-488-0488)
(1-800-989-3600)

The Story of Benjamin Burro (video)
Brown-ROA
2460 Kerper Blvd.
P.O. Box 539
Dubuque, IA 52004-0539
(1-800-922-7696)

Lesson Plan: Beginning

Objectives

To help the children

- know the meaning of Lent;
- appreciate Lent as a time for growing;
- choose to grow closer to Jesus during Lent.

Focusing Prayer

Let the children share any experience they have of seeing something grow. Have them share their feelings about it. Then lead them in the prayer at the top of page 131.

Our Life

Reflecting on Pictures

Give the children a few minutes to examine the pictures on page 131. Then divide them into three groups and have each group choose one picture to talk about in responding to the directives in the *Our Life* section. List on the chalkboard or a large piece of paper other things that grow and change.

Sharing Life

Using Our Imaginations

Have the children close their eyes and picture a world where everything was just as it is now and nothing ever changed. Have them tell what it would be like to live in this kind of world.

Have the children look at their hands, their arms and legs, and so forth. Ask if they would like them to remain this same size forever. Then have them think about their ideas and feelings. Ask if they would like them to remain exactly the same as they are today, without ever changing. Have them respond to the follow-up questions in the *Sharing Life* section.

---

20 Lent

Jesus, help us to grow and change during Lent.

Our Life

Look at the pictures.
Take turns telling how each thing grows and changes.
Accept reasonable responses.
Name other things that grow and change. people; plants; animals; all living things

Sharing Life

Imagine a world where nothing ever grew or changed. What would it be like? dull; not very exciting; always the same; boring; etc.
Suppose you never grew.
Would you always want to be just the way you are right now?
Tell why or why not.
Encourage the children to share the feelings about growing and changing.

131

Lesson Plan: Middle

Our Catholic Faith

A Time to Prepare

Display a flash card with the word *Lent.* Show the children on a calendar the dates that Lent begins and ends. Recall for them how we prepare for Christmas during Advent. Then explain that Lent is the time when we prepare for the great feast of Easter, when the Church celebrates the resurrection of Jesus.

Materials needed: flash card with the word *Lent*

Learning About Lent

Read with the children the paragraph at the top of page 132. If your parish has catechumens being prepared through the RCIA for reception of the sacraments of initiation at Easter, tell the children a little about them and about their preparation.

Explain that during the Easter vigil, when we remember the new life Jesus won for us through His resurrection, we promise to continue growing in this life. Ask the children if they remember being baptized. Tell them that you don't remember either, because we were all probably baptized as infants. But our parents promised that they would help us to live our faith and grow closer to Jesus each day. Explain that during the Easter vigil, we make this promise again.

ENRICHMENT

Pictures of Growth

Give each child a sheet of drawing paper. Invite the children to draw a picture of some living thing showing its growth in stages—for example: a plant; an animal; a person; a frog from a tadpole; a butterfly from a cocoon; etc. When they are finished, have them share their drawings and tell why they think it is important for the living thing they drew to continue growing.

Materials needed: drawing paper; pencils or markers

OUR CATHOLIC FAITH

Lent Is a Time to Grow

Lent is a special time before Easter. It is a time for us to change things we need to change, and to grow in our Catholic faith. During the forty days of Lent, we prepare for Easter. We also pray for those who are preparing for Baptism.

During Lent we can do something special for someone else. We can:

- do extra chores at home;
- take care of a younger brother or sister;
- pray for someone preparing for Baptism.

We can decide to be more generous. We can:

- be kind to everyone we meet;
- give in and let others watch their favorite TV program;
- share our snacks and toys;
- with our family, help a poor or needy person.

132

Lesson Plan: Middle

Ways in Which to Grow

Have the children contribute their own ideas about ways in which they might live their faith and grow closer to Jesus during Lent. Then take time to go over the lists at the bottom of page 132. Give your own examples or have them give examples of how they might do each of the things suggested.

You may also wish to use pages 45–46 in the activity book.

Coming to Faith

Teaching About Lent

Invite one of the children to pretend he or she is teacher. Let the "teacher" come to the front of the room, take the flash card that says *Lent,* and tell the group everything he or she remembers learning about it. Then suggest that the "teacher" call on someone in the class to respond to the second directive in the *Coming to Faith* section. Praise the child who took the role of "teacher." If there is time, allow other children to do the same.

Faith Summary

Turn to the *Faith Summary* on page 135. Use the annotations to see if the children can express in their own words what they have learned today.

Practicing Faith

Writing How You Will Grow

Have the children look at the picture of the fountain at the bottom of page 133. Remind them of the symbolism of the water used in Baptism. Then have them follow the directive.

FAITH WORD

Lent is the forty days before Easter.

(1) Lent means a time to change and grow in our Catholic Faith.

Coming To Faith

Tell someone what Lent means. (1)

Share how we can come closer to Jesus during Lent.
Possible responses: do extra chores at home; be especially kind to someone; help the poor; pray for those preparing for Baptism.

Practicing Faith

In the fountain pool, write how you will show you are trying to grow in friendship with God and others.

Possible responses: Get up on time for school. Say my bedtime prayers. Write a letter or send a card to a sick relative or friend.

Share my toys and games. Play with someone I don't like. Help out at home.

133

Enrichment

A Letter of Welcome

Obtain the names of those persons enrolled in the RCIA who will be received into your parish family at Eastertime. Let the children write letters to them, telling them that they welcome them into their parish family and promise to pray for them. Have the children sign these letters, and give them to your parish RCIA coordinator to distribute.

You may wish to use pages 33–34 of the *Celebrating Our Seasons and Saints* level 2 book from William H. Sadlier, Inc.

Lesson Plan: End

A Lenten Prayer

Have the children turn to page 134. Talk to them briefly about the picture of Jesus with the children. Let the children comment on the meaning of Lent. See the annotation. Then lead them in the Lenten prayer service.

Evaluating Your Lesson

- Do the children know the meaning of Lent?
- Do they appreciate Lent as a time of growth?
- Have they decided to grow closer to Jesus during this time?

(1) Have the children memorize their responses.

† Lenten Prayer Service

Leader: Let us think about ways we can change and grow in our Christian faith this Lent. Jesus, we want to come closer to You this Lent.
All: Jesus, help us to come closer to You. (1)

Leader: We want to be kind like You.
All: Jesus, help us to come closer to You.

Leader: Jesus said, "Love God with all your heart. Love others as you love yourself."
All: Jesus, help us to come closer to You.

Leader: Help us, Jesus, to love God and others by being kind and fair to everyone.
All: Amen.

Talk to the children about ways they and their families might use the "Faith Alive" pages. Encourage them to do the Lenten activity with a family member.

A Liturgy Activity

Display pictures of trees, plants, and flowers. Invite the children to choose their favorite and draw themselves as that tree or plant. Mount their drawings at the bottom of a Growth Chart which will be displayed throughout Lent.

Pray together each week for those who will be baptized at Easter, for newborns, for family members, and for the parish. Have the children extend their drawings week by week, showing how prayer enables them to grow closer to God.

Materials needed: Growth Chart; magazines; drawing paper; crayons or markers; glue

A Justice and Peace Activity

The Lenten Growth Chart may also be used to symbolically record the children's growth in loving service to others. Have a basket of construction paper leaves and flowers on hand. Print on each a good deed to be accomplished by the child who draws it out of the basket. (These deeds may be acts of sharing, helping, forgiving, making peace, cooperating, and listening well.)

Each week have the children mount the completed leaves and flowers on their Growth Chart trees or plants.

Materials needed: basket; construction paper leaves and flowers

Do It Yourself

Use this space to create your own Lenten activity.

FAITH ALIVE AT HOME AND IN THE PARISH

In this lesson your child was led to a deeper understanding of the meaning of Lent in the life of the Church and in his or her own life. Lent is a time of ongoing conversion to the way of Jesus Christ. At the beginning of the Lenten season, we receive ashes to remind us of our mortality. We are encouraged to repent for our sins and failings through prayer, sacrifice, and fasting. We join with our parish in praying for those preparing for Baptism.

Lent is a penitential journey toward the Easter renewal of our own baptismal promises. It is a time to take stock of our lives and to reflect on our participation in the passion, death, and resurrection of Jesus. We renew our efforts to live our Baptism by following the way of Jesus.

You might ask yourself:

- *How will our family make Lent a season of spiritual growth?*
- *How can I help my child grow in the way of Jesus during Lent?*

Learn by heart

Faith Summary

- Lent is a time to grow in our Christian faith.

  What is Lent?
- Lent is a special time to show our love for God, others, and ourselves.

  What will you do during Lent?

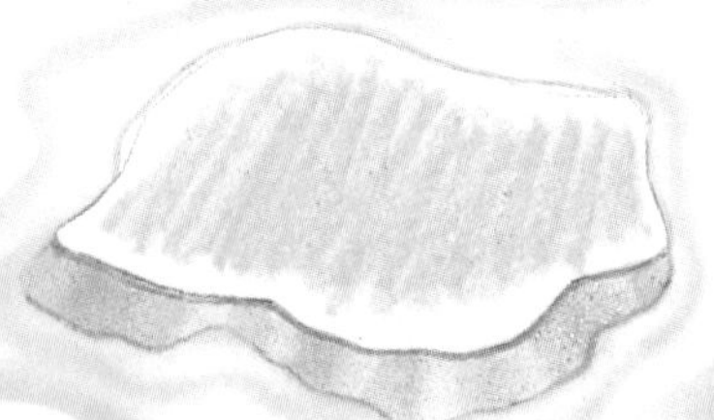

pray to Jesus

go to Mass

help cheerfully

share and play fairly

clean up

listen to God's word

Lenten Thaw

Lent is a time to let selfish, icy ways melt.
Color each chunk of ice blue
when you do what is written inside.
Will all the ice blocks have melted by Easter?

Review

Go over the *Faith Summary* together before your child completes the *Review.* The answers for questions 1–3 appear on page 200. The response to number 4 will show you whether your child understands the basic meaning of Lent. When the *Review* is completed, have your child place a sticker on this page.

sticker

Color the circle beside the correct answer.

1. Lent is a special time before

○ Christmas. ● Easter.

2. In Lent there are

● forty days. ○ four weeks.

3. We try during Lent to do things for

○ ourselves. ● others.

4. Tell what you will do to come closer to Jesus during Lent.

Possible responses: I will be kind to my friends.
I will share my toys.

Encourage the children to gather with their families to share the *Family Scripture Moment.*

FAMILY SCRIPTURE MOMENT

As you **Gather** invite family members to give examples of times when they have put others first to show love and respect. Then **Listen** to the words of Jesus.

Jesus said to His disciples, "If people want to come with Me, they must forget themselves, carry their cross, and follow Me. For those who want to save their life will lose it; but those who lose their life for My sake will find it. Will they gain anything if they win the whole world but lose their life? Of course not!"

From Matthew 16:24–26

Share What stood out for you in this reading? What are some crosses you carry?

Consider for family enrichment:

- Having told His disciples that He would soon have to suffer and die, Jesus warns them that they, too, must be willing to "die to themselves" if they hope to gain eternal life with Him.
- Dying to self does not mean hating or hurting oneself. It means putting God's will first, which is the best way to love ourselves and others.

Reflect and **Decide** What does it mean to carry our cross and follow Jesus? As a family, how will we help one another to do that during Lent?

21 EASTER

The Theme of This Chapter Corresponds with Paragraph 1169

For the Catechist: Spiritual and Catechetical Development

Our Life

Since 1945 millions of readers have been awakened from their apathy by a modest little bulletin called "Christopher News Notes." Founded by Father James Keller, the Christophers are known by their motto: "It is better to light one candle than to curse the darkness." They firmly believe in each person's power to change the world through constructive action. And they believe that power resides in every Christian as a bearer of the risen Christ.

Ask yourself:

- What "candles" have I lit?
- How have they improved the world?

Sharing Life

How do I hope my celebration of Easter will enable me to light more candles and curse the darkness less often?

Our Catholic Faith

Easter is the most important feast of the Church. In addition to Sunday as the celebration of the resurrection, the followers of Jesus in the early centuries had an annual celebration of death/resurrection of Jesus.

The paschal mystery is the fundamental fact of our faith, and all liturgical feasts are related to it. Easter is not only the commemoration of the death and resurrection of Jesus Christ, it is the manifestation of the new life in which we share by reason of our union with Jesus Christ. Easter is our celebration of the salvation and transformation of all creation.

Coming to Faith

Envision yourself as a paschal candle. Where do you hope to shed new light?

How will you help those whose candles are not yet lit?

Practicing Faith

How will you celebrate your new life in Jesus Christ at Easter?

In what ways will you encourage your group's faith to shine at Easter?

Teaching Resources

Teaching Hints

Spring is the perfect season to introduce Easter as the celebration of new life in Jesus. If possible, take the children outdoors to experience the wonders of nature's "resurrection" at this time of the year. Enter into the joy of this experience with them. Help the children to see that Easter is not simply a one-day celebration, but that, like spring, it is a whole season during which we celebrate the new life Jesus won for us through His own resurrection.

Special-Needs Child

Encourage and support any special-needs child to take part in the Easter play.

Visual Needs

- samples of symbols so children can feel them (cloves, candles, etc.)

Auditory Needs

- headphones, tape recording of "Alleluia"

Tactile-Motor Needs

- practice their part in the play ahead of time

Supplemental Resources

The Easter Story (video)
from Hanna-Barbera
Vision Video
2030 Wentz Church Road
Worcester, PA 19490
(1-800-523-0226)

The Easter Story (video)
God's Story series
Mass Media Ministries
2116 North Charles Street
Baltimore, Maryland 21218
(1-800-828-8825)

Lesson Plan: Beginning

OBJECTIVES

To help the children

- know the true meaning of Easter;
- appreciate Easter as a time to celebrate our new life in Jesus;
- choose to celebrate Jesus' new life.

Focusing Prayer

Tell the children that today they will learn about celebrating the most wonderful happening in Jesus' life. Then lead them in the prayer at the top of page 137.

Our Life

Writing a Poem

Guide the children in completing the poem about springtime on page 137. Share with them what you like best about the season of spring, and then have them respond to the follow-up question in the *Our Life* section.

Sharing Life

Learning from Spring

Have the children examine the picture on page 137. See how many examples of being alive they can name that are shown there. Then have them respond to the follow-up questions. Help them to see that because God is so loving, God created us for life. Each spring we are reminded that even though things die, as some things do in the winter, God can bring new life out of death.

Lesson Plan: Middle

Our Catholic Faith

The Holiest Time of Year

Explain to the children that Easter is the holiest and most special time of the year for followers of Jesus. Ask if the children know why. Read aloud the first paragraph on page 138. Have the children recall what they learned about the catechumens who are baptized during the Easter vigil.

Easter Symbols

Write the word *symbol* on the chalkboard or a large piece of paper. Ask the children if they know what symbols are. Explain that symbols are signs or objects that remind us of something else. Have them look at the pictures on pages 138 and 139 and name the symbols they see. Let the children talk about their experience of coloring eggs at Eastertime.

Read aloud the next two paragraphs. Explain the symbols on the Easter candle to the children: the cross stands for Jesus, and the five grains of incense at the four corners and in the middle stand for the five wounds of Jesus as He hung on the cross. The letters above and below the cross are the first and last letters of the Greek alphabet (alpha and omega). They are signs of Jesus, who is the beginning and end of our

Enrichment

From Death to Life

Show the children a bare tree branch. Talk with them about how in some places the blossoms and leaves on trees die during the autumn and winter seasons. Tell them to decorate the tree branch with new life to show that it has come alive again. Have them make small blossoms out of pink and green crepe paper and attach these to the branch with tape or glue. Place the decorated branch in a prominent place with the sign that says: GOD GIVES US NEW LIFE.

Materials needed: bare tree branch; pink and green crepe paper; scissors; glue or tape; sign: GOD GIVES US NEW LIFE

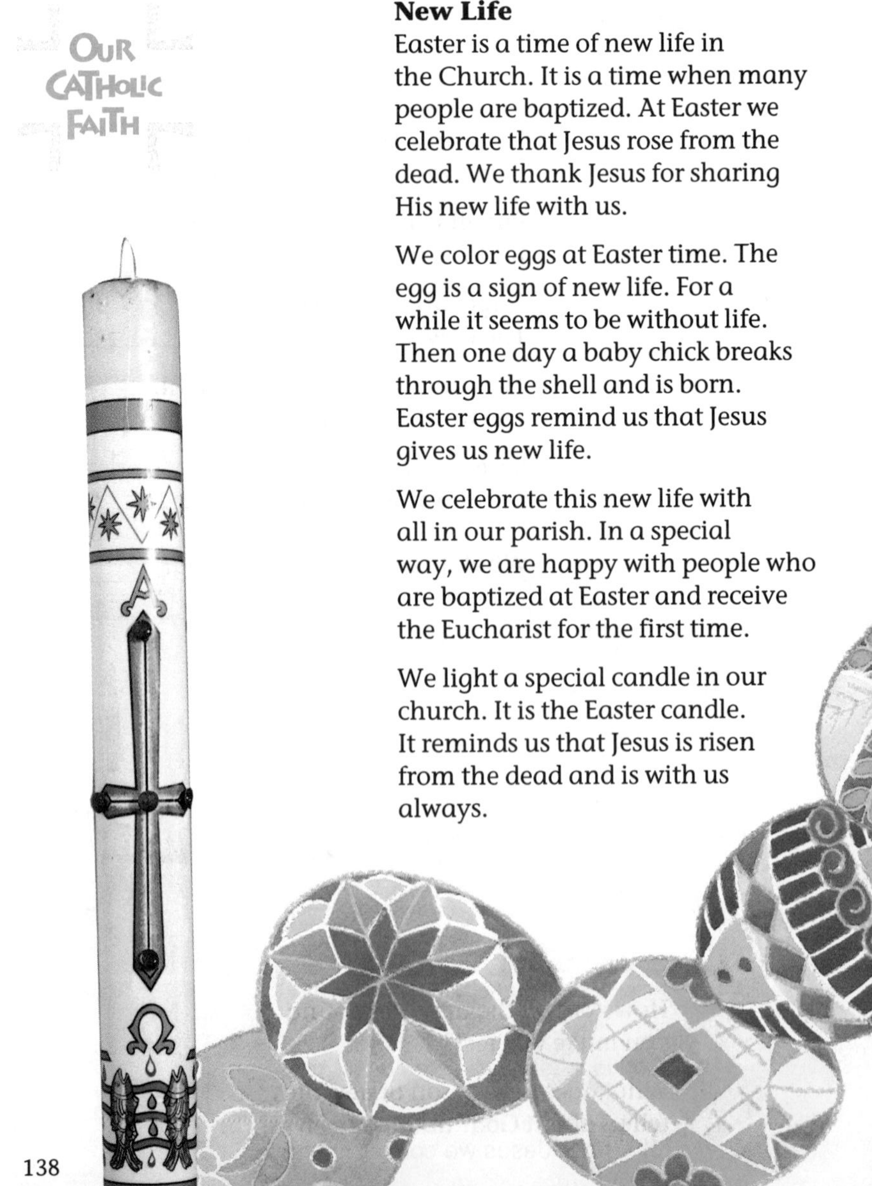

Our Catholic Faith

New Life

Easter is a time of new life in the Church. It is a time when many people are baptized. At Easter we celebrate that Jesus rose from the dead. We thank Jesus for sharing His new life with us.

We color eggs at Easter time. The egg is a sign of new life. For a while it seems to be without life. Then one day a baby chick breaks through the shell and is born. Easter eggs remind us that Jesus gives us new life.

We celebrate this new life with all in our parish. In a special way, we are happy with people who are baptized at Easter and receive the Eucharist for the first time.

We light a special candle in our church. It is the Easter candle. It reminds us that Jesus is risen from the dead and is with us always.

138

Lesson Plan: Middle

life in God. Ask the children if they have ever noticed the candle lit during Mass. The lighted candle reminds us that the resurrected Jesus is still with us.

You may also wish to use pages 47–48 in the activity book.

You may wish to use pages 35–36 of the *Celebrating Our Seasons and Saints* level 2 book from William H. Sadlier, Inc.

Coming to Faith

Why We Celebrate

Have a decorated egg and an Easter candle cut out of construction paper, each with one of the questions in the *Coming to Faith* section written on the back. Call on volunteers to come and choose one and answer the question. Then let them talk about the symbol they have picked. Invite the rest of the group to add any additional information they remember.

Faith Summary

Turn to the *Faith Summary* on page 141. Use the annotations to see if the children can express in their own words what they have learned today.

Practicing Faith

Finding the Missing Word

Explain the missing-letter activity on page 139. Help the children complete the first part. Then let them copy, at the bottom of the page, the word that is formed from the missing letters.

Coming to Faith

Why do we celebrate Easter? (1)

What is your favorite Easter sign of new life? Why?
Encourage the children to share and affirm their responses.
(1) It reminds us that Jesus is risen from the dead and is with us always.

Practicing Faith

What will you do to celebrate Jesus' new life at Easter?

Find the word we say on Easter.

1. __A__ is in bat but not in bet.
2. __L__ is in let but not in pet.
3. __L__ is in lake but not in take.
4. __E__ is in met but not in mat.
5. __L__ is in lap but not in cap.
6. __U__ is in luck but not in lick.
7. __I__ is in sit but not in sat.
8. __A__ is in beat but not in beet.

Write the word here.

A	L	L	E	L	U	I	A
1	2	3	4	5	6	7	8

Jesus Christ is risen!

Share this Easter word with someone you love.
Say together,
Christ is risen! ____ALLELUIA____!

Enrichment

Decorating an Easter Candle

Give each child a white candle, some construction paper, five cloves, and some very small artificial flowers or cut-out paper flowers. Invite each one to make an Easter candle, using the construction paper for the cross and letters and the cloves for the five wounds of Jesus. Let them decorate the candle with the flowers and construction paper as they wish. Use pins or glue to attach the materials to the candle.

Materials needed: white candles; construction paper; scissors; small artificial flowers or flowers cut from paper; cloves; pins or glue

Lesson Plan: End

An Easter Play

Let the children act out the play on page 140. Teach them a melody or chant for the triple "Alleluia." You may wish to use the grade 2 *Coming to Jesus in Song* cassette from William H. Sadlier, Inc. You may also wish to invite another class in to witness their play.

Evaluating Your Lesson

- Do the children know the meaning of Easter?
- Do they appreciate it as a time to celebrate Jesus' new life?
- Have they decided to celebrate Jesus' new life?

An Easter Play

Reader: Early on Sunday morning, Mary Magdalene, a friend of Jesus, went to visit the tomb.

Mary: (crying) Oh, I can't believe He's gone. I miss Him so much!

Reader: When Mary got to the tomb, the big rock was moved away.

Mary: (surprised) The tomb is empty! Where is Jesus?

Reader: Mary went running to Peter and John.

Mary: Peter! John! They have taken away the body of Jesus!

Peter and John: What are you talking about? That's impossible!

Reader: Peter and John raced to Jesus' tomb. John reached the tomb first and looked in. Then Peter went in. He saw the burial cloths.

Peter and John: Jesus is risen! Let us rejoice!

All: (sing) Alleluia, alleluia, alleluia!

From John 20: 1–10

Talk to the children about ways they and their families might use the "Faith Alive" pages together. Encourage them to tell the Easter story to a family member.

140

A Liturgy Activity

If possible, use an electric candle. Give each child a white paper flower, or a stole cut from an old sheet to wear. Gather at the prayer table and invite the children to raise their arms and sing "Alleluia!" in response to the following:

- Risen Jesus, give us joy!
- Risen Jesus, give us peace!
- Risen Jesus, give us faith!
- Risen Jesus, fill our world!

Materials needed: paper flowers; old sheet; scissors; electric candle

A Justice and Peace Activity

Talk with the children about who may be missing the Light of Jesus at Easter time. Is it a child who is in the hospital? An aged parishioner who lives alone? A neighbor who no longer goes to church?

List and plan ways in which the children can be "living candles" who brighten others' lives by visiting them, giving small cards or gifts, singing or telling stories, and/or asking Jesus to bless the one who is in "darkness."

Do It Yourself

Use this space to plan your own Easter festival.

AT HOME AND IN THE PARISH

In this lesson your child was drawn more deeply into the Easter story. The paschal mystery (the life, death and resurrection of Jesus) is a fundamental belief of our Christian faith, and all our liturgical feasts are related to it. It is at the center of our whole Christian life.

Easter is not only the commemoration of the death and resurrection of Jesus, it is the manifestation of the new life we share through Him. That is why this is the time for the Church to welcome new members through the sacraments of initiation—Baptism, Confirmation, and Eucharist.

You might ask yourself:

- *How does your belief in the resurrection give you hope?*
- *How will your family celebrate new life in Christ at Easter?*

The Easter Story

Encourage your child to tell you the Easter story. You might enjoy acting it out together. If you do not have your child's book, you can find it in the Bible, John 20:1–10.

Learn by heart

Faith Summary

- Jesus rose from the dead on Easter.
  What happened on Easter?
- We celebrate Jesus' new life.
  What do we celebrate on Easter?

An Easter Butterfly

The butterfly is a symbol of Easter. For a while it lies in a cocoon. Finally it is changed into a beautiful butterfly. Trace this butterfly. Color it with bright springtime colors. Send the butterfly message to someone who is ill or lonely.

Review

Go over the *Faith Summary* together before your child completes the *Review.* The answers for questions 1–3 appear on page 200. The response to number 4 will show you whether your child is learning about the meaning of Easter. When the *Review* is completed, have your child place a sticker on this page.

sticker

Color the circle beside the correct answer.

1. Jesus rose from the dead on

○ Christmas. ● Easter.

2. On Easter we celebrate

● Jesus' new life. ○ Jesus' death.

3. At Easter the Church welcomes new members in

○ Lent. ● Baptism.

4. Imagine you meet Jesus on the first Easter. What will you say to Him?

____

____

Encourage the children to gather with their families to share the Family Scripture Moment.

Gather and **Listen** to the story of the first Easter morning.

After the Sabbath, as Sunday morning was dawning, Mary Magdalene and the other Mary went to look at the tomb. An angel spoke to the women. "Go quickly, now, and tell His disciples, 'Jesus has been raised from death, and now He is going to Galilee ahead of you; there you will see Him!' Remember what I have told you." So they left the tomb in a hurry, afraid and yet filled with joy, and ran to tell His disciples. Suddenly Jesus met them and said, "Peace be with you. Go and tell My brothers to go to Galilee, and there they will see Me."

From Matthew 28: 1, 5, 7–10

Share Imagine you are with the women at the tomb. How do you respond to the risen Christ?

Consider for family enrichment:

- The resurrection of Jesus is at the heart of our faith. Through the passion, death, and resurrection of the Lord we have been saved and share in His new life.
- Like the women at the tomb, we are called to proclaim the risen Lord joyfully and courageously.

Reflect and **Decide** How will we share with others in our family and parish the joy of Jesus' new life?

UNIT 3 • REVIEW

Use the annotations on this page to review the major points of Unit 3.

Jesus Gives Us the Mass

At Mass, we listen to the word of God. The bread and wine become Jesus Himself. At Mass we remember and celebrate that Jesus lived and died and rose for us. Jesus is our Savior.

Ask: What do we remember and celebrate at Mass?

We Prepare for Eucharist

We celebrate the Eucharist at Mass. Mass is our greatest prayer of thanks to God.

Ask: What happens during the Liturgy of the Word?

We Celebrate the Liturgy of the Word

We listen to God's word from the Bible during the Liturgy of the Word. The priest or deacon reads the gospel to us and gives a homily or sermon. We say what we believe in the Creed. We pray for our own needs and the needs of others in the Prayer of the Faithful.

Ask: What happens during the Liturgy of the Eucharist?

We Celebrate the Liturgy of the Eucharist

In the Eucharist, we give thanks to God. Through the power of the Holy Spirit, our gifts of bread and wine become the Body and Blood of Christ. We can receive Jesus in Holy Communion.

Ask: How can we live the Eucharist?

We Are Sent to Love and Serve

At the end of Mass, we are sent to love and serve the Lord and one another. We bring the peace and love of Christ to others.

ACTIVITY: Have the children create a mural to illustrate these key ideas:

- the Last Supper;
- praise and thanksgiving;
- listening to God's word;
- Consecration;
- Holy Communion;
- peacemakers.

UNIT 3 • TEST

Circle the correct answer.

1. Jesus gave us the gift of His Body and Blood at

   Easter   (the Last Supper)   Pentecost

2. The Mass is another name for the sacrament of

   (the Eucharist)   Reconciliation   Baptism

3. We listen to God's word at Mass during

   Holy Communion   (the Liturgy of the Word)   the Liturgy of the Eucharist

4. During the Liturgy of the Eucharist, our gifts of bread and wine

   stay the same   (become Jesus Himself)

Child's name ____________________

Your child has just completed Unit 3. Have your child bring this paper to the catechist. It will help you and the catechist know better how to help your child grow in the faith.

____ My child needs help with the part of the Review/Summary I have underlined.

____ My child understands what has been taught in this unit.

____ I would like to speak with you. My phone number is ____________.

(Signature) ____________________

22 We Celebrate First Holy Communion

For the Catechist: Spiritual and Catechetical Development

Adult Background

Our Life

At table one in Brown's Family Restaurant, Maria and Ricardo are lifting their wine glasses as they look into each other's eyes. At table two the entire Chen family is seated elbow to elbow, enjoying a long-awaited reunion. At table three Father Pat McAvoy is chuckling at the joke four of his parish staff members have just put over on him.

Ask yourself:

- How does this scene illustrate communion?
- In what ways do I experience communion?

Sharing Life

What do I want Holy Communion to mean in my life?

Our Catholic Faith

The last meal that Jesus shared with His friends must have recalled for them other times of closeness. The first Christians continued this simple intimacy with Jesus and one another. "Day after day they met as a group in the Temple, and they had their meals together in their homes, eating with glad and humble hearts, praising God, and enjoying the good will of all the people" (Acts 2:46–47). Each time they met as the community of beloved disciples, the early Christians experienced communion with the risen Christ and with one another.

The first Christians met commonly to celebrate the Lord's Supper, and frequent reception of Communion was the norm for the Christian community. They carried the consecrated bread home to those who were sick and unable to attend the eucharistic celebration. Gradually, as social and political circumstances changed, taking the Eucharist to the sick became a responsibility reserved for priests. A change in the concept of intimacy with Jesus occurred as well. As time passed, not only did the Christian community become united with Jesus in Communion, but the custom of reserving the Eucharist for adoration developed. This practice of venerating the consecrated Host led to the custom of exposing the Blessed Sacrament and the devotion of Benediction. Other traditions developed that involved the Christian community in the adoration of Jesus Christ present in the consecrated Host. Corpus Christi processions, for example, involved whole villages and towns as the Host was carried along the streets.

While these devotions encouraged attitudes of reverence and awe for the Blessed Sacrament, they also encouraged feelings of unworthiness. The reception of Communion became less and less frequent. In 1215 the Fourth Lateran Council decreed that all Christians had to receive Holy Communion at least once each year.

When Saint Pius X became pope in 1903, he issued decrees encouraging frequent and daily reception of Communion and early First Communion for children.

During the Second Vatican Council (1962–1965), the Constitution on the Sacred Liturgy emphasized Communion as a sign of our union with Jesus Christ and with one another. By receiving Communion frequently, we grow in our union with Christ and one another.

Coming to Faith

Why does the Church encourage frequent reception of Communion?

How will you encourage others to seek communion with Jesus?

Practicing Faith

How will you deepen your relationship with Jesus?

How will you help your group see First Communion as a new and wonderful way to become better friends with Jesus?

Catechism of the Catholic Church

The Theme of This Chapter Corresponds with Paragraph 1391

Liturgical Resources

The Sacred Congregation for Divine Worship issued these guidelines in the "Directory on Children's Masses" (1973):

> The preparation of children for their First Communion deserves special consideration. It should be aimed not only at teaching them the truths of their faith concerning the Eucharist, but also at explaining how from now on they are going to be able to share the Eucharistic activity with the people of God and have a share in the Lord's table and in the community of their fellow Christians.

Invite parents to participate in a First Communion invitations workshop with their children. Provide colored paper, markers, envelopes, and eucharistic stickers if possible. Have parents and children together decide who will receive these invitations.

Sing a Communion song as a group, and share simple refreshments.

Justice and Peace Resources

Help the children to appreciate that once they have celebrated their First Holy Communion they will have taken a big step forward as followers of Jesus. Ask:

How do you think we can show that Jesus is really present with us?

Who might Jesus want us to show His special love and care for?

You may want to use an illustrated children's Bible to recall several stories of how Jesus cares for the sick (Matthew 8:14–15), feeds the hungry (Matthew 14:13–20), and blesses children (Matthew 19:13–15). Then decide how the children can serve one of these groups which Jesus loves so well.

Teaching Resources

Overview of the Lesson

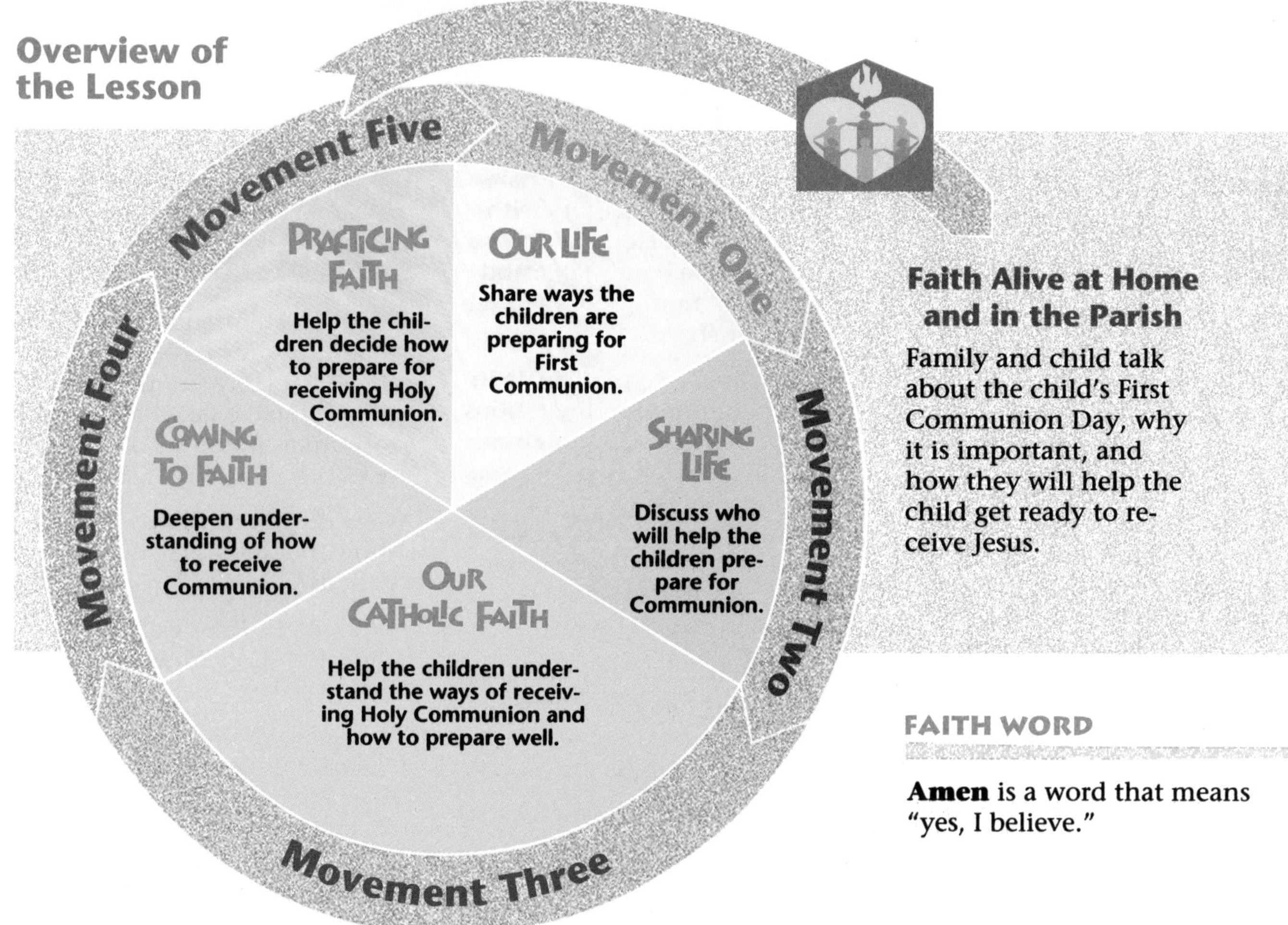

Faith Alive at Home and in the Parish

Family and child talk about the child's First Communion Day, why it is important, and how they will help the child get ready to receive Jesus.

FAITH WORD

Amen is a word that means "yes, I believe."

Teaching Hints

Help the children understand that their reception of the Eucharist is a cause of joy to the whole parish. It might be helpful to invite some parishioners to express this joy to the children personally. Explain carefully that they may receive communion either in the hands or on the tongue. Let them experience both ways and then make their choice.

Special-Needs Child

Assign to the special-needs child a partner who is accepting of his/her differences and can help the child understand how to make the prayer mat.

Visual Needs

- a host and chalice that they can feel

Auditory Needs

- tape recording of how to receive Holy Communion

Tactile-Motor Needs

- large copy of prayer taped to desk

Supplemental Resources

First Eucharist (video)
St. Anthony Messenger/
Franciscan Communications
1615 Republic Street
Cincinnati, OH 45210
(1-800-488-0488)
(1-800-989-3600)

Lesson Plan: Beginning

OBJECTIVES

To help the children

- know the importance of preparing well to receive Holy Communion;
- appreciate the fact that we receive Jesus Himself;
- decide to prepare well.

Focusing Prayer

Introduce the prayer at the top of page 145 by talking with the children about how when we love someone very much, we want to be with her or him. Then lead them in saying the prayer together.

Our Life

We Get Ready for Jesus

Talk about what the children would do to prepare for a visit with a very important person. Ask: "Would someone help you prepare for the visit? Who?" Explain that you have a picture of a wonderful Person who is coming to visit them soon. Ask if they can guess who it is. Show a picture of Jesus. Have the children examine the illustration on page 145 and read the parish bulletin shown there. Have the children respond to the question in the *Our Life* section on page 145.

Materials needed: picture of Jesus.

Sharing Life

Our Parish Helps Us Prepare

Have the children respond to the question at the bottom of the page. Talk about some ways their parish family might help them prepare for receiving Jesus.

ENRICHMENT

A Letter to the Parish

Guide the children in composing and writing a group letter to the parish asking that parishioners pray for them. Have them write the letter on white paper and paste it on a large sheet of construction paper. Allow each child to sign her or his name to it. Post the letter at the entrance of the church.

Materials needed: large sheet of construction paper; paste; pencils; white paper

22 We Celebrate First Holy Communion

Jesus, we love You. Stay with us.

OUR LIFE

Jimmy and his mom are reading this notice. Read with them.

(1) Possible responses: participating in the Mass; learning my prayers; etc.

How are you preparing for First Communion? (1)

SHARING LIFE

Who will help you prepare for Holy Communion? Help the children identify those who will help them at home and in the parish.

145

Lesson Plan: Middle

Our Catholic Faith

We Prepare by Fasting

Write the word *fasting* on the chalkboard. Elicit from the children what their understanding of the word is. Then read aloud the first paragraph on page 146. Recall for the children some of the things they mentioned they would do in preparing for the visit of an important personage.

Emphasize the fact that fasting before Communion is a sign of respect and a way of preparing our bodies for Jesus' visit.

We Prepare Our Hearts

Ask the young people to read quietly to themselves the first sentence in the next paragraph on page 146. Then ask them how else they prepare that is even more important. Recall for them what they learned in the previous lessons about participating in the prayers and singing at Mass. Explain that these are some ways we can prepare our hearts for Jesus. Let them suggest other things they might do.

We Learn How to Receive Jesus

Ask the children to look at the pictures as you read to them the rest of page 146 and the first paragraph on page 147, about how they receive Jesus in

OUR CATHOLIC FAITH

Receiving Holy Communion

Stress the underlined text.

As a sign of respect for Jesus, Catholics fast before receiving Holy Communion. This means that we do not eat or drink anything for one hour before Communion time. Drinking water does not break our fast.

All during the Mass, we prepare our hearts to welcome Jesus, who comes to us in Holy Communion. When Communion time comes, the priest or eucharistic minister holds the Host up to each of us and says, "The body of Christ." Ask: What do we believe about Holy Communion?

<u>We believe that Jesus is really present in Holy Communion.</u>

We say, "Amen." Ask: How can you receive Holy Communion?

You can choose to receive the Host in your hand. To do this you put your right hand under the left and hold your hands out, palms up, to receive the Host. You then use your right hand to put the Host in your mouth.

146

Lesson Plan: Middle

Holy Communion. Use gestures as you explain the procedure for receiving. Use the annotations. Direct the children's attention to the faith word at the top of page 147 to explain the meaning of *Amen*.

If the young people in your parish receive from the chalice at First Communion, explain the procedure for this also.

Multicultural Awareness

Have the children note the persons from various cultures portrayed in the pictures. Then read aloud the second paragraph on page 147. Explain how important it is that we realize that in Jesus, all people are united together. Remind the children that Jesus gave His life for all of us and that He wants us to love and respect one another as sisters and brothers in Jesus.

We Give Thanks for Jesus

Share with the children some of your own awe at the realization that in the Eucharist Jesus is really present to us. Read aloud the third paragraph on page 147, and stress the importance of talking to Jesus in our hearts after receiving Him in Holy Communion. Have the children read together the prayer at the bottom of the page. Encourage them to memorize it and say it as a daily prayer. Then give them time to complete the prayers at the end of the page.

You may also wish to use pages 49–50 in the activity book.

FAITH WORD

Amen is a word that means "yes, I believe."

You can also choose to receive the Host on your tongue. You hold your head up and gently put out your tongue. The priest puts the Host on your tongue.

After we receive Jesus in Holy Communion, we return to our places to pray and sing. The word *Communion* means that we are united with Jesus Christ and one another.

Jesus is really present with us. We can tell Jesus whatever is in our hearts. We can say this special prayer or make up our own prayer.

† Stay with me, Jesus.
Help me do what is right.
Stay with me, Jesus,
Each day and each night.

Thank You, Jesus, for coming to me.

Please bless Possible responses: me; my family; my friends; etc.

Please help me to Possible responses: become Your friend and follower; help out at home; learn to be a peacemaker; etc.

147

Practicing How to Receive

If possible, take the children to church to practice receiving Communion. Use unconsecrated hosts (and altar wine if the children receive from the chalice in your parish). Explain once more to the children that these have not yet been changed into Jesus. Be sure they understand that even though the bread and wine will become Jesus after the consecration, they will taste the same as they did before. Then go through the procedure slowly and reverently. Allow the children to ask any questions they might have.

Lesson Plan: End

Coming to Faith

Sharing How We Receive

Divide the children into two groups. Have one group pretend to be kindergartners coming to visit. Suggest that those in the other group explain simply about receiving Jesus in Holy Communion. Let them act out for the "kindergarten" children their responses to the directive and questions in the *Coming to Faith* section. See the annotations.

Faith Summary

Turn to the *Faith Summary* on page 149. Use the annotations to see if the young people can express in their own words what they have learned today.

Practicing Faith

Our Amen to Jesus

Have the children examine the illustrated heart on page 148 and read what it says. Explain how they are to complete the heart, and let them share with one another some things they might do during the week. Then lead them in the prayer at the bottom of the page. Let each child contribute an ending to the petition.

Evaluating Your Lesson

- Do the children know the importance of preparing well to receive Holy Communion?
- Do they appreciate the gift of Jesus in the Eucharist?

Enrichment

A Church Banner

Have the children make a large banner to display in church on the day of their First Holy Communion. Let them decide what should be on the banner and what they would like the banner to say. Some examples might be: a large host and chalice with the words *Come Jesus* and the children's names around it, or a large heart with Jesus' name in it and smaller hearts with their names on them.

Materials needed: markers; paste; posterboard or felt; scissors

Coming to Faith

Act out the ways we can receive Holy Communion. Children should practice receiving in hand or on the tongue.

What do we do after receiving Jesus?
Possible responses: thank Jesus; tell Him whatever is in our hearts; etc.

What can we say to thank Jesus for being really present in Holy Communion? Share your thoughts. Possible responses: Jesus, I love You; I will try to live as I should; etc.

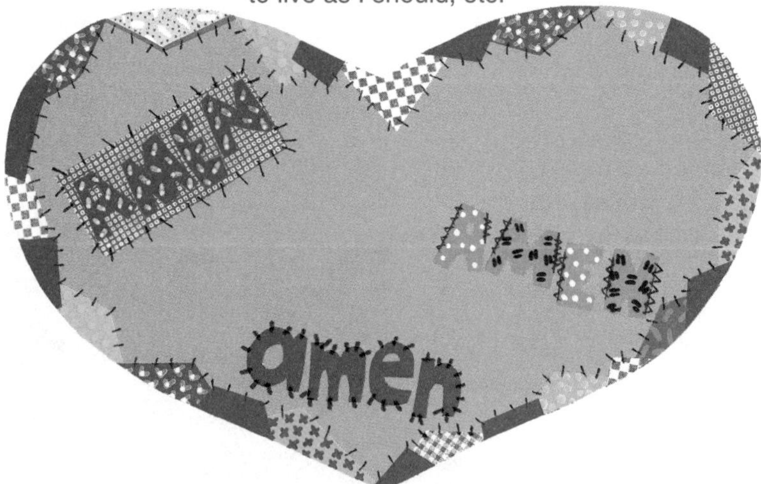

Practicing Faith

Each time this week you do something to get ready for Holy Communion write the word *Amen* in the heart. Tell one another what you hope to do.

† Then take turns praying,
Jesus, help us to prepare for You by
Possible responses: helping my family; helping someone in need; praying to God; going to Mass, etc.

Talk to the children about ways they and their families might use the "Faith Alive" pages. Encourage them to write their own Communion prayer and to share it with a family member.

148

Bookmarks (for use with page 145)

Suggest that the children choose a "faith friend" to help them prepare for their First Communion. It might be a parent, sibling, neighbor, or relative. Have them make a bookmark for this faith friend.

Give each child a strip of construction paper about 5″ long and $3\frac{1}{2}$″ wide. Have each child trace the pattern of a cross on the construction paper and cut it out. Have them use markers to decorate their crosses with ribbon-like designs, starting at the edges and moving toward the middle, using different colors. Have them print on the back: FOR MY FAITH FRIEND, and add a brief message.

Materials needed: construction paper; markers; scissors

Missionary for a Day (for use with page 146)

Show a globe or a world map to the children. Recall for them that Jesus asked his followers to go all over the world to tell people about Jesus and the good news. Invite the children to come up one at a time, cover their eyes, and point to a location on the globe or map. Have each one pretend she or he is a missionary sent to that country to tell the children there about Jesus and prepare them for their first Holy Communion. Have the others act as the children from other countries while each "missionary" acts out her or his part.

Materials needed: globe or world map

A Communion Chain (for use with page 147)

Have each child draw herself or himself, with arms extended to the sides, on a sheet of colored construction paper. Have them draw identification chains around their necks and print their names on them. Then have them carefully cut out their drawings. Attach these together by the hands with staples or tape to make a chain. Tape a beautiful picture of Jesus in the center of the chain. Hang the chain on the bulletin board or across the top of the chalkboard as a reminder that communion means being united together in Jesus.

Materials needed: construction paper; markers; scissors; stapler or tape; a beautiful picture of Jesus

A Thank-You Prayer Card (for use with page 148)

Distribute 5-inch square cards. Invite the children to write a short Thank-You prayer to Jesus to pray after receiving communion. Explain that this is their secret prayer and that they do not need to share it with anyone else. Let them make an attractive border around the prayer card by pasting strips of lace or ribbon along the edges, or have them glue braided yarn around it. Encourage them to bring it to church each weekend and to say the prayer after they receive Jesus in Holy Communion.

Materials needed: 5-inch square cards; lace, ribbon, or braided yarn; pencils; glue

FAITH ALIVE AT HOME AND IN THE PARISH

In this lesson your child has learned how to receive Jesus in Holy Communion. For many adult Catholics, the day of their First Holy Communion is still a fond memory. It can be a milestone in the personal relationship your child is developing with Jesus.

Your child needs the enthusiastic and prayerful support of your family and parish at this time. This will help your child understand and appreciate more fully what it means to receive Jesus for the first time in Holy Communion. Talk to your child about

- your feelings when you receive Holy Communion;
- what you say to Jesus;
- how you want to live your Catholic faith.

Then talk about the fact that receiving Jesus is more important than new Communion clothes or a party, though these have their place. Have your child show you how he or she will receive Holy Communion.

Ask the members of your family to write individual notes to your child, telling what they will do to help him or her get ready to receive Jesus for the first time. Then help your child to do the following activity.

Celebration Scroll

You may wish to make a scroll for your child's First Communion. Include your child's name, the date, and the name of your parish. Leave room for her or his Communion picture and for all who share in the celebration to sign the scroll.

Here is a suggestion to help the children do the activity at home. Explain that they start with two pieces of paper. Show them how to cut one piece with slits and the second piece in strips. Let a few children weave the strips into the slits.

Learn by heart

Faith Summary

- We believe that Jesus is really and truly present in Holy Communion.

  Who do we believe is really present in Holy Communion?

- After we have received Holy Communion, we thank Jesus for coming to us.

  What do we do after we have received Holy Communion?

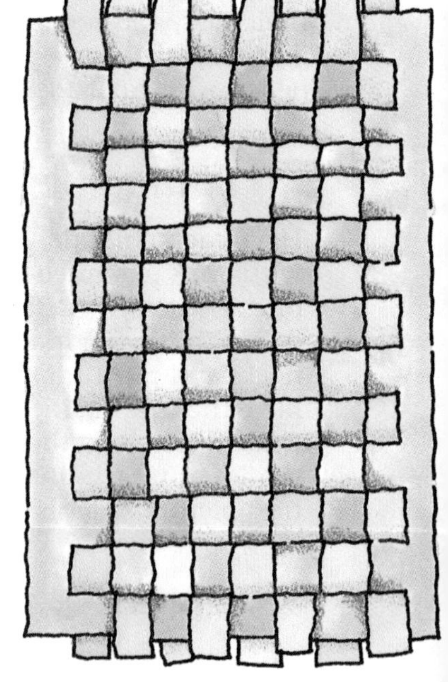

Make a prayer placemat to help you and your family get ready for your First Holy Communion. The pictures show you how. As you weave each paper strip into the mat pray "Jesus, we love You. Stay with us." Put the mat where it will remind you to pray often.

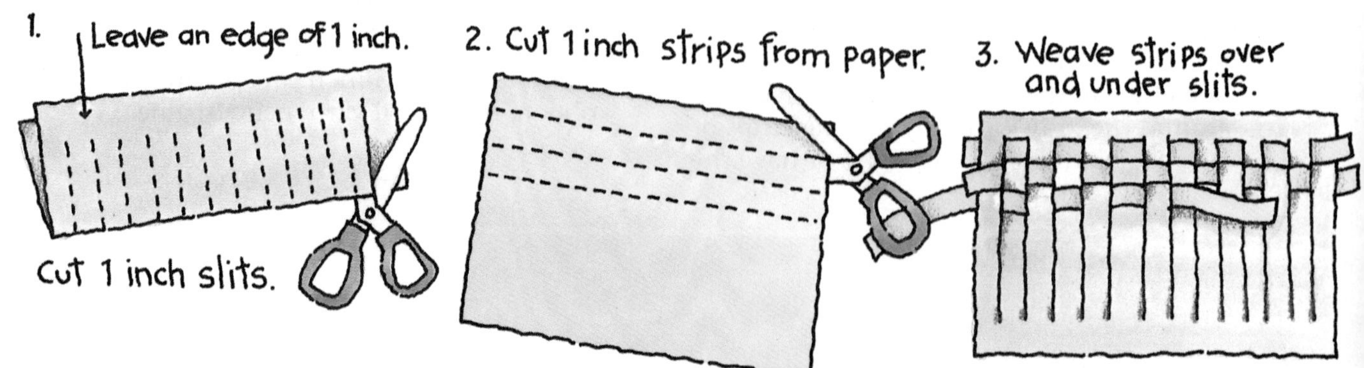

Review

Go over the *Faith Summary* together before your child completes the *Review*. The answers for questions 1–3 appear on page 200. The response to number 4 will show you whether your child understands what it means to receive Jesus for the first time. When the *Review* is completed, have your child put a sticker on this page.

sticker

Circle the correct answer.

1. We receive Jesus in Holy (Celebration, Communion).
2. We do not eat or drink for (five hours, one hour) before Communion.
3. When we receive Holy Communion, we say ("Forgive me," "Amen").
4. Tell what you will say to Jesus after you receive Holy Communion.

Possible responses: I love You; I want to be Your friend; help me to share my toys with others; etc.

Encourage the children to gather with their families to share the *Family Scripture Moment.*

Gather and invite family members to tell about times when they felt close to Jesus. **Listen** to a story about Jesus and children.

Some people brought children to Jesus for Him to place His hands on them and to pray for them, but the disciples scolded the people. Jesus said, "Let the children come to Me and do not stop them, because the kingdom of heaven belongs to such as these." He placed His hands on them and then went away.

From Matthew 19:13–15

Share Why does Jesus say that the kingdom of God belongs to children?

Consider for family enrichment:

- Just as Jesus welcomed children into His arms, He welcomes them into the Church at Baptism and touches them in a deep and personal way in Holy Communion.
- Jesus invites us to come to Him with the simplicity and honesty of children.

Reflect and **Decide** Reread the Scripture passage. Then ask: what can we do in our family and in our parish to imitate Jesus' love for children?

23 We Celebrate Our Life with Jesus

For the Catechist: Spiritual and Catechetical Development

Adult Background

Our Life

An old Celtic proverb says, "Anyone without a soul-friend is a body without a head." A soul-friend is one who shares our spiritual journey. He or she knows and accepts us as we are, offering enthusiastic praise or gentle correction as needed. Binding the two (or more) together is their mutual love for Jesus Christ. They know in their hearts that true friendship "begins in Christ, continues in Christ, and is perfected in Christ" (Saint Aelred of Rievaulx, 12th-century Cistercian).

Ask yourself:

- Do I have (or have I had) a soul-friend?
- How would I characterize him or her?

Sharing Life

In what ways are soul-friends present to one another?

How is Christ the bond between them?

Our Catholic Faith

At the Last Supper, Jesus gave His disciples a new name that signified their future relationship with Him. "I do not call you servants any longer," He said, "because a servant does not know what his master is doing. Instead, I call you friends, because I have told you everything I heard from my Father" (John 15:15).

The loving presence of God to God's people is echoed throughout the Old Testament. In Isaiah, we read "Do not be afraid—I will save you. I have called you by name—you are mine.... Do not be afraid—I am with you!" (Isaiah 43:1, 5). At Bethlehem, God's presence is intensified and deepened in Jesus. Jesus' name speaks the eternal truth: Emmanuel means God-is-with-us.

At times in our history the concept of "God-with-us" has been misconstrued. The idea of God waiting to spot our errors, to catch us, was sometimes communicated. God as "watching to catch us" is a far cry from the God of Scripture who announced God's presence: "Do not be afraid!"

Isaiah says that God has called us by name. What an incredible notion! God—who created the universe, the wonders of nature, the miracle of humanity—this God calls us by name. Such a God is obviously not an impersonal one, but one who calls us into a personal relationship.

The birth of God's own Son reiterates God's concern and desire to be involved in our human lives. The title "Christ" means Savior. Jesus Christ comes to save His people, to make His dwelling with us and within us. Jesus Christ, God-with-us, seeks intimate union with us. By His death and resurrection, Jesus Christ radically transformed all of creation and the whole history of humanity. Jesus Christ united Himself to all creation in such a way that He became permanently a part of human history. Despite this, however, His presence often goes undetected. Although Jesus is present to us, we do not recognize Him. We are more concerned with the affairs of our daily lives. We need to have our eyes of faith opened so that we may recognize our Friend and Brother Jesus the Christ present in our lives.

Coming to Faith

Who or what helps you to believe that God-is-with-us?

What does it mean for your relationship with Jesus that He has named you "friend"?

Practicing Faith

How will you be more attentive to Jesus as your primary Soul-Friend?

How will you encourage the children to see themselves in a relationship with Jesus, who has called each of them "friend"?

The Theme of This Chapter Corresponds with Paragraph 1404

LITURGICAL RESOURCES

At a celebration of the liturgy, the celebrant took the congregation by surprise. Instead of the customary "The Lord be with you," he announced with great feeling, "The Lord is with you." Slightly taken aback by this declaration, the people hesitatingly mumbled, "And also with you." While the priest's greeting was not liturgically correct, it did convey a truth. "The Lord be with you" sounds like a blessing, a hope. "The Lord is with you" states the fulfillment of that hope. Jesus is with us in the Eucharist, the Scripture, and His people.

Make it a habit to say to the children as a group and as individuals, "The Lord is with you when you ... " Complete the greeting with phrases like: "pray," "are peaceful," "help others," and "receive Jesus in Holy Communion."

JUSTICE AND PEACE RESOURCES

When Jesus taught His followers to pray, He said that they should call God "Our Father." In naming God "Our Father," we implicitly name all people our sisters and brothers. Our role in the work of peace and justice is based on our recognition of this relationship with all people and our response to all of those sisters and brothers in need. Our name "Christian" is a global family name. To live up to it we must examine our prejudices and grow to embrace as brothers and sisters any persons whom we now reject.

Help your students to have a sense of themselves in relationship with all God's children. Use photos of people of many races and ethnic groups to talk about how we are all part of God's creation and should help and love each other regardless of skin color. Distribute pieces of colored construction paper. Have the students trace their hands on the paper and then carefully cut out the paper hands. Join all of the hands together as a way of linking together all the peoples of the world.

Teaching Resources

Overview of the Lesson

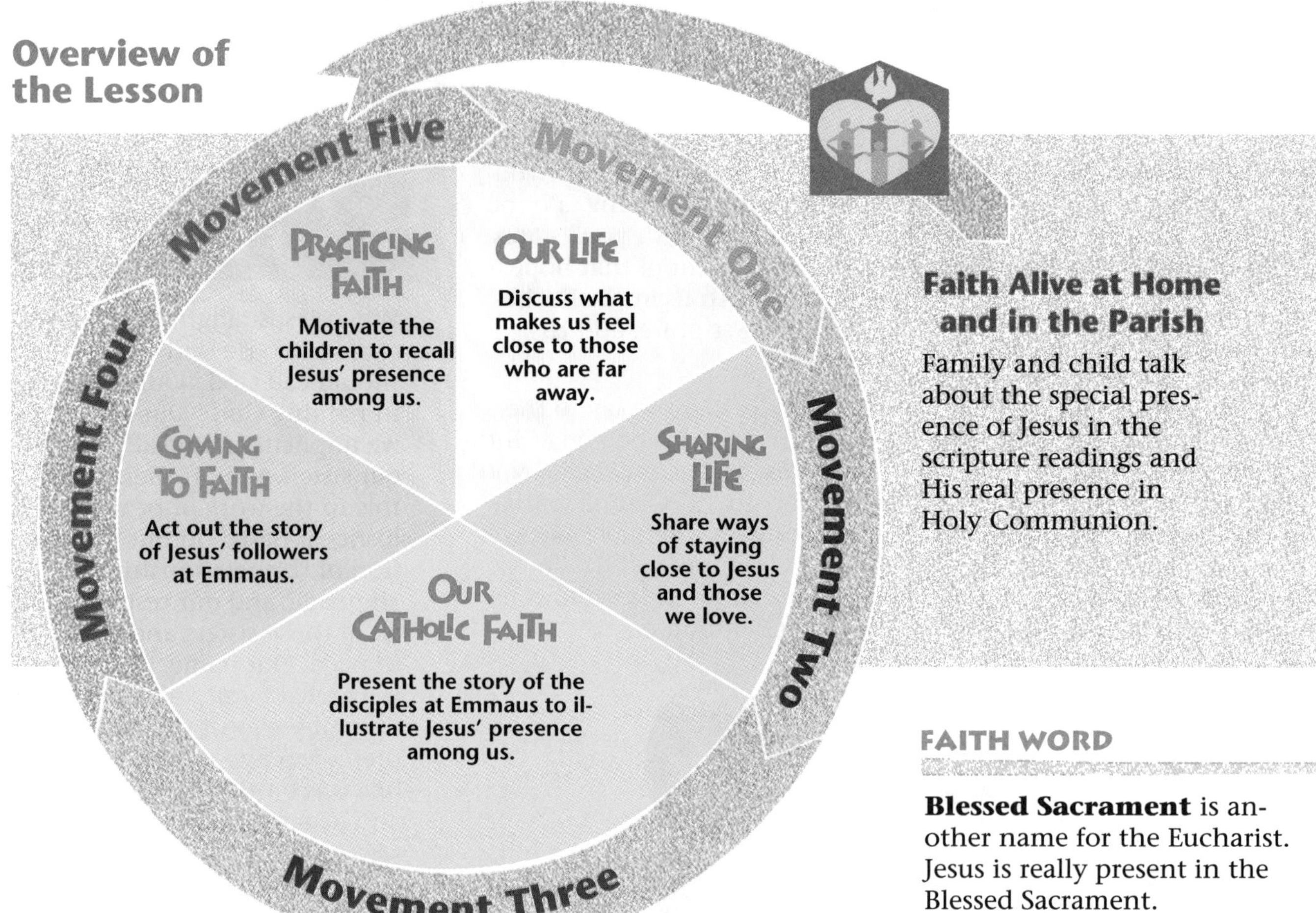

Faith Alive at Home and in the Parish

Family and child talk about the special presence of Jesus in the scripture readings and His real presence in Holy Communion.

FAITH WORD

Blessed Sacrament is another name for the Eucharist. Jesus is really present in the Blessed Sacrament.

Teaching Hints

It is important for children at this age, especially in today's world, to feel they are not alone. In this lesson, they will be reminded of the many different ways in which Jesus keeps His promise to be with us always. Try to instill in them a sense of joyful gratitude for this gift of Jesus' presence. Encourage them to reflect often on it.

Special-Needs Child

Affirm the children for who they are and for their many gifts and talents.

Visual Needs

- enlargement of *Faith Summary* statements

Auditory Needs

- tape recording of scripture story, *Faith Summary* statements, and faith words

Tactile-Motor Needs

- peer helpers to assist in acting out the story

Supplemental Resources

Eucharist: Mass Video
(Ages 6-8)
W.H. Sadlier
9 Pine Street
New York, NY 10005
(1-800-221-5175)

Lesson Plan: Beginning

OBJECTIVES

To help the children

- know the ways that Jesus is with us;
- appreciate Jesus' presence with us;
- often recall Jesus' presence among us.

Focusing Prayer

Tell the children that in this lesson they will learn about the many ways Jesus is with us. Then lead them in the prayer at the top of page 151.

Our Life

Responding to a Story

Invite the children to follow along as you read the story of Jenny and Andrew on page 151. Give them time to comment on the pictures. Then have them respond to the follow-up questions. Emphasize the fact that our relatives and friends continue to love us even when they are far away.

Sharing Life

Focusing on Loved Ones

Call on volunteers to share the name of someone they love who is far away. Have them respond to the first two questions in the *Sharing Life* section. Ask the remaining questions and write the children's responses on the chalkboard or a large piece of paper. Then read back their responses and add some of your own.

23 We Celebrate Our Life with Jesus

Jesus, thank You for being with us always.

(1) Possible responses: thinking about them; sharing your thoughts and experiences with them, etc.

OUR LIFE

Jenny's and Andrew's father was a scientist in Antarctica. He had to be away for a long time. They promised to keep in touch with him by sending him a cassette each week. They filled their cassettes with all the news from home.

What do you think they told him? about school; their friends; things happening at home; etc.

What helps you to feel close to those you love? (1)

(2) Possible responses: write letters to them; phone them; receive letters and phone calls from them; etc.

SHARING LIFE

How do you feel when someone you love is far away? Why? sad; lonely; because I love them and miss them.

What are some ways we can be close to people we love when they are far away? (2)

How can we stay close to Jesus? talk to Jesus in our hearts

151

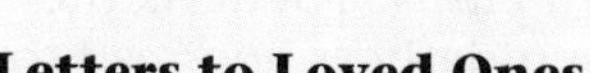

ENRICHMENT

Letters to Loved Ones

Talk with the children about how wonderful it is to receive a letter or card from someone you love who is far away. Let them share any experiences they may have had of this. Then give each child a sheet of writing paper and suggest that they write a letter to someone they love who is far away. Encourage them to tell these persons how much they care for them and how they miss them. Let them decorate their letters with drawings if they wish. Let those who wish share their letters with the group.

Materials needed: writing paper; pencils; crayons

Lesson Plan: Middle

Our Catholic Faith

Remembering Jesus' Promise

Write the word *promise* on the chalkboard or a large sheet of paper. Ask the children if they can remember an important promise Jesus made to His apostles before He died. If they don't know the answer, have them read it together in the first sentence on page 152. Then read the rest of the paragraph. Explain that even though His friends forgot what Jesus had said, He still kept His promise to them.

Listening to an Easter Story

On the chalkboard or a large piece of paper, print a large letter *E,* followed by five dashes. Invite the children to come and write on the chalkboard a letter that will help spell the name of the day on which Jesus kept His promise to His friends. Let as many children as possible help to complete the word *Easter.* Then ask them to listen quietly as you read to them a wonderful story about Jesus.

Read the story from Luke on page 152 with great expression. As you mention the village of Emmaus, write the word on the chalkboard or a large piece of paper and have the children repeat it after you. Comment on the excitement the disciples must have felt when they realized the stranger was Jesus.

Jesus Is with Us Today

Give the children time to examine carefully the picture on pages 152 and 153. Let them comment on it. Ask them what is happening in the small inset. Recall for them what they learned about the Mass. Explain that after Jesus' resurrection, His followers gathered together, as He had asked them to do, to remember and celebrate what Jesus had done at the Last Supper. At that time, they called this the "breaking of the bread." Today, we call it the Mass. Point out that just as the disciples recognized Jesus in the breaking of the bread, so

OUR CATHOLIC FAITH

Activity: Have the children memorize the underlined text on page 153.

Jesus Is with Us

Jesus promised His friends that He would rise from the dead. But after Jesus died and was buried, His friends forgot Jesus' promise. They were sad and afraid.

On Easter morning, two of Jesus' disciples were walking from Jerusalem to a village called Emmaus. As they walked along, Jesus Himself joined them and walked with them. They saw Jesus but they did not recognize Him. They thought He was a stranger.

When they came near Emmaus, Jesus started to leave them. They said, "Please stay with us."

Jesus sat down with them to eat. He took some bread and said the blessing. Then He broke the bread and gave it to them just the way He had done at the Last Supper. At that minute, Jesus' friends recognized Him.

From Luke 24:13–35

152

Lesson Plan: Middle

too at Mass we recognize that Jesus is with us as our Bread of Life. Have the children read the first paragraph on page 153 with you.

Faith Word

Read aloud the second paragraph and pause to explain the meaning of consecrated Hosts: those that have been changed into the Body and Blood of Jesus through the words and actions of the priest. Focus the children's attention on the faith word and have them read the meaning of *Blessed Sacrament* together. Talk about times when they might visit Jesus in the Blessed Sacrament.

Our Catholic Identity

Use the *Our Catholic Identity* on page 12 in the back of the book. Have the children examine the picture showing the tabernacle and sanctuary lamp. If time permits, give the children materials to make their own tabernacles.

Jesus Is Present in Others

Guide the children to an understanding that because Jesus loves us so much, He wants to be with us in every way possible. Show a picture illustrating poor persons or someone who is sick. Read aloud the last two paragraphs, and have the children join in the reading of Jesus' words from Matthew. You may also wish to use pages 51–52 in the activity book.

Materials needed: pictures

FAITH WORD

Blessed Sacrament is another name for Eucharist. Jesus is really present in the Blessed Sacrament.

Jesus' friends recognized Him when He broke the bread. We also recognize Jesus when He comes to us in Holy Communion. He is with us as our Bread of Life.

Jesus remains present in our parish church. We call the consecrated Hosts left over from Mass the Blessed Sacrament. We keep the Blessed Sacrament in a special place called the tabernacle. We can visit Jesus present in the Blessed Sacrament.

Jesus is always with us. He is present in a special way in the poor and the sick. He helps us to live as His disciples and grow in our Catholic faith.

Jesus said, "Wherever two or three of My friends meet together in My name, I will be present with them."
From Matthew 18:20

153

Enrichment

A Visit to Jesus

Take the children to church to visit Jesus in the Blessed Sacrament. If possible, let them stand in the sanctuary, and explain reverently that Jesus is present in the tabernacle. Show the children the sanctuary light and explain that it is a sign that Jesus is present with us in the Eucharist. Kneel near the tabernacle and lead the children in a quiet prayer to thank Jesus for His presence among us.

Lesson Plan: End

Coming to Faith

Acting Out a Story

Let the children look again at the picture on pages 152 and 153. Call on volunteers to act out the story as you read it. Then have them do the imagining activity in the *Coming to Faith* section on page 154 and respond to the follow-up questions.

Faith Summary

Turn to the *Faith Summary* on page 155. Use the annotations to see if the children can express in their own words what they have learned today.

Enrichment

A Reminder of Jesus

Guide the children in making a small holy card. Give each child a piece of posterboard 6″ wide by 11″ long. Help them fold it in three equal parts so that it can stand up. Give each child a small picture of Jesus to paste in the middle section. Have them print across the front of the card *I am with you always.* Let them decorate the card if they wish. Tell them to place it somewhere at home—on their desk or dresser, for example—where they will see it and remember these words of Jesus and be happy knowing that He is with us always.

Materials needed: posterboard; small picture of Jesus for each child; paste; markers

Practicing Faith

Remembering Jesus

Read aloud the *Practicing Faith* section. Have the children join in on the prayer at the bottom of the page. Encourage them to recall Jesus' presence as often as possible each day.

Evaluating Your Lesson

- Do the children know the many ways Jesus is with us today?
- Do they appreciate Jesus' presence?
- Have they decided to remember Jesus is with us always?

Coming to Faith

Act out the story of Jesus and His followers at Emmaus.

Imagine that a new child has come into your group and has no friends. How will you treat her or him? What do you think Jesus would want you to do? Possible responses: be friendly; invite him or her to join you at play, lunch; etc.

How do you feel knowing that Jesus is always with you? Possible responses: happy; glad to have Jesus as my friend; happy not to be alone; etc.

Practicing Faith

Color a stone on the prayer walk each time you remember that Jesus is with you.

Jesus, You are with me

- when bread and wine become Your Body and Blood at Mass.
- when I receive Holy Communion.
- when my friends and I pray together.
- when I try to be fair to everyone.

154

Talk to the children about ways they and their families might use the "Faith Alive" pages. Encourage them to share their prayer walk with someone at home.

A Love Cassette (for use with page 151)

Have a blank cassette and cassette recorder available. With the children, decide on a person they might send a love message to: a classmate who is ill, a person in a nursing home, their pastor, or someone else. Have each child take a turn telling that person's name and speaking a caring message into the cassette. When finished, play back the cassette so the children can hear their messages. Talk about the good effect these messages will have on the person to whom they are sending them.

Materials needed: cassette player; blank cassette

An Emmaus Mural (for use with page 152)

Have the children make a mural of the Emmaus story with two scenes: Jesus and the disciples on the road, and Jesus eating with the disciples.

Tape a long sheet of heavy paper across a wall. Designate Jerusalem at one end, and Emmaus at the other. Have folded slips of paper with the following written on them: trees; grass; Jesus; first disciple; second disciple; birds and sky; mountains; house; table; bread and wine. Place these slips in a box and let the children pick one to see which part of the mural they will draw. If there are more children than strips of paper, let the children suggest other things they might add to the mural.

Materials needed: heavy paper; markers

An Artist's Sketch (for use with page 153)

Talk with the children about how artists often sketch persons and objects with pencil or ink before they paint them.

Take the children to church and invite them to sketch the tabernacle. Guide them with instructions as they go along. Have them notice the lighted sanctuary candle and explain how this tells visitors that Jesus is truly present. Explain that we call Jesus' presence here the Blessed (or Holy) Sacrament. Then return to your room and have the children color and then share their drawings.

Materials needed: drawing paper; pencils

Being a Eucharistic Minister (for use with page 154)

Recall the great privilege eucharistic ministers have, such as carrying Jesus in Holy Communion to the sick or helping to distribute Holy Communion at Mass. Ask how many would like to be eucharistic ministers someday.

Explain that even though they cannot yet carry Jesus in Holy Communion to others, they do have ways of bringing Jesus to others. Give examples, such as comforting someone who is sad, sharing candy, games, and so forth.

Have each child decide how he or she will be a "eucharistic minister" to someone. Distribute sheets of yellow construction paper. Have them cut out a chalice with a host showing above the rim. Let them write on this how they will "carry" Jesus to someone during the coming week.

Materials needed: yellow construction paper; marker's scissors

FAITH ALIVE AT HOME AND IN THE PARISH

Your child has learned that Jesus is with us always. After we receive Jesus in Holy Communion, He continues to be with us in our daily lives. Jesus is present in the Blessed Sacrament reserved in our parish churches. We encounter Jesus in the people we meet. The Church also reminds us that we encounter the risen Christ when we reach out to people in need. Above all, the family should be the place where your child continues to find Jesus.

You might ask yourself:

- *Do I believe that Jesus is present to me always? Or do I forget when I am tired, cranky, or upset?*
- *What will my family and I do this week to show our conviction that Jesus is with us?*

If possible, try to participate in the Eucharist as a family this week. Before Mass, remind the family of the special presence of Jesus in the Scripture readings and His real presence in Holy Communion.

Learn by heart

Faith Summary

- Jesus is really present in the Blessed Sacrament.
  Where is Jesus really present?
- Jesus is with us whenever we come together in His name.
  When is Jesus with us?

A Family Blessing

Ask your family to gather in a circle. As a sign of blessing, ask everyone to raise their right hands as shown. Remind your family that Jesus is with all of you as you pray together.

Leader: When we are with each other, help us remember You are with us.
All: Jesus, bless us with Your peace and love.

Leader: When we are at work or play with others,
All: Jesus, bless us with Your peace and love.

Leader: Jesus, help us to see You in everyone we meet.
All: Jesus, bless us with Your peace and love.

After praying, share together a special family treat.

Review

Go over the *Faith Summary* together before your child completes the *Review*. The answers for questions 1–3 appear on page 200. The response to number 4 will show you whether your child understands that Jesus is with us always. When the *Review* is completed, have your child place a sticker on this page.

sticker

Write the correct answer on each line.

Jesus Life Blessed Sacrament

1. When we help someone in need,

J esus ____________ is with us.

2. Jesus is really present in the

B lessed ____________ Sacrament ____________ .

3. In Holy Communion Jesus is our Bread of

L ife ____________ .

4. Tell how you will remember that Jesus is with you always.

By receiving Jesus in Holy Communion; by sharing Jesus' love with others; etc.

Encourage the children to gather with their families to share the *Family Scripture Moment.*

As you **Gather** invite family members to imagine how they would respond if Jesus unexpectedly dropped in on them. Then **Listen** to Jesus' words.

Whoever welcomes you welcomes Me; and whoever welcomes Me welcomes the one who sent Me. Whoever welcomes God's messengers because they are God's messengers, will share in their reward. And whoever welcomes good people because they are good, will share in their reward. You can be sure that whoever gives even a drink of cold water to one of the least of these My followers because that person is My follower, will certainly receive a reward.

From Matthew 10:40–42

Share Ask: Who comes to us that reminds us of Jesus?

Consider for family enrichment:

- Here Jesus identifies Himself with God, and His disciples with Himself. To show hospitality to a disciple is to earn a lasting reward in heaven.
- Even a drink of cold water given in the name of Jesus will receive a reward.

Reflect and **Decide** Who might be some of Jesus' "least followers" in our parish and community? How will we welcome them as messengers of God to us?

24

Jesus Christ Is with Our Community

For the Catechist: Spiritual and Catechetical Development

Adult Background

Our Life

The people of Holy Cross Parish were taken by surprise when their pastor announced a "hospitality time" to precede each liturgy. Father Ray asked them to stand up and reach out to someone near them—even if it meant leaving their pews! "Introduce yourself to someone new," he advised, "or renew an old acquaintance. Let someone know you are happy they are here. After all, we are all members of the same family."

Like icebergs breaking loose at the spring thaw, the parishioners rose from their habitual places and moved towards each other. A murmur of greetings punctuated by laughter suddenly warmed the church. "I'm glad someone finally suggested that we do this," a catechist observed.

Ask yourself:

- When and how have I experienced the Church as a community or a family?

Sharing Life

Why are Catholics sometimes slow to express their unity in action?

How do we make Jesus present to one another in the faith community?

Our Catholic Faith

The Constitution on the Church of the Second Vatican Council describes the Church as a sign and a sacrament. The Church is a visible sign of the union between God and all people, brought about by the life, death, and resurrection of Jesus Christ. The Church also acts as an instrument of unity. With the help of the Holy Spirit, the Church builds up the body of Christ by uniting all baptized persons to Christ and to one another.

Although we are all members of a diocese or local church, our primary experience of the Church is probably defined by our own parish. It is in the parish that we are called by name; our gifts are affirmed, and we are invited to minister to others. The parish is the community that supports us and reminds us of Jesus' presence in our midst. The parish is the community that directly challenges us to respond to Jesus.

Yet the seed of faith planted by God finds its most fertile ground in the family. In our own homes we first learn the meaning of love, forgiveness, service, and celebration. In the family we form our concept of God, our neighbors, and our life values. Although as we mature we are better able to come to a sense of the whole world as our global community, the family remains our core community.

In his 1994 New Year's Message, Pope John Paul II observes: "The Church is home and family for all. She opens wide her doors and welcomes in all who are alone or abandoned; in them she sees the specially beloved children of God, whatever their age, and whatever their aspirations, difficulties or hopes." This is the Church in which Jesus makes Himself at home with us.

Coming to Faith

What is your vision of a hospitable Church?

How will you work to achieve it?

Practicing Faith

What will you do to make Jesus present to the children in your group this week?

How will you help them to experience the Church as their home?

The Theme of This Chapter Corresponds with Paragraph 1369

LITURGICAL RESOURCES

To introduce the children to some of their ancestors in faith, display a large family tree labeled "Our Church Family." Invite the children to draw out of a basket pictures, symbols, or name cards of saints or other people whose lives were examples of saintly living. On the back of each card write one sentence about how the saint followed Jesus or helped our Church family.

Examples:

- Saint Thérèse encouraged us to do little things well out of love for Jesus.
- Saint Francis praised God for making such a beautiful world.
- Saint Elizabeth Seton founded Catholic schools for teaching our faith.
- Saint Peter Claver served slaves and treated them with respect.
- Archbishop Oscar Romero stood up for the poor who were treated unjustly.

Have each child add a saint to the tree.

JUSTICE AND PEACE RESOURCES

In their 1993 pastoral message to families, *Follow the Way of Love*, the U.S. Catholic Bishops write:

> There are so many ways in which families can give life, especially in a society that devalues life... Each generation of a family is challenged to leave the world a more beautiful and beneficial place than it inherited.

One way you can affirm the families of the children is by soliciting help to produce a simple newsletter called "Our Families Give Life." Have each child who chooses to do so introduce his or her family in the newsletter by telling something about them. If possible, photocopy family photos. Carry brief stories about how families give life to each other, the parish, and the community.

Teaching Resources

Overview of the Lesson

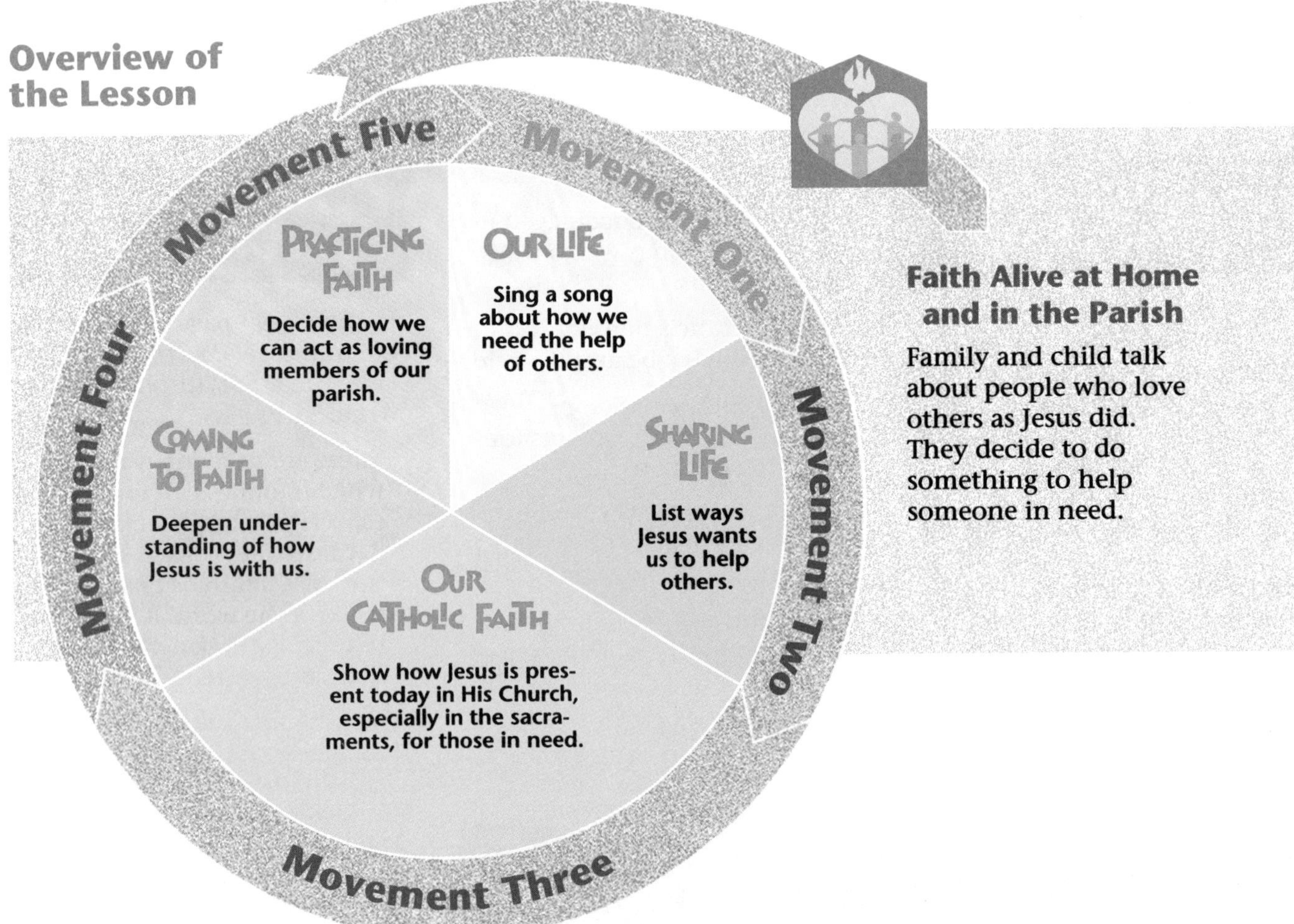

Teaching Hints

This lesson will focus on the ways Jesus is present with us in our community, the Church. Help the children realize that the sacraments are dynamic actions of Jesus, His way of being present personally at important moments in our lives. Guide them in understanding also that when we help others in need, we are helping Jesus.

Special-Needs Child

When giving directions, first gain the special-needs child's attention. Make sure you give the directions slowly, one at a time. Then quietly repeat the directions.

Visual Needs

■ sandpaper letters for the word *sacraments*

Auditory Needs

■ headphones, tape recording of song

Tactile-Motor Needs

■ peer helper to assist in writing activity

Supplemental Resources

Martin the Cobbler (video)
Mass Media Ministries
2116 North Charles Street
Baltimore, MD 21218
(1-800-828-8825)

Lesson Plan: Beginning

Objectives

To help the children

- know the many ways Jesus is with us in the Church;
- appreciate Jesus' presence among us;
- choose to be loving members of their parish.

Focusing Prayer

Recall for the children what they learned in a previous lesson about Jesus' promise to be with us to help us love one another. Then lead them in the prayer at the top of page 157.

Our Life

We Need One Another

Have the children look at the adults in the illustrations on page 157. Ask what they are doing and why. Talk with them about the boy and girl in the picture who are learning to play instruments but can't do it alone, and about the boy who needs someone to hold the stake he is hammering into the ground. Go over the melody for "Frère Jacques" briefly, and then teach the words to the song. Have the children sing the song as they point to each picture in turn. Then have the children respond to the follow-up directive and question. See the annotation.

You may wish to use the grade 2 *Coming to Faith in Song* cassette.

Sharing Life

Making a List

Invite the children to respond to the questions in the *Sharing Life* section. Have them respond to the directive, then list their answers on the chalkboard or a large piece of paper.

Enrichment

A Helpers' Chain

Guide the children in tracing the outlines of their hands on sheets of construction paper. Have each one print his or her name on the hand and cut it out. Make a long chain of their "hands" by stapling them together. Hang it up at the front of the room as a reminder that Jesus wants all of us to help one another.

Materials needed: construction paper; markers; scissors; stapler

24 Jesus Christ Is with Our Community

Jesus, help us to serve one another.

Repetition of the words and melody will help the children remember the song.

Our Life

Let's sing about each picture.
(To the tune of "Frère Jacques")

♫ I can't play it, I can't play it.
It's too hard, it's too hard.
Need someone to help me.
Who will come to help me?
Tell me who, tell me who.

I can't do it, I can't do it.
Don't know how, don't know how
Need someone to help me.
Who will come to help me?
Tell me who, tell me who. ♫

Tell about some of the people who help you.
Whom do you help?

(1) Yes; because sometimes we need help in learning and doing new things.

Sharing Life

Is it easier to do some things when people help us?
Why or why not? (1)

Together make a list of the ways that Jesus wants us to help other people.

Lesson Plan: Middle

Our Catholic Faith

Jesus Helps Us

Recall for the children the promise Jesus made to be with us always. Explain that Jesus helps us do many special things. See if the children can name what these are. Then have them read together with you the first two paragraphs on page 158.

Some Sacraments

Display a flash card with the word *sacraments*. Explain to the children that sacraments are special gifts Jesus gave to His Church so that we could be helped in special ways.

Read the next four paragraphs on pages 158 and 159 carefully with the children. Have them underline the name of each of the sacraments mentioned. Ask them to share any knowledge they have about the sacraments of Baptism and Confirmation, and use the pictures on this page to further the discussion. Try to develop in them a sense of eagerness to receive the sacraments of Reconciliation and Eucharist.

Ways Jesus Is with Us

Begin a list on the chalkboard or large piece of paper entitled "Ways Jesus Is with Us." Recall for the children what they learned in the last lesson—that Jesus is with us in the Blessed Sacrament and in a special way when we serve the poor and sick. Put these on the list. Add the word *sacraments*.

Our Catholic Faith

Stress the underlined text.

In Our Church

Disciples of Jesus are ready to help all people. This shows that we are members of Jesus' community, the Church.

Jesus helps us to pray, love, and serve others as He did. He is with our Church in a special way when we celebrate the sacraments.

Ask: What does our Church do that Jesus did?

Jesus welcomed everyone to be His friend. In the sacrament of Baptism, the Church welcomes all people to share the new life we have with Jesus.

Jesus sent the Holy Spirit to help His Church. In the sacrament of Confirmation, the Holy Spirit comes to us in a special way to help us live as Jesus' disciples.

Jesus forgave people who sinned. In the sacrament of Reconciliation, the Catholic Church celebrates God's forgiveness.

Lesson Plan: Middle

Help the children appreciate that Jesus shares with us God's life and love.

Studying Pictures

Give the children a few minutes to examine the pictures on page 159. Talk about what is happening in each one. Then read aloud the rest of page 159. Recall for them what they learned about the parish family celebrating Eucharist together. Explain that this is the great "get-together" moment for our parish family and that Jesus is with us in a very special way at that time.

Help the children recall the importance of living out during the week the Mass they celebrated on Sunday. Ask how the boy in the lower picture is doing this. Have them read together again Jesus' words from Matthew, and emphasize the importance of always remembering them. You may also wish to use pages 53–54 in the activity book.

Our Catholic Identity

Use the *Our Catholic Identity* page 13 in the back of the book. Introduce the story by telling the children that many of the prayers we say at Mass can be found in the Bible. Read the story with great feeling. Pause to have the children repeat the words of the important person mentioned in the story. Have the children make a prayer card similar to the one on the page. Explain that God loves us so much that by His Word we become good enough and can receive Jesus, God's Son, into our hearts. Suggest that they bring their prayer card to Mass.

The sacraments are powerful signs through which Jesus shares with us God's life and love. Jesus is with us in the sacrament of the Eucharist. We can ask His help to live our Catholic faith when we receive Him in Holy Communion.

In Our Parish and Family

Our parish is our home in the Catholic Church. Jesus Christ is with us when we gather with our parish family to pray and worship God.

Jesus wants us to celebrate the sacraments often with our parish family. Most of all, Jesus is with our parish family when we celebrate the sacrament of the Eucharist.

Jesus is also with us when we work together in our parish and in our families to love and serve one another and those in need. If people need food to eat or a place to live, our parish must try to help.

Remember, Jesus says, "When you do something good for someone, you do it for Me."

From Matthew 25:40

Enrichment

An Exchange of Gifts

Have prepared two large gift boxes and some wrapping paper. Let the children cover the sides and tops of the boxes by pasting wrapping paper to them, then give them ribbons for the top. Make two large tags, one that reads, *From Jesus to Us,* and another that says, *From Us to Jesus.* Divide the children into two groups and distribute paper and drawing materials. Have one group draw pictures of things they learned about today that are gifts from Jesus. Let the other group draw pictures of gifts they can give to Jesus by helping others. Have them place their pictures ceremoniously in the boxes.

Materials needed: two large boxes; wrapping paper; glue; drawing paper; markers; gift tags; ribbons

Lesson Plan: End

Coming to Faith

Remembering Jesus Is with Us

Have prepared slips of paper—enough copies for the entire group—on each of which is written one of the following letters: *B; C; E; R; AT*. Fold the papers and give one to each child. Then have them turn to page 160 and find in the *Coming to Faith* section the word beginning with their letter that tells of a way Jesus is with us. (Have them find the words *another time* in the last sentence.) Each child should respond to the directive by explaining the word that begins with his or her letter.

Materials needed: slips of paper with letters

Faith Summary

Turn to the *Faith Summary* on page 161. Use the annotations to see if the children can express in their own words what they have learned today.

Enrichment

Making a Promise Note

Let each child cut a large heart out of red construction paper. Give each one a piece of note paper. Ask them to think of someone who might need their help during the week. Have them write a short note promising to help this person. Have them attach the note to the heart and give the note to this person.

Materials needed: construction and note paper; scissors

Practicing Faith

Deciding What We Will Do

Help the children decide what they will do to show they are loving members of their parish. Guide them in writing their plans inside the helping hands outlined at the bottom of page 160. Then end with the last verse of the song, sung to the tune of "Frère Jacques."

Evaluating Your Lesson

- Do the children know the many ways Jesus is with us in the Church?
- Do they appreciate Jesus' presence with us?
- Have they decided to be loving members of their parish?

Coming to Faith

Tell how Jesus is with us in each of these sacraments.

Baptism **Confirmation**
Reconciliation **Eucharist**

Tell about another time when you know that Jesus is with you.
Possible responses: when I pray; when I live the Law of Love; etc.

Practicing Faith

What will you do to show that you are a loving member of your parish? of your family? Write your plans in the helping hands. Then join hands and sing.

♫ We can do it, we can do it.
Yes we can, yes we can!
We can love like Jesus.
He will always help us.
Yes He will, yes He will! ♫

member of my parish
participate at Mass

member of my family
help, share, pray

Talk to the children about ways they and their families might use the "Faith Alive" pages. Encourage them especially to talk with their families about helping others. Then pray the *Family Prayer* as a closing faith response.

160

A Stick Puppet and a Song (for use with page 157)

Distribute drawing paper and have the children draw the face and shoulders of a boy or girl on it. Let them cut out the drawing and attach it with masking tape to a ruler or long stick. Let them use these stick puppets to respond to the questions on page 157.

Call on volunteers to sing their responses by changing the words of the song, using the same melody. For example:

I can ______, I can ______,

It's not hard, it's not hard.

______________ came to help me,

He/She ___________________

So, it's not hard, it's not hard.

On the first two lines have them indicate what it is they can do because another person helped them. On the third line, have them add the name of the person who helped them, and on the fourth line, they might add how the person helped them.

Materials needed: drawing paper; markers; scissors; rulers or long sticks; tape

Adopting New Parish Members (for use with pages 158–159)

Obtain from your RCIA coordinator or from the parish bulletin the names of those persons who were baptized or received into full communion with the Church at Eastertime. Let each child "adopt" one of these new parish members to pray for.

Give each child a sheet of drawing paper. Have them make a card to send to their "adopted" friend. Have them tell the person something about themselves and that they will pray for them.

Materials needed: drawing paper; markers; list of new parish members

Parish Buttons (for use with page 159)

Talk with the children about how the Church is divided into parish families. Have the children tell what their parish name is, and write it on the chalkboard.

Distribute pieces of posterboard about $5\frac{1}{2}''$ x 8″ to each child. Let each one trace a circle on their posterboard. Then have the children print on the button: "I belong to ______ parish," adding their parish name. Let them decorate the buttons with markers and attach them to their shirts or dresses with masking tape.

Materials needed: posterboard; markers; scissors; tape

Conversing with Jesus (for use with page 160)

Explain to the children that Jesus wants all of us to be happy in our parish family. One of the things that can make us happy is living by Jesus' words. Tell the children you are going to read a sentence that contains some of Jesus' words, and that you want them to finish it by saying how they can live those words. Read the following to the children:

If I met Jesus on my way home from school today, and He said to me: "As long as you did something good for someone, you did it for Me!" I would tell Jesus that I ______.

Let each child contribute an ending to the story. Then conclude with a prayer asking for Jesus' help in living their responses.

FAITH ALIVE AT HOME AND IN THE PARISH

Your child has learned that Jesus is with us in our Church, our parish, and our family. Each time we pray together as a family, Jesus is with us. We can do this each morning and evening and before and after our meals. Most of all, we can pray together with our whole parish family at Mass.

Each time our family reads the Bible, Jesus is with us. Jesus is with us especially when we help other families who are hurting or who are in need of food, clothing, friendship, or other assistance.

After First Holy Communion, encourage your child to receive the Eucharist at Mass every weekend. After they have celebrated the sacrament of Reconciliation for the first time, help them to develop the practice of celebrating it regularly.

Friends of Jesus

Give your child examples of people who love others as Jesus does. You might share stories of the saints. It is important that your child understand saints as ordinary people whose love of God enabled them to do extraordinary things. Help your child with the activity below.

† Family Prayer

Jesus, help my family to help others.

Learn by heart

Faith Summary

- The Catholic Church helps us to grow in our life with Jesus.
  Who helps us grow in our life with Jesus?
- Jesus is with us when we celebrate the sacraments, pray together, and help those in need.
  When is Jesus with us?

Trace the card below. Send the message to someone who needs comfort and love.

Review

Go over the *Faith Summary* together before your child completes the *Review.* The answers for questions 1–3 appear on page 200. The response to number 4 shows whether your child really understands that Jesus is present in the life of your family. When the *Review* is completed, have your child place a sticker on this page.

sticker

Circle the letter next to the correct answer.

1. Our Church welcomes

   (a.) everyone. **b.** some people.

2. Jesus is with our Church

   (a.) forever. **b.** sometimes.

3. Jesus wants us to help

   a. only our parish. (b.) all those in need.

4. Tell how Jesus is with you in your family and parish.

   Jesus is with us in the sacraments, at Mass, when we pray together, and when we help one another.

Encourage the children to gather with their families to share the *Family Scripture Moment.*

Gather and ask: What leaders do we admire most? Whom do we most want to follow? Then **Listen** to Jesus' words.

You know that the rulers of the Gentiles have power over them, and the leaders have complete authority. This, however, is not the way it shall be among you. If one of you wants to be great, that person must be the servant of the rest; and if one of you wants to be first, that person must be your slave—like the Son of Man, who did not come to be served, but to serve and to give His life to redeem many people.

From Matthew 20:25–28

Share What do you think of Jesus' advice about becoming "great"?

Consider for family enrichment:

- When two of Jesus' disciples wanted the highest places of honor in His community, He corrected them. The greatest followers of Jesus are those who serve with humility and love.
- By imitating Jesus' example, we can be among the greatest in God's kingdom.

Reflect and **Decide** How can we support the leaders of our Church? What will we do as a family to practice the kind of greatness that Jesus describes?

25 Mary, Our Mother

For the Catechist: Spiritual and Catechetical Development

Adult Background

Our Life

The story of a friendship between a young Irish Catholic boy and a Jewish girl is told in the film "Hand in Hand." Each decides to go to the other's worship service as a test of their friendship. Although Michael is terrified in the synagogue, the rabbi calms him by praying one line from a Psalm in English rather than Hebrew: "The Lord is with you. Have no fear."

When Rachel attends Mass, she is equally terrified by the foreign prayers and the unfamiliar ritual. Then a statue of a lovely Lady catches her eye. A few minutes later, Rachel smiles and says, "It's alright, Michael. The Lady likes me."

Ask yourself:

- How has Mary made her presence known in my life?

Sharing Life

In what ways might Mary unite rather than divide people of different faiths?

How does your relationship with Mary affect your present spirituality?

Our Catholic Faith

From the time of the earliest failures of people to live as God wanted them to live, the promise of the Messiah was God's gift of hope to humanity. The prophet Isaiah reiterates God's promise in Genesis and the significance of the woman who will be instrumental in its fulfillment: "Well then, the Lord himself will give you a sign: a young woman who is pregnant will have a son and will name him 'Immanuel'" (Isaiah 7:14).

At the Annunciation, both the will of God and the character of Mary as a faithful Jewish girl are revealed. To God's request, the Virgin Mary responds immediately with trust. She does not waver indecisively. She does not delay her answer until she has consulted with Joseph or her parents. She is not a passive vessel, submitting to others' opinions and decisions. She makes her choice with confidence and faith.

Certainly Our Lady had a close relationship with God and a strong, healthy sense of self-identity to say "Yes" so naturally. She knew that her "Yes" meant a change in her own plans and uncertainty for her future. Yet she did not regret her response, but rejoiced in God's plan and proclaimed His greatness and glory in the Magnificat. She expressed no self-pity or helplessness. She did not complain of lost opportunity or unfulfillment. Our Lady never used her position as the Mother of Jesus to draw crowds. Her focus was within, on her relationship to God and her willingness to respond joyfully to Him. Mary is, indeed, a great sign of discipleship.

Jesus must have found great encouragement in the faith of His Mother. Perhaps that is why, as His earthly life ended, He turned to John and said, "Behold your mother." He gave Mary as Mother to John and to all of us. How privileged we are to have Mary as our mother and model of discipleship! It is good for us to know that "The Lady likes us."

Coming to Faith

What image of Mary is most meaningful for you?

How can Our Lady be a model for you?

Practicing Faith

How will you reflect Mary as mother or disciple in your life?

How will you encourage the children to have devotion to our Blessed Mother?

The Theme of This Chapter Corresponds with Paragraph 494

LITURGICAL RESOURCES

The Church celebrates the life of Jesus Christ throughout the liturgical year. The Church also teaches that we should honor the Blessed Mary, Mother of God, with a special love.

Distribute calendars to your group. Tell them about some of the following feasts as you list them on the chalkboard:

September 8, Birth of Mary;

October 7, Our Lady of the Rosary;

November 21, Presentation of Mary;

December 8, Immaculate Conception;

December 12, Our Lady of Guadalupe;

January 1, Mother of God;

February 11, Our Lady of Lourdes;

March 25, Annunciation;

May 31, Visitation.

Have the children color in each feast day on the calendar. During the year, help them to become familiar with Mary by observing her feast days. Recall the story of the particular feast and pray the Hail Mary or an original litany together.

JUSTICE AND PEACE RESOURCES

Mary's Song, the Magnificat (Luke 1:46–55), is a powerful and prophetic statement of God's compassion for the least ones. The Mother of Jesus praises God, who:

> has brought down mighty
> kings from thrones, and
> lifted up the lowly.
> He has filled the hungry
> with good things,
> and sent the rich away with
> empty hands.
> (From Luke 1:52–53)

Share these lines with your group. Explain that Mary was a poor person and that her people, the Jews, had suffered many unjust things. Invite the children to name those who are hungry or treated unfairly today. Decide together how to honor Mary by helping someone they have named.

Teaching Resources

Overview of the Lesson

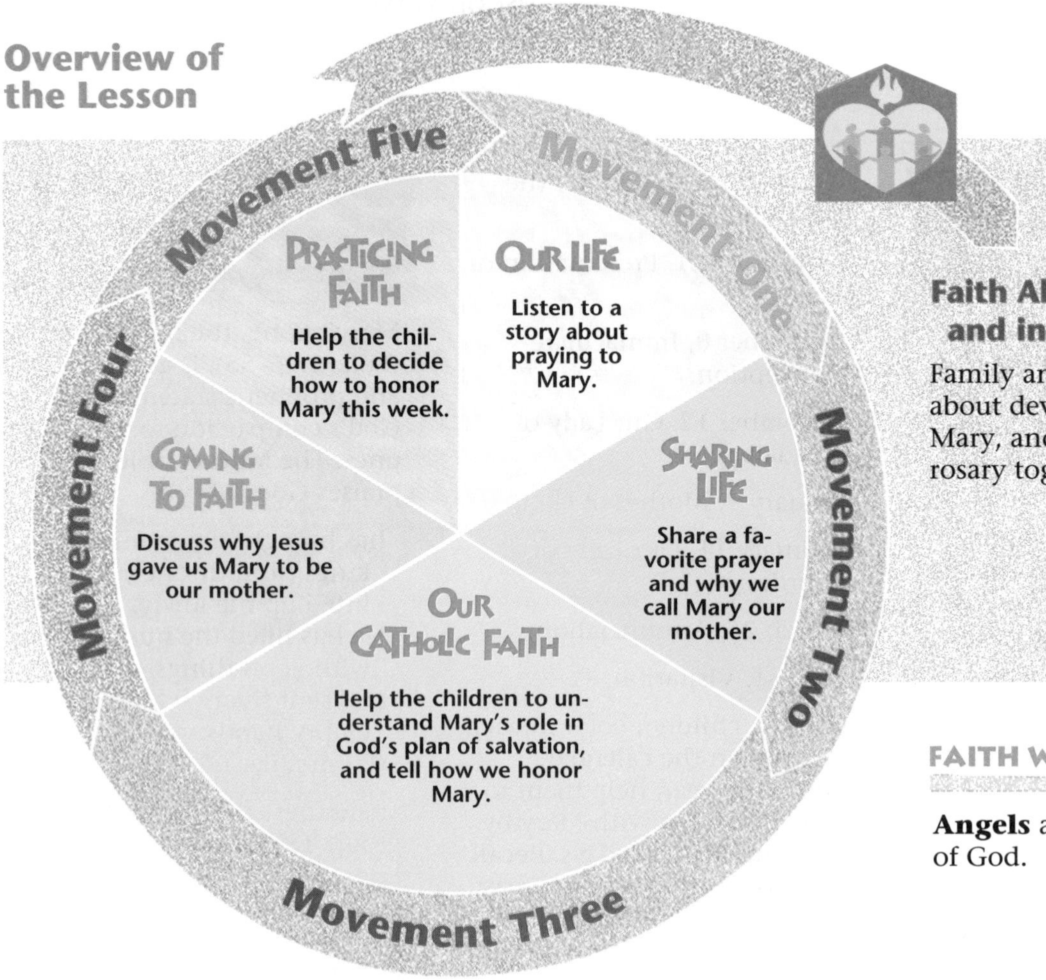

Faith Alive at Home and in the Parish

Family and child talk about devotion to Mary, and pray the rosary together.

FAITH WORD

Angels are special messengers of God.

Teaching Hints

Devotion to Mary is an important part of our Catholic heritage. In this lesson, help to develop in the children a love and respect for Mary as the mother of Jesus and as an example of all we are called to become. Make a Mary shrine or decorate a special corner of your room as a Mary corner where the children may go and speak quietly to her in prayer. Help them to understand that Mary loves us as her own children.

Special-Needs Child

It is important to assign only one task at a time to the special-needs child.

Visual Needs

- peer helper to assist in making a decade of the rosary

Auditory Needs

- headphones and tape of the Hail Mary

Tactile-Motor Needs

- peer helper to assist in making a decade of the rosary

Supplemental Resources

Mary, Our Friend (video)
Brown-ROA
2460 Kerper Blvd.
P.O. Box 539
Dubuque, IA 52004-0539
(1-800-922-7696)

Lesson Plan: Beginning

Objectives

To help the children

- know Mary's part in God's plan for us;
- appreciate Mary's role in our lives;
- decide to honor Mary.

Focusing Prayer

Tell the children that in today's opening prayer we will speak to someone who was very close to Jesus during His earthly life. Then lead them in the beginning of the Hail Mary at the top of page 163.

Our Life

A Story About Good News

Have the children look at the picture at the bottom of page 163 as you read the story to them. Some of them may have experienced something similar. Allow them to share their stories if they wish. Then have the children respond to the follow-up question.

Sharing Life

Thinking About Mary

Show a beautiful picture of Mary. Help the children recall what they learned about Mary in previous lessons. Give each child the opportunity to respond to the questions in the *Sharing Life* section. Share your own favorite prayer to Mary with the children.

Materials needed: picture of Mary

25 Mary, Our Mother

Hail Mary, full of grace, the Lord is with you.

Our Life

Chris was almost ready for bed. His mom came in to say good night. She was smiling. "I have wonderful news to tell you, Chris," she said. "Someone new will be coming to our family. We're going to have a baby."

Chris jumped out of bed with excitement. "Great!" he said. "When will the baby come? Will it be a girl or a boy?"

Mom hugged him. She said, "We'll see. But for now let's ask Mary to take care of the baby and all of us."

So Chris and his mom prayed to Mary. What do you think they said?

Sharing Life

What is your favorite prayer to Mary?
Possible response: Hail Mary

Why can we call Mary our mother, too?
Possible response: Jesus gave Mary to us to be our mother, too.

163

Enrichment

Praying for Unborn Babies

Have the children gather in a prayer circle around a table on which you have placed a statue of Mary. Tell the children that we want all mothers and all families to feel as happy as Chris and his mom did when a new baby is about to be born to them. Have the children join hands and say a prayer to Mary, asking her to ask Jesus to help families welcome new babies.

Materials needed: statue of Mary

Lesson Plan: Middle

Our Catholic Faith

An Answer to God's Promise

Have the children turn to page 164 in their books. Read aloud the introductory paragraph and see what the children remember about the first sin. Then read the rest of the page. Emphasize the fact that the first people had said no to God but that Mary's answer was always yes.

Mary Visits Her Cousin

Ask the children to share with you the names of some of their cousins. Ask whether they live close by or far away and if they ever get to visit them. Tell them that Mary had a cousin named Elizabeth who lived very far from Mary. Have them listen as you read aloud the first paragraph on page 165, the story of Mary's visit to Elizabeth.

Studying a Picture

Have the children study the picture of Mary and Elizabeth on pages 164 and 165. Ask what they think Elizabeth and Mary might be talking about and how they can tell how much they loved each other.

The Hail Mary

Ask how many of the children know the Hail Mary. Read aloud the second paragraph on page 165. See if the children can go back and find Elizabeth's words in the paragraph above. Then have them turn to the Hail Mary prayer in the back of their books and find Elizabeth's words there.

Mary Our Mother

Tell the children that the Hail Mary is a very special prayer for followers of Jesus, first because Mary is Jesus' mother, and for another reason too. Have them read the last sentence on the page to find the other reason.

Stress the underlined text.

Mary the Mother of Jesus

In a Bible story we learned that the first people turned away from God's love and sinned. But God still loved them and promised to send a Savior.

The Savior would be the Son of God. To become one of us, the Son of God would need a human mother. <u>So God chose Mary, even before she was born, to be the mother of Jesus.</u>

One day an angel came to Mary with a message. God wanted Mary to be the mother of His Son. Mary said yes to God. She said, "I am the Lord's servant. May it happen to me as you have said."

From Luke 1:38

164

Lesson Plan: Middle

Our Catholic Identity

Use the *Our Catholic Identity* on page 14 in the back of the book. If possible, have some inexpensive rosaries available for the children to examine, or show them one of your own. Have them follow along on the diagram as you explain the rosary and how to pray it. If time permits have the children make a decade of the rosary using string and plastic beads or pieces of macaroni.

Multicultural Awareness

Talk with the children about the fact that Jesus gave Mary to be the mother of all of His followers, from every country of the world. If possible, show pictures of Mary that are unique to other cultures, for example: Our Lady of Guadalupe (Mexico); Our Lady of Fatima (Portugal); Our Lady of Czestochowa (Poland); and so forth.

Special Feasts to Honor Mary

Explain to the children that because we love and respect Mary so much, the Church has chosen special days on which to honor Mary, our mother. Read each date listed at the bottom of page 165 and have the children say the name of the feast that occurs on that day. Explain each feast as simply as possible.

You may also wish to use pages 55–56 in the activity book.

FAITH WORD

Angels are special messengers of God.

Mary, Our Mother

Mary had a cousin named Elizabeth. Elizabeth was very old, but she was going to have a baby, too. When Elizabeth saw Mary coming to visit, she knew Mary had been chosen to be the mother of God's own Son. Elizabeth was filled with joy. She said to Mary, "Blessed are you among women, and blessed is the fruit of your womb."

From Luke 1:42

Today we pray a beautiful prayer in which we hear Elizabeth's words. We also hear the words of the angel to Mary. This prayer is called the Hail Mary. The Hail Mary is our very special prayer to Mary.

Before Jesus died on the cross, He gave Mary to us to be our mother, too.

Special Feasts To Honor Mary

Mary, Mother of God	January 1
Annunciation	March 25
Visitation	May 31
Assumption	August 15
Immaculate Conception	December 8
Our Lady of Guadalupe	December 12

Enrichment

A Mary Shrine

Have the children work with you to create a Mary shrine in your room. Place the statue and table used for the previous enrichment activity against a wall. Attach strips of blue and white crepe paper to the wall above the statue and twist them together in pairs. Then attach them to the front of the table to make a "canopy" over the statue. Place some flowers or leaves in front of the statue. You may wish to hang more crepe-paper strips from the sides of the table. Tell the children that they may come and say a prayer to Mary when they wish or bring flowers to place before the shrine.

Materials needed: statue of Mary; blue and white crepe paper; tape; flowers/leaves

Lesson Plan: End

Coming to Faith

Reflecting on Reasons

Ask the children to sit quietly in a circle for a few minutes and to imagine that Jesus is there in the middle of the circle. Ask the question in the *Coming to Faith* section on page 166. Tell the children to think of an answer Jesus might give. Let them take turns sitting in the middle of the circle to answer for Jesus.

Faith Summary

Turn to the *Faith Summary* on page 167. Use the annotations to see if the children can express in their own words what they have learned today.

Practicing Faith

Praying to Mary

Have the children respond to the three questions in the *Practicing Faith* section. Then invite them to gather around the Mary shrine they helped make and sing together the Hail Mary.

Evaluating Your Lesson

- Do the children know why we honor Mary?
- Do they appreciate the role Mary plays in our lives?
- Have they decided to honor Mary?

Enrichment

Making a Rosary

Let the children each make a decade of a rosary. Distribute string and plastic beads (small pieces of macaroni can also be used). Have the children tie a knot at one end of the string. Have them separate the beads by tying knots between each one, and tie three knots at the end of the decade. There should be one bead for the Our Father and ten beads for the Hail Marys. Explain the procedure for praying a decade of the rosary (one Our Father, ten Hail Marys, and one Glory to the Father). Then gather with the children around the Mary shrine and pray a decade of the rosary.

Materials needed: string; plastic beads or macaroni

Coming to Faith

Why do you think Jesus gave us Mary to be our mother?

Possible responses: Mary helps us live as followers of her Son, Jesus; when we pray to Mary, we can ask her to pray to Jesus for us; etc.

Practicing Faith

What prayer can we pray to Mary? (1) the Hail Mary; the rosary.

How can you show that you are Mary's child? Try to live as followers of Jesus; celebrate Mary's feast days; pray.

When will you pray the Hail Mary this week?

Answers will vary.

Now gather together in a circle, holding hands. As our closing prayer, let us sing the Hail Mary.

Talk to the children about ways they and their families might use the "Faith Alive" pages. Show them a rosary and demonstrate how we pray the Hail Mary, Our Father, and Glory to the Father in the appropriate places.

A Prayer Card for New Mothers (for use with page 163)

Have the children make prayer cards to give as gifts to women in the parish who are expecting children or who are new mothers.

Distribute posterboard and have the children paste a picture of Mary on the front. Use small pictures of Mary from greeting cards, old religion texts, or magazines to decorate the cards; or have the children draw a picture of Mary on it. On the front, have them write a short prayer, for example, "Mary, help me raise my child as God wants." On the back of the card, have them write "Congratulations! I'm praying for you and the baby" and sign their name. Have the children offer a prayer together for these mothers or mothers-to-be, and then arrange to have the cards distributed to the expectant or new mothers in the parish.

Materials needed: posterboard; small pictures of Mary; scissors; paste; crayons

A Mary Performance (for use with pages 164–165)

Have the children invite a group of younger children in and let them act out the stories of the angel's visit to Mary and Mary's visit to Elizabeth. You may want to have simple costumes—a white veil for Mary, a gold headband for the angel, another veil for Elizabeth. Have one child read the story on page 164 and another child the story on page 165, while the "actors" portray the actions silently. Let the children suggest their own gestures to use. As a finale to the performance, have all the children join hands and recite together the Church's prayer that contains parts from each of the happenings that were portrayed: the Hail Mary. You may want to play some soft, reflective music in the background.

Materials needed: two veils; "gold" headband; soft music

Mary Feast Posters (for use with page 165)

Distribute large sheets of drawing paper and markers or crayons. Let the children select one of the Mary feasts mentioned on page 165 in their books and make a poster to illustrate it. When all are finished, have them take turns coming to the front of the room, showing their poster, and explaining something about the feast day depicted on it.

Materials needed: posterboard; markers or crayons

Mini-Book of Prayers to Mary (for use with page 166)

Give each child two sheets of white drawing paper $5\frac{1}{2}''$ x $8\frac{1}{2}''$. Have them fold each sheet in half and staple the sheets together to make a small booklet. Distribute small pictures of Mary and have them paste them on the cover. Have them print on the cover, "My Book of Prayers to Mary." Explain that prayers do not have to be long to be special to Mary, and that we can talk in prayer to Mary just as we would talk to our own mothers. Then give the children time to write their own prayers for special occasions; for example: My Morning Prayer to Mary; A Birthday Prayer; A Nighttime Prayer to Mary.

Materials needed: drawing paper; stapler; small pictures of Mary; paste; markers

FAITH ALIVE AT HOME AND IN THE PARISH

Your child has learned that Mary is the mother of Jesus and our mother, too. Fostering devotion to Mary early in life may help your child to understand and appreciate Mary's place in our Catholic faith. Devotion to Mary has always been a rich aspect of Catholic spirituality.

Before Jesus died on the cross, He gave Mary to us to be our mother. Mary, who is in heaven with God forever, loves each one of us. She asks Jesus to help us live as His disciples.

If you have a Church calendar, use it to find the many times we honor Mary throughout the liturgical year. Make a list of all her feast days.

Help your child learn the special prayer to Mary that we call the rosary. The activity below will help you. (Do not expect your child to know the Apostles' Creed yet.)

A Song to Mary

Encourage your child to teach you the Hail Mary song learned in this lesson. Then sing it together.

Learn by heart

Faith Summary

- Mary is the mother of Jesus.
  Who is the mother of Jesus?
- Mary is our mother, too.
  Who is our mother, too?

Color and pray the Rosary

Our Father

Hail Mary

Glory to the Father

Apostles' Creed

Review

Go over the *Faith Summary* together before your child completes the *Review*. The answers for questions 1–3 appear on page 200. The response to number 4 will help you find out whether your child is growing in his or her devotion to Mary.

When the *Review* is completed, have your child place a sticker on this page.

sticker

Complete the following sentences. Use these words.

mother   Hail Mary   our

1. God chose Mary to be Jesus' mother __________.

2. Mary is our __________ mother, too.

3. Our special prayer to Mary is the Hail ______ Mary ______.

4. How will you honor Mary this week? What will you do?

Possible response: I will pray the Hail Mary each night before going to sleep.

Encourage family involvement.

Gather and ask: Who are the people who have nurtured us in faith? Then **Listen** to the story of Jesus' birth.

Mary was engaged to Joseph, but before they were married, she found out that she was going to have a baby by the power of the Holy Spirit. While Joseph was thinking about this, an angel of the Lord appeared to him in a dream and said, "Joseph, descendant of David, do not be afraid to take Mary to be your wife. For it is by the Holy Spirit that she has conceived. She will have a son, and you will name Him Jesus—because He will save His people from their sins."

From Matthew 1:18, 20–21

Share Imagine you are present in this scene. Retell the story in your own words.

Consider for family enrichment:

- Mary cooperated fully with God's plan for our salvation by giving birth to Jesus. Together with Joseph, Mary was willing to face any challenge in following God's invitation.
- Jesus gave Mary to us as our mother. We can always ask her to pray for us.

Reflect and **Decide** What place do we want Mary to have in our family? Do you have a statue or picture of her? Pray the Hail Mary together.

26 Jesus Christ Is with Us Forever

For the Catechist: Spiritual and Catechetical Development

Adult Background

Our Life

Consider the following images of growth:

- an amaryllis bulb sprouting its first green leaves;
- a child's height chart marking many milestones;
- a favorite shirt that is now too small;
- a vineyard at harvest time;
- a beloved book that once seemed unintelligible or "beyond" you.

Ask yourself:

- Which of these images (or another I have thought of) best fits my experiences of personal growth?
- How have I grown during the past year?

Sharing Life

What evidence do you detect of growth in your relationship with Jesus?

What evidence do you hope to see in the coming year?

Our Catholic Faith

One of the signs of spiritual growth is our increasing awareness of the presence of Jesus in our daily lives. He is always there. But we must make a clearing for Him in the midst of our activities and multiple responsibilities and promises:

> "Listen! I stand at the door and knock; if anyone hears my voice and opens the door, I will come in and eat with him."
> (From Revelation 3:20)

Our faith teaches us that Jesus is present to us in Scripture. By reading the Gospels and reflecting prayerfully on them, we come to know Jesus' actions and words. We also grow not only to know Him as He was on earth, but to recognize His presence in our lives.

The sacraments of the Church are signs that Jesus shares with us God's life and love. Through them we celebrate His presence both in the significant events of our lives and every day. In Baptism we celebrate His presence in the newness of life. In the Eucharist we celebrate His presence as nourishment. His presence is felt in the sacraments of Matrimony and Holy Orders as we make commitments of love and service. Jesus speaks to us through our sacramental experiences. His message is simple and clear: "I am with you."

Through its love and concern, acceptance, forgiveness, and support, our faith community, the Church, witnesses to the presence of Jesus so that we might recognize Him. We hear the voice of Jesus through the support of others. Our faith is strengthened through the living example of those who serve as Jesus did. They inspire us to serve as well.

Through Scripture, the sacraments, and our parish community, His love touches us gently and encourages us to allow ourselves to be nurtured by Him. When we choose to respond, then we will recognize the echoes of His love all around us, in the faces of those we meet and in the lives of those with whom we interact with kindness, generosity, and love. The familiar warmth of His presence will be enough.

Coming to Faith

How will you "open the door" to Jesus in your daily life?

How will you nourish others' spiritual growth by sharing His presence?

Practicing Faith

What will you do this week to help yourself grow in faith?

How will you help the children begin to recognize Jesus' presence for themselves?

The Theme of This Chapter Corresponds with Paragraph 1716

LITURGICAL RESOURCES

Like our Jewish ancestors in faith, most of us enjoy singing "psalms, hymns, and sacred songs" as an expression of our communal worship. We "sing to God with thanksgiving in our hearts" at our eucharistic feasts. (See Colossians 3:16.) And in this embodied prayer we more deeply experience the presence of Jesus.

Plan with the children a "We Sing to God" songfest. Review the songs they have learned this year and invite them to choose several favorites. Teach or recall one familiar psalm response sung in the parish. Invite families or another group of children to come to the songfest. (If possible, make available simple instruments like bells, drums, and tambourines.)

JUSTICE AND PEACE RESOURCES

Despite the storms that assail it, the contemporary Christian family remains the primary community in which Jesus shares His good news. Our Church sees family life itself as "an itinerary of faith and in some way a Christian initiation and a school of following Christ" (Pope John Paul II, "Apostolic Exhortation on the Family," 39).

Let the children know that Jesus wants them to serve their families by praying for them and choosing to do what God wants them to do. Invite them to pray for each family member by name, using this prayer:

Jesus, keep______ in Your loving care.

Suggest that each day they do one thing to show their loving care for their families (help with chores, entertain younger children, wait on someone who is sick or tired, be cheerful, patient, and cooperative).

Teaching Resources

Overview of the Lesson

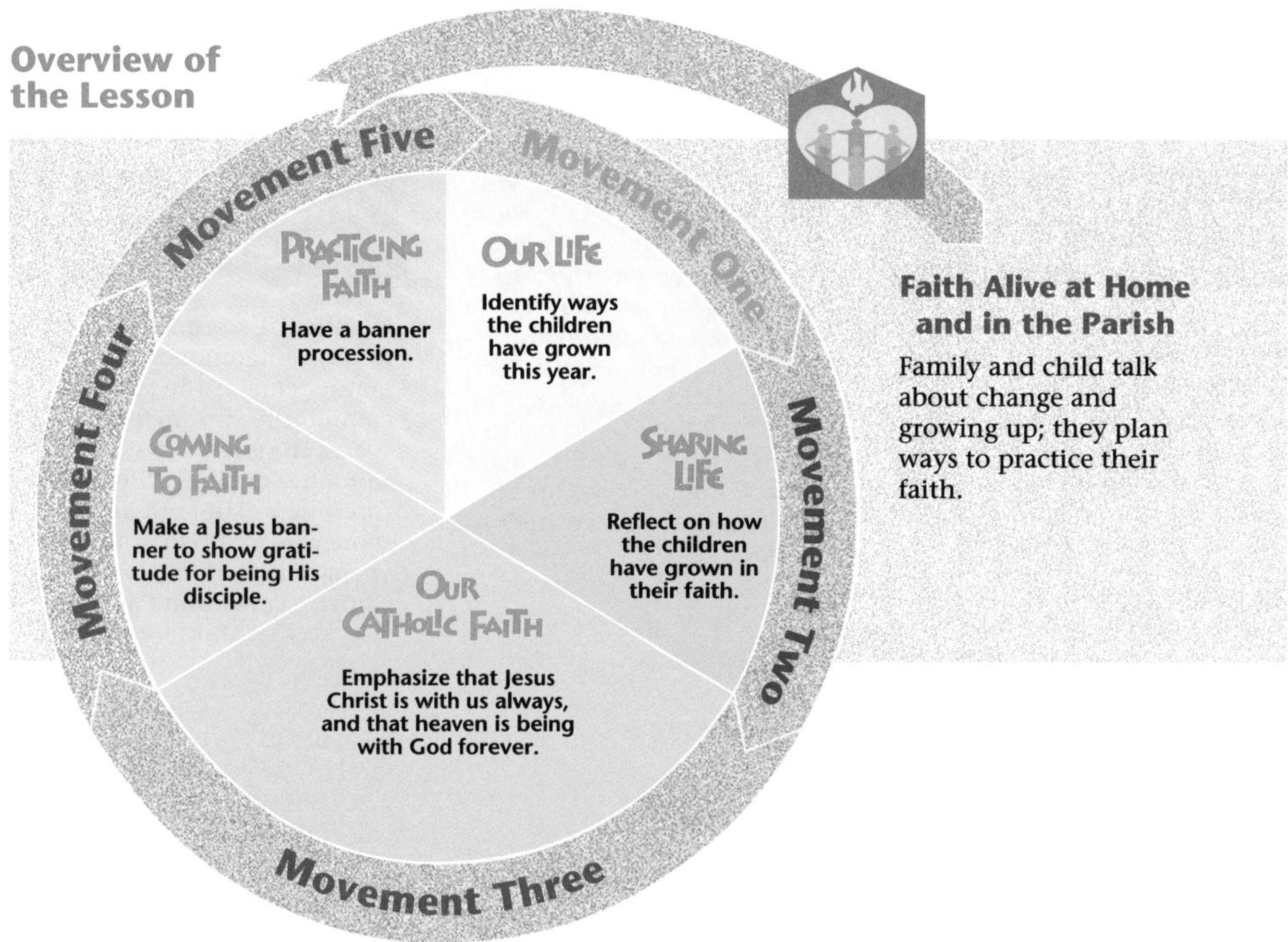

Faith Alive at Home and in the Parish

Family and child talk about change and growing up; they plan ways to practice their faith.

Teaching Hints

In this lesson, help the children to reflect joyfully on their growth. End your class with a blessing ceremony and send the children away with an awareness that Jesus will continue to be with them. Encourage them to reflect often on His presence, and to be faithful to prayer and to celebrating the Eucharist during the summer months.

Special-Needs Child

Help the children with motor difficulties by practicing the parade with them ahead of time.

Visual Needs

- thick letters to make the banner

Auditory Needs

- headphones and tape of song

Tactile-Motor Needs

- a peer helper to help make the banner

Supplemental Resources

Our Friend Is Always With Us... Everywhere (video)
Mass Media Ministries
2116 North Charles Street
Baltimore, MD 21218
(1-800-828-8825)

Lesson Plan: Beginning

Objectives

To help the children

- know that Jesus is with them forever;
- appreciate God's loving care for them;
- decide to continue growing in their faith during the summer.

Focusing Prayer

Recall for the children what they have learned this year about God's loving care for us. Then lead them in the prayer at the top of page 169.

Our Life

Reflecting on Growing Up

Have the children examine the pictures on page 169. Ask what is happening in the pictures. Talk about ways in which people grow up: in their bodies, their minds, their feelings, and so forth. Then ask the questions in the *Our Life* section.

Sharing Life

Reflecting on the Year

Gather the children around you in a circle. Ask the questions in the *Sharing Life* section. Talk with the children about ways in which you, too, have grown this year.

26 Jesus Christ Is with Us Forever

Jesus, keep us in Your loving care.

Our Life Possible responses:

How can you tell that you are growing up? growing taller; learning more; able to do more things; able to receive Communion.

What things can you do now that you could not do when you began the second grade? Individual responses will vary according to child and readiness level.

Sharing Life Possible responses:

What did you like best about being in second grade? My friends; math; science; reading; etc.

What are some favorite things you have learned in your religion group this year? Jesus' love for me; to receive Jesus in Holy Communion; Act of Contrition; Hail Mary; etc.

How have you grown in living your Catholic faith? I received Jesus in Holy Communion; I learned God's forgiveness in Reconciliation; I learned to be a peacemaker; etc.

169

Enrichment

A Reaching for the Sky Display

Invite the children to make a commitment to grow in some special way during the summer—for example: put the needs of others before my own; try to learn something new each day; eat the right kind of foods.

Reach your arm upward toward the sky to tell the children how much you hope they will grow during the summer months. Let them choose partners, and have them trace, on a sheet of posterboard, each other's arms reaching up to the sky. Let them write on the drawing one thing they will do to grow during the summer, then have them sign their names to it. Stand these drawings along a wall with a flash card over it that reads: *Reaching for the Sky.*

Materials needed: sheets of posterboard; flash cards with words *Reaching for the Sky;* markers; scissors

Lesson Plan: Middle

Our Catholic Faith

A Special Year

Talk with the children about what a special year this has been for you and how much you have enjoyed being with them and teaching them. Remind them that it has been special for them, too. Invite them to listen as you read to them the first paragraph on page 170, telling why.

We Share a Wonderful Message

Tell the children that many, many years ago, when Jesus' followers first went all over the world to tell people about Jesus, the most important message they brought is the very same message about our faith that we have learned this year. Have them read this message together with you in the second paragraph on page 170.

A Game to Help Us Remember

Read the sentence that comprises the third paragraph on page 170. Then explain the directions for the game that will

Jesus Is with Us Forever

This was a very special year for you, for your family, and for your parish family. You celebrated the Eucharist fully with your parish family. You received Jesus in Holy Communion. How much you have grown as a disciple, or follower, of Jesus!

As Christians we believe that Jesus died and rose for us. He has given us His new life that lasts forever. Jesus promises that we, too, can be with God forever in heaven.

We know that Jesus is with us wherever we are.

Play this game with a partner. It will help you remember that Jesus Christ is with us always.

Start at number 1. Take turns completing the sentences. Use the words in the list above. Don't forget to talk about the pictures! When you are finished, share your answers with the group.

170

Lesson Plan: Middle

help them remember that Jesus is with us always. Divide the children into eight groups and have each group respond together with one of the answers.

Our Catholic Identity

Use the *Our Catholic Identity* on page 15 in the back of the book. Point out to the children that Jesus taught us that prayers do not have to be long. Aspirations are like quick prayers that come right from the heart. Share with the children any favorite aspirations that you might have. Help them to see how easy it is to make up their own aspirations—like breathing!

You may also wish to use pages 57–58 in the activity book.

Enrichment

A Jesus Remembrance

Make copies, one for each child, of a sheet of paper with "I am with you always" printed in large letters, with each sheet cut into jigsaw puzzle shapes. Give each child a sheet of construction paper to use as a "board" for the puzzle. Have them arrange their puzzle pieces on their "boards." Once the children have discovered the message, have them paste the puzzle pieces onto the "board." Have the children color and decorate their puzzles.

Materials needed: papers inscribed with "I am with you always"; construction paper; glue; crayons

Lesson Plan: End

Coming to Faith

Making a Jesus Banner

Give each child a large sheet of construction paper, some markers, and a long stick. Have them look at the pictures of banners on page 172, then let the children design their own personal banners and decorate them as they wish.

Faith Summary

Turn to the *Faith Summary* on page 173. Use the annotations to see if the children can express in their own words what they have learned today.

Practicing Faith

A Song to Help Us Remember

Teach the children the song on page 172. Encourage them to sing it throughout the summer as a reminder of how they can remember and live all that they have learned this year. Then lead them in a procession as you sing it together.

You may wish to use the grade 2 *Coming to Faith in Song* cassette.

You may wish to use pages 43–44 of the *Celebrating Our Seasons and Saints* Level 2 book.

Evaluating Your Lesson

- Do the children remember that Jesus is with them always?
- Do they appreciate God's love for them?
- Have they decided to grow in faith during the summer?

Enrichment

A Blessing for All

Gather the children in a circle around a table on which you have placed a picture of Jesus. Begin with a reverent Sign of the Cross. Then invite the children to join hands and remind them of some of the wonderful things they have learned during the year about Jesus and about God's love for them.

Then ask them to stand quietly as you raise your hands and pray a blessing over them, such as, "May the Lord bless you and keep you in peace and happiness, now and forever." Have them respond, "Amen."

Coming to Faith

Make a Jesus banner. On the back, tell Him how you feel about being one of His disciples.

Practicing Faith

Carry your banner as you sing this song to help you remember how to live as Jesus' disciples.

(To the tune of "Down by the Station")

Chorus: All through our lifetime
We'll stay close to Jesus.
All through our lifetime
We'll stay close to Him.

1. We will go to Mass each week.
We'll receive the Eucharist.
We'll remember, yes, we will! (Chorus)

2. We'll be kind to those in need
Especially the sick and poor.
We'll remember, yes, we will! (Chorus)

3. We will say our prayers each day
And be kind at home and play.
We'll remember, yes, we will! (Chorus)

Talk to the children about ways they and their families might use the "Faith Alive" pages. Encourage them to make and keep their summer plan for God. Pray your favorite prayer as a closing faith response.

A Little Yearbook (for use with page 169)

Distribute two sheets of $8\frac{1}{2}''$ x $11''$ paper to each child. Have them fold and staple them together to make a four-page book, with the headings: 1) *Friends I Have Made,* 2) *A Message From My Teacher,* 3) *A Favorite Story I Learned,* 4) *How I Will Live What I Learned.* On the first page, have them collect autographs from the other children. Recall some stories they have learned this year, and talk about simple ways they might live what they have learned. Then while the children work on their responses to pages three and four, circulate around the room and write a brief, personal message on page two of each one's book. Let the children decorate the books and take them home as remembrances of their year.

Materials needed: drawing paper; stapler; crayons or markers

Daydreaming About Heaven (for use with pages 170–171)

Have the children gather in a circle and sit quietly for a few minutes. Talk to them about how wonderful it will be when we all meet in heaven someday with Jesus and with all those whom we love. Invite them to share at least one thing they imagine heaven will be like by closing their eyes, "daydreaming" about it, and taking turns speaking their daydreams out loud. Record the children's thoughts on a cassette player. When all are finished, play back their responses.

Materials needed: cassette recorder

A Special Picture Frame (for use with pages 170–171)

Talk with the children about someone who has made you feel Jesus' presence in a special way. Ask them to think quietly about someone in their own life who has made them feel the same way. Pass out sheets of drawing paper, $4\frac{1}{2}''$ x $7\frac{1}{2}''$, to each child. Invite them to draw a picture of this person. Then give each one a sheet of construction paper $8\frac{1}{2}''$ x $11''$ and have them fold it in half. Let them trace a border on it $1\frac{1}{4}''$ wide on all four sides and cut this out to make a "frame" for their picture. Let them slip the pictures between the folded pages and paste the edges down. Have them decorate the frame.

Materials needed: drawing paper; markers; construction paper; scissors; rulers; paste

A Time Machine Ride (for use with page 172)

Have the children sit in a circle on the floor. Place a beautiful picture or statue of Jesus in the middle. Tell the children to close their eyes and imagine they are in a time machine. Explain that you will be travelling together through the summer months ahead. Invite the children to take turns telling one thing they "see" as you name each month they are passing through. Start with an example such as: "I see my family travelling in our car to _______." Then add softly the words: "Jesus is here." Repeat these words softly after each child's contribution. When all have finished, "return" to your classroom and talk with the children about how wonderful it is to know that no matter where we are at any time, Jesus is present there with us.

Materials needed: picture or statue of Jesus

FAITH ALIVE AT HOME AND IN THE PARISH

Your child has now completed the second grade book, *Coming to Jesus*. He or she has learned what it means to follow Jesus at home and in your parish and has been encouraged to practice and live our faith. Help your child continue to grow in the love and practice of our faith. Use this chart to help you continue to "come to Jesus." Add your own ideas.

Growing Up

Show your child some of his or her baby pictures. Talk about what your child was like as an infant and about the ways he or she has changed. Stress the positive aspects of growing up.

Remind your child that receiving the Eucharist and celebrating Reconciliation help us grow in learning to love God, ourselves, and others.

Learn by heart

Faith Summary

- Jesus Christ promises to be with us forever.
  How long does Jesus promise to be with us?
- We try to grow closer to Jesus each day.
  When will we try to grow closer to Jesus?

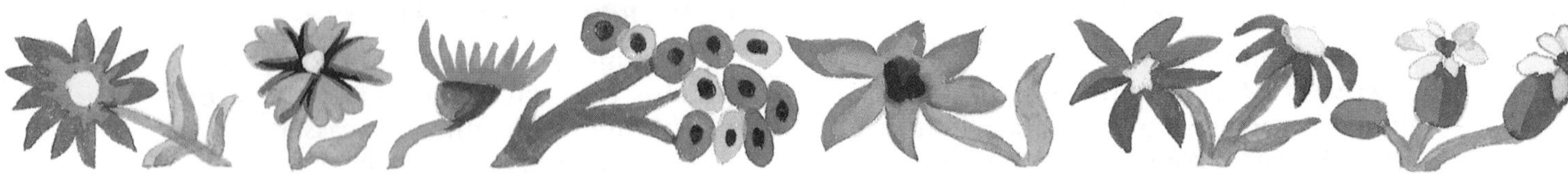

Our Family Plan for Coming to Jesus

We will take part in Mass by
- ☐ singing
- ☐ praying with the priest and the assembly
- ☐ receiving Holy Communion

We will serve others by
- ☐ visiting someone who is sick
- ☐ being friendly to someone who is lonely

We will pray as a family
- ☐ in the morning
- ☐ before meals
- ☐ at bedtime

We will read from the Bible together
- ☐ at least once during the week
- ☐ before or after Mass

We will help in the parish by
- ☐ taking part in a Church activity such as

____

Review

Go over the *Faith Summary* together before your child completes the *Review*. The answers for questions 1–3 appear on page 200. The response to number 4 will help you see whether your child is growing in his or her desire to do God's will. When the *Review* is completed, choose a sticker together to place on this page.

sticker

Circle the correct answer.

1. Jesus promised heaven only to a few people. Yes **(No)**

2. Jesus is with us at Mass. **(Yes)** No

3. Jesus is with us forever. **(Yes)** No

4. Tell about something you will do for God today.

Possible responses:
I will try to be fair; I will say my evening prayers; etc.

Encourage the children to gather with their families to share the *Family Scripture Moment.*

FAMILY SCRIPTURE MOMENT

Gather and **Listen** as Jesus sends us off with a challenge worthy of true disciples.

You are like salt for all humankind. But if salt loses its saltiness, there is no way to make it salty again. You are like light for the whole world. A city built on a hill cannot be hidden. No one lights a lamp and puts it under a bowl; instead you put it on the lamp stand, where it gives light for everyone in the house. In the same way, your light must shine before people, so that they will see the good things you do and praise your Father in heaven.

From Matthew 5:13–16

Share what special light Jesus wants each family member to share with others.

Consider for family enrichment:

- Jesus compares His disciples to salt, which is necessary for preserving and flavoring food. He also compares them to a bright light on a lamp stand. We are like salt and light when we do the good works of God's reign.
- Everyone can recognize the light of faith in us when we really live it.

Reflect and **Decide** Consider ways family members may have hidden their light under a bowl. How will you let your faith shine this week?

A Reconciliation Celebration

The Theme of This Chapter Corresponds with Paragraph 1465

For the Catechist: Spiritual and Catechetical Development

Our Life

There are days when parents and teachers wish certain children would "get lost"—if only for ten minutes—so that peace might reign once again. Any list of "Common Provocations By Young Children" would include: refusing to share, excluding or making fun of others, being lazy or failing to do simple chores, and being uncooperative in a communal setting.

Ask yourself:

- What item on the list do I find most provoking?
- What would I add to the list?

Sharing Life

What is my usual response when children choose do these things? How do I model the opposite virtues of generosity, inclusiveness, reliability, and having a cooperative spirit?

Our Catholic Faith

If the sacrament of Reconciliation is to be a saving experience, it must connect to our deepest needs to make right the relationships in our lives. We are all imperfect, but we can make amends for our mistakes and choose to grow.

Children need to be given regular opportunities to be reconciled. Along with occasional sacramental celebrations, informal prayer services of reconciliation and healing can be offered.

These services will be times of renewing the peace between us, restoring relationships, and enabling children to grow by recognizing the ways in which they are both "hitting the mark" and "missing the mark" on doing God's will for them.

Coming to Faith

How can you be reconciled with others in your life right now?

Are there any "lost ones" you may need to seek out?

Practicing Faith

How will you help the children in your group grow in the virtues they need?

How will you be a "good shepherd" for them?

Teaching Resources

Teaching Hints

This prayer service is intended to be used as a preparation for the celebration of the sacrament of Reconciliation.

The lesson is divided into two parts: preparation and celebration. If time permits, use a few minutes of each lesson for a given week to prepare for the celebration, and use the last day of the week to conduct the celebration.

You might want to have a snack prepared for the conclusion of the celebration.

Special-Needs Child

When conducting the prayer service, be sure to give the mainstreamed children whatever assistance they need to participate.

Visual Needs

- preferential seating for celebration

Auditory Needs

- opportunities to role-play "Good Shepherd" story

Tactile-Motor Needs

- peer-assistance in acting out story

Supplemental Resources

The Stray (video)
Mass Media Ministries
2116 North Charles Street
Baltimore, Maryland 21218
(1-800-828-8825)

The Little Lost Lamb (video)
St. Paul Books and Media
50 St. Paul's Ave.
Boston, MA 02130
(1-800-876-4463)

Lesson Plan: Beginning

Focusing Prayer

Gather the children around you and explain that today we will celebrate and thank God for God's loving forgiveness. Then lead them in the prayer of thanks at the top of page 175.

Setting the Tone

Begin by asking volunteers to act out these or similar situations:

- You are in a video store and see a movie you would like to borrow. You don't have the money, so you take the video when the clerk isn't looking.
- Your little brother gets you in trouble so you decide to get even by breaking one of his toys.
- Your mom asks you to hurry home after school because she has an important errand for you to run, but instead you stop to play ball with your friends.

After acting out the situations, have each person tell how he or she felt. Talk about the importance of saying "I'm sorry" when we have hurt someone in any way. Explain that this helps to "heal" the hurt we or someone else has felt.

27 A Reconciliation Celebration

Jesus, thank You for Your caring love.

You might want to take the children to the church for the celebration part of this lesson. (See page 178 of wraparound text.)

All: Jesus, You are the Good Shepherd. You take care of us always and show us how much God loves us. We come together today to ask God's forgiveness for times that we turned away from You by hurting one another.

Leader: Jesus told us that God loves us forever, no matter what we do. Even when we sin, God always forgives us when we are sorry.

Jesus told this to us in the Bible story of the Good Shepherd.

Reader: Once there was a good shepherd who had a very large flock of sheep. He knew every one of his sheep by name.

One day, one of the sheep got lost. The shepherd left the rest of the sheep and went to find the lost sheep.

When he found his lost sheep, the shepherd called all his friends together to celebrate.

From Luke 15:4–6

Lesson Plan: Middle

Preparation

Have the children open their books to page 175. Tell them you would like to celebrate a Reconciliation service with them. See the annotations. It will help them remember that Jesus, our Good Shepherd, is always ready to forgive us when we're sorry.

Go over the prayer service briefly with the children. Choose a leader and a reader, or choose several and have them alternate parts. Let others act out the story as it is read. Practice any appropriate songs you wish to sing. Place a picture of the Good Shepherd on the prayer table.

(You might want to use "Sometimes It's Not Easy" from the grade 2 cassette for *Coming to Jesus in Song* from William H. Sadlier, Inc.)

Begin by going over the words with the children.

Sometimes It's Not Easy

Sometimes it's not easy to care for ev'rybody.
Sometimes it's not easy to share with ev'rybody.
Sometimes it's not easy to do the things we should.
Sometimes it's not easy to be good.
Sometimes it's not easy to do the things we're taught to.
Sometimes it's not easy to do the things we ought to.
Sometimes it's not easy to do the things we should.
Sometimes it's not easy to be good.
Sometimes it's not easy to be good.

Play the hymn and have the children listen. Then play it once more and invite them to join in.

Talk about the picture on this page. Invite the children to tell how they feel about Jesus, our Good Shepherd.

Look at the picture on this page. Think about these questions:

- How do you think the shepherd felt when he discovered one sheep was lost?
- How do you think the shepherd felt once he found the lost sheep?
- How would you feel if you were lost?
- How would you feel when someone you love finds you?

Leader: After telling this story, Jesus says that He is the Good Shepherd. Jesus is the one whom God sent to love and forgive us.

We ask Jesus to help us love God and others always.

Leader: Jesus, You are our Good Shepherd who takes care of us always.

All: For this we thank You.

176

Lesson Plan: Middle

Examination of Conscience

Help the children to examine their consciences. Explain that we think carefully about the choices we have made, to decide whether they are right or wrong. Encourage the children to ask themselves: "What would Jesus think about this choice?" Then ask them to respond quietly in their hearts as you ask the following questions:

- Do I pray and remember how important God is in my life?
- Do I show love and respect to my parents and teachers?
- Have I selfishly refused to share with others?
- Have I been unkind or spiteful toward anyone?
- Have I taken care of my body as God's gift to me?
- Have I always been honest and truthful?
- Do I take care of the world God has given us?
- Am I content with the gifts God has given me, or do I want or take what others have?

Leader: Jesus, You came to show us God's love and forgiveness.
All: For this we thank You.

Leader: Jesus, You help us to make good choices.
All: For this we thank You.

Leader: Jesus, when we do wrong things, You help us to be sorry.
All: For this we thank You.

Leader: Jesus, You help us to forgive those who hurt us.
All: For this we thank You.

Leader: In the quiet of our hearts let us each tell Jesus we are sorry for anything we may have done wrong. (Pause.)
All: Jesus, we are sorry.

Lesson Plan: End

Celebrating

Gather the children around the prayer table. Ask them to look at the picture of the Good Shepherd as you read the opening prayer on page 175. Then have the children continue with the readings and story.

Slowly read aloud the meditation questions at the top of page 176 and have the children reflect quietly on each one. Continue the service. You may wish to have the children join hands as they respond to the thank-you "litany" on pages 176 and 177. Close with "Sometimes It's Not Easy."

(1) Encourage the children to reverently make the sign of the cross on each other's forehead.

Leader: Jesus, our Good Shepherd, we are sorry for the times we have turned away from You. We ask You to help us love God and other people always.

All: Help us love everyone.

Leader: Let us bless one another to show that we forgive one another. (Sign each other's foreheads with a cross.) (1)

All: Bless us, God.

Leader: Let us go in peace.

All: Thanks be to God.

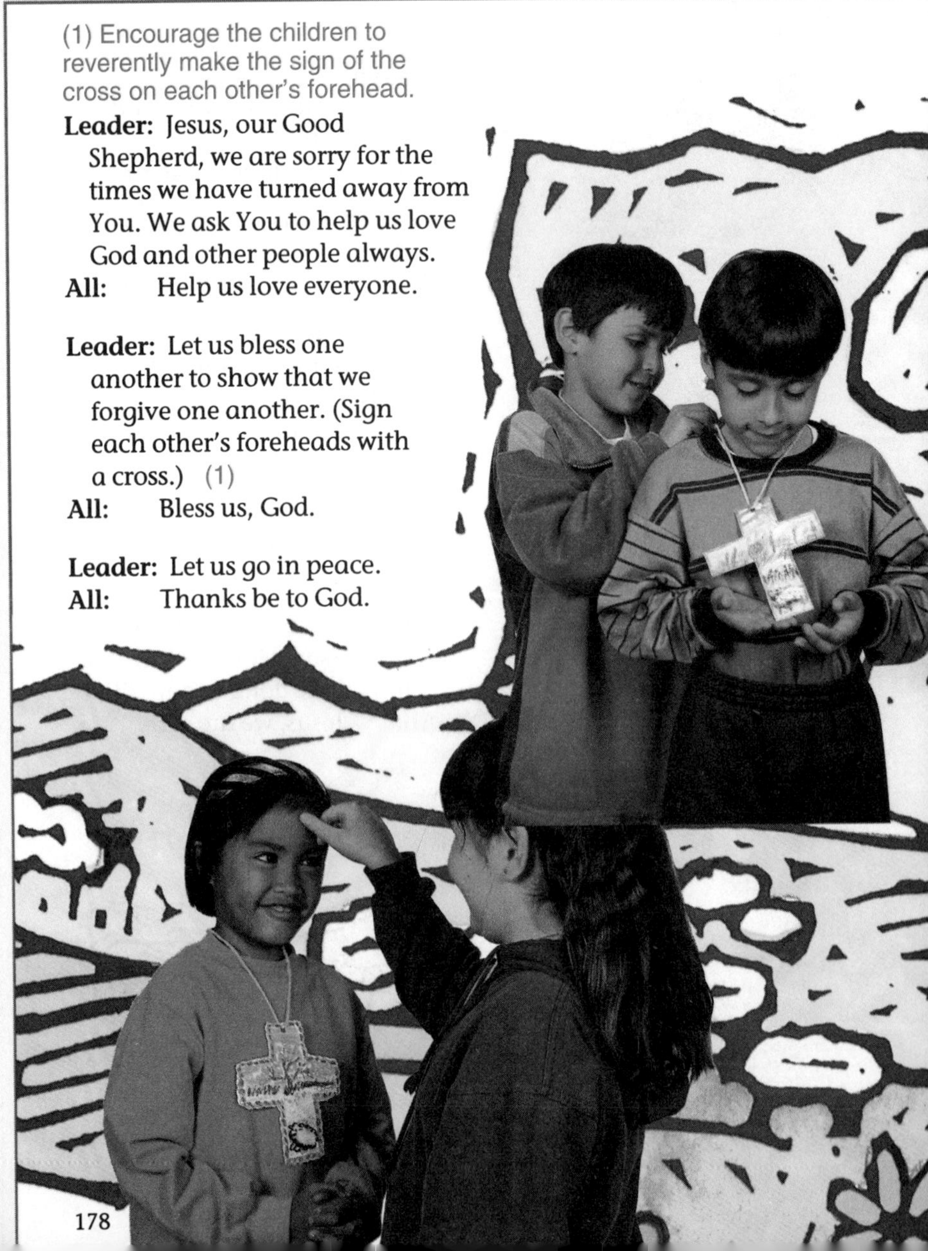

178

A Liturgy Activity

To emphasize the reconciling ministry of Jesus, the Good Shepherd, you might choose to create a shepherd's staff to be displayed above the prayer table. The staff may be fashioned from a walking stick or a broomstick, with a large white bow attached. When a child has separated himself or herself from the group through misbehavior, the shepherd (staff in hand) welcomes the child back into the group. An expression of sorrow is invited but not demanded.

Materials needed: walking stick or broomstick; white bow

A Justice and Peace Activity

Social sin is the result of the collective behavior of a social group. Such a sin is rooted in and is the result of many personal sins, since the group itself does not act morally or immorally. Situations cannot in themselves be considered to be good or bad.

Groups of children may be guilty sometimes of social sin when they treat others with intolerance, hatred, or ridicule. If the destructiveness of these habits is not confronted in childhood, it may carry into adult life. Help your group to recognize how these situations arise. Give them practice in showing tolerance and patience with those who provoke or who are different.

Do It Yourself

Use this space to create your own Reconciliation activity.

SUMMARY 2 • REVIEW

Use the annotations on this page to review the major points of Units 3 and 4.

The Sacrament of the Eucharist

Ask: What are the two main parts of our Mass celebration?

The Mass is our celebration of Jesus' special meal and sacrifice. Eucharist means "giving thanks." The Mass is the great thanksgiving prayer of the Catholic Church.

Ask: What happens in the Liturgy of the Word? the Liturgy of the Eucharist?

In the Liturgy of the Word, we listen to God's word from the Bible, especially the gospel, Jesus' good news. In the Liturgy of the Eucharist, we give thanks to God. The gifts of bread and wine become the Body and Blood of Christ. We can receive Jesus in Holy Communion. After Mass we go in peace to love and serve the Lord and other people.

Ask: What do we do after Mass?

We Celebrate the Eucharist

When we receive Communion, Jesus is really present with us as our Bread of Life. After Communion we thank Jesus for coming to us. Jesus is always present in the Blessed Sacrament, which is reserved in the tabernacle.

Ask: When is Jesus with us?

Jesus is with us in our Church, our parish, and our families. He is with us when we celebrate the sacraments, pray together, and help those in need.

God chose Mary to be the mother of our Savior, Jesus Christ. Mary is our mother, too.

Ask: Whose mother is Mary?

By following Jesus, we can be happy with God forever in heaven.

SUMMARY 2 ▪ TEST

Circle the correct answer.

1. At Mass (the bread and wine, only the bread) become Jesus Himself.

2. During the Liturgy of the Word, we (receive Holy Communion, listen to God's Word).

3. In the Liturgy of the Eucharist, we offer to God gifts of (oil and water, bread and wine).

4. After Mass, we are sent in peace to love and serve (only people we like, everyone who needs us).

5. Tell how you will be a peacemaker.

Possible responses:

I will share my toys with others.
I will pray for peace.

The Mass Ends

The priest blesses us. Then he or the deacon may say,
"Go in peace
to love and serve the Lord."

We answer:
"Thanks be to God."

Cut on this line.

Fold on this line.

Help the children to cut and fold pages 181–184 to make their Mass books.

We pray,
"Lord, I am not worthy
to receive you,
but only say the word
and I shall be healed."

Guide pages 181–199 duplicate the child's text but cannot be used to make models. If you wish to make models from these pages, use a child's text.

We Begin the Mass

We stand and pray,
"In the name of the Father,
and of the Son,
and of the Holy Spirit."

We ask God to forgive us,
"Lord, have mercy,
Christ, have mercy,
Lord, have mercy."

We praise God,
"Glory to God in the highest
and peace to his people
on earth."

Welcome

We gather with family and friends to celebrate the Mass. The Mass is our greatest prayer of thanks to God.

✂ Cut on this line.

Fold on this line.

At Holy Communion we hear,
"The body of Christ."
We answer:
"Amen."

"The blood of Christ."
We answer:
"Amen."

Liturgy of the Word

We listen to God's word from the Bible.
We pray the psalm.

The reader says:
"The word of the Lord."
We answer:
"Thanks be to God."

Ask: After listening to God's word what do we say?

The priest or deacon asks everyone to share a sign of peace.

We pray the prayer
that Jesus taught us:

"Our Father, who art in heaven,
hallowed be thy name;
thy kingdom come;
thy will be done on earth
as it is in heaven.
Give us this day our daily bread;
and forgive us our trespasses
as we forgive those
who trespass against us;
and lead us not into temptation,
but deliver us from evil."

Cut on this line.

Fold on this line.

We stand for the gospel.
The priest or deacon says:
"The Lord be with you."
We answer:
"And also with you."
The priest or deacon then says:
"A reading from the
holy gospel. . . ."
We say:
"Glory to you, Lord."
After the gospel, we say:
"Praise to you, Lord Jesus Christ."

Ask: What do we do when it is time for the Gospel?

The priest says the words of Jesus,
"This is my body which
will be given up for you."
"This is the cup of my blood.
Do this in memory of me."

Ask: What gifts are brought to the altar?

Liturgy of the Eucharist

Our gifts of bread and wine
are carried to the altar.

The priest prepares our gifts
to be offered to God.

Together we pray the Creed. We tell what we believe as Catholics. Then we pray for the Church and the world. We can say:
"Lord, hear our prayer."

The priest asks us to pray with him for the whole Church. At the end of the prayer we answer, "Amen."

Fold on this line.

Cut on this line.

Ask: What does the priest invite us to do? What do we answer?

The priest invites us to pray:
"Lift up your hearts."

We answer:
"We lift them up to the Lord."

We give thanks and praise to God.

We pray,
"Holy,
holy,
holy Lord,
God of power and might . . . "

Ask: What do we remember at the Liturgy of the Eucharist?

We remember what Jesus said and did at the Last Supper.

By the power of the Holy Spirit and the actions of the priest, the bread and wine become the Body and Blood of Christ.

This faith book is a special way to review *Coming to Jesus*. It highlights many faith facts that are important for the children's journey of faith.

For the Family

As your child's second grade experience ends, we celebrate with you the ways in which your child has grown as a disciple of Jesus Christ. You have guided your child's growth in the wisdom of our Catholic faith, including a love for Scripture. You have helped prepare your child to celebrate the sacraments of Eucharist, Reconciliation, and perhaps Confirmation. During this year, your child has learned and experienced some very important truths of our faith as they are contained in the Catechism of the Catholic Church. For example:

- **Creed:** Jesus Christ is the Son of God. He died and rose to give us new life. The Holy Spirit came to Jesus' friends on Pentecost. We belong to the Catholic Church. In the Eucharist, we share in and celebrate the meal and sacrifice of Jesus Christ. In the Eucharist, Jesus is really present.
- **Sacraments:** Through Baptism, we are freed from sin, share in God's life of grace, and are welcomed as members of the Church. In Confirmation, the Holy Spirit comes to us in a special way. In the Eucharist, we are nourished with the Body and Blood of Christ and sent forth to share Jesus' love and peace. In Reconciliation, we celebrate receiving God's forgiveness.
- **Morality:** We try to follow the Law of Love and the Ten Commandments. We try not to make sinful choices. We try to love and serve God and bring the peace and love of Christ to others.
- **Prayer:** In prayer, we praise God, thank God, ask God for help, or tell God we are sorry. We pray the Our Father, Hail Mary, Act of Contrition, Creed, and many other prayers.

Continue to encourage your child to grow in faith by going to Mass together every weekend, by celebrating Reconciliation frequently, and by reading Scripture and praying together often.

†Family Prayer

Jesus, help our family to continue to grow in faith as Your disciples. May the Holy Spirit help us choose to love God, ourselves, and others. Amen.

My Catholic Faith Book

C R E E D

You might suggest that the children read one of these paragraphs each night at bedtime.

This is what we believe . . .

God created everyone and everything good. There are three Persons in one God: the Father, the Son, and the Holy Spirit. We call the three divine Persons in one God the Blessed Trinity.

Jesus Christ is the Son of God. Jesus is also human, as we are. Jesus died and rose from the dead to give us new life.

The Holy Spirit came to the friends of Jesus on Pentecost. The Holy Spirit gave them courage to live and tell everyone the good news of Jesus. The Holy Spirit helps us today.

We belong to the Catholic Church. The Catholic Church is the community of Jesus' followers, or disciples, led by the pope and bishops.

Encourage the children to refer to this page throughout the summer months.

This is how we pray . . .

We pray when we praise God, thank God, ask God for help, or tell God we are sorry.

We pray in our own words or say special prayers of the Church, such as the Glory to the Father.

Jesus taught us the Our Father. We pray the greeting of the angel to Mary when we pray the Hail Mary.

We pray an Act of Contrition to tell God we are sorry for our sins.

We say what we believe when we pray the Creed.

P R A Y E R

MORALITY

This is how we live . . .

We ask the Holy Spirit to guide us in making good choices.

We try to follow the Ten Commandments, and we try to live the Law of Love by loving God, ourselves, and one another.

We follow Jesus' teachings by loving and serving others. We treat people fairly. We are also to pray and worship together at Mass. At the end of the Mass, we are sent to love and serve the Lord and one another.

Sin is disobeying God's law on purpose. We try not to sin. We forgive those who have hurt us and we ask forgiveness of those we have hurt.

We try to live as peacemakers, as Jesus taught us.

Sacraments are powerful signs that Jesus is with us, sharing God's life and love.

At Baptism we are freed from sin, welcomed into the Church, and receive God's own life and love.
In Confirmation the Holy Spirit comes to us in a special way.

In the Eucharist, we give thanks to God. Through the power of the Holy Spirit, our gifts of bread and wine become the Body and Blood of Christ.

The Catholic Church celebrates God's forgiveness in the sacrament of Reconciliation. God always forgives us if we are sorry for our sins.

God's love for us will never end. We can live forever in heaven with God.

This is how we celebrate . . .

We celebrate the sacrament of Baptism. It is the sacrament that brings us into the life of the Church.

In the sacrament of Confirmation, the Holy Spirit comes to us in a special way.

We celebrate the sacrament of the Eucharist at Mass. In the Eucharist, we share Jesus' gift of Himself. Jesus is truly present in the Eucharist under the forms of bread and wine.

We celebrate the sacrament of Reconciliation. We confess our sins to the priest and tell God that we are sorry for them. We receive absolution and know that our sins are forgiven.

The Mass is our greatest prayer of thanks to God. It is both a meal and a sacrifice.

In the Liturgy of the Word, we listen to God's word from the Bible. We say what we believe in the Creed. We pray for our own and others' needs in the Prayer of the Faithful.

In the Liturgy of the Eucharist, we give thanks to God. Through the power of the Holy Spirit, our gifts of bread and wine become the Body and Blood of Christ. We receive the Body and Blood of Christ in Holy Communion.

Prayer of Quiet

Sit in a comfortable position.
Relax by breathing in and out.
Shut out all sights and sounds.
Each time you breathe in and out, say the name "Jesus."

Psalm of Praise

O God,
Your greatness is seen in all the world.
From Psalm 8:9

Psalm of Sorrow

Remember, God, Your kindness and constant love.
Forgive my sins.
From Psalm 25:6–7

Psalm of Thanksgiving

I thank You, God, with all my heart.
I sing praises to You.
From Psalm 138:1

Psalm of Trust

May Your constant love be with us, O God,
as we put our hope in You.
From Psalm 33:22

Psalm for Help

Remember me, O God, when You help Your people.
From Psalm 106:4

Encourage the children to memorize one of the Scripture passages. Explain that they can pray these words often during the day.

FOLD

A Doorway to Prayer

Directions:

1. Fold all sections.
2. Glue side A to side B. Glue only the shaded area.

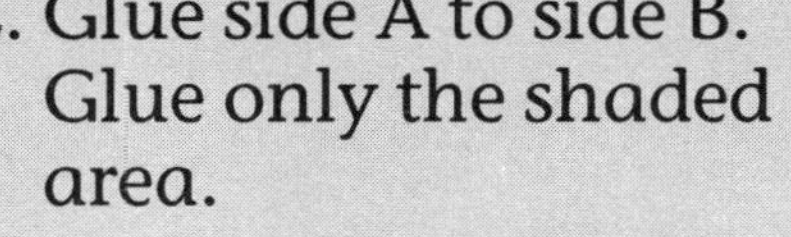

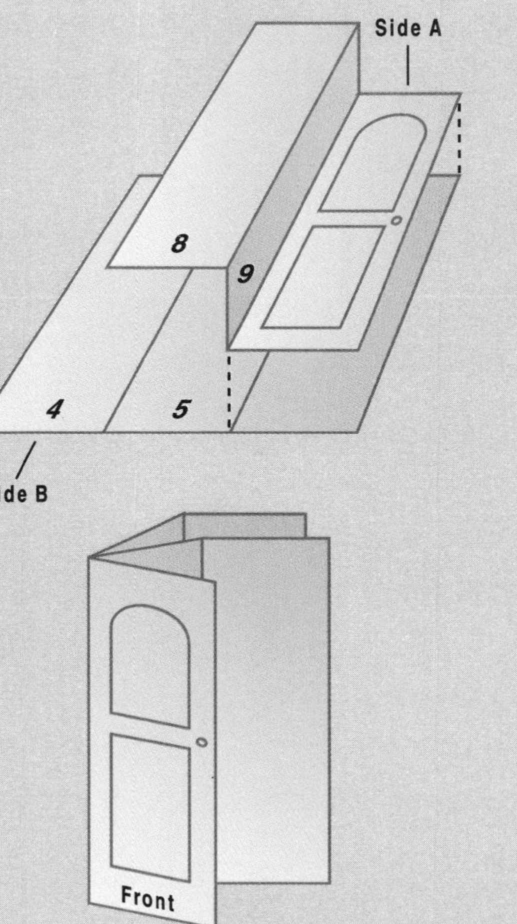

FOLD

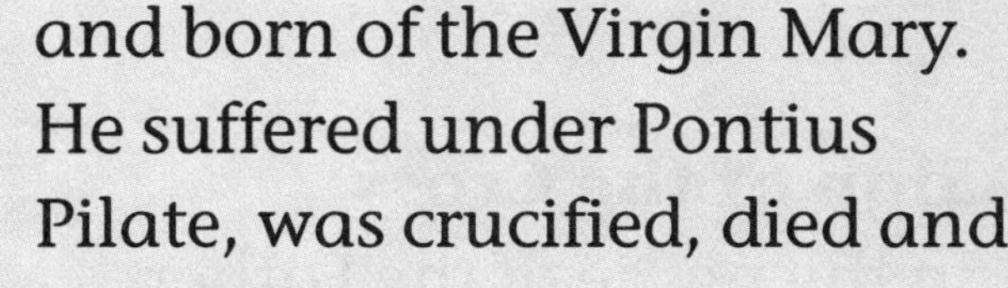

Hail Mary

Hail Mary, full of grace,
the Lord is with you;
blessed are you among women,
and blessed is the fruit of your
womb, Jesus.
Holy Mary, Mother of God,
pray for us sinners now
and at the hour of our death.
Amen.

Apostles' Creed

I believe in God, the Father
almighty,
creator of heaven and earth.

I believe in Jesus Christ,
his only Son, our Lord.
He was conceived by the power
of the Holy Spirit

FOLD

and born of the Virgin Mary.
He suffered under Pontius
Pilate, was crucified, died and
was buried.
He descended to the dead.
On the third day he rose again.
He ascended into heaven,
and is seated at the right hand
of the Father.
He will come again to judge
the living and the dead.

I believe in the Holy Spirit,
the holy catholic Church,
the communion of saints,
the forgiveness of sins,
the resurrection of the body,
and the life everlasting.
Amen.

Sign of the Cross

In the name of the Father,
and of the Son,
and of the Holy Spirit.
Amen.

Glory to the Father

Glory to the Father,
and to the Son,
and to the Holy Spirit:
as it was in the beginning,
is now, and will be for ever.
Amen.

FOLD

Our Father

Our Father, who art in heaven,
hallowed be thy name;
thy kingdom come;
thy will be done on earth
as it is in heaven.
Give us this day our daily bread;
and forgive us our trespasses
as we forgive those
who trespass against us;
and lead us not into temptation,
but deliver us from evil.
Amen.

FOLD

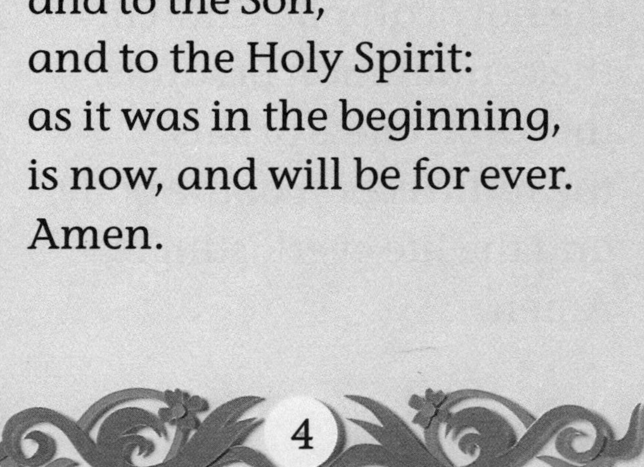

Jesus says,
Listen, I stand at the door and knock; whoever hears My voice and opens the door, I will come into their house and eat with them, and they will eat with Me.
From Revelation 3:20

FOLD

Morning Offering

My God, I offer you today
all I think and do and say,
uniting it with what was done
on earth by Jesus Christ,
Your Son.

Evening Prayer

Dear God, before I sleep I want to thank you for this day so full of your kindness and your joy. I close my eyes to rest safe in your loving care.

A Vocation Prayer

God, I know you will call me for special work in my life. Help me to follow Jesus each day and be ready to answer your call.

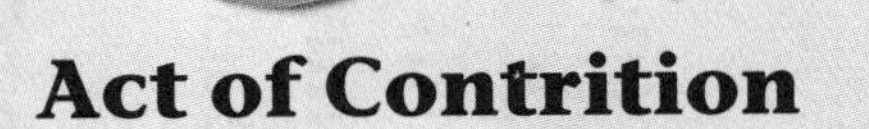

FOLD

Act of Contrition

My God,
I am sorry for my sins with all my heart.
In choosing to do wrong
and failing to do good,
I have sinned against you
whom I should love above all things.
I firmly intend, with your help,
to do penance,
to sin no more,
and to avoid whatever leads me to sin.
Our Savior Jesus Christ
suffered and died for us.
In his name, my God, have mercy.

We Celebrate the Church Year

Make a Church year calendar to help you remember to celebrate and pray during each season.

1. Cut out the chart and the pointer.
2. Use a paper fastener to attach the pointer.
3. During the Church year, move the pointer on the chart as you begin to celebrate each Church season.
4. Say often the prayer for each season on the back of the chart. Use your own words to tell Jesus how you will share His love each day of the season. >

Cut on this line.

Advent

† Come, Lord Jesus!

The Church year begins on the First Sunday of Advent. We begin Advent four Sundays before December 25. The color violet is used in the priest's vestments and decorations, telling us that Advent is a time of waiting for Christmas and for Christ's coming at the end of time.

Christmas

† Jesus, You bring us peace.

Christmas is our celebration of Jesus' birth. The season begins at the Christmas Vigil Mass and ends on the feast of the Baptism of the Lord. We remember and celebrate that Jesus was born to be our Savior. The season's joyful color is white.

Lent

† Jesus, help us to grow as Your disciples.

During the season of Lent, we try to grow and change to follow Jesus more closely. We also remember those preparing for Baptism. Lent begins on Ash Wednesday and ends on Thursday of Holy Week. The color violet is a sign of our sorrow and need for reconciliation.

Easter Triduum

† Jesus, we remember the new life You won for us.

This is the most important time of the Church year. Beginning on Holy Thursday evening and ending Easter Sunday night, we remember Jesus' saving death and resurrection.

Easter

† Alleluia!

We celebrate the resurrection of Jesus from the dead and the new life He gives us. We use signs of new life from the world around us. The priest wears white at Mass to show joy in new life.

Ordinary Time

† Jesus, You are with us always.

All the other weeks during the year make up Ordinary Time. We celebrate Ordinary Time between Christmas and Lent and after the Easter season until Advent. The color green is used as a sign of hope and trust in God.

We honor our Saints.
Welcome, Friends of Jesus.
Saints of God, pray for us.
Saint Rose of Lima
Saint Anne
Saint Patrick

Guide the children in recalling that a saint is someone who lives as God wants him or her to live, with love for God, for self, and for others.

Saint Patrick brought the good news of God's love to others. He trusted that God's love would protect him.

Patrick went to Ireland where many people did not know about God. He used a shamrock to teach about the Blessed Trinity, the three Persons in one God.

Saint Patrick, help me bring the good news of God's love to others.

Hang these saints' signs on your doorknob at home. Use them to remind you to pray often to these friends of Jesus.

Cut on this line.

Saint Anne was the mother of Mary, our Blessed Mother. She showed Mary how to love God and others. Saint Anne taught her daughter to say yes to God. We celebrate the feast of Saint Anne on July 26.

Saint Anne, help us to always say yes to God.

Help the children cut out and put together their Saints cards.

Cut on this line.

Saint Rose of Lima spent her life comforting people who had troubles. She helped her parents. She visited the poor and she prayed to God to forgive all sinners. Saint Rose of Lima is the patroness of South America. We celebrate her feast day on August 23.

Saint Rose, help me to help those most in need.

GLOSSARY

Help the children to turn to the lesson page that is referenced for each word in the Glossary. Challenge them to find the word on the lesson page. Then ask a child to use the word in a sentence.

Absolution (page 77)
The prayer of the priest sharing God's forgiveness of our sins.

Advent (page 88)
The name we give to the four weeks of waiting time before celebrating Jesus' birth at Christmas. We continue to wait until Jesus comes again.

Baptism (page 27)
The sacrament by which we are freed from sin, become children of God and members of the Church.

Bible (page 51)
The book in which we read the word of God for our lives.

Bishop (page 32)
A bishop is the leader of a diocese.

Blessed Sacrament (page 153)
The consecrated hosts left over from Mass kept in the tabernacle. Jesus is really present in the Blessed Sacrament.

Blessed Trinity (page 15)
The three Persons in one God: the Father, the Son, and the Holy Spirit.

Catholic Church (page 32)
The baptized followers of Jesus Christ who are joined together by the Holy Spirit under the leadership of the pope and bishops.

Christians (page 27)
Followers of Jesus Christ.

Christmas Day (page 93)
The day (December 25) we celebrate the birth of Jesus.

Confirmation (page 39)
The sacrament in which the Holy Spirit comes to us in a special way.

Contrition (page 71)
The word *contrition* means "sorrow." The Act of Contrition is a special prayer for saying "I am sorry" to God.

Creed (page 115)
A prayer that tells what we believe.

Disciple (page 9)
A disciple is a follower of Jesus.

Divine (page 15)
A word used only to describe God.

Easter Sunday (page 138)
The day we celebrate Jesus' rising from the dead and giving us new life.

Eucharist (page 108)
The word *Eucharist* means "to give thanks." It is the sacrament in which we receive the Body and Blood of Christ.

Examination of Conscience (page 76)
A way to prepare for the sacrament of Reconciliation. We ask ourselves if we have been living as disciples of Jesus.

Gospel (page 115)
The good news that God loves us and gives us Jesus Christ, the Son of God.

Holy Communion (page 102)
The Body and Blood of Christ.

Holy Spirit (page 59)
The third Person of the Blessed Trinity.

Jesus Christ (page 20)
The Son of God and the Son of Mary.

Law of Love (page 58)
The Law of Love is "You must love God with all your heart. You must love others as yourself."

Lent (page 133)
The special time before Easter. We pray and try to grow as followers of Jesus Christ.

Liturgy of the Eucharist (page 120)
The second part of the Mass in which we give thanks to God. The bread and wine that we offer become the Body and Blood of Christ.

Liturgy of the Word (page 114)
The first part of the Mass in which we listen to God's word from the Bible.

Mass (page 103)
Our celebration of Jesus' special meal and sacrifice. At Mass we hear God's word and share the Body and Blood of Christ.

Distribute balloons and markers with string or dowels for the balloons. Then have the children write their favorite word on the balloons. Have one child at a time come up and ask the group to name and define the word.

Parish (page 38)
Our special home in the Catholic Church where we come together to pray, to celebrate the sacraments, and to share our faith.

Penance (page 77)
Something good we can do or prayers we can say to show we are sorry for our sins.

Pope (page 32)
The leader of the whole Catholic Church.

Prayer (page 45)
Prayer is talking and listening to God.

Reconciliation (page 70)
The sacrament in which we celebrate God's mercy and forgiveness of our sins.

Sacrament (page 39)
A powerful sign in which Jesus shares God's life and love with us.

Saints (page 195)
People who loved God very much, and who are now happy with God forever in heaven.

Sin (page 65)
The act of freely choosing to do what we know to be wrong. We disobey God's law on purpose.

Tabernacle (page 153)
A special place in our parish church where the Blessed Sacrament is kept.

Ten Commandments (page 65)
Laws that tell us what God wants us to do, help us obey the Law of Love, and live for God's kingdom.

Designing Vestments

(for use with page 110A)

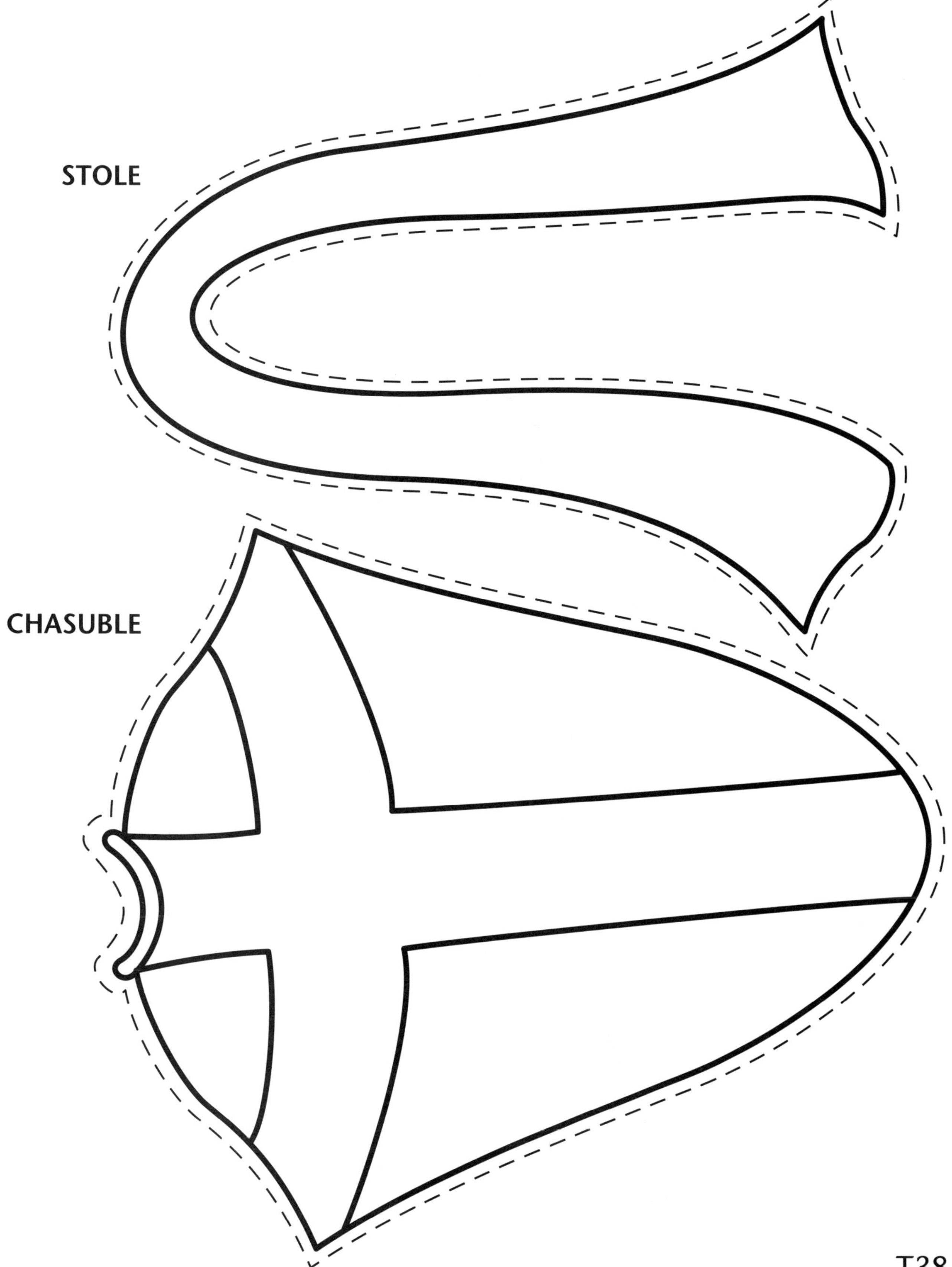

A Doorknob Reminder

(for use with page 110A)

(for use with page 110A)

A Mass Spinner

(for use with page 122A)

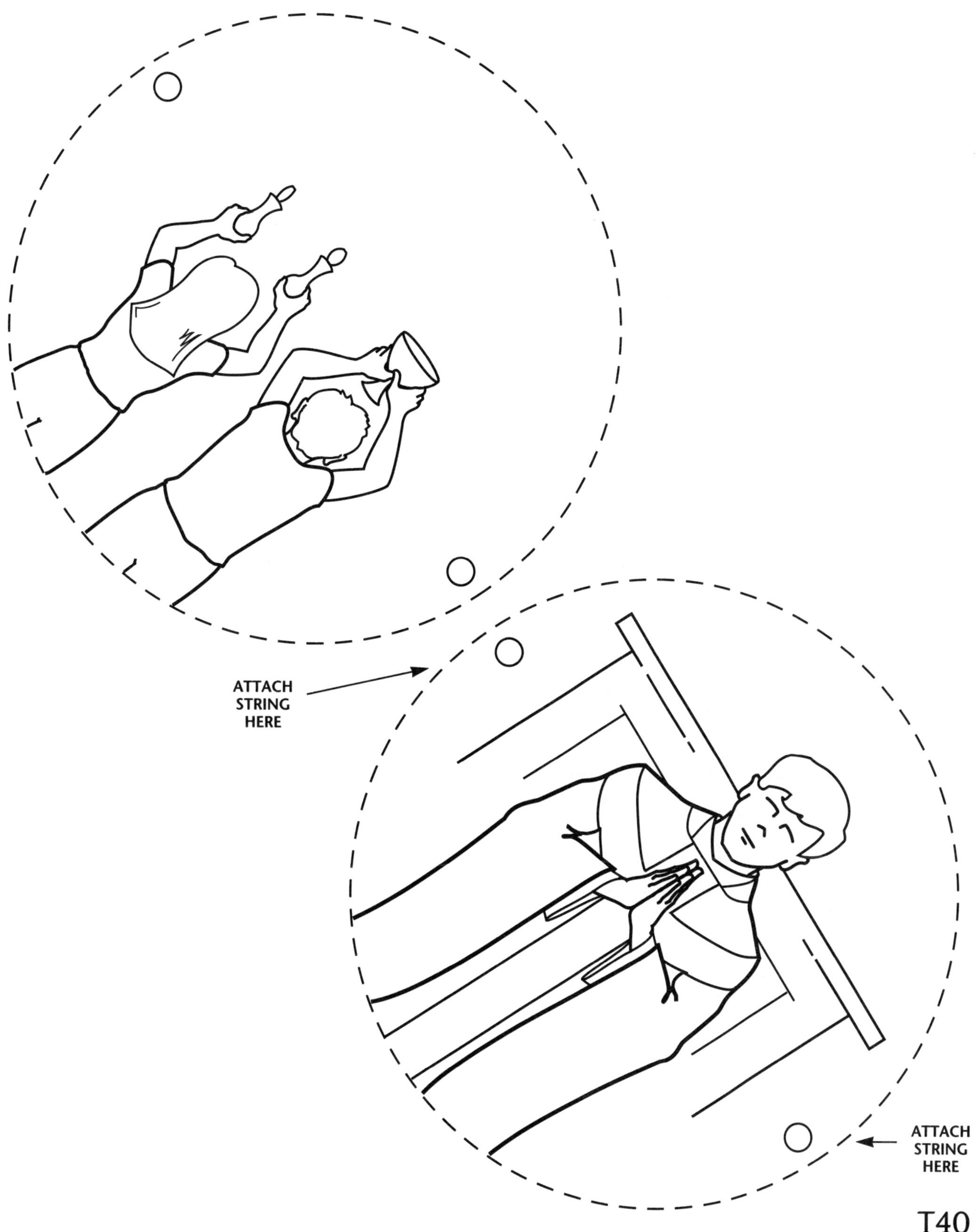

A Eucharist Puzzle

(for use with page 122A)

1 2 3 4 5 6 7

A Eucharist Puzzle

(for use with page 122A)

ACROSS

1. We offer gifts of ______ and wine at Mass.
4. After the consecration, the bread and wine become the Body and Blood of ______.
5. This happens through the ______ of the priest and the power of the Holy Spirit.
7. At Mass, the priest says and does what Jesus did at the Last ______.

DOWN

1. At Mass, the priest says over the bread: "This is my ______."
2. The part of the Mass that follows the Liturgy of the Word is called the Liturgy of the ______.
3. At Mass, the priest says over the ______, "This is the cup of my blood."
5. ______ the priest, we give praise to the Father through Jesus Christ.
6. We proclaim our faith and say: "Christ has ______, Christ is risen, Christ will come again."

INDEX

The following is a list of topics that appear in the pupil text. *Italic* indicates family pages. **Boldface** indicates an entire chapter.

SCRIPTURE REFERENCES

Family Pages

Family Pages (cont.)

Our Catholic Identity

The Blessed Trinity

Long, long ago, Saint Patrick traveled to bring the good news of God's love to others. When Patrick went to Ireland he met many people who did not know about the one true God.

The story is told that he used a shamrock to teach them about the Blessed Trinity—three Persons in one God. There are three leaves on one stem. There are three Persons in one God.

Pretend you are Saint Patrick and you are holding a shamrock. Use the shamrock to help you tell someone about the Blessed Trinity.

Learn by heart **Faith Summary**

- God created everyone and everything good.
- The Blessed Trinity means the three Persons in one God, the Father, the Son, and the Holy Spirit.

The Holy Spirit

No one has ever seen the Holy Spirit. There are no pictures of the Holy Spirit.

Sometimes in our churches you will see a beautiful, white dove in paintings and in stained-glass windows. The Church often uses the picture of a dove to remind us that the Holy Spirit is with us.

The next time you see a picture of the dove in church, thank the Holy Spirit for being your Helper.

Learn by heart **Faith Summary**

- The Holy Spirit came to the followers of Jesus Christ on Pentecost.
- The Holy Spirit helps us to believe in Jesus and to live as Jesus shows us.

The Holy Father

The leader of the whole Catholic Church is the pope. He is the bishop of Rome. The pope continues the leadership that began with Peter the apostle. He serves and cares for people in the Church all over the world. With the other bishops, he teaches us how to follow Jesus.

Catholics call the pope by a special title. Begin by coloring the letter "A" and color every other tile piece. Read the uncolored tiles to find the title.

Write what we call our pope.

Faith Summary

Learn by heart

- The Catholic Church is our home in the Christian family.
- As Christians we try to live as Jesus taught.

Mary in Our Family and Parish

Catholic families and parishes show love and respect for Mary, the mother of Jesus. She is the most important saint of all. Jesus gave Mary to us to be our mother, too.

When Jesus was dying on the cross, He looked down with love on his mother Mary. He told her that she was now to be a special mother to all His followers.

Look in your parish church. Is there a statue or a picture of Mary? What does Mary look like? Tell about it.

Maybe your group can go to see it together. When you do, pray the Hail Mary. Ask Mary to pray for everyone in your family and parish.

Learn by heart

Faith Summary

- Our parish is a special family in the Catholic Church.
- Our parish helps us live together as a community of Jesus' friends.

What Is a Shepherd?

People who care for sheep are known as shepherds. During the time that Jesus lived, many people were shepherds.

The life of shepherds was not easy. Most of the year was spent outside in all kinds of weather. Everyday they took care of their sheep, leading them to water and food. Good shepherds loved and cared for their flocks.

Jesus called Himself the Good Shepherd. Your parish church might have a window or a statue of the Good Shepherd. Look at the picture of the Good Shepherd. Imagine that you are the lamb on Jesus' shoulders. Why is He carrying you?

Learn by heart **Faith Summary**

- We must love God with our whole heart. We must love others as ourselves.
- The Holy Spirit helps us to make good choices.

Our Catholic Identity

Vestments

For the celebration of the sacraments, the priest wears special clothes called vestments.

One of the vestments the priest wears is a stole. A stole is like a long narrow scarf. The priest always wears the stole around his neck when he leads us in worshiping God. When you receive the sacrament of Reconciliation, you will see the priest wearing a stole. The stole reminds us that the priest forgives sins in the name of God. The priest brings us God's mercy.

See if you can find out what other vestments the priest wears this week at Mass.

- The Church celebrates God's forgiveness in the sacrament of Reconciliation.
- We celebrate the sacrament of Reconciliation with our parish family.

Our Catholic Identity

A Sign of Forgiveness

Jesus often stretched out His hands when He healed or forgave people. In the sacrament of Reconciliation, the priest stretches out his hand when he gives us absolution. This means that we are being forgiven by God.

When we hear the priest absolving us in the name of the Father, and of the Son, and of the Holy Spirit, we make the sign of the cross, and we answer, "Amen."

How can you thank God for this gift of forgiveness?

Learn by heart **Faith Summary**

- We can celebrate Reconciliation either by ourselves with the priest or with others in our parish and the priest.
- Celebrating Reconciliation helps us to grow in our love for God, others, and ourselves.

Blessed Be God Forever

How wonderful! At Mass the simple gifts of bread and wine become the Body and Blood of Christ. When the priest prepares the bread and wine he says,

Blessed are you, Lord, God of all creation.
Through your goodness we have this bread to offer,
which earth has given and human hands have made.
It will become for us the bread of life.

Blessed are you, Lord, God of all creation.
Through your goodness we have this wine to offer,
fruit of the vine and work of human hands.
It will become our spiritual drink.

After each prayer, we say,

"Blessed be God forever."

Remember to pray these words at Mass.

Learn by heart **Faith Summary**

- The Mass is both a meal and a sacrifice.
- Jesus gives us the gift of Himself in Holy Communion.

Why Catholics Genuflect

Catholics genuflect in church to show respect for Jesus present in the Blessed Sacrament. When we genuflect, we bend our right knee to the floor.

Out of love and respect for Jesus, we want to genuflect the right way. We should genuflect slowly, looking toward the tabernacle. Some people like to say a short prayer when genuflecting. They might say, for example, "Jesus, I love You."

Practice genuflecting.
What prayer will you say to Jesus?

Learn by heart **Faith Summary**

- Eucharist means "giving thanks."
- Mass is the great thanksgiving prayer of the Catholic Church.

Our Communion Prayer

After receiving Holy Communion, we can say to Jesus whatever is in our hearts. We can talk to Jesus, just as we talk to our best friend.

We can thank Jesus for coming to us.
We can tell Him about anything that worries us.
We can pray for our families and friends.
We can ask Jesus to help those in need.

What would you like to say to Jesus after Holy Communion?

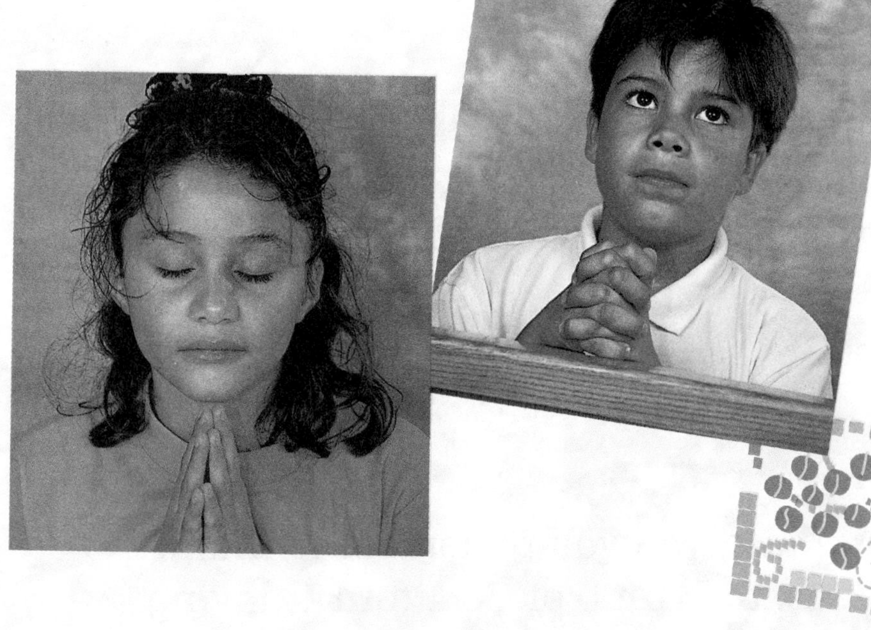

Our Catholic Identity

Learn by heart **Faith Summary**

- At Mass we offer gifts of bread and wine to God.
- During the Eucharistic Prayer, our gifts of bread and wine become the Body and Blood of Christ.

Lamb of God

A long time ago, people often offered a lamb as a sacrifice to God. This was their way of asking God to forgive their sins. John the Baptist said of Jesus, "Here is the Lamb of God who takes away the sin of the world."

From John 1:29

Why do you think John called Jesus "the Lamb of God"?

Jesus offered Himself to God to free us from our sins. At Mass we ask Jesus to have mercy on all people. We pray,

Lamb of God, you take away the sins
of the world:
have mercy on us. (Pray twice.)

Lamb of God, you take away the sins
of the world:
grant us peace.

At Mass, will you remember to thank Jesus, the Lamb of God, for His loving sacrifice for us?

Learn by heart

Faith Summary

- We receive Jesus Christ, our Bread of Life, in Holy Communion.
- After Mass we continue to love and serve God and one another.

The Tabernacle

After Holy Communion has been given to the people at Mass, sometimes there are Hosts that remain. These Hosts are put in a special place. It is called the tabernacle. *Tabernacle* means "tent." The tabernacle looks like a small tent-like box. It is usually on a side altar.

Catholics genuflect in front of the tabernacle. In this way we show reverence for Jesus, who is present in the Blessed Sacrament.

A special light called the sanctuary lamp is always kept burning near the tabernacle. The burning lamp reminds us that Jesus is present in the Blessed Sacrament.

The next time you enter your parish church, look for the tabernacle and sanctuary lamp. Remember to genuflect and talk to Jesus, who is present there.

Learn by heart

Faith Summary

- Jesus is really present in the Blessed Sacrament.
- Jesus is with us whenever we come together in His name.

Lord I Am Not Worthy

Here is a story from the Bible.

An important person had a servant who became very sick. He sent a message to Jesus, saying, "Lord, I am not worthy to have you enter my house. Just say the word, and my servant will be healed." Jesus was amazed at the man's strong faith. And from that moment, the servant was healed.

From Luke 7:1–10

As Catholics we remember this beautiful story of faith each time we receive Holy Communion. The priest leads us in saying these words:

> Lord, I am not worthy to receive you,
> but only say the word and I shall
> be healed.

Learn this prayer by heart so you can pray it with your parish community.

Faith Summary

- The Catholic Church helps us to grow in our life with Jesus.
- Jesus is with us when we celebrate the sacraments, pray together, and help those in need.

Our Catholic Identity

The Rosary

A beautiful way Catholics honor Mary is by praying the rosary. The rosary is made up of groups of beads and a cross.

The rosary begins with a cross followed by one large bead and three small ones. Then there are five groups of ten small beads called "decades." Beginning each decade is one large bead.

To pray a decade of the rosary pray the Our Father on the large bead. Pray a Hail Mary on each of the ten smaller beads. At the end of the decade, pray the Glory to the Father.

Do you have a rosary?
Pray a decade of the rosary with a friend.

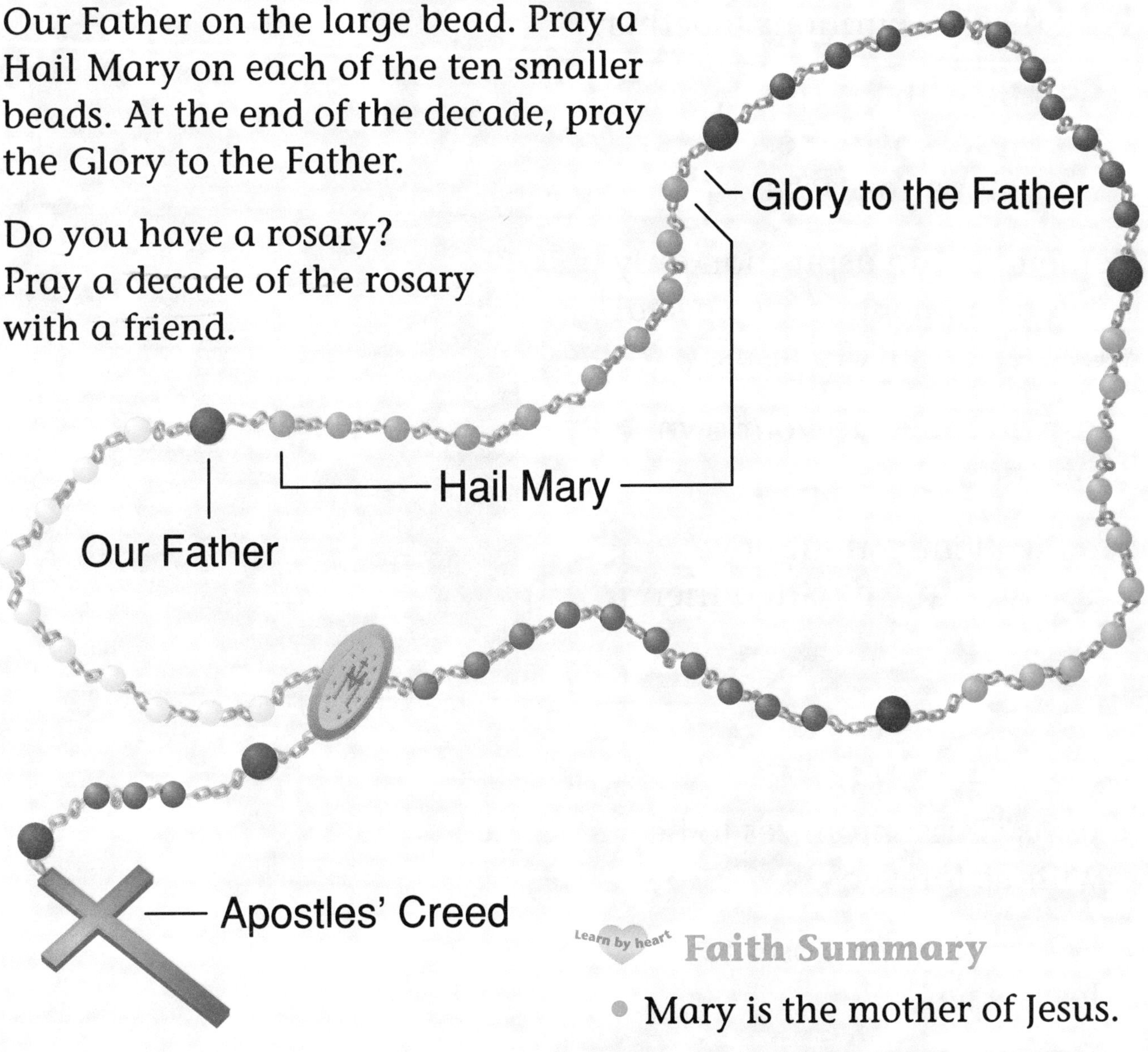

Glory to the Father

Hail Mary

Our Father

Apostles' Creed

Learn by heart

Faith Summary

- Mary is the mother of Jesus.
- Mary is our mother, too.

Aspirations

Say "Jesus" slowly and softly. Do you know that you just prayed an aspiration? *Aspiration* comes from a word meaning "breath." Aspirations are prayers that are so short they can be said in one short breath. Aspirations can be said at any time and in any place. We can say them quietly to ourselves.

Pray these aspirations together:

† Be with me, Jesus.
† Jesus, help me.
† I love You, Jesus.

Remember, an aspiration only takes a moment. It is a special way we can talk to Jesus.

Can you make up your own aspiration?

Pray it silently, right now.
Can you share it with a friend?

Learn by heart

Faith Summary

- Jesus Christ promises to be with us forever.
- We try to grow closer to Jesus each day.